D0382092

WOMEN IN PERSPECTIVE

WOMEN IN PERSPECTIVE
A Guide for Cross-Cultural Studies

SUE-ELLEN JACOBS

UNIVERSITY OF ILLINOIS PRESS
Urbana   Chicago   London

©1974 by the Board of Trustees of the University of Illinois
Manufactured in the United States of America
Library of Congress Catalog Card No. 72-93987
Cloth: ISBN 0-252-00299-7
Paper: ISBN 0-252-00345-4

to

Ruth M. Cain Jacobs(M)
Lacy A. Neal Cain(MM)
M. Lois Cain Williams(MZ)
William D. Jacobs(F)

for the education they gave me

and to my

Sisters (real and fictive)
Brothers
Nieces
and Nephews

for a better world for each of us and all of us

74450

Preface

In my research in the Southwest, Canada, California, and the Midwest on poverty, health, and education problems, social structure, and ethnocommunications, I have had the opportunity to direct a portion of my research attention to the roles of women in diverse cultural and social settings. On the whole, my research interests did not permit isolation of design features that would allow an exclusive focus on women. Instead, I established rapport with women and men while focusing on larger sociocultural problems. During parts of the past two years, however, I have conducted research on the everyday life of Southwest Indian women of different generations: grandmothers, mothers, unmarried young women not yet mothers, and small girls. The research was specifically female-centered, but this did not preclude interaction with the men in the village. In these instances, I was able to test the worth of basic research on women with respect to the contribution such studies can make to the understanding of everyday life and to the total ethnographic record. I found that focusing specifically on women gave me a different perspective for understanding mechanisms of social order. Comparing my findings with those of other researchers who have dealt primarily with men in the same village, I have found that there are differences in basic data and the interpretation of data as these relate to presentation of a description of the culture. The experience has been extremely revealing.

We are trained in our respective fields to ask specific sets of questions that will lead toward solution of research problems. Most of us use a male-based epistemology, since that is the point of view which constrains Western thought, especially in scholarly or academic work. The kinds of questions we raise, then, are based not necessarily on pragmatics of daily living, but on "models" for inquiry. We can become lost in seeking solutions to problems (or answers to questions) that are mere manipulations of data around a prior framework. I believe that participation in the mundane but necessary aspects of daily life gives the researcher an opportunity to ask questions relating practical survival to social order. Some "hard" scientists accuse social scientists of lacking rigor in their research strategies; further, they suggest that until we can build formal models for analysis, we shall never be able to demonstrate the scientific validity of our work. Social scientists who agree recognize the limitations which the current "scientific" tools hold, since these do not allow for free variation in the actual on-the-ground behavior of people. Still others suggest that social scientists should be concerned not with scientific rigor, but with accurate descriptions of behavior in cultural context. Only in this latter way, it is suggested, will they be able to understand the "mind of man," the reality of variation in the "cultural expressions of man." Perhaps a significant proportion of social and behavioral scientists are interested in building a comprehensive Science of Man, and so they must strive to define the nature of that inquiry. I am more interested in building a comprehensive Science of Humanity, where inquiry leads us into the domains of women and men, to all areas of human interaction.

Conducting research with a sex bias, or concentrating on a sex-set, may be interesting in terms of getting at specific sex-based data; nevertheless, members of either sex-set (except in specific cloistered circumstances) do not operate contextually, on a day-to-day basis in society, without interaction with members of the opposite sex. If one uses more, or only, members of a given sex to obtain data, and relegates information obtained from a few members of the opposite sex to a lower category (as uninformative or uninteresting), then one is gathering only half the data needed to present a complete picture of the problem in question. In the case of studies of societies, or individuals in societies, and of cross-cultural analysis of various cultural norms, limitations arise resulting from the concentration of researchers on males to provide answers to questions derived from male-oriented epistemologies. We do not yet have sufficient data obtained through research designed from women's points of view and directed, on the one hand, toward the study of women, and, on the other, toward society as a whole. When Sally Linton (1971) speaks of the "male bias in anthropology," she could well be speaking of male bias in all behavioral and social sciences. When Beverly Chiñas (1971) notes the differences between the findings of male colleagues who have conducted research on economic structures in Mexico and those she and other women anthropologists have obtained, she is advising other male researchers to be cautious in defining situations without adequate and accurate regard for the roles of women. Women often relate to other women in one fashion and to men in another, as do men. When these differences occur in research, two sets of results are obtained and reported. There is a further problem: women may enter research designed to deal with problems deemed interesting by men. That is to say, some women who conduct research may be equally guilty of presenting descriptions of cultures based entirely on interviews and social inter-action with men in the society, since "educated" women from outside a culture are often given considerable freedom to interact with men in the host culture. The advantage

which the woman scholar has in another culture is that more
often than not she has greater freedom of mobility among
men, women, and children than her male counterpart, who is
frequently limited in interview contact to men only, or
sometimes men and children (if the children are separated
from the women). In 1969 Margaret Mead said: "Native men
may be afraid that a male anthropologist will take their
women. . . men cannot study children without a great deal
of difficulty, because children are where women are and if
men get too close to women. . . they get into other complications with men of the tribe."

Mead also pointed out that women who go into the field
usually do not threaten other women. In some areas of my
research I have been able to move freely between women and
men; in others, specifically, urban areas, I have found
that it required longer to establish a position non-
threatening to local women in my interaction with the men.
Once credibility was established, I received the same assistance in seeking key male informants as in seeking
female ones. Certainly some women have noted the ease of
transition from male to female groups in field work, and
others have documented difficulties (see, for example,
Golde, "Women in the Field"). Still others have noted that
they were able to discuss topics with women that men could
not because of local taboos regarding such discussion
across sex lines.

Although there has been a proliferation of papers and
books related to the cross-cultural study of women since I
began compiling this bibliography in 1970, there are
numerous areas for research which have not been touched.
Recently more major grants have been made to women interested in doing research specifically on women, indicating
at least some recognition of the need to fill the gaps in
the record on human animals. Perhaps someone will take
advantage of the interest expressed by funding agencies to
conduct a study of society from women's points of view.
Not only should we consider working toward filling the gaps
in the ethnographic records, toward understanding the
socialization processes for females and males, toward
further understanding the varieties of cognitive development and orientations, etc.; we should also begin looking
at areas assumed to be relatively well documented.

For example, are we willing to use our own sex bias and
look for alternative explanations for the primatological
and archaeological records? Are we willing to look for
logical analogies and intuitive clues based on our own experiences (as do our male colleagues, though they will
seldom admit it) and rational judgments? Are we willing to
use an experiential model for seeking answers to questions,
as well as what might contrastively be called "formal"
models? Are we willing to shed the bias of male thought
that we learned as professionals and seek a broader

epistemology which allows us to ask questions pertaining to the whole of life? In reference to this, Sally Linton (1971:20) stated: "This paper stems from asking a simple question: What were the females doing while the males were out hunting? It was only possible for me to ask this question after I had become politically conscious of my-self as a woman. Such is the prestige of males in our society that a woman, in anthropology or any other profession, can only gain respect or be attended to if she deals with questions deemed important by men." By learning to ask questions of importance to women too, we can begin to deal with the other half of humanity. Once we have asked the questions, recorded the data, and analyzed it, we should seek avenues of publication, as difficult as this latter may be.

Potential success in building alternative futures depends largely on success in overcoming deficiencies in the publications which serve to guide decision-makers in our society. While Beverly Chiñas (1971:23) has noted that women are expected to center research around problems of culture which interest men, she has also noted that "women anthropologists often gather a great deal of data about women in the course of their fieldwork centering around other problems, data which too often gathers dust in raw-data files and is thus effectively lost to the scientific community." Some of the material previously held in files is beginning to appear in various professional journals and some in feminist or liberation magazines (e.g., Evans-Pritchard for the former, Kathleen Gough for the latter).

There is one further concern that needs mentioning. In the entries which deal with views of women in specific non-Western societies, there have been at least two warnings against making judgments about the "conditions" of women. In 1937, Camilla H. Wedgewood (pp. 401-2) criticized the use of standards for judging the position of women in society and noted that "the standard which is usually, and perhaps unconsciously, adopted is that of the upper-middle classes of western Europe or North America, a standard which is of very little value to the study of a community whose cultural background differs so greatly. . ." Dr. Wedgewood was specifically concerned with the representations of Melanesian women. But, thirty-six years later, there is still a problem. Baron von Ehrenfels has noted that in recent publications "feminism is being treated as though it were an almost exclusively Western affair. . . feminism all over the world, and especially in Afro-Asiatic countries, is at the same time widely neglected, even though it is in the Afro-Asiatic countries that some of the most striking changes in the conditions of women are now occurring." (von Ehrenfels 1973:1.) I believe it is crucial that we attempt to collect data on the changing roles of women by working <u>with</u> women to obtain answers to questions and insights they seek in the communities where we conduct research. I am a proponent of the insider-outsider, or polyocular, approach to research, and I believe that unless we are willing to bring to consciousness the cultural biases we take to our research problem, we will continue to represent a one-sided point of view (Jacobs 1971). Racism and chauvinism are not male prerogatives, yet because of my interactions with women of various cultural backgrounds I believe we can, by working together, create a more egalitarian future.

This sourcebook contains numerous references which further attest to the problems outlined in the preceding paragraphs. The increase in numbers of new and reprinted materials about women does not necessarily mean that there has been a proliferation of <u>knowledge</u> about women. True, there is much that has been <u>said about</u> women and there is, in essence, a tradition to deal with women in various genres of writing. Some authors write with personal and negative biases, others with romantic idealism, and others "treat the subject scientifically." There are those who attempt to mask sexist bias with scientific language, making irresponsible extrapolations from poor scientific premises, and still others who write in pseudo-scientific jargon "to appeal to the sensibilities" of scholars and lay people. Then there are those of us who wish to separate truths from fantasies by searching for on-the-ground data. In our work we must sort through a great deal of trivia. We may choose to deal with trivia as points of departure for further research, or we may wish to attack such writings from either moral or scholarly points of view. There are very few sources which provide empirically tested alternatives to previous theories and methods for analysis of women in societies, or for societies in general. There is much yet to learn about women in all our diverse conceptualized and acted-out postures. When we have concentrated our energies in this direction, we may then begin to fill gaps in the human record so that understanding mankind means understanding all of humanity. I hope this bibliography will stimulate further research in the areas noted, and that its use will suggest even others.

This sourcebook does not pretend to be all encompassing; rather, it represents research into special areas by myself, colleagues, and students who are seeking answers to specific questions about women. Thus it becomes slanted toward those interest areas. It is intended for use by students and faculty interested in women's studies in general and in analysis of women in cross-cultural perspective specifically. A perusal of the contents will quickly show that women in various periods and in diverse cultural circumstances have been "examined" by a variety of researchers and authors. Consequently, the materials here may be found useful not only by anthropologists, but also by sociologists, political scientists, psychologists, and others interested in turning their attention to or incorporating materials on women in their research, teaching, or writing.

The sources have been divided into two main categories. Part I, "Geographical Topics," has sources arranged by culture areas and countries; Part II, "Subject Topics," has sources arranged according to the major theme in the article or book listed. The user can turn to a specific area of interest or can, by checking through the listings, note areas where information seems to be lacking or outdated. At a more general level, the user will note the broad range of materials available on women. But it is important to keep in mind that we still do not know what constitutes the whole of humanity, because publications concerned with many cultures have not included valid studies of the "other half"--women.

In preparing this work, I have had the opportunity to meet and correspond with a number of people who are equally concerned with the issues raised here. Nearly all entries have been seen by one or all of us who have contributed basic and smaller bibliographies for women's studies or the study of women. Although I am ultimately responsible for errors, this work is the result of an informal consortium of women and men interested in centralizing data concerned with women. The successfulness in reaching a broader understanding of women is dependent on all of us working together to keep the record of our writing up to date. I therefore request that users of this bibliography write to me to offer further suggestions, note errors or inconsistencies in the entries, and identify new sources so that we can keep an up-to-date record of our work.

I am grateful to all who have helped me organize this book. I wish to give thanks especially to the students at California State University, Sacramento, for diligently working with me in the initial collection of material for a course on women in cross-cultural perspective; to Mario Bick, Dana Raphael, and Mobin Shorish for sending their bibliographies and copies of some of

their writings; to Beverly Litzler-Chiñas for maintaining
correspondence with me throughout preparation of the previous version of the sourcebook (and her article therein),
and for sending me several bibliographies and suggestions
for this version; to Sally Linton for her contributions;
to Michelle (Shelly) Rosaldo and Joanna Kirkpatrick for
their comments and suggestions; and to Pam Bailey for her
assistance in verifying and transliterating Russian
sources. I am also grateful to Michael P. Brooks, head of
the department of urban and regional planning at the
University of Illinois, for giving me both financial and
moral support during the preparation of the bibliography.
Special thanks go to Chris Rich, who, in addition to
other demanding responsibilities associated with her work
for women, spent long and tedious hours helping me sort
and verify references. Finally, I express my sincere ap-
preciation to the editorial staff at the University of
Illinois Press for their long hours of careful attention
to the bibliography.

Sue-Ellen Jacobs
University of Illinois,
Urbana-Champaign

TABLE OF CONTENTS

Part I. Geographical Topics

WOMEN IN PERSPECTIVE

PART ONE: GEOGRAPHICAL TOPICS

AFRICA

Introductory Texts

Bohannan, Paul. Africa and Africans. Garden City, N.Y.:
    Doubleday, 1964.
Gibbs, James L., Jr., ed. Peoples of Africa. New York:
    Holt, Rinehart & Winston, 1965.
Murdock, George Peter. Africa: Its Peoples and Their
    Cultural History. New York: McGraw-Hill, 1959.
Ottenberg, Simon, and Ottenberg, Phoebe, eds. Cultures
    and Societies of Africa. New York: Random House, 1960.

General References

African Bibliographic Center. Contemporary African Women:
    An Introductory Bibliographical Overview and a Guide to
    Women's Organizations, 1960-1967. Washington, D.C.:
    Women's African Committee of the African-American
    Institute, 1968-69.
"African Women: From Old Magic to New Power." Time,
    Aug. 31, 1971, pp.28-33.
"African Women Help in Rural Education and Training."
    UNESCO Information Bulletin 22 (Feb. 1, 1966):12-13.
Anderson, J. N. D. Family Law in Asia and Africa. New
    York: Frederick A. Praeger, 1967.
Carley, Verna A. African Women Educators Project Report.
    Washington, D.C.: U.S. Agency for International
    Development, Bureau for Africa and Europe, Office of
    Institutional Development, 1962.
Clignet, Remi. Many Wives, Many Powers: Authority and
    Power in Polygynous Families. Evanston: Northwestern
    University Press, 1970.
Dipoko, Mbella. Because of Women. African Writers
    Series, 57. New York: Humanities Press, 1970.
Douglas, Mary. "Is Matriliny Doomed in Africa?" In Man
    in Africa, ed. Mary Douglas and P. Kaberry, pp. 121-35.
    London: Tavistock, 1969.
Ehrenfels, U. R. "The African Woman: Between Apartheid
    and the Brideprice." United Asia 13 (1961):129-33.
Fuchs, Peter. Das Antlitz der Afrikanerin. First
    published, 1928. Reprint, Stuttgart: Deutsche
    Verlags-Anstalt, 1966.
Gluckman, Max. "Estrangement in the African Family." In
    A Modern Introduction to the Family, ed. Norman W.
    Bell and Ezra F. Vogel, pp. 464-68. New York: Free
    Press, 1968.
Hope, Marjorie. "Family Life in Africa: A Look at
    Another Culture." Parents Magazine 45 (1970):46-47.

Isaac, S. "Pour la promotion sociale de la femme."
    African Documents 59 (1962):216-29.
Kuper, Leo. An African Bourgeoisie. New Haven: Yale
    University Press, 1965.
Lebeuf, Annie M. D. "The Role of Women in the Political
    Organization of African Societies." In Women of
    Tropical Africa, ed. Denise Paulme, pp. 93-120.
    Berkeley: University of California Press, 1971.
Leith-Ross, Sylvia. African Women. New York: Frederick
    A. Praeger, 1965.
Letourneau, Charles. "La femme en Papouasie et en
    Afrique." Paris Revue de l'Ecole d'Anthropologie 12
    (1902):373-88.
LeVine, R. A. "Sex Roles and Economic Change in Africa."
    Ethnology 5 (1966):186-93.
Maistriaux, Robert. La femme et le destin de l'Afrique;
    les sources psychologiques de la mentalité dite
    primitive. Elisabethville: Editions Cepsi, 1964.
Marie-André du Sacre Coeur. "La femme dans la famille
    africaine." African Contemporary Monographs 4 (Nov.-
    Dec. 1965):15-18.
Mayer, Philip, and Mayer, Iona. "Women and Children in
    the Migrant Situation." In Townsmen or Tribesmen.
    Capetown: Oxford University Press, 1963.
Munroe, Robert L.; Munroe, Ruth H.; and LeVine, Robert A.
    "Africa." In Psychological Anthropology, new ed., ed.
    Francis L. Hsu, pp. 71-120. Cambridge, Mass.:
    Schenkman, 1972.
Nadel, S. F. "Witchcraft in Four African Societies: An
    Essay in Comparison." American Anthropologist 54
    (1952):18-29.
Ogot, Grace. "Family Planning for African Women."
    Development Digest 6 (Apr. 1968):37-40.
Paulme, Denise, ed. Women of Tropical Africa. First
    published, 1960. Reprint, Berkeley: University of
    California Press, 1971.
Phillips, Arthur, ed. Survey of African Marriage and
    Family Life. London: Oxford University Press, 1953.
Plisnier-Ladame, F. La condition de l'Africaine en
    Afrique noire. Brussels: Centre de Documentation
    Economique et Sociale Africaine, 1962.
Radcliffe-Brown, A. R., and Forde, Daryll, eds. African
    Systems of Kinship and Marriage. First published,
    1950. Reprint, New York: Oxford University Press,
    1964.
Schapera, I. Married Life in an African Tribe. New
    York: Sheridan House, 1951.
Scobie, Alastari. Women of Africa. London: Cassell,
    1960.
Seabury, R. I. Daughter of Africa. Boston: Pilgrim
    Press, 1945.

Segal, Ronald. Political Africa: A Who's Who of
    Personalities and Parties. New York: Frederick A.
    Praeger, 1961.
Smirnova, Raisa Mikhaĭlovna. Polozhenie zhenshchin v
    stranakh Afriki. Moscow: Vostochnoĭ Literaturi, 1967.
Social Implications of Industrialization in Africa South
    of the Sahara. Paris: International African
    Institute, UNESCO Publications, 1956.
Southall, Aiden. "The Position of Women and the
    Stability of Marriage." In Social Change in Modern
    Africa, ed. A. Southall, pp. 46-66. London: Oxford
    University Press, 1961.
____, ed. Social Change in Modern Africa. London: Oxford
    University Press, 1961.
Sunons, Harold. African Women. Evanston: Northwestern
    University Press, 1968.
Taylor, Sidney, ed. The New Africans. New York: G. P.
    Putnam's Sons, 1967.
Tuden, A., and Plotnicov, L. Social Stratification in
    Africa. Oxford: Oxford University Press, 1966.
Welch, Galbraith. Africa before They Came: The Continent
    North, South, East, and West, Preceding the Colonial
    Powers. New York: William Morrow, 1965.
Women in Africa and the Sixties: A Preliminary Survey.
    Washington, D.C.: African Bibliographic Center, 1965.
Women Today: A Journal for Women in Changing Societies.
    London: Department of Education in Tropical Areas,
    University of London Institute of Education, Dec. 1954.

North Africa: Algeria, Libya, Morocco, Tunisia (Islamic Women: see also Egypt, Middle East, India, Pakistan)

Ammar, Sleim, and M'barak, Ezzedine. "Hysteria in
    Tunisian Women." La Tunisie Medicale II (1961):479-94.
Anderson, J. N. D. "Reforms in Family Law in Morocco."
    Journal of African Law 2 (1958):146-59.
Celarie, Henriette. Behind Moroccan Walls, trans.
    Constance Lily Morris. First published, 1931. Reprint,
    Freeport, N.Y.: Books for Libraries, 1970.
Crapanzano, Vincent. "The Transformation of the Eumenides:
    A Moroccan Example." A paper presented at the 70th
    Annual Meeting of the American Anthropological
    Association, New York, 1971. Mimeo. Princeton
    University.
Daumas, General Eugene. Women of North Africa, trans.
    A. G. H. Kreiss. San Diego: A. G. H. Kreiss, 1943.
Des Villettes, Jacqueline. "La vie des femmes dans un
    village Maronite Libanais: Aïn al Kharoube."
    L'Institut des Belles Lettres Arabes 23 (1960):151-207,
    271-79.
Devulder, M. "Ritual magique des femmes Kabyles." Revue
    Africaine 101 (1957):299-361.

Forget, Nelly. "Attitudes towards Work by Women in Morocco." International Social Science Journal 14 (1962):92-123.

Fuchs, K. L. "'Mutterrechtliche' Spuren bei Berberstammen Nordwestafrikas." Wiener völkerkundliche Mitteilungen 3 (1956):167-75.

Gaudry, Mathea. La femme Chaouia de l'Aures: étude de sociologie Berbere. Paris: Geuthner, 1929.

___. La société feminine au Djebel Amour et au Ksel: étude de sociologie rurale. Algiers: Société Algerienne d'Impressions Diverses, 1961.

Goichon, Amelia-Marie. "La vie feminine au Mzab." Révue du Monde Musulman 62 (1925):27-38.

___. La vie feminine au Mzab: étude de sociologie musulmane. Paris: Geuthner, 1927.

Gordon, David C. Women of Algeria: An Essay on Change. Harvard Middle Eastern Monograph Series. Cambridge: Harvard University Press, 1968.

Holland, Clive. "North Africa." In Women of All Nations, vol. 2, ed. T. A. Joyce, pp. 215-33. New York: Funk & Wagnalls, 1915.

Howe, S. E. "Touareg Women and the Veiled Men." Muslim World 18 (1928):34-44.

Jacobs, Milton. A Study of Culture Stability and Change: The Moroccan Jewess. Washington, D.C.: Catholic University of America Press, 1956.

Larson, Barbara. "The Tunisian Woman: A Veiled Threat." A paper presented at the 70th Annual Meeting of the American Anthropological Association, New York, 1971. Mimeo. CUNY, Lehman.

LeFebvre, G. "La toilette feminine dans deux villages de Petite Kabylie." Libyca 11 (1963):199-220.

___. "Le portage de l'eau dans deux villages de Petite Kabylie." Libyca 9, 10 (1961-62):199-204.

Lelong, M. "Femmes tunisiennes d'aujourd'hui." l'Institut des Belles Lettres Arabes 22 (1959):354-57.

___. "La personalité de la femme tunisienne." l'Institut des Belles Lettres Arabes 19 (1956):423-28.

Leis, Nancy. "Women in Groups: Virilocality, Polygyny and Women's Associations in Africa." A paper presented at the 70th Annual Meeting of the American Anthropological Association, New York, 1971. Mimeo. Central Michigan University.

Mohsen, Safia K. "La consommation des familles musulmanes d'Algerie." Population 16 (1961):117-22.

___. "The Legal Status of Women among Awlad'Ali." Anthropological Quarterly 40 (1967):153-66.

Montely, Henri de. Femmes de Tunisie. Paris: Mouton, 1958.

Noualer, K. "The Changing Status of Women and the Employment of Women in Morocco." African Women 5 (Dec. 1962): 17-22.

___. "The Changing Status of Women and the Employment of Women in Morocco." International Social Science Journal 14 (1962):124-29.

Sfar, L. "Tunisia: Prevocational Training for Girls." CIRF Abstracts 8 (1969).

Sfeir, G. N. "The Tunisian Code of Personal Status." Middle-East Journal 11 (1957):309-18.

Stratton, F. "Women of Tunisia." African Women 5 (June 1963):31-34.

Suter, K. "Die Ortsgebundenheit der Frau bei den Mozabiten" [The residential restriction of women among the Mozabits]. Geographica Helvetica 12 (1957):102-14.

Westermarck, Edvard Alexander. Marriage Ceremonies in Morocco. London: Macmillan, 1914.

Women of Algeria: An Essay on Change. Middle Eastern Monograph 19. Cambridge: Harvard University Press, 1968.

Egypt (Islamic Women: see also North Africa, Middle East, India, Pakistan)

Abu Lugbod, Janet. "Egyptian Marriage Adjustment: Microcosm of a Changing Society." Marriage and Family Living 23 (1961):127-38.

Ammar, Hamed. Growing Up in an Egyptian Village. London: Routledge & Kegan Paul, 1954.

Anderson, J. N. D. "The Problem of Divorce in the Sharia Law of Islam: Measures of Reform in Modern Egypt." Journal of the Royal Central Asian Society 37 (1950): 168-85.

Awad, B. A. "The Status of Women in Islam." Islamic Quarterly 8 (Jan.-June 1964):17-24.

Blackman, Winifred. The Fellahin of Upper Egypt. London: George Harrap, 1927.

Cooper, Elizabeth. The Women of Egypt. New York: Frederick A. Stokes, 1914.

Dickerman, Lysander. "The Condition of Women in Ancient Egypt." Bulletin of the American Geographical Society 26 (1894):494-527.

Douglass, Joseph H., and Douglass, Katherine W. "Aspects of Marriage and Family Living among Egyptian Peasants [Fellaheen]." Marriage and Family Living 16 (1954): 45-48.

Harby, Mohammed Khayri, and Zeinab, Mahmoud Mehrez. Education for Women in the U.A.R. Cairo: General Organisation for Government Printing Offices, 1961.

Hohenwart-Gerlachstein, A. "The Legal Position of Women in Ancient Egypt." Wiener völkerkundliche Mitteilungen 3 (1956):90-93.

Hussein, Aziza. "The Role of Women in Social Reform in Egypt." Middle East Journal 7 (1953):443-50.

Kahle, P. "A Gypsy Woman in Egypt in the Thirteenth Century." Journal of Gypsy Lore Society 29 (1950): 11-15.

Kazem, Mohamed I. "Autobiographies of Five Egyptian Young
    Women." Primary Records in Culture and Personality,
    vol. 2, ed. Bert Kaplan. Madison: Microcard
    Foundation, n.d.
Kennedy, John G. "Mushahara: A Nubian Concept of Super-
    natural Danger and the Theory of Taboo." American
    Anthropologist 69 (1967):685-702.
Klunzinger, C. B. Upper Egypt: Its People and Its
    Products. London: Blackie & Son, 1878.
Lane, E. W. Manners and Customs of Modern Egyptians.
    London: Dent & Sons, 1954.
Lichtenstadter, I. "The Muslim Woman in Transition, Based
    on Observations in Egypt and Pakistan." Sociologus 7
    (1957):23-38.
Nelson, Cynthia. "Changing Roles of Men and Women:
    Illustrations from Egypt." Anthropological Quarterly
    41 (1968):57-77.
Nervall, Gerard de. The Women of Cairo: Scenes of Life
    in the Orient. 2 vols. London: Routledge, 1929.
Patrick, Mary Mills. "The Emancipation of Mohammedan
    Women." National Geographic (1909):42-66.
Sedki, L. K. "Egyptian Women." African Women 3 (Dec.
    1959):53-55.
Shafig, Doria. The Egyptian Woman. Cairo, 1955.
Tomich, Nada. "Egyptian Women in the First Half of the
    Nineteenth Century." In Conference on the Beginnings
    of Modernization in the Middle East in the 19th Century,
    ed. William Polk and Richard L. Chambers. Chicago:
    University of Chicago Press, 1966.
Tralins, Robert. Cairo Madam. New York: Paperback
    Library, 1968.
Wenig, Steffen. Woman in Egyptian Art. New York: McGraw-
    Hill, 1970.

Eastern Sudan: Chad, Sudan

Calame-Griaule, G. "Le rôle spirituel et social de la
    femme dans la société soudanaise traditionnelle."
    Diogene 37 (Jan.-Mar. 1962):81-92.
Ciccacci, I. "Mamme Denka." Nigrizia 84 (Jan. 1966):
    28-29.
Driberg, J. H. "The Status of Women among the Nilotics
    and Nilo-Hamitos." Africa 5 (1932):404-21.
Kashif, H. "The Sudanese Women's Movement." African
    Women 3 (Dec. 1959):55-56.
Nadel, S. F. "Dual Descent in the Nuba Hills." In
    African Systems of Kinship and Marriage, ed. A. R.
    Radcliffe-Brown and Daryll Forde, pp. 333-59. New
    York: Oxford University Press, 1950.
Reyna, Stephen. "Fertility and Divorce among the North-
    western Barma of Chad." A paper presented at the 70th
    Annual Meeting of the American Anthropological Association,
    New York, 1971. Mimeo. Columbia University.

Sanderson, Lillian. "Careers for Women in the Sudan Today."
African Women 5 (June 1963):25-29.
———. "The Khartoum Girls' Secondary School." Overseas
Education 34 (Jan. 1963):153-57.

Western Sudan: Gambia, Mali, Mauritania, Niger, Portuguese Guinea, Senegal, Upper Volta

Ames, D. W. "The Economic Base of Wolof Polygyny."
Southwestern Journal of Anthropology 11 (1955):391-403.
Carreira, A. "As primeiras referencias estritasa excisao
clitoridiana no Ocidente Africano" [Early written
sources on clitoridectomy in West Africa]. Boletim
cultural de Guiné Portugesa 20 (1965):147-50.
Dupire, Marguerite. "The Position of Women in a
Pastoral Society." In Women of Tropical Africa, ed.
Denise Paulme, pp. 47-92. Berkeley: University of
California Press, 1971.
Falade, Solange. "Women of Dakar and the Surrounding
Urban Area." In Women of Tropical Africa, ed. Denise
Paulme, pp. 217-30. Berkeley: University of California
Press, 1971.
Fongeyrallas, Pierre. Television and the Social Education
of Women: A First Report on the UNESCO-Senegal Pilot
Project at Dakar. Paris: UNESCO Publications, 1967.
Gamble, D. P. "Changes in Wolof Way of Life." West
African Review 30 (Mar. 1959):211-13.
Gessain, Monique. "A propos de l'evolution actuelle des
femmes Coniagui et Bassari." Journal de la Société
Africanistes 34 (1965):257-76.
———. "Coniagui Women." In Women of Tropical Africa, ed.
Denise Paulme, pp. 17-46. Berkeley: University of
California Press, 1971.
Grandmaison, Colette LeCour. "Activites economiques des
femmes Dakaroises." Africa 39 (1969):138-52.
Hanry, P. "La clitoridectomie rituelle en Guinee:
motivations, consequences, psychopathologies." Africa
1 (1965):261-67.
Lurin, G. "La condition de la femme au Niger." Revue
Internationale de l'Education des Adultes et de la
Jeunesse 15 (1963):133-37.
Schweeger-Hefel, A. "Die Stellung der Frau bei den
Kurumba, Ober-Volta, West-Afrika" [The position of
women among the Kurumba,Upper Volta, Western Africa].
Anthropos 57 (1963):725-47.
Stenning, Derrick J. "Household Viability among the
Pastoral Fulani." In The Developmental Cycle in
Domestic Groups, ed. Jack Goody, pp. 92-119.
Cambridge: Cambridge University Press, 1958.

West Africa: Dahomey, Ghana, Guinea, Ivory Coast, Liberia, Nigeria, Sierra Leone, Togo

Acquah, Ionie. Accra Survey. London: University of
     London Press, 1958.
Andreski, Iris, ed. Old Wives' Tales: Life-Stories of
     African Women. Sourcebooks in Negro History. New
     York: Schocken Books, 1970.
Ariwoola, O. The African Wife. London: O. Ariwoola,
     1965.
Baba of Karo. Baba of Karo, Woman of the Muslim Hausa.
     Autobiographical record by Mary F. Smith. New York:
     Philosophical Library, 1955.
Banton, M. West African City: A Study of Tribal Life in
     Freetown. New York: Oxford University Press, 1957.
Basden, G. T. Among the Ibos of Nigeria. London: Seeley,
     Service, 1921.
_____. Niger Ibos. London: Frank Cass, 1966.
Baumann, Hermann. "The Division of Work According to Sex
     in African Hoe Culture." Africa 1 (1928):289-317.
Beier, H. U. "The Position of Yoruba Women." Présence
     Africaine 1-2 (Apr.-July 1955):39-46.
Birmingham, W., Neustadt, I., and Omaboe, E. N., eds. A
     Study of Contemporary Ghana. Evanston: Northwestern
     University Press, 1967.
Bohannan, Laura. "Dahomean Marriage: A Revaluation."
     First published 1949. Reprint, Marriage, Family and
     Residence, ed. Paul Bohannan and John Middleton,
     pp. 85-108. New York: Natural History Press, 1968.
Bowen, Eleanor Smith. Return to Laughter. New York:
     Harper & Row, 1955.
Burness, H. M. "Women in Katsina Province, Northern
     Nigeria." Overseas Education 29 (Oct. 1957):185-89.
Busia, K. A. "The Conflict of Cultures." In Africa,
     Continent of Change, ed. Peter R. Gould. Belmont,
     Calif.: Wadsworth, 1961.
Buxton, J. "Girls' Courting Huts in Western Mandari."
     Man 63 (Apr. 1963):49-51.
Caldwell, John Charles. "The Erosion of the Family in
     Ghana." Population Studies 20 (1966):5-26.
_____. "Extended Family Obligations and Education."
     Population Studies 19 (1965):183-99.
_____. "Fertility Attitudes in Three Economically Con-
     trasting Rural Regions of Ghana." Economic Development
     and Cultural Change 15 (1967):217-38.
_____. "Fertility Differentials as Evidence of Incipient
     Fertility Decline in a Developing Country: The Case of
     Ghana." Population Studies 21 (1967).
_____. Population Growth and Family Change in Africa: The
     New Urban Elite in Ghana. Canberra: Australian
     National University Press, 1968.

Carreira, A. "As primeiras referencias estritasa excisao clitoridiana no Ocidente Africano" [Early written sources on clitoridectomy in West Africa]. Boletin cultural de Guiné Portugesa 20 (1965):147-50.

Carter, M. "Professional Women of Sierra Leone." African Women 3 (June 1959):41-42.

Christian, A. "The Place of Women in Ghana Society." African Women 3 (Dec. 1959):57-59.

Clignet, Remi. "Environmental Change, Types of Descent and Child Rearing Practices." In The City in Modern Africa, ed. H. Miner. London: Frederick A. Praeger, 1967.

____. "Introduction to the Inquiry on the Attitude of Society towards Women on the Ivory Coast." International Social Science Journal 14 (1962):137-48.

____. "Les attitudes de la société à l'égard des femmes en Côte d'Ivoire." Revue Internationale des Sciences Sociales 14 (1962):139-50.

Cohen, Ronald. Dominance and Defiance. Washington, D.C.: American Anthropological Association, 1971.

Dobert, Margarita. "Civic and Political Participation of Women in French-Speaking West Africa." Master's thesis, George Washington University, 1970.

Dorjahn, Vernon R. "Fertility, Polygyny and Their Interrelations in Temne." American Anthropologist 60 (1958):838.

Forde, Daryll. "Double Descent among the Yako." In African Systems of Kinship and Marriage, ed. A. R. Radcliffe-Brown and Daryll Forde, pp. 285-332. New York: Oxford University Press, 1950.

Fortes, Meyer. "Kinship and Marriage among the Ashanti." In African Systems of Kinship and Marriage, ed. A. R. Radcliffe-Brown and Daryll Forde, pp. 252-84. New York: Oxford University Press, 1950.

Gamble, David. "The Temne Family in a Modern Town in Sierra Leone." Africa 33 (1963):209-26.

Goody, Esther N. "Conjugal Separation and Divorce among the Gonja of Northern Ghana." In Marriage in Tribal Societies, ed. Meyer Fortes, pp. 14-54. Cambridge: Cambridge University Press, 1962.

____. Contexts of Kinship: An Essay in the Family Sociology of the Gonja of Northern Ghana. New York: Cambridge University Press, 1973.

Green, M. M. Ibo Village Affairs. New York: Frederick A. Praeger, 1947.

Henderson, Helen. "Ritual Roles of Women in Onitsha Ibo Society." Ph.D. dissertation, University of California, 1969.

Herskovits, Melville J. Dahomey. New York: J. J. Augustin, 1938.

____. "A Note on 'Woman Marriage' in Dahomey." Africa 10 (1937):335-41.

Hoffer, Carol P. "Women's Role: What Male Anthropologists Say vs. What Women Paramount Chiefs Do." A paper presented at the 70th Annual Meeting of the American Anthropological Association, New York, 1971. Mimeo. Franklin and Marshall College.

Huber, H. "Initiation to Womanhood among the Se (Ghana)." Nigerian Field 23 (July 1958):99-119.

Izzett, Alison. "Family Life among the Yoruba, in Lagos, Nigeria." In Social Change in Modern Africa, ed. A. Southall, pp. 305-15. London: Oxford University Press, 1961.

Jahoda, Gustav. "Love, Marriage and Social Change: Letters to the Advice Column of a West African Newspaper." Africa 29 (1958):177-90.

_____. "The Social Background of a West African Student Population." British Journal of Sociology 5, 6 (1954-55):355-69, 71-79.

Jakande, L. K., ed. West African Annals 1966. London: John West, 1966.

Joseph, Ceston. "Condition de la femme en Côte d'Ivoire." Société d'Anthropologie de Paris, Bulletins et Mémoires 4 (1913):385-89.

Kaye, Barrington. Bringing Up Children in Ghana. London: Allen & Unwin, 1962.

Kelly, John V. "The Influence of Native Customs on Obstetrics in Nigeria." Obstetrics and Gynecology 30 (1967):608-12.

Leis, Nancy B. "Economic Independence and Ijaw Women: A Comparative Study of Two Communities in the Niger Delta." Ph.D. dissertation, Northwestern University, 1964.

_____. "Women in Groups: Virilocality, Polygyny and Women's Associations in West Africa." A paper presented at the 70th Annual Meeting of the American Anthropological Association, New York, 1971. Mimeo. Central Michigan University.

Leith-Ross, Sylvia. African Conversation-piece. New York: Hutchinson, 1944.

_____. African Women: A Study of the Ibo of Nigeria. New York: Frederick A. Praeger, 1965.

LeVine, R. A.; Klein, N. H.; and Deven, C. R. "Father-child Relationships and Changing Life-styles in Ibadan Nigeria." In The City in Modern Africa, ed. H. Miner, pp. 215-55. New York: Frederick A. Praeger, 1967.

Lison Tolosana, C. "La condition de la femme au Niger." Revue Internationale de l'Education des Adultes et de la Jeunesse 15 (1963):133-37.

Little, Kenneth L. "The Changing Position of Women in the Sierra Leone Protectorate." Africa 18 (1948): 1-17.

_____. "Some Urban Patterns of Marriage and Domesticity in West Africa." Sociological Review 7 (1959):65-97.

MacLean, Una. "In Defense of Their Children." New Society 10 (July 1969):52-54.

McCall, Daniel F. "Family Structure and Changing Economic Activities of Women in a Gold Coast Town." Ph.D. dissertation, Columbia University, 1955.

___. "Trade and the Role of Wife in a Modern West African Town." In Social Change in Modern Africa, ed. A. Southall, pp. 284-99. London: Oxford University Press, 1961.

Marie-Andre du Sacre Coeur. The House Stands Firm: Family Life in West Africa, trans. Alba I. Zizzamia. Milwaukee: Bruce, 1962.

Marris, Peter. Family and Social Change in an African City: A Study of Rehousing in Lagos. London: Institute of Community Studies, 1962.

Marshall, Gloria. "In a World of Women: Field Work in a Yoruba Community." In Women in the Field: Anthropological Experiences, ed. Peggy Golde, pp. 167-94. Chicago: Aldine, 1970.

___. "Women, Trade and the Yoruba Family." Ph.D. dissertation, Columbia University, 1964.

Muller, Jean-Claude. "Preferential Marriage among the Rukuba of Benue-Plateau State, Nigeria." American Anthropologist 71 (1969):1057-62.

___. "Ritual Marriage, Symbolic Fatherhood and Initiation among the Rukuba, Plateau-Benue State, Nigeria." Man 7 (1972):283-95.

Netting, Robert McC. "Women's Weapons: The Politics of Domesticity among the Kofyar." American Anthropologist 71 (1969):1037-46.

Nigerian Broadcasting Corporation. Eminent Nigerians of the Nineteenth Century. New York: Cambridge University Press, 1960.

Ogunsheye, F. A. "Les femmes du Nigeria." Présence Africaine 32-33 (June-Sept. 1960):120-38.

Okediji, F. O. "Some Social Psychological Aspects of Fertility among Married Women in an African City." Nigerian Journal of Economic and Social Studies 9 (1967):67-79.

Okpewho, Isidore. The Victims: A Novel of Polygamy in Modern Africa. Garden City, N.Y.: Doubleday, 1971.

Omari, Peter. "Changing Attitudes of Students in West African Society towards Marriage and Family Relationships." British Journal of Sociology 11 (1960):197-210.

___. "Role Expectations in the Courtship Situation in Ghana." Social Forces 42 (1963):147-56.

Ottenberg, Simon. Double Descent in an African Society. Seattle: University of Washington Press, 1968.

Owusu, Maxwell. Uses and Abuses of Political Power: A Case Study of Continuity and Change in the Politics of Ghana. Chicago: University of Chicago Press, 1970.

Paulme, Denise. Une société de Côte d'Ivoire hier et aujourd'hui: les Bete. Paris: Mouton, 1962.

Ross, S. V. B. "Women in the Guianese Society." African Women 5 (Dec. 1962):21-22.

13

Sangree, Walter H. "Going Home to Mother: Traditional Marriage among the Kofyar." American Anthropologist 71 (1969):1046-57.
____. "Secondary Marriage and Tribal Solidarity in Irigwe, Nigeria." American Anthropologist 74 (1972): 1234-43.
Scarbrough, E. M. "Women of Liberia." African Women 3 (June 1959):35-37.
Smith, Mary. Baba of Karo: A Woman of the Moslem Hausa. New York: Philosophical Library, 1955.
Stratton, F. "West Africa's Women." West African Review 33 (Feb. 1962):10-13.
Talbot, D. Amaury. Woman's Mysteries of a Primitive People: The Ibibios of Southern Nigeria. New York: Cassell, 1915.
Thomas, Northcote Whitridge. "The West Coast of Africa." In Women of All Nations, vol. 1, ed. T. A. Joyce, pp. 333-59. New York: Funk and Wagnalls, 1915.
Usoro, E. J. "The Place of Women in Nigerian Society." African Women 4 (June 1961):27-30.

Congo: Angola, Burundi, Cameroun, Central African Republic, Congo, Gabon, Malawi, Rwanda, Zaire, Zambia

Albert, Ethel M. "Women of Burundi: A Study of Social Values." In Women of Tropical Africa, ed. Denise Paulme, pp. 179-216. Berkeley: University of California Press, 1971.
Balandier, Georges. Daily Life in the Kingdom of the Congo. New York: Random House, Pantheon Books, 1968.
Balsan, F. Chez les femmes à crinières du Sud-Angola. Paris: Faynard, 1964.
Binet, J. "Le statut des femmes au Cameroun forestier." Recueil Société Jean Bodin 11 (1959):45-62.
Brandel, M. "Urban Lobala Attitudes." African Studies 17 (1958):34-51.
Campbell, Henry D. A Congo Chattel: The Story of an African Slave Girl. New York: Christian Alliance, 1917.
Codere, Helen. "Field Work in Rwanda, 1959-1960." In Women in the Field: Anthropological Experiences, ed. Peggy Golde, pp. 143-66. Chicago: Aldine, 1970.
Collard, J. "La femme dans la sensibilité bantoue." Syntheses 2 (June 1956):288-91.
Comhaire-Sylvain, Suzanne. Femmes de Kinshasa: hier et aujourd'hui. Ecole Pratique des Hautes Etudes, le Monde d'Outre-Mer Passe et Present, troisième ser. Paris: Mouton, 1968.
David, Nicholas, and Hennig, Hilke. "The Ethnography of Pottery: A Fulani Case Seen in Archaeological Perspective." Module 21. Reading, Mass.: Addison-Wesley, 1972.

Dorsingfang-Smets, A. "Le statut de la femme dans la société primitive, spécialement en Afrique centrale." Recueil Société Jean Bodin 11 (1960):23-43.
Douglas, Mary. "A Form of Polyandry among the Lele." Africa 21 (1951):1-12.
Eby, O. "Zambian Women Recommend Reform in Marriage Laws." Christian Century 88 (Sept. 22, 1971):1112-14.
Evans-Pritchard, E. E. "Sexual Inversion among the Azande." American Anthropologist 72 (1970):1428-34.
Gluckman, Max. "Kinship and Marriage among the Lozi of Northern Rhodesia and the Zulu of Natal." In African Systems of Kinship and Marriage, ed. A. R. Radcliffe-Brown and Daryll Forde, pp. 166-206. New York: Oxford University Press, 1950.
Harris, Grace. Review of Femmes de Kinshasa: hier et aujourd'hui by Suzanne Comhaire-Sylvain. American Anthropologist 72 (1968):1484-86.
Kaberry, Phyllis M. Women in Grassfields: Study of the Economic Position of Women in Bamenda, British Cameroons, 2nd. ed. New York: Humanities Press, 1969.
Laurentin, Anne. "Nzakara Women." In Women of Tropical Africa, ed. Denise Paulme, pp. 121-78. Berkeley: University of California Press, 1971.
Lawman, T. "Civilizing Influence on the Copperbelt." Times British Colonies Review 36 (1959):23.
Mitchell, J. C. "Social Change and the Stability of African Marriage in Northern Rhodesia." In Social Change in Modern Africa, ed. A. Southall, pp. 316-29. London: Oxford University Press, 1961.
Powdermaker, Hortense. "Social Change through Imagery and Values of Teen-age Africans in Northern Rhodesia." American Anthropologist 58 (1959):783-813.
Retif, A. "Vers la liberation de la femme camerounaise." Etudes 284 (Jan. 1955):80-88.
Richards, Audrey I. Chisungu: A Girl's Initiation Ceremony among the Bemba of North Rhodesia. New York: Humanities Press, 1961.
___. "Some Types of Family Structure amongst the Central Bantu." In African Systems of Kinship and Marriage, ed. A. R. Radcliffe-Brown and Daryll Forde, pp. 207-51. First published, 1950. Reprint, New York: Oxford University Press, 1965.
Strangway, A. K. "The Advance of African Women in Angola." African Women 1 (1956):79-84.
Torday, Emil. "The Congo Free State." Women of All Nations, vol. 2, ed. T. A. Joyce, pp. 311-32. New York: Funk & Wagnalls, 1915.
Turnbull, Colin M. The Forest People. Garden City, N.Y.: Vantage Books, 1961.
___. "The Mbuti Pygmies of the Congo." In Peoples of Africa, ed. J. L. Gibbs, Jr., pp. 279-318. New York: Holt, Rinehart & Winston, 1965.

Turner, Victor. The Forest of Symbols: Aspects of
    Ndembu Ritual. Ithaca: Cornell University Press,
    1967.

East Horn: Ethiopia, Somalia

Bartels, Lambert. "Birth Customs and Birth Songs of the
    Macha Galla." Ethnology 8 (1969):406-22.
Cook, Alan (U.S. Peace Corps volunteer). Unpublished
    personal journal of Ethiopia. 1966-68.
"Ethiopian Woman's Status." Times Educational Sup-
    plement 2495 (Mar. 1963):510.
Greenfield, Richard. Ethiopia. New York: Frederick A.
    Praeger, 1965.
Huntingford, G. W. B. The Galla of Ethiopia. London:
    Hazzel Watson & Viney, 1955.
Levine, Donald N. Wax and Gold. Chicago: University
    of Chicago Press, 1965.
Messing, Simon D. "The Highland Plateau Amhara of
    Ethiopia." Ph.D. dissertation, University of
    Pennsylvania, 1957.
Reminick, Ronald A. "Ritual of Defloration: The
    Symbolic Expression of the Heterosexual Union Within
    the Institution of Marriage among the Amhara of
    Ethiopia." A paper presented at the 70th Annual
    Meeting of the American Anthropological Association,
    New York, 1971. Mimeo. Cleveland University.
U.N. Commission on Status of Women. Seminar on Par-
    ticipation of Women in Public Life, Addis Ababa, 1960.
    Report. New York: United Nations, 1961.

East African Cattle Area: Kenya, Mozambique, Rhodesia, Swaziland, Tanzania, Uganda

Beidelman, T. O. The Kaguru: A Matrilineal People of
    East Africa. New York: Holt, Rinehart & Winston,
    1971.
Bell, F. L. S. "Male and Female in Tanga." Mankind 5
    (May 1957):137-48.
Carlebach, J. Juvenile Prostitutes in Nairobi.
    Kampala: Institute of Social Research, 1963.
Child, H. F. "Family and Tribal Structure: Status of
    Women." Nada 35 (1958):65-70.
Earthy, Emily Dora. "Initiation of Girls in the
    Masiyeni District, Portuguese East Africa." In Annal
    of the Transvaal Museum 11 (1925):103-17.
_____. Valenge Women: The Social and Economic Life of
    the Valenge Women of Portuguese East Africa: An
    Ethnographic Study. First published, 1933. Reprint,
    London: Cass, 1968.

Edgerton, Robert E. "Pokot Intersexuality: An East
    African Example of Resolutions of Sexual Incongruity."
    American Anthropologist 66 (Dec. 1964):6.
Ember, Carol. "'Feminine' Task-Assignment and Its
    Effect on the Social Behavior of Boys." A paper
    presented at the 69th Annual Meeting of the American
    Anthropological Association, San Diego, 1970. Mimeo.
    Hunter College.
Evans, Maurice S. Black and White in Southeast Africa:
    A Study in Sociology. New York: Negro Universities
    Press, 1911.
Felkin, R. W. "East Africa." In Women of All Nations,
    vol. 2, ed. T. A. Joyce. New York: Funk &
    Wagnalls, 1915.
Fox, L. K., ed. East African Childhood. New York:
    Oxford University Press, 1967.
Glazier, Jack. "Sexuality and Ritual in Mbeare, Kenya."
    A paper presented at the 70th Annual Meeting of the
    American Anthropological Association, New York, 1971.
    Mimeo. Oberlin College.
Gray, R. F. "Sonjo Bride Price and the Question of
    African 'Wife Purchase.'" American Anthropologist
    62 (1960):34-57.
Henrigues, F. Figueira. Contribuição para o estudo de
    fertilidade da mulher indígena no ultramar português.
    Estudos, Ensaios e Documentos 38. Lisbon: Junta de
    Investigações do Ultramar, 1957.
Kisosonkole, P. "La femme africaine dans l'Ouganda
    moderne." Way Forum 32 (1959):48-51.
Klima, G. "Jural Relations between the Sexes among the
    Barabaig." Africa 34 (Jan. 1964):9-20.
Kuper, Hilda. "Kinship among the Swazi." In African
    Systems of Kinship and Marriage, ed. A. R. Radcliffe-
    Brown and Daryll Forde, pp. 86-110. New York:
    Oxford University Press, 1950.
    ___. A Witch in My Heart: A Play about the Swazi
    People. London: Oxford University Press, 1970.
Landberg, Pamela. "Women's Roles and Spirit Possession
    Cults: Bitchcraft or a Question of Options?" A paper
    presented at the 70th Annual Meeting of the American
    Anthropological Association, New York, 1971. Mimeo.
    University of California, Davis.
Lessing, Doris. The Grass Is Singing. London: M.
    Joseph, 1950.
LeVine, Robert A. "Witchcraft and Co-wife Proximity in
    Southwestern Kenya." Ethnology 1 (1962):39-45.
    ___. "Gusii Sex Offenses: A Study in Social Control."
    American Anthropologist 61 (1959):965-90.
    ___, and LeVine, Barbara B. Nyansongo: A Gusii Com-
    munity in Kenya. New York: John Wiley, 1966.
"Literacy Program for the Women of Uganda." UNESCO
    Features 433 (Feb. 1964):7.
McVicar, Thomas. "The Position of Woman among the
    Wanguru." Primitive Man 7 (1934):17-22.

Marce, M. E.   "The Nyasa Woman at Home and in Southern
    Rhodesia."   In Proceedings of the Missionary Con-
    ference of Southern Rhodesia.   Salisbury, 1928.
Molnos, A.   Attitudes towards Family Planning in East
    Africa.   Munich: Weltforum Verlag, 1968.
Oloo, Celina Nyai, and Cone, Virginia.   Kenya Women Look
    Ahead.   Nairobi: East African Literature Bureau, n.d.
Perlman, Melvin L.   "The Changing Status and Role of
    Women in Toro, Western Uganda."   Cahiers d'Etudes
    Africaines 6 (1966):564-91.
Thurnwald, Richard.   Black and White in East Africa.
    London: Routledge, 1935.
Uganda Commission on Marriage, Divorce and the Status of
    Women.   Report.   Entebbe: Government Printer, 1965.
Whiting, Beatrice B.   "Mothers and Their Preschool
    Children in a Period of Rapid Social Change."   Paper
    prepared for UNICEF publication on the preschool
    child, April, 1972.
____, and Whiting, John W.   "Task Assignment and Per-
    sonality: A Consideration of the Effect of Herding
    on Boys."   A paper presented at the University of East
    Africa Social Science Conference, Dar-es-Salaam, 1968.
Wilson, Monica.   "Nyakyusa Kinship."   In African Systems
    of Kinship and Marriage, ed. A. R. Radcliffe-Brown
    and Daryll Forde, pp. 111-39.   New York: Oxford
    University Press, 1950.

South Africa: Botswana, Lesotho,
South Africa, Southwest Africa

Blacking, John.   "Songs, Dances, Mimes, and Symbolism of
    Venda Girl's Initiation Schools."   African Studies 28
    (1969):3, 35.
Brandel, M.   "The African Career Woman in South Africa."
    African Women 2 (June 1957):36-38.
Draper, Patricia.   "The Hunting and Gathering Mode of
    Subsistence and Its Relation to Child Rearing: A
    Review of the Bacon, Barry and Child Hypothesis."   A
    paper presented at the 70th Annual Meeting of the
    American Anthropological Association, New York, 1971.
    Mimeo.   Harvard University.
Eiselen, Werner M.   "Die posisie von die weduwee by die
    heidense en by die Kristelika Baton."   Bantu Studies
    9 (1935):281-85.
Hunter, Monica.   "The Effects of Contact with Europeans
    on the Status of Pondo Women."   Africa 6 (1933):259-76.
Kriege, Eileen Jensen.   "Girls' Puberty Songs and Their
    Relation to Fertility, Health, Morality and Religion
    among the Zulu."   Africa 38 (1968):173-98.
____, and Kriege, J. D.   The Realm of the Rain Queen: A
    Study of the Pattern of Lovedu Society.   London:
    International African Institute, 1943.

Lewin, J. "The Legal Status of African Women." Race
    Relations Journal 26 (Oct.-Dec. 1959):152-59.
Longmore, Laura. The Dispossessed: A Study of the Sex-
    life of Bantu Women in Urban Areas in and around
    Johannesburg. London: J. Cape, 1959.
Marshall, Lorna. "Marriage among the Bushmen." Africa
    29 (1959):335-64.
Reyher, Rebecca Houruich. Zulu Woman. Preface by Ruth
    Benedict. New York: Columbia University Press, 1948.
Schapera, I. "Kinship and Marriage among the Tswana."
    In African Systems of Kinship and Marriage, ed. A. R.
    Radcliffe-Brown and Daryll Forde, pp. 140-65. New
    York: Oxford University Press, 1950.
___. Western Civilization and the Natives of South
    Africa. London: Routledge & Kegan Paul, 1967.
Simons, H. J. African Women: Their Legal Status in South
    Africa. Evanston: Northwestern University Press,
    1968.
"Swaziland's Women Prepare for the Future." UNESCO
    Features 502 (May 1967):21.
Theal, George McCall. The Yellow and Dark-skinned People
    of Africa South of the Zambesi. New York: Negro
    Universities Press, 1969.
van den Berghe, Pierre. Social Structure of a South
    African Town. Connecticut: Wesleyan University Press,
    1964.
___. South Africa: A Study in Conflict. Middletown,
    Conn.: Wesleyan University Press, 1965.
Werner, Alice. "South and Southwest Africa." In Women
    of All Nations, vol. 2, ed. T. A. Joyce, pp. 272-310.
    New York: Funk & Wagnalls, 1915.

Malagasay Republic

Auber, J. "La femme dans les traditions et les moeurs
    malgaches." Revue Madagascar 22 (1955):43-48.
Benedict, Burton. "The Equality of the Sexes in the
    Seychelles." In Social Organization: Essays in
    Honor of Raymond Firth, ed. M. Freedman, pp. 43-65.
    Chicago: Aldine, 1967.
Razafyadriamihaingo, S. "La femme a Madagascar."
    Africa 16 (Feb. 1961):29-32.
___. "The Position of Women in Madagascar." African
    Women 3 (June 1959):29-33.
VanGennep, Arnold. "Madagascar." In Women of All
    Nations, vol. 2, ed. T. A. Joyce, pp. 209-14. New
    York: Funk & Wagnalls, 1915.

MIDDLE EAST

Introductory and General Islamic Texts

Abbot, Nabia. Aishah, the Beloved of Mohammed. Chicago:
University of Chicago Press, 1942.
___. "Women and the State in Early Islam." Journal of
Near Eastern Studies 1 (1942):106-26, 341-68.
Anderson, J. N. D. "Recent Developments in Shari^{c}a Law."
Muslim World 40 (1950):244-56;41(1951):34-48,113-26,
186-98,277-88;42(1952):33-47,124-40,190-206,257-76.
Bouvat, L. "Le code familial Ottoman de 1917." Revue du
Monde Musulman 43 (1921):5-26.
deBellefonds, Linant. "La repudiation dans l'Islam
d'aujourd'hui." Revue Internationale de Droit Comparé
14 (1962):521-48.
Feroze, M. R. "The Reform of Family Laws in the Muslim
World." Islamic Studies 1 (1962):107-30.
Flory, Vera E. "Women and Culture in Islam." Muslim
World 30 (Jan. 1940).
Gaudio, A. La revolution des femmes en Islam. Paris:
Julliard, 1957.
Hassum, H. C. "Social Rights of Muslim Women." Asian
Review 198 (Apr. 1956):158-60.
Hussein, A. "Women in the Muslim World." World Muslim
League Monthly 1 (May 1964):22-36.
Ibn ou Alfourat. "Quelques reflexions sur la femme
musulmane à travers les ages." Afrique et l'Asie 51
(1960):46-50.
Khuri, Faud L. "Parallel Cousin Marriage Reconsidered:
A Middle Eastern Practice That Nullifies the Effects
of Marriage on the Intensity of Family Relationships."
Man 5 (Dec. 1970):597-618.
Kilibanov, L. A. Islam i zhenshchina [Islam and the
woman]. Frunze, Kirgiz SSR: Kirgizgosizdat, 1963.
Lichtenstadter, Ilse. Islam and the Modern Age: An
Analysis and an Appraisal. New York: Twayne, 1960.
Malik, Fida Hussain. Wives of the Prophet. Lahore:
Sh. Muhammad Ashraf, 1961.
Melek-Hanum. Thirty Years in the Harem; or The Auto-
biography of Melek-Hanum, Wife of H. H. Kibriz-
limehemet-Pasha. New York: Harper, 1872.
Patrick, Mary Mills. "The Emancipation of Mohammedan
Women." National Geographic 20 (1909):42-66.
Rosenfeld, Henry. "An Analysis of Marriage and Marriage
Statistics for a Moslem and Christian Arab Village."
Internationales Archiv für Ethnographie 48 (1957):
32-62.
Roussier, J. "La femme dans la société islamique:
droit malikite maghribin." Recueil Société Jean
Bodin 11 (1959):223-36.
Salman, A. "Polygamy and the Status of Women in
Islamic Society." Majallat at-Azhar 33 (1961):17-24.
Shaltout, M. "The Position of Women in Islam."
Majallat al-Azhar 32/1 (1961):4-13; 32/2:6-15; 32/7:
6-23.

"Shedding the Veil." Newsweek, October 25, 1971.
Siddiqi, Mohammad Mazharuddin. Women in Islam. Lahore:
    Institute of Islamic Culture, 1959.
Sweet, Louise E., ed. "Appearance and Reality: Status
    and Roles of Women in Mediterranean Societies."
    Anthropological Quarterly 10 (1967):95-183.
____. The Central Middle East: A Handbook of Anthropology
    and Published Research on the Nile Valley, the Arab
    Levant, Southern Mesopotamia, the Arabian Peninsula
    and Israel. New Haven: Human Relations Area Files
    Press, 1971.
Woodsmall, Ruth Frances. Moslem Women Enter a New World.
    New York: Round Table Press, 1936.

                Arabia: Kuwait, Saudi Arabia, Yemen

Abu-Zahra, Nadia M. "On the Modesty of Women in Arab
    Muslim Villages: A Reply." American Anthropologist
    72 (1970):1079-92.
"Access of Girls to Education in the Arab States."
    UNESCO Chronicle 10 (May 1964):173.
Antoun, Richard T. "Antoun's Reply to Abu-Zahra."
    American Anthropologist 72 (1968):1088-92.
____. "On the Modesty of Women in Arab Muslim Villages:
    A Study of the Accommodation of Traditions."
    American Anthropologist 70 (1968):671-97.
Chelhod, J. "Notes sur le marriage chez les Arabes du
    Kowet." Journal de la Société des Africanistes 26
    (1956):255-67.
Final Report: Meeting of Experts on the Access of Girls
    and Women to Technical and Vocational Education in the
    Arab States, Kuwait. Paris: UNESCO Publications,
    1970.
Hansen, Henry Harold. "The Patterns of Women's Seclusion
    and Veiling in a Shia Village (Bahrain)." Folk 3
    (1961):23-42.
Lichtenstadter, Ilse. Women in the Aiyam al-'Arav: A
    Study of Female Life during Warfare in Pre-Islamic
    Arabia. London: Royal Asiatic Society, 1935.
Muhyi, Ibrahim Abdulla. "Women in the Arab Middle East."
    Journal of Social Issues 15 (1959):45-57.
"New Women in the Arab World." UNESCO Information
    Bulletin 19 (Nov. 1964):14.
Serjeant, R. B. "Recent Marriage Legislation from al-
    Mukalla with Notes on Marriage Customs." Bulletin of
    the School of Oriental and African Studies (University
    of London) 25 (1962):472-98.
Vernier, Pierre. "Education for Arab Girls, Economic
    Expansion, Changing Attitudes Favour Progress."
    UNESCO Features 437 (Apr. 1964):14-17.

Iran

Mahludji, M. Die Frauenbildung in Iran und ihr
kulturgeschichtlicher Hintergrund. Cologne, 1965.
Rice, Clara Colliver Hammond. Persian Women and Their
Ways: The Experiences and Impressions of a Long
Sojourn amongst the Women of the Land of the Shah,
with an Intimate Description of Their Characteristics,
Customs and Manner of Living. London: Seeley,
Service, 1923.
Serin. "La femme persane." Civilisations 1 (1951):4,
41-44.
Spooner, B. "Kinship and Marriage in Eastern Persia."
Sociologus 15 (1965):22-37.
Sykes, Ella C. "Persia." In Women of All Nations, vol. 4,
ed. T. A. Joyce, pp. 633-845. New York: Funk &
Wagnalls, 1915.
Yohannan, Jacob Baba. Woman in the Orient. St. Louis:
A. R. Fleming, 1901.

Iraq

Drower, E. S. "Woman and Taboo in Iraq." Iraq 5 (1938):
105-17.
Fernea, Elizabeth Warnock. Guests of the Sheik: An
Ethnography of an Iraqi Village. Garden City, N.Y.:
Doubleday, Anchor Books, 1965.
Hansen, Henry Harold. Daughters of Allah: Among the
Muslim Women in Kurdistan. London: Allen & Unwin, 1960.
____. "Growing Up in Two Different Areas: Field Research
in Iraqi Kurdistan and Bahrain." Folk 5 (1963):143-56.
____. The Kurdish Woman's Life: Field Research in a
Muslim Society, Iraq. Copenhagen: National Museum,
1961.
Jean, C. F. "De la condition de la femme, dans la Bosse-
Mesopotamie, d'après les documents sumeriens et
akkadiens anterieurs au XVIIe siècle au J.-C." In
Fifteenth International Congress of Anthropology and
Prehistoric Archaeology, pt.2, pp. 698-700. Paris,
1931.

Israel

Agress, Eliyahu. Golda Meir: Portrait of a Prime
Minister, trans. Israel I. Taslitt. New York: Sabra
Books, 1969.
Auerbach, H. A. "Social Stratification in Israel's
Collectives." Rural Sociology 18 (Mar. 1953):25-34.
Baldensperger, Philip J. "Birth, Marriage and Death among
the Fellahin of Palestine." Palestine Exploration
Fund Quarterly Statement (1894):127-44.

Barad, Mirram. "Women as Managers in Israel." Public
    Administration in Israel and Abroad, 1966 (1967):
    78-87.
Bar Joseph, Rikvak. "The Pattern of Early Socialization
    in the Collective Settlements in Israel." Human
    Relations 12 (1959):345-60.
Ben-Gurion, David. "How Is Israel Different?" Jewish
    Frontier 29 (Aug. 1962):7-14.
Bentwich, Norman. Israel Resurgent. New York:
    Frederick A. Praeger, 1960.
Ben-Yosef, A. C. "The Woman in the Kibbutz." Israel
    Horizons (1957):16-19.
Bettelheim, Bruno. The Children of the Dream. New York:
    Macmillan, 1969.
de Beauvoir, Simone. "On Israeli Woman." New Outlook
    10 (May 1967):14-26.
Diamond, Stanley. "Collective Child-rearing: The
    Kibbutz." In The Family: Its Structure and Functions,
    ed. Rose Coser. New York: St. Martin's Press, 1964.
____. "Kibbutz and Shtetl: The History of an Idea."
    Social Problems 5 (1957):71-94.
Dowty, Nancy. "To Be a Woman in Israel." Women in
    Education, Special Issue. School Review 80 (1972).
Drabkin, Haim. The Other Society. London: Gollancz,
    1962.
Eaton, Joseph W. "Gadna: Israel's Youth Corps." Middle
    East Journal 23 (Autumn 1969):471-83.
Eisenstadt, S. N. Israeli Society. New York: Basic
    Books, 1967.
Elston, D. R. Israel: The Making of a Nation. London:
    Oxford University Press, 1963.
Etzioni, A. "The Fundamental Differentiation of Elites
    in the Kibbutz." American Journal of Sociology 64
    (Mar. 1959):476-87.
Fitch, Florence Mary. The Daughters of Abd Salam: The
    Story of a Peasant Woman of Palestine. Somerville,
    Mass.: Bruce Humphries, 1934.
Gervasi, Frank. The Case for Israel. New York: Viking,
    1967.
Goshen-Gottstein, Esther R. Marriage and First Preg-
    nancy: Cultural Influences on Attitudes of Israeli
    Women. London: Tavistock, 1966.
Granquist, Hilma Natalia. Birth and Childhood among the
    Arabs: Studies in a Muhammedan Village in Palestine.
    Helsingfors: Söderstrom, 1947.
____. Child Problems among the Arabs: Studies in a
    Muhammedan Village in Palestine. Helsingfors:
    Söderstrom, 1950.
____. Marriage Conditions in a Palestinian Village. 2.
    Helsingfors: Akademische Buchhandlung, 1931-35.
Irvine, E. R. "Observations on the Aims and Methods of
    Child-rearing in Communal Settlements in Israel."
    Human Relations 5:247-75.

Karovsky, Eliyahu. The Economy of the Israeli Kibbutz. Cambridge: Harvard University Press, 1966.

Larteguy, Jean. The Walls of Israel, trans. Ormonde de Kay, Jr. New York: M. Evans, 1969.

Leon, D. The Kibbutz. Tel Aviv: Israel Horizons, 1964.

McDonald, James G. My Mission in Israel. New York: Simon & Schuster, 1951.

Marshall, S. L. A. "The Army of Israel." Military Review 48 (Apr. 1968):3-9.

Miller, Irving. Israel: The Eternal Ideal. New York: Farrar, Straus & Cudahy, 1955.

Neubauer, Peter B., ed. Children in Collectives: Child-rearing Aims and Practices in the Kibbutz. Springfield, Ill.: Charles C. Thomas, 1965.

Nussbaum, Elizabeth. Israel. London: Oxford University Press, 1968.

Patai, Raphael. Israel between East and West. Philadelphia: Jewish Publication Society of America, 1953.

Prittle, Terence. Israel: Miracle in the Desert, rev. ed. New York: Frederick A. Praeger, 1967.

Rabin, A. I. "Attitudes of Kibbutz Children to Parents and Family." American Journal of Orthopsychiatry 29 (1959):172-79.

____. Growing Up in a Kibbutz: Comparison of Children Brought Up in the Kibbutz and of Family-reared Children. New York: Springer, 1965.

____. "Infants and Children under Conditions of Intermittent Mothering." American Journal of Orthopsychiatry 28 (1958):577-86.

Rabkin, L. Y. "A Very Special Education in the Israeli Kibbutz." Journal of Special Education 2 (1967): 251-61.

Rosenfeld, E. "Institutional Change in the Kibbutz." Social Problems 5 (1957):110-36.

Rosenfeld, H. "On Determinants of the Status of Arab Village Women." Man 60 (May 1960):66-70.

Rosner, M. "Women in the Kibbutz." Asian and African Studies 3 (1967):35-68.

Samuel, Edwin. Structure of Israeli Society. New York: Random House, 1969.

Shain, Rochelle. "The Sexual Division of Labor on Mishpati, an Israeli Kibbutz." A paper presented at the 69th Annual Meeting of the American Anthropological Association, San Diego, 1971. Mimeo. University of California, Berkeley.

Shuval, Judith T. "Perceived Role Components of Nursing in Israel." American Sociological Review 28 (Feb. 1963):37-46.

Spiro, Melford E. Children of the Kibbutz. New York: Schocken Books, 1965.

_____. "Education in a Collective Settlement in Israel."
American Journal of Orthopsychiatry 25 (1955):283-92.
_____. Kibbutz: Venture in Utopia. Cambridge: Harvard
University Press, 1956.
Stern, Bernhard. The Scented Garden: Anthropology of
the Sex Life in the Levant, trans. David Berger.
New York: American Ethnological Press, 1934.
Stern, Boris. The Kibbutz That Was. Washington, D.C.:
Public Affairs Press, 1965.
Stern, Geraldine. Daughters from Afar: Profiles of
Israeli Women. New York: Bloch, 1958.
Syrkin, Marie. Golda Meir: Israel's Leader. New York:
G. P. Putnam's Sons, 1969.
Talmon-Garber, Yonina. "The Family in a Revolutionary
Movement: The Case of the Kibbutz in Israel." In
Comparative Family Systems, ed. M. Nimhoff, pp. 257-
86. Boston: Houghton Mifflin, 1965.
_____. "Family vs. Community: Patterns of Divided
Loyalties in Israel." In Comparative Perspectives on
Marriage and the Family, ed. H. Rent Girger. Boston:
Little, Brown, 1968.
_____. "Sex-role Differentiation in an Equalitarian
Society." In Life in Society, ed. Harold Lasswell
et al., pp. 144-55. Glenview, Ill.: Scott
Foresman, 1964.
_____. "Social Structure and Family Size." Human
Relations 12 (1959):2.
Waagenaar, Sam. Women of Israel. New York: Schocken
Books, 1962.
Weingarten, Murray. Life in a Kibbutz. New York:
Reconstructionist Press, 1955.
Weintraub, D.; Lissak, M.; and Azman, Y. Moshava,
Kibbutz, Moshav: Patterns of Jewish Rural Settlement
and Development in Palestine. Ithaca: Cornell
University Press, 1969.
Willner, Dorothy. Nation-Building and Community in
Israel. Princeton: Princeton University Press, 1969.
Zweig, Ferdynand. Israel: The Sword and the Harp.
Cranbury, N.J.: Associated University Presses, 1969.
_____. The Israeli Worker: Achievements, Attitudes and
Aspirations. New York: Herzl Press, 1959.

Turkey

Anderson, J. N. D. "The Family Law of the Turkish
Cypriots." World of Islam 5 (1958):161-87.
Brown, Demetra Vaka. Haremlik: Some Pages from the
Life of Turkish Women. Boston: Houghton Mifflin,
1909.

____. *The Unveiled Ladies of Stamboul*. Boston: Houghton Mifflin, 1923.

Decourdemanche, J. A. *The Wiles of Women*, trans. J. and S. F. Mills Whitham. London: Golden Dragon Library, 1928.

Dobkin, Marlene. "Social Ranking in the Woman's World of Purdah: A Turkish Example. *Anthropological Quarterly* 40 (1967):65-72.

Edif, Halide. "Woman's Part in Turkey's Progress." *The Opencourt* 46 (1932):343-60.

Ellison, Grace Mary. *Turkey To-day*. London: Hutchinson, 1928.

Esenkova, P. "La femme turque contemporaire: education et rôle social." *l'Institut des Belles Lettres Arabes* 14 (1951):255-77.

Fitzpatrick, William. *Istanbul after Dark*. New York: Macfadden Bartell, 1970.

Garnett, Lucy M. "Turkey and Greece." In *Women of All Nations*, vol. 4, ed. T. A. Joyce. New York: Funk & Wagnalls, 1908.

____. *The Women of Turkey and Their Folklore*. London: David Nutt, 1890-91.

Guntekin, Resat Nuri. *The Autobiography of a Turkish Girl*. London: Allen & Unwin, 1949.

Inan, Afet. *The Emancipation of the Turkish Woman*. Paris: UNESCO Publications, 1962.

Jaschke, G. "Die Frauenfrage in der Turkei." *Saeculum* 10 (1959):360-69.

Jean, C. F. "De la condition de la femme, dans la Bosse-Mesopotamie, d'après les documents sumeriens et akkadiens anterieurs au XVIIe siècle au J.-C." In *Fifteenth International Congress of Anthropology and Prehistoric Archaeology*, pt.2, pp. 698-700. Paris, 1931.

Jenkins, Hester Donaldson. *Behind Turkish Lattices: The Story of a Turkish Woman's Life*. London: Chatto & Windus, 1911.

Johnson, Clarence R. "Courtship and Marriage Customs of the Turks and Greeks." *Journal of Applied Sociology* 10 (1925).

____. "Evil Eye and Other Superstitions in Turkey." *Journal of Applied Sociology* 9 (1925):259-68.

League of Nations. *Report of the Commission for the Protection of Women and Children in the Near East, July 1, 1925 - June 30, 1926*. Geneva: Imp. d'Ainbilly, 1926.

Lewis, Bernard. "Men, Women and Traditions in Turkey." *Geographical Magazine* 32 (1959):346-54.

Meakin, Annette. "Turkestan." In *Women of All Nations*, vol. 4, ed. T. A. Joyce, pp. 646-53. New York: Funk & Wagnalls, 1915.

Orga, Irfan. Portrait of a Turkish Family. New York:
    Macmillan, 1950.
Paris, Pierre. Quatenus feminae res publicas in Asia
    Minore, Romanis imperantibus, attigerint. Paris:
    Apud Ernestum Thorin, 1891.
Penzer, Norman Mosley. The Harem. London: Spring
    Books, 1965.
Ramsey, Lady. "Asia Minor." In Women of All Nations,
    vol. 4, ed. T. A. Joyce, pp. 654-63. New York:
    Funk & Wagnalls, 1915.
Schreiner, George Abel. From Berlin to Bagdad: Behind
    the Scenes in the Near East. New York: Harper, 1918.
Sonmez, Emel. "Turkish Women in Turkish Literature of
    the Nineteenth Century." Die Welt des Islams 12
    (1969):1-73.
Stirling, A. Paul. "Land, Marriage and the Law in
    Turkish Villages." International Social Science
    Bulletin 9 (1957):21-33.
Zeyneb, Lanum. A Turkish Woman's European Impressions,
    ed. Grace Ellison. London: Seeley, Service, 1913.

Jordan, Lebanon, Syria

Anderson, J. N. D. "The Syrian Law of Personal Status."
    Bulletin of the School of Oriental and African
    Studies (University of London) 17 (1955):34-49.
Gulick, John. "Social Structure and Culture Change in a
    Lebanese Village." Viking Fund Publications in
    Anthropology 21 (1951):1-191.
Joly, Gertrude. "The Women of the Lebanon." Journal of
    the Royal Central Asian Society 38 (1951):177-84.
Khairullah, Ibrahim A. The Law of Inheritance in the
    Republics of Syria and Lebanon. Beirut: American
    Press, 1941.
Khalaf, Samir. Prostitution in a Changing Society: A
    Sociological Survey of Legal Prostitution in Beirut.
    Beirut: Khayats, 1965.
Klima, J. "Die Stellung der ugaritischen Frau." [The
    position of Ugaritic woman]. Archiv Orient 25 (1957):
    313-33.
Prothro, E. T. Child-rearing in the Lebanon. Harvard
    Middle Eastern Monographs, 8. Cambridge: Harvard
    University Press, 1961.
Sweet, Louise E. "The Women of 'Ain Dayr." Anthro-
    pological Quarterly 40 (1967):167-83.
Vatuk, Ved Prakash. "The Position of Women in Hittite
    Laws and Manusmurti." Journal of Asian and African
    Studies 2 (1967):251-65.
Williams, Herbert H. "Sixteen Autobiographical Dream
    Series of Moslem Maronite Men and Women." In Primary
    Records in Culture and Personality, vol. 4, ed. Bert
    Kaplan. Madison: Microcard Foundation, n.d.

27

ASIA

Introductory Texts

Reischauer, Edwin, and Fairbank, John K. East Asia:
The Great Tradition, vol. I. Boston: Houghton
Mifflin, 1960.
Ward, Barbara E., ed. Women in the New Asia: The
Changing Social Roles of Men and Women in South and
Southeast Asia. Paris: UNESCO Publications, 1963.

General References

Aldaba-Lim, Estefania. "The Role and Status of Young
Asian Women Today." UNESCO Philippines 4 (May–June
1965):156-63.
Andersen-Rosendal, Jørgen. The Moon of Beauty: Woman
and Love in the East, trans. Eiler Hanson and J. F.
Burke. New York: John Day, 1958.
Anderson, J. N. D. Family Law in Asia and Africa. New
York: Frederick A. Praeger, 1967.
Breitenbach, Josef. Women of Asia. Introduction by
Spurgeon M. Keeny. New York: John Day, 1968.
Burton, Margaret Ernestine. Women Workers of the
Orient. West Medford, Mass.: Central Committee on
the United Study of Foreign Missions, 1918.
"Conditions of Employment of Women Workers in Asia."
Geneva: International Labour Office, 1955. Reprinted
from International Labour Review 70 (Dec. 1954).
Cousins, Margaret E. The Awakening of Asian Womanhood.
Madras: Ganesh, 1922.
Fisher, Marguerite J. "Higher Education of Women and
National Development in Asia." Asia Survey 8 (Apr.
1968):263-69.
Houghton, Ross C. Women of the Orient. New York:
Nelson & Phillips, 1877.
Meeting of Experts on the Access of Girls and Women to
Education in Rural Areas in Asia (Bangkok, Feb. 26-
Mar. 8,1962). Final Report 193. Paris: UNESCO
Publications, 1962.
Paul, Radha. "Equipping Women for Participation in
Economic Life." In Long Term Educational and
Training Programmes for the Advancement of Women in
Asia. Bombay: International Seminar, 1967.
Peerbhoy, Homai. "Civic Education for Women." In Long
Term Educational and Training Programmes for Advance-
ment of Women in Asia. Bombay: International
Seminar, 1967.

Pernell, Ruby B. "Training for Professions and Careers." In Long Term Educational and Training Programmes for the Advancement of Women in Asia. Bombay: International Seminar, 1967.

Report of the Asian Conference and Seminar on the Role of Women's Voluntary Organizations in Economic, Social and Cultural Development (Kuala Lumpur, Mar. 27-Apr.7, 1961). London: Associated Country Women of the World, 1961.

Report to the Governments of Ceylon, India, Indonesia, Japan, Pakistan, the Philippines and Thailand on Conditions of Women's Work in Seven Asian Countries. Geneva: International Labour Office, 1958.

U.N. Commission on Status of Women. Seminar on the Civic Responsibilities and Increased Participation of Asian Women in Public Life. Bangkok, 1957. Report. New York: United Nations, 1957.

Wattel, J. Harem: Vrouwenleven in het Oosten. Meppel: Boom und Zoon, 1955.

YWCA, U.S. National Board, Education and Research Division. Women in Industry in the Orient: A Source Book. New York: Woman's Press, 1926.

Zinkin, Taya. "The Position of Women in Asia." In Asia: A Handbook, ed. Guy Wint, pp. 581-86. New York: Frederick A. Praeger, 1966.

Japan

Ackermann, Jessie. "The Ainu." In Women of All Nations, vol. 3, ed. T. A. Joyce. New York: Funk & Wagnalls, 1915.

Akimoto, Shunkichi. Family Life in Japan. Tokyo: Maruzen, 1937.

Ariga, Kizaeman. "The Contemporary Japanese Family in Transition." In Transactions of the Third World Congress of Sociology, vol. 4. Amsterdam: International Sociological Association, 1956.

Azuma, T. Yome no tengoku: Shima no inkyo-no-jo-sei [Paradise for "yome"--young wife--retiring system of Shima area]. Tokyo: Miraisha, 1959.

Bacon, Alice M. Japanese Girls and Women. Boston: Houghton Mifflin, 1902.

Beard, Mary. Force of Women in Japanese History. Washington, D.C.: Public Affairs Press, 1953.

Beardsley, Richard; Hall, John W.; and Ward, Robert E. Village Japan. Chicago: University of Chicago Press, 1959.

Bellah, R. Tokugawa Religion. Glencoe, Ill.: Free Press, 1957.

Benedict, Ruth. The Chrysanthemum and the Sword. Boston: Houghton Mifflin, 1946.

Black, Lydia T. "Relative Status of Wife Givers and Wife Takers in Gilyak Society." American Anthropologist 74 (1972):1244-48.

Borton, Hugh, ed. Japan. Ithaca: Cornell University Press, 1951.

Burch, Thomas. "Induced Abortion in Japan." Eugenics Quarterly 2 (1955):140-51.

Burton, Margaret. The Education of Women in Japan. New York: Fleming H. Revell, 1914.

Caudill, William. "Tiny Dramas: Vocal Communication between Infants and Mothers in Japan and America." A paper presented at the 68th Annual Meeting of the American Anthropological Association, New Orleans, 1969. Mimeo. National Institute of Mental Health.

___, and Frost, Lois. "A Comparison of Maternal Care and Infant Behavior in Japanese-American, American, and Japanese Families." A paper presented at the 70th Annual Meeting of the American Anthropological Association, New York, 1971. Mimeo. National Institute of Mental Health.

Corassel, F. "Die Stellung der Ehefrau in Japan." Anthropos 3 (1908):533-55.

Cressy, E. H. Daughters of Changing Japan. London: Gollancz, 1955.

DeMente, Boye. Some Prefer Geisha: The Lively Art of Mistress Keeping in Japan. Rutland, Vt.: C. E. Tuttle, 1966.

DeVos, George, and Wagatsuma, Hiroshi. "Value Attitudes toward Role Behavior of Women in Two Japanese Villages." American Anthropologist 63 (1961): 1204-30.

Dore, R. P. City Life in Japan: A Study of a Tokyo Ward. Berkeley: University of California Press, 1958.

___. Education in Tokugawa Japan. Berkeley: University of California Press, 1965.

___, ed. Aspects of Social Change in Modern Japan. Princeton: Princeton University Press, 1967.

Faust, Allen Klein. The New Japanese Womanhood. New York: George H. Doran, 1926.

Fueto, Toshi. "Discrepancy between Marriage Law and Morals in Japan." American Journal of Comparative Law 5 (Spring 1956):256-66.

Fujita, Taki. Japanese Women in Post War Years. Kyoto: 12th Conference, Institute of Pacific Relations, Sept.-Oct. 1959.

Goodman, Mary Ellen. "Values and Attitudes and Social Concepts of Japanese and American Children." American Anthropologist 59 (1957):979-99.

Gulick, Sidney Lewis. Evolution of the Japanese. New York: Fleming H. Revell, 1903.

___. Working Women of Japan. New York: Missionary Education Movement of the U.S. & Canada, 1915.

Haldeman, C. The Sun's Attendant. New York: Simon & Schuster, 1964.

Hasegawa, Nyozekan. The Japanese Character. Palo Alto, Calif.: Kodansha International, 1966.

Hatsumi, Reiko. Rain and the Feast of the Stars. Boston: Houghton Mifflin, 1959.

Hearn, Lafcadio. "A Woman's Tragedy." Transactions and Proceedings of the Japanese Society, Oct. 1902.

Holland, Clive. "Japan." In Women of All Nations, vol. 3, ed. T. A. Joyce, pp. 489-515. New York: Funk & Wagnalls, 1915.

Hoppe, E. "Le statut de la femme ainu." Société Royale Belge d'Anthropologie et de Prehistoire de Bruxelles, Bulletin 68 (1957):75-82.

Hunt, Chester L. "Female Occupational Roles and the Urban Sex Ratios in the United States, Japan and the Philippines." Social Forces 43 (Mar. 1965):407-16.

Institute of Advanced Projects. Women's Movements in Postwar Japan. Honolulu: East-West Center, 1968.

Japan Ministry of Labor. Statistical Materials Relating to Japanese Women, 13. Tokyo: Women's and Minors' Bureau, 1962.
_____. The Status of Women in Japan. Tokyo: Women's and Minors' Bureau, 1962.

Kadono, Chakuro. "The Bringing Up of Japanese Girls." Transactions and Proceedings of the Japanese Society 6 (1903-4):308-15.

Kaibara, Ekken. Women and Wisdom of Japan. First published, 1905. Reprint, London: J. Murray, 1914.

Kawai, Michi. Japanese Women Speak: A Message from the Christian Women of Japan to the Christian Women of America. Boston: Central Committee on the United Study of Foreign Missions, 1934.

Koya. "A Study of Induced Abortion in Japan and Its Significance." Millbank Memorial Fund Quarterly 32 (July 1959):282-93.

Koyama, Takashi. The Changing Social Position of Women in Japan. Paris: UNESCO Publications, 1961.

Kuchler, L. W. "Manage in Japan." Transactions of the Asiatic Society of Japan 13 (1885):116-40.

Kuznets, Simon; Moore, Wilbert; and Spengler, Joseph. Economic Growth: Brazil, India, Japan. Durham, N.C.: Duke University Press, 1955.

Lanham, Betty B. "Aspects of Child Care in Japan: Preliminary Report." In Personal Character and Cultural Milieu, 3rd rev. ed., ed. Douglas G. Harding. Syracuse: Syracuse University Press, 1956.

Lifton, R. J. "Individual Patterns in Historical Change." Comparative Studies in Society and History 6 (1964): 369-83.
_____. "On Contemporary Man and Woman: Woman as Knower." In Lifton, History and Human Survival. New York: Random House, 1971.

Longford, Joseph H. Japan of the Japanese. New York:
    Charles Scribner's Sons, 1914.
Longstreet, Stephen, and Longstreet, Ethel. Yoshiwara:
    City of the Senses. New York: David McKay, 1970.
Matsue, A. "Role de la femme dans la nouvelle societe
    japonaise." Rhythmes du Monde 33 (1960):201-10.
Matsumoto-Yoshihar, S. "Contemporary Japan--the
    Individual and the Group." Transactions of the
    American Philosophical Society 52 (1960).
Mead, Margaret, and Metraux, Rhoda, eds. The Study of
    Culture at a Distance. Chicago: University of
    Chicago Press, 1971.
Mishima, Sumie Seo. The Broader Way: A Woman's Life in
    the New Japan. First published, 1954. Reprint,
    Westport, Conn.: Greenwood Press, 1971.
Morris, Ivan. The World of the Shining Prince: Court
    Life in Ancient Japan. New York: Alfred A. Knopf,
    1964.
Murasaki, Lady. The Tale of Genji. Garden City, N.Y.:
    Doubleday, 1960.
Nakane, Chie. Japanese Society. Berkeley: University
    of California Press, 1967.
Norbeck, Edward. Changing Japan. New York: Holt,
    Rinehart & Winston, 1965.
___. Takashima: A Japanese Fishing Village. Salt Lake
    City: University of Utah Press, 1954.
___, and Norbeck, Margaret. "Child Training in a
    Japanese Fishing Community." In Personal Character
    and Cultural Milieu, 3rd rev. ed., ed. Douglas G.
    Harding. Syracuse: Syracuse University Press, 1956.
Nuita, Yoko. "Trends in Continuing Education of Women
    in Japan." Indian Journal of Adult Education 30
    (Oct. 1969):5-7.
Ohnuki-Tierney, Emiko. "The Status of Women and Speech
    Variation in Japan: A Problem and Method in Socio-
    linguistics." A paper presented at the 70th Annual
    Meeting of the American Anthropological Association,
    New York, 1971. Mimeo. Beloit College.
Okamura, Kimi, and Takei, Yoko. "A Study on the Process
    of Establishment and Practice of Home-making
    Educational System in the Girls' Secondary Education
    in the Meiji Period." Bulletin of Tokyo Gakugei
    University 21 (Oct. 1969):88-111.
Raper, Arthur. The Japanese Village in Transition.
    Tokyo: General Headquarters, Supreme Commander of
    Allied Powers, 1950.
Sand, Chiye. Changing Values of the Japanese Family.
    Washington, D.C.: Catholic University of America
    Press, 1958.
Sarashina, Lady. As I Crossed a Bridge of Dreams: The
    Recollections of a Woman in 11th Century Japan, trans.
    Ivan Morris. New York: Dial Press, 1971.

Sato, Toshihiko. "Emancipation of Women in Japan."
   Asian Student 17 (Jan. 11, 1969):5.
___. "Ibsen and the Emancipation of Women in Japan."
   UNESCO Features 535, 536 (Sept.-Oct. 1968):8-11.
✓ Scott, A. C. The Flower and Willow World: A Study of
   the Geisha. New York: Orion Press, 1960.
Shonagon, Sei. The Pillow Book of Sei Shonagon, ed. A.
   Waley. New York: Barnes & Noble, 1959.
Singleton, John. Nichu: A Japanese School. New York:
   Holt, Rinehart & Winston, 1966.
Smith, R., and Cornell, J. B. Two Japanese Villages.
   Ann Arbor: University of Michigan Press, 1956.
Smith, R. F., and Beardsley, R. Japanese Culture.
   Chicago: Aldine, 1962.
Sofue, Takao. "Childhood Ceremonies in Japan: Regional
   and Local Variations." Ethnology 4 (1965):148-64.
Stoetzel, Jean. Without the Chrysanthemum and the
   Sword: A Study of the Attitudes of Youth in Post-
   war Japan. New York: Columbia University Press,
   1955.
Straelen, Henricus van. The Japanese Woman Looking
   Forward. Tokyo: Kyobunkwan, 1940.
Sugimoto, Etsu Inagaki. A Daughter of the Samurai.
   First published, 1926. Reprint, Garden City, N.Y.:
   Doubleday, 1934.
Sykes, John. A Japanese Family. London: Allan
   Wingate, 1957.
Vogel, Ezra. "Democratization of Family Relationships
   in Japanese Urban Society." Asian Survey 1 (1961):
   19.
___, and Vogel, Susan. "Family Security, Personal
   Immaturity and Emotional Health in a Japanese Sample."
   Marriage and Family Living 23 (1961):161-66.
Ward, Robert E., and Rustow, D. A., eds. Political
   Modernization in Japan and Turkey. Princeton:
   Princeton University Press, 1964.
Wilionson, T. O. "Family Structure and Industrialization
   in Japan." American Sociological Review 27 (1962):
   678-82.
"Working Women and Prostitution." Current Japanese
   Public Opinion Surveys 2 (1948), 15 (1949). Tokyo:
   General Headquarters, Supreme Commander of Allied
   Powers.
Yanagida, Kunio. Japanese Manners and Customs, trans.
   S. Terry. Tokyo: O. Bruska, 1957.

Korea

Ackermann, Jessie. "Korea." In Women of All Nations,
   vol. 3, ed. T. A. Joyce. New York: Funk & Wagnalls,
   1915.

Chun Koh, Hesung, and Steffens, Joan. Korea: An
     Analytical Guide to Bibliographies. New Haven:
     Human Relations Area Files Press, 1971.
Hwang-Kyung, Ko. "Korean Women and Education." Korea
     Journal 4 (Feb. 1964):10-13.
Pak, Hwa-song. The Heroines of Korea, trans. Kim
     Dongsung. Seoul: Omungak, 1965.
"Women in Korea." Korea Journal 4 (Feb. 1964):4-43.

China

"Access of Girls in Higher Education." UNESCO Infor-
     mation Bulletin 38 (June 1, 1967):7-13.
"Access of Girls in Secondary Education." UNESCO
     Information Bulletin 26 (June 1, 1966):8-10.
Arduini, Alberto. Dame al Macao. Rome: Cultura
     Moderna, 1945.
Ayscough, Florence. Chinese Women: Yesterday and
     Today. Boston: Houghton Mifflin, 1937.
Belden, Jack. Gold Flower's Story: Women's Liberation
     in Revolutionary China. Boston: New England Free
     Press.
Benn, Rachel R. Ping-Kua: A Girl of Cathay. Boston:
     Woman's Foreign Missionary Society, Methodist
     Episcopal Church, 1912.
Boggs, Lucinda Pearl. Chinese Womanhood. Cincinnati:
     Jennings & Graham, 1913.
Burton, Margaret Ernestine. The Education of Women in
     China. New York: Fleming H. Revell, 1911.
     . Notable Women of Modern China. New York: Fleming
     H. Revell, 1912.
Chao, Pu-Wei Yang. Autobiography of a Chinese Woman.
     New York: Greenwood Press, 1970.
Chinese Women in the Great Leap Forward. Peking:
     Foreign Languages Press; San Francisco: China Press
     and Periodicals, 1960.
Chung, Shou-Ching, ed. Women in Industry in the
     Chapei, Hongkew and Pootung Districts of Shanghai.
     Shanghai: National Committee, YWCA of China, 1931.
Chung-Cheng, Chow. The Lotus Pool. New York:
     Appleton-Century-Crofts, 1961.
Colquhoun, A. R. "China." In Women of all Nations,
     vol. 3, ed. T. A. Joyce. New York: Funk & Wagnalls,
     1915.
     . "Manchuria, Mongolia and Tibet." In Women of All
     Nations, vol. 3, ed. T. A. Joyce. New York:
     Funk & Wagnalls, 1915.
Conger, Sarah Pike. Letters from China, with Particular
     Reference to the Empress Dowager and the Women of
     China. Chicago: A. C. McClurg, 1910.

Cooper, Elizabeth. The Love Letters of a Chinese Lady.
Edinburgh & London: T. N. Foulis, 1919.
_____. My Lady of the Chinese Courtyard. New York:
Frederick A. Stokes, 1914.
Cusack, Dymphna. Chinese Women Speak. Sydney: Angus &
Robertson, 1958.
Diamond, Norma. "Fieldwork in a Complex Society:
Taiwan." In Being an Anthropologist: Fieldwork in
Eleven Cultures, ed. George D. Spindler. New York:
Holt, Rinehart & Winston, 1970.
Eichinger, F. "Frauenarbeit bei den tibetischen Nomaden
im Kukonor-Gebiet" [Women's work among the Tibetan
nomads in the Kukonor area]. Anthropos 50 (1955):
837-847.
Epstein, Israel. From Opium War to Liberation. Peking:
New World Press, 1956.
_____. The Unfinished Revolution in China. Boston:
Little, Brown, 1949.
Fisher, Welthy Honsinger. A String of Chinese Pearls:
Ten Tales of Chinese Girls Ancient and Modern. New
York: Woman's Press, 1924.
Frick, J. "Mutter und Kind bei den Chinesen in Tsinghai"
[Mother and child among the Chinese in Tsinghai].
Anthropos 5 (1957):1055-63.
Gamarekian, E. "Hong Kong's Forgotten Girls." United
Asia 15 (June 1963):432-35.
Greene, Felix. Awakened China. Garden City, N.Y.:
Doubleday, 1961.
_____. Curtain of Ignorance: How the American Public Has
Been Misinformed about China. Garden City, N.Y.:
Doubleday, 1965.
_____. A Divorce Trial in China. Boston: New England
Free Press.
Grosbois. "La femme chinoise en 1960." Academie des
Sciences d'Outre-Mer 20 (1960):304-8.
Headland, Isaac Taylor. Court Life in China: The
Capital, Its Officials and People. New York:
Fleming H. Revell, 1909.
Hibbert, Eloise Talcott. Embroidered Gauge: Portraits
of Famous Chinese Ladies. First published, 1941.
Reprint, Freeport, N.Y.: Books for Libraries, 1969.
Highbaugh, Irma. Family Life in West China. New York:
Agricultural Missions, 1948.
Hinton, William. Fanshen: A Documentary of Revolution
in a Chinese Village. New York: Random House, 1966.
Horner, Isaline Blew. Women under Primitive Buddhism:
Laywomen and Almswomen. London: Routledge, 1930.
Hosie, Lady Dorothea Soothill. The Pool of Ch'ien Lung:
A Tale of Modern Peking. London: Hodder & Stoughton,
1948.
Huang, Jen Lucy. "A Re-evaluation of the Primary Role of
the Communist Chinese Woman: The Homemaker or the
Worker." Marriage and Family Living 25 (1963):162-66.

Kirkpatrick, Joanna. "Some Unexamined Aspects of Child-
    hood Association and Sexual Attraction in the
    Chinese Minor Marriage." Originally prepared for
    discussion and debate, American Anthropologist, 1971.
    Mimeo. Bennington College.
Levy, Howard Seymour. Chinese Footbinding: The History
    of a Curious Erotic Custom. New York: W. Rawls,
    1966.
___, ed. Warm-Soft Village: Chinese Stories, Sketches
    and Essays. Tokyo: Dai Nippon Insatsu, 1964.
Lewis, Ida Belle. The Education of Girls in China.
    New York: Columbia University, Teachers College,
    1919.
Li, Yu (1611-1680). Die Volkommene Frau; das
    chinesische Schönheitsideal von Li-Li-Weng. Berlin:
    W. de Gruyter, 1961.
Mao Tse-tung. Quotations from Chairman Mao: The "Little
    Red Book." New York: Frederick A. Praeger, 1957.
Mead, Margaret, and Metraux, Rhoda, eds. The Study of
    Culture at a Distance. First published, 1953.
    Reprint, Chicago: University of Chicago Press, 1971.
Morgan, W. P. Triad Societies in Hong Kong. Hong Kong:
    Government Press, 1960.
O'Hara, Albert Richard. The Position of Woman in Early
    China According to the Lieh nu chuan, "The Biog-
    raphies of Eminent Chinese Women." Washington, D.C.:
    Catholic University of America Press, 1945.
Pruitt, Ida. A Daughter of Han: The Autobiography of
    a Chinese Working Woman. New Haven: Yale University
    Press, 1945.
Russell, Maude. "Chinese Women Liberated!" Far East
    Reporter, n.d.
Snow, Edgar. Red Star over China. New York: Random
    House, 1938.
Snow, Helen. Women in Modern China. New York:
    Humanities Press, 1968.
Snow, L. W. "How Chinese Women Live and Work." Vogue,
    Dec. 1971.
Strong, Anna Louise. China's Communes. New York:
    Marzani & Munsell, 1960.
___. The Chinese Conquer China. Garden City, N.Y.:
    Doubleday, 1949.
___. One-fifth of Mankind. New York: Modern Age Books,
    1938.
Suyin, Han. China: 2001. New York: Basic Books, 1967.
T'ai T'ai, Ning L. Daughter of Han, ed. Ida Pruitt.
    Stanford: Stanford University Press, 1945.
Topley, Marjorie. "Immigrant Chinese Female Servants
    and Their Hostels in Singapore." Man 59 (1959):
    213-15.
U.N. Commission on Status of Women. Seminar on the Par-
    ticipation of Women in Public Life. Ulan Bator.
    1965. Report. New York: United Nations, 1966.

"UNESCO's Triple Campaign for Illiterates, Women and Youth." UNESCO Information Bulletin 19 (Nov. 1, 1965):11-13.

Wolf, Arthur P. "Adopt a Daughter-in-law, Marry a Sister: A Chinese Solution to the Problem of the Incest Taboo." American Anthropologist 70 (1968): 864.

———. "Childhood Association and Sexual Attraction: A Further Test of the Westermarck Hypothesis." American Anthropologist 72 (1970):503-15.

———. "Childhood Association, Sexual Attraction and the Incest Taboo: A Chinese Case." American Anthropologist 68 (1966):883-98.

Wolf, Margery. The House of Lim: A Study of a Chinese Farm Family. New York: Appleton-Century-Crofts, 1968.

———. Women and the Family in Rural Taiwan. Stanford: Stanford University Press, 1972.

Women in New China. Peking: Foreign Languages Press, 1949.

"Women Inside China." Introduction by S. Attwood and J. Garavente. McCalls, Nov. 1971.

Women of China (periodical). Peking: National Women's Federation of the People's Republic of China, 1970--.

The Women's Representative: Three One-Act Plays. Peking: Foreign Languages Press, 1956.

Wong, Su-ling [pseud.], and Cressy, Earl Herbert. Daughter of Confucius: A Personal History. New York: Farrar, Straus & Young, 1952.

Yang, Chiing-K'un. Chinese Communist Society: The Family and the Village. Cambridge: M.I.T. Press, 1965.

Yieni Tsao Li. "The Life of a Girl in China." Annals of the American Academy of Political and Social Science 39 (Jan. 1912):62-70.

Southeast Asia: Burma, Cambodia, Laos, Thailand, Vietnam

Benitez, Helena Z. "Cultural Educational Differentials: A Challenge." Southeast Asia Quarterly 4 (July 1969): 1-12.

Brant, Charles S., and Khaing, MiMi. "Burmese Kinship and the Life Cycle: An Outline." Southwestern Journal of Anthropology 7 (1951):437-54.

Brown, Grant R. "Burma." In Women of All Nations, vol. 3, ed. T. A. Joyce, pp. 559-74. New York: Funk & Wagnalls, 1915.

Cooper, Elizabeth. Harim and the Purdah: Studies of Oriental Women. First published, 1915. Reprint, Detroit: Gale Research Co., n.d.

Coughlin, R. J. "The Position of Women in Vietnam."
New Haven: Southeast Asia Studies, Yale University,
1950. Mimeo.

Democratic Republic of Vietnam, Education Office.
"Vietnamese Women." Vietnamese Studies 10 (1966).
San Francisco: China Press and Periodicals.

"Education of Girls." In Some Socio-economic Problems
of Educational Development in Asia. Bangkok:
Economic Commission for Asia and the Far East, 1965.

Grant, Zalin. "Mobilization of Women in Vietnam." New
Republic 158 (June 1968):11-13.

Hart, Donn V.; Rajadhon, Phya Anuman; and Doughlin,
Richard J. Southeast Asian Birth Customs: Three
Studies in Human Reproduction. New Haven: Human
Relations Area Files Press, 1965.

LeBar, Frank M. Ethnic Groups in Insular Southeast
Asia, vol. 1. New Haven: Human Relations Area
Files Press, 1971.

_____. Ethnic Groups in Insular Southeast Asia, vol. 2.
New Haven: Human Relations Area Files Press,
forthcoming.

_____; Hickey, Gerald C.; and Musgrave, John K.,
eds. Ethnic Groups of Mainland Southeast Asia.
New Haven: Human Relations Area Files Press, 1964.

Leblanc, Maria. "Acculturation of Attitude and Personality among Katangese Women." Journal of Social
Psychology 47 (1958):257-64.

Mi Mi Khaing, Daw. Burmese Family. Bombay: Longmans,
Green, 1946.

Panbanyong, S. "Sidti lae tana king ying Thai" [The
rights and status of Thai women]. Kahasestasart 1
(Aug.-Sept. 1955):13-20.

Pelzer, Karl J. West Malaysia and Singapore: A
Selected Bibliography. New Haven: Human Relations
Area Files Press, 1971.

Phansi Wichakorakun. "Development of Education for
Thai Women." Master's thesis, Chulalongkorn
University, Bangkok, 1957.

Senalak, Thatchanaphon. "Development of Education and
Vocations for Thai Women in the Rattanakosin Bangkok
Period." Master's thesis, Chulalongkorn University,
Bangkok, 1963.

Skeat, Walter W. "Siam and Cambodia." In Women of All
Nations, vol. 3, ed. T. A. Joyce, pp. 550-58. New
York: Funk & Wagnalls, 1915.

Soysa, Nita. Fact-finding among Rural Families as a
Basis for Training Women Workers and Home-makers for
Improvement of Rural Homes and Communities. Bangkok:
Food and Agriculture Organization of the United
Nations, Regional Office for Asia and the Far East,
1961.

___. The Role of Women's Voluntary Organizations in
Community Development. Bangkok: Food and Agri-
culture Organization of the United Nations, Regional
Office for Asia and the Far East, 1961.
___. Training of Women for Home Improvement and Rural
Development. Bangkok: Food and Agriculture Or-
ganization of the United Nations, Regional Office
for Asia and the Far East, 1962.
Stahlie, T. D. "Pregnancy and Childbirth in Thailand."
Tropical and Geographical Medicine 2 (1960):127-37.
Thailand Women and Employment. Bangkok: Department of
Public Welfare, 1960.
Tirabutana, P. A Simple One: The Story of a Siamese
Girlhood. Ithaca: Cornell University Press, 1958.
Win, Kyi Kyi, and Dju, D. C. "Access of Girls and
Women to Education in Rural Areas in Asia: A
Working Document." A paper presented at a Meeting
of Experts on the Access of Girls and Women to
Education in Rural Areas in Asia, Feb. 26-Mar. 8,
1962. Bangkok: UNESCO Regional Office for Education
in Asia, 1962.
Women in Vietnam: Selected Articles from Vietnamese
Periodicals: Saigon, Hanoi 1957-1966, trans. Cheim
T. Kein. Honolulu: East-West Center Press, 1967.

Afghanistan, Bangladesh, Pakistan

Afzal, Mohammed. The Fertility of East Pakistani
Married Women: A Study Based on 1961 Census.
Karachi: Pakistan Institute of Development Economics,
1966.
Ahmed, Tahrunessa. Women's Education and Home Develop-
ment. Comilla: Pakistan Academy for Rural
Development, 1966.
Ali, Z. A. "The Status of Women in Pakistan." Pakistan
Quarterly 6 (1956):46-55.
All Pakistan Women's Association. Annual Report for
1961-62. Karachi: Information and Research Bureau,
1962.
___. Participation of Women in Public Life in Pakistan,
Report of the Seminar, Lahore, Nov. 21, 1960. Karachi:
Information and Research Bureau, 1961.
___. The Role of Women in the Developing Economy of
Pakistan. Karachi: Information and Research Bureau,
1961.
___. Women's Movement in Pakistan. Karachi: Information
and Research Bureau, 1963.
Chughtie, Ghayas-u-din. An Up-to-date Commentary on West
Pakistan Control of Goondas Ordinance, 1959, with
Control of Goondas Rules, 1961, Suppression of Pros-
titution Ordinance, 1961 and Prevention of Gambling
Ordinance, 1967. Lahore: Shah Nawaz, 1967.

Coulson, N. J. "Reform of Family Law in Pakistan."
    Studia Islamica 7 (1957):133-55.
Dhunjibhoy, R. "La condition de la femme dans le nouveau
    Pakistan." Temps Moderne 12 (June 1957):1930-42.
"East Pakistan School Prepares Girls for Public Life."
    UNESCO Features 449 (Dec.4, 1966):6.
Family Life in Pakistan: A Report of the Proceedings
    and Recommendations of Seminar. Karachi: Social
    Services Coordinating Council, 1963.
Honigman, John. "Women in Pakistan." In Pakistan:
    Society and Culture, ed. Stanley Maron, pp. 159-76.
    New Haven: Human Relations Area Files Press, 1957.
Hussain, Asaf. The Educated Pakistani Girl: A Socio-
    logical Study. Karachi: Ima, 1963.
Ikramullah, S. S. "Pakistani Women." African Women 1
    (June 1958):89-92.
    . "The Role of Women in the Life and Literature of
    Pakistan." Asian Review 55 (1959):14-26.
Mirza, Sarfaraz Hussain. Muslim Women's Role in the
    Pakistan Movement. Lahore: University of Punjab,
    1969.
Papanek, Hannah. "The Woman Fieldworker in a Purdah
    Society." Human Organization 23 (1964):160-63.
Salas, Irma. Education of Women in Pakistan: Pre-
    liminary Report of the UNESCO Mission on the Access of
    Women to Education. Mexico: UNESCO Publications,
    1954.
Serignan, C. "La condition des femmes en Afghanistan et
    son evolution recente." Orient 14 (1960):33-56.
Sherazee, M. H. Girl Guiding in West Pakistan. Lahore:
    West Pakistan Bureau of Education, 1960.

Ceylon, India, Nepal

Access of Women and Girls to Education in Rural Areas:
    A Comparative Study. Paris: UNESCO Publications,
    1964.
Adivar, Halide Ebid. Inside India. London: Allen &
    Unwin, 1941.
Aiyer, K. B. "Industrial Institute for Blind Women,
    Bombay." Social Welfare 16 (Oct. 1969):16.
Alteker, Anent S. Position of Women in Hindu Civili-
    zation from Prehistoric Times to the Present Day.
    First published, 1938. Rev. ed. Mystic, Conn.:
    Lawrence Verry, 1962.
Armstrong, Ruth Gallup. Sisters under the Sari. Ames:
    Iowa State University Press, 1964.
Associated Country Women of the World. The Place of
    Rural Women's Organisations in Their Country's Develop-
    ment; Past, Present and Future. Report of the
    International Seminar, Kandy (Ceylon), 1957. London,
    1957.

Athavale, Parvatibai. My Story: The Autobiography of a
  Hindu Widow. New York: G. P. Putnam's Sons, 1930.
Aziz, Wahida. Careers. Allahabad: Kitab Mahal, 1945.
Babb, Lawrence A. "Marriage and Malevolence: The Uses
  of Sexual Opposition in a Hindu Pantheon." Ethnology
  9 (1970):137-48.
Bader, Clarisse. Women in Ancient India: Moral and
  Literary Studies. 2nd ed. Benares: Chowkhamba
  Sanskrit Series Office, 1964.
Berreman, Gerald D. "On the Role of Women." Bulletin
  of the Atomic Scientists (Nov. 1966):26-28.
_____. "Pahari Polyandry." In Marriage, Family and
  Residence, ed. Paul Bohannan and John Middleton,
  pp. 147-68. New York: Natural History Press, 1968.
Bhattacharyya, Pancharan. Ideals of Indian Womanhood.
  Calcutta: Goldgwin, 1921.
Billington, Mary Frances. Woman in India. London:
  Chapman & Hall, 1895.
Bista, Khem Bahadur. "Tîj ou la fête des femmes."
  Objets et Mondes 9 (1969):7-18.
Brayne, Frank Lugard. Village Uplift in India.
  Allahabad: Pioneer Press for the Rural Community
  Council, Aurgaon, 1928.
Central Social Welfare Board. Family Life Education for
  Ladies and Marriageable Girls: Course Outline.
  Lucknow: Family Life Institute, 1969.
_____. National Council for Women's Education, Annual
  Reports, 4 vols. New Delhi: Ministry of Education,
  1960-66.
_____. Report of the Committee for Review and Evaluation
  of the Programme of "Condensed Courses of Education
  of Adult Women." New Delhi: Ministry of Education,
  1964.
Chakraborty, Usha. Condition of Bengali Women around
  the Second Half of the Nineteenth Century. Calcutta:
  Chakraborty, 1963.
_____. "Women in Bengali Society." Bulletin of
  Ramakrishna Mission Institute Culture 15 (Nov. 1964):
  372-80.
Chakravarty, Syam Sunder. My Mother's Picture: An
  Attempt to Get at the Hindu Spirit in Connection with
  the Mayo Challenge. Calcutta: Sanjiboni Book Depot,
  1930.
Chaltopadhyaya, Kamaladevi. The Awakening of Indian
  Women. Madras: Everyman's Press, 1970.
Chaudhary, Roop Lal. Hindu Woman's Right to Property,
  Past and Present. Calcutta: K. L. Mukhopadhyay,
  1961.
Chimnabai II, Maharani of Baroda, and Mitra, S. M. The
  Position of Women in Indian Life. London: Longmans,
  Green, 1911.

Geographical Topics

Chopra, Sharda. "Gandhiji on Women, Children and Rural
India." Social Welfare 16 (Oct. 1969):25-26.
Cormack, M. L. The Hindu Woman. London: Asia Pub-
lishing House, 1962.
Crawford, E. A. "Ceylon." In Women of All Nations, vol.
4, ed. T. A. Joyce. New York: Funk & Wagnalls, 1915.
Crooke, W. "The Land and Island of Women." Man in
India 2 (1922):216-19.
Das, M. N. "Female Infanticide among the Bedees and the
Chouhans: Motives and Modes." Man in India 36
(Oct.-Dec. 1956):261-66.
_____. "Movement to Supress the Custom of Female Infan-
ticide in the Punjab and Kashmir." Man in India
37 (Oct.-Dec. 1957):280-83.
Das, Parimal. "Women under India's Community Develop-
ment Programme." Geneva: International Labour
Office, 1959. Reprinted from International Labour
Review 80 (July 1959).
"Democratic India and Women's Education." Education
Quarterly 13 (1961):117-220.
Dhindsa, Bagwinder Kaur. "Changing Status of Women in
Rural India." Master's thesis, University of
Illinois, 1968.
Dube, S. C. India's Changing Villages. Ithaca: Cornell
University Press, 1955.
Durand, E. M. "La condition de la femme dans la
société annamite." In L'Ethnographie 21, 22 (1930):
93-97.
Dutt, Beulah. "Women's Education." New Delhi: Asian
Institute for Educational Planning and Administration,
1964. Mimeo.
Education Commission. Recommendations on Women's
Education. New Delhi: Central Social Welfare Board,
1965.
Edwardes, Stephen Meredyth. Crime in India: A Brief
Review of the More Important Offences Included in the
Annual Criminal Returns, with Chapters on Prostitution
and Miscellaneous Matters. New York: H. Milford,
Oxford University Press, 1924.
Ehrenfels, U. R. Mother Right in India. Toronto:
Oxford Press, 1941.
Elder, Joseph. "Industrialism and Hinduism." Ph.D.
dissertation, Harvard University, 1959.
Epstein, T. S. Economic Development and Social Change
in South India. New York: Humanities Press, 1962.
Field, Harry Hubert. After Mother India. London: J.
Cape, 1929.
Gadgil, D. R. Women in the Working Force in India. New
York: Asia Publishing House, 1965.
Gandhi, Mohandas Karamchand. The Role of Women, ed.
Anand T. Hingorani. Bombay: Bharatiya Vidya Bhavan,
1964.

42

____. Woman's Role in Society, comp. R. K. Prabhu.
Ahmedabad: Navajivan, 1959.
____. Women. First published, 1958. Reprint,
Ahmedabad: Navajivan, 1964.
____. Women and Social Injustice, 3rd ed. Ahmedabad:
Navajivan, 1947.
Gedge, Evelyn C., ed. Women in Modern India: Fifteen
Papers by Indian Women Writers. Bombay: D. B.
Taraporewala, 1929.
Geldens, Maria. Report to the Government of India on a
Programme of Practical Education for Rural Women in
Uttar Pradesh. Rome: Food and Agriculture Organi-
zation of the United Nations, 1958.
Gemini, P. "The Place of Khadduh: The Youngest
Daughter in Khasi and Synteng Society." Vanyajati
4 (Apr. 1956):82-84.
Gideon, Helen. "A Baby Is Born in the Punjab."
American Anthropologist 64 (Dec. 1962):1220-34.
Gokulanathan, K. S., and Verghese, K. P. Child Care in
a Developing Community. New York: Vantage Press,
1970.
Goswami, M., and Majumdar, D. N. "A Study of Women's
Position among the Garo of Assam." Man in India 45
(Jan.-Mar. 1965):27-35.
Gough, E. Kathleen. "Female Initiation Rites on the
Malabar Coast." Journal of Royal Anthropological
Institute 85 (1955):45-80.
____. "Incest Prohibitions and Rules of Exogamy in Three
Matri-lineal Groups of the Malabar Coast." Inter-
national Archives of Ethnology 46 (1952).
____. "The Nayars and the Definition of Marriage."
Journal of the Royal Anthropological Institute 89
(1959):23-34.
A Guide to Gram Sevikasad Mukhya Sevikas. New Delhi:
Ministry of Community Development and Cooperation,
Department of Community Development, 1961.
Harper, Edward B. "Fear and the Status of Women."
Southwestern Journal of Anthropology 25 (1969):81-95.
Hate, Chandrakala Anandrao. Changing Status of Women
in Post Independence India. New York: Paragon Book
Reprint, 1969.
____. Hindu Woman and Her Future. Bombay: New Book
Co., 1948.
Indian Women's League for Peace and Freedom. Inter-
national Seminar on Women's Education and Community
Development. Final Report. New Delhi: Women's
International League for Peace and Freedom, 1966.
Indra, V. V. The Status of Women in Ancient India.
Benares: Motilal Banarsidass, 1955.
International Alliance of Women, South East Asia Regional
Group. Report of the Inaugural Conference, Colombo,
1954. Colombo: Association of the All-Ceylon Women's
Conference, 1954.

Jambagi, Sadanand, and Jambagi, Sulochana. "Life and Activities of Lingayat Widows in Mysore State." Social Welfare 17 (May 1970):11-12.

Jones, Violet Stanford. Woman in Islam: A Manual with Special Reference to Conditions in India. Lucknow: Lucknow Publishing House, 1941.

Jumunabai, J. "Women's Education: The Roles and Content of Education in the Changing Social Pattern with Special Reference to Women's Education." Indian Journal of Adult Education 23 (Feb. 1962): 15-16.

Kannangara, Inrogen. "Women's Employment in Ceylon." International Labour Review 93 (Feb. 1966):117-26.

Kaur, Manmohan. Role of Women in the Freedom Movement, 1857-1947. New Delhi: Sterling, 1968.

Khwaja, B. A. "Attitudes towards Purdah among Muslim Girl Students of Kanpur." Man in India 45 (July-Sept. 1965):223-27.

Kirkpatrick, Joanna. "Autobiography: A Source for the Analysis of Intersexual Conflict in North India." A paper presented at the 70th Annual Meeting of the American Anthropological Association, New York, 1971. Mimeo. Bennington College.

Kuznets, Simon; Moore, Wilbert; and Spengler, Joseph, eds. Economic Growth: Brazil, India, Japan. Durham, N.C.: Duke University Press, 1955.

Lajpat Rai, Lala. Unhappy India: Being a Reply to Miss Katherine Mayo's "Mother India." Calcutta: Banna, 1928.

Leach, E. R. "Did the Wild Veddahs have Matrilineal Clans?" In Studies in Kinship and Marriage: Essays Dedicated to Brenda Z. Seligman on Her 80th Birthday, ed. I. Schapera, pp. 68-78. London: Royal Anthropological Institute, 1963.

_____. "A Critique of Yalman's Interpretation of Singhalese Girls' Puberty Ceremonial." In Echanges et Communications. Paris: Mouton, 1970.

Luschinsky, Mildred Stroop. The Life of Women in a Village of North India: A Study of Role and Status. Ann Arbor: University Microfilms, 1962.

Majumdar, D. N. Himalayan Polyandry: Structure, Functioning and Culture Change: A Field Study of Jaunsar-Bawar. London: Asia Publishing House, 1962.

Mandelbaum, David G. "Polyandry in Kota Society." American Anthropologist 40 (1938):574-83.

_____. Society in India. 2 vols. Berkeley: University of California Press, 1970.

Mann, R. S. "Acculturation and Woman's Standing." Indian Journal of Social Work 22 (1961):77-80.

Marain, Dhirendra. "Growing Up in India." Family
    Process 3 (1964):127-54.
Mathur, A. S., and Gupta, B. L. Prostitutes and Pros-
    titution. Agra: Ram Prasad, 1965.
Mayo, Katherine. Slaves of the Gods. London: J.
    Cape, 1929.
Mehta, R. The Western Educated Hindu Woman. London:
    Asia Publishing House, 1970.
Mehta, S. V. "The Hindu Widow: With Special Reference
    to Gujerat." Journal of the University of Bombay 26
    (July 1957):50.
Mehta, Sushila. "Literacy among Women." Indian
    Journal of Adult Education 25 (Dec. 1964):11-12.
Meyer, Johann Jakob. Sexual Life in Ancient India: A
    Study in the Comparative History of Indian Culture.
    London: Routledge, 1930.
Misra, Rekha. Women in Mughal India: 1546-1748 A.D.
    Mystic, Conn.: Lawrence Verry, 1967.
Mitter, Dwarka Nath. "The Position of Women in Hindu
    Law." Master's thesis, University of Calcutta, 1912.
Mukherjee, P. "Some Notes on the Study of the 'Woman
    Question' in Ancient India." Man in India 44 (July-
    Sept. 1964):264-74.
Mukhopadhyay, A. "Sati as a Social Institution in
    Bengal." Bengal Past and Present 76 (1957):99-115.
Nag, Moni. "Sex, Culture and Human Fertility: India
    and the United States." Current Anthropology 13
    (Apr. 1972):231-37.
Nanda, Savitri Devi. The City of Two Gateways: The
    Autobiography of an Indian Girl. London: Allen &
    Unwin, 1950.
Nath, Kamla. "Women in the New Village." Economic
    Weekly 17 (1965):813-16.
National Council for Women's Education. Sixth Annual
    Report. New Delhi: Ministry of Education, 1966.
National Council of Women in India. Bulletin. Nagpur,
    1932--.
Nehru, Shyam Kumari, ed. Our Cause: A Symposium by
    Indian Women. Allahabad: Kitabistan, 1938.
Nimbkar, Krishna Bai. Development of Work among Rural
    Women: A Guidebook. New Delhi: Indian Adult
    Education Association, 1958.
___. "Voluntary Organization and Women's Education."
    Indian Journal of Adult Education 22 (Mar. 1961):5-7.
Noble, Margaret. The Web of Indian Life, by the Sister
    Nivedita of Ramakrishna-Vivekananda. London: W.
    Heinemann, 1904.
Noronha, George E. "Backgrounds in the Education of
    Indian Girls." Master's thesis, Catholic University
    of America, 1939.

Obeyesekere, G. "Pregnancy Cravings (Dola-Duka) in
    Relation to Social Structure and Personality in a
    Sinhalese Village." American Anthropologist 65 (1963)
    323-42.
Orenstein, Henry. "Death and Kinship in Hinduism:
    Structural and Functional Interpretations." American
    Anthropologist 72 (1970):1357-77.
Paranavitana, S. "Matrilineal Descent in the Sinhalese
    Royal Family." Ceylon Journal of Science 2 (1933):
    235-40.
Peiris, W. "Women in Buddhism." Ceylon Today 9 (Sept.
    1960):6-9.
Penny, F. "South India." In Women of All Nations,
    vol. 4, ed. T. A. Joyce, pp. 605-25. New York: Funk
    & Wagnalls, 1915.
Peter, Prince of Greece and Denmark. "The Mother Sibs
    of the Todas of the Nilgiris." Eastern Anthropologist
    5 (1951):65-73.
Pinch, Trevor. Stark India. London: Hutchinson, 1930.
Pinkham, Mildreth Worth. The Status of Women in Hinduism
    as Reflected in the Puranas, the Mahabharata, and the
    Ramayana. New York: Columbia University Press, 1941.
Prakash, P. "The Role of Women among Car-Nicobarese."
    Vanyajati 6 (Jan. 1958):31-33.
Prakash, Ram. "Unprogressive Pattern of Women's Employ-
    ment in India." Social Welfare 16 (Aug. 1969):4.
Prasad, T. "Fate of a Barren Woman in Hindu Society."
    Indian Folklore 2 (Apr. 1959):15-19.
Punekar, S. D. A Study of Prostitutes in Bombay, with
    Reference to Family Background. Bombay: Lalvani,
    1967.
Radhakrishnan, Sarvepalli. Religion and Society. 2nd
    ed. New York: Barnes & Noble, 1966.
Rama Devi, B. "Indian Woman and Her Attitude toward
    Traditional Values." Journal of Psychological Research
    7 (1963):72-78.
Ramabai, Sarasvati. The High-caste Hindu Woman. New
    York: Revell, 1887.
Ranade, R. Himself: Autobiography of a Hindu Lady.
    London: Longmans, Green, 1938.
Rothfield, Otto. Women of India. Bombay: D. B.
    Taraporevala, 1928.
Ryan, Bryce, and Fernando, Sylvia. "The Female Factory
    Worker in Ceylon." International Labour Review 64
    (1951):438-61.
Saran, Raksha. Education of Girls and Women in Rural
    Areas, India. New Delhi: Ministry of Education, 1962.
    _____. "Twenty Years of Women's Welfare Activities in
    India." Social Welfare 17 (May 1970):22.
Sen Gupta, Padmini. The Portrait of an Indian Woman.
    Calcutta: YMCA Publishing House, 1956.
    _____. The Role of Women in Indian Public Life in Modern
    Times. Ann Arbor: University Microfilms, 1959.

___. Women in India. New Delhi: Information Service of India, 1964.

___. Women Workers of India. New York: Asia Publishing House, n.d.

___. Women's Education in India. New Delhi: Ministry of Education, 1960.

Sen Gupta, Sankar. Women in Indian Folklore: A Short Survey of Their Social Status and Position: Linguistic and Religious Study. Foreword by Indira Gandhi. Calcutta: Indian Publications, 1969.

Sheth, Jyotsna. "College Education: Take-off Stage to Wider Culture: An Interview with Dr. Premlila Thackersey, Vice-Chancellor of S.N.D.T. Women's University." Times of India, Nov.30, 1969.

Shridevi, S. A Century of Indian Womanhood. Mysore: Rao & Raghavan, 1965.

Singer, Milton, and Cohn, B. S., eds. Structure and Change in Indian Society. Chicago: Aldine Atherton, 1968.

Singh, Amrit Kaur. Challenge to Women. Allahabad: New Literature, 1946.

Sivachandra, Vasu. The Hindoos as They Are: A Description of the Manners, Customs, and Inner Life of Hindoo Society in Bengal. Calcutta: Thacker, Spink, 1881.

Sorabji, Cornelia. Between the Twilights: Being Studies of Indian Women by One of Themselves. London: Harper, 1908.

___. India Recalled. London: Nisbet, 1936.

Stanford, John K. Ladies in the Sun: The Memsahibs' India, 1790-1860. London: Galley Press, 1962.

Stern, Elizabeth Levin. The Women in Gandhi's Life. New York: Dodd, Mead, 1953.

The Suppression of Immoral Traffic in Women and Girls Act, 1956, with Rules of States by V. Sriramamohara Rao. Hyderabad: Andhra Law Times, 1966.

Tampoe, R. "The Women of India." Contemporary Review 1117 (Jan. 1959):23-26.

Thomas, Paul. Indian Women through the Ages: A Historical Survey of the Position of Women and the Institutions of Marriage and Family in India from Remote Antiquity to the Present Day. New York: Asia Publishing House, 1964.

Tuxen, Paul. Kvinden i det gamle Indien, et udkast. Copenhagen: B. Lunos Bogtrykkeria, 1944.

Urquhart, Margaret M. Women of Bengal: A Study of the Hindu Pardanasins of Calcutta. Calcutta: Association Press, 1925.

Vatuk, Sylvia J. "Trends in North Indian Urban Kinship: The 'Matrilateral Asymmetry' Hypothesis." Southwestern Journal of Anthropology 27 (1971):287-307.

Vreede de Stuers, Cora. Parda: A Study of Muslim Women's Life in Northern India. Foreword by W. F. Wertheim. Asson, The Netherlands: Royal Van Gorcum, 1940.

Wilde, Mrs. Frank. "The Kukis and Magas of the North
    Cachar Hills, Assam." In Women of All Nations, vol.
    3, ed. T. A. Joyce, pp. 575-84. New York: Funk &
    Wagnalls, 1915.
Williams, Gertrude L. Marvin. Understanding India. New
    York: Coward-McCann, 1928.
Wiser, William, and Wiser, Charlotte. Behind Mud Walls,
    1930-1960, With a Sequel: The Village in 1970.
    Berkeley: University of California Press, 1970.
Yalman, Nur O. "On the Purity of Women in the Castes of
    Ceylon and Malabar." Journal of the Royal Anthro-
    pological Institute 93 (1963):25-58.
    . Under the Bo Tree: Studies in Caste, Kinship, and
    Marriage in the Interior of Ceylon. Berkeley:
    University of California Press, 1971.
Young, Miriam. Among the Women of the Punjab: A Camping
    Record. London: Carey Press, 1916.

EUROPE

General References

Almond, Gabriel, and Verba, Sidney. The Civic Culture:
    Political Attitudes and Democracy in Five Nations.
    Princeton: Princeton University Press, 1963.
Congres International des Oeuvres et Institutions
    Feminines. "2e Congrès International des Oeuvres et
    Institutions Féminines tenu au palais des Congrès de
    l'Exposition Universelle de 1900 sous la présidence
    d'honneur de M. Léon Bourgeois et sous la présidence
    de Mademoiselle Sarah Monod." Paris: Impr. Typ. C.
    Blot., 1902.
DuVerger, Maurice. The Political Role of Women. Paris:
    UNESCO Publications, 1955.
Leser, C. E. V. "An International Survey of Part-time
    Employment." International Labour Review 88 (1963):
    380, 490.
    . "Trends in Women's Work Participation."
    Population Studies 12 (1958-59):100-110.
    . "Women in the Labour Force." International Labour
    Review 77 (Mar. 1958):254-72.
Luckey, Eleanor B., and Vass, Gilbert. "A Comparison of
    Sexual Attitudes and Behavior in an International
    Sample." Journal of Marriage and Family Living 31
    (May 1969):364-79.
Martin, Louis Auguste. Histoire de la femme, sa con-
    dition politique, civile, morale et religieuse. Paris:
    Didier, 1862-63.
Navarre, Octave Lucien Louis. Les femmes dans la société
    grecque; étude de moeurs antiques. Paris: Editions
    Universitaires, 1937.

Tingston, Herbert. Political Behavior: Studies in Election Statistics. London: P. S. King and Son, 1937.

Great Britain

Acton, William. Prostitution, Considered in Its Moral, Social and Sanitary Aspects, in London and Other Large Cities and Garrison Towns, with Proposals for the Control and Prevention of Its Attendant Evils. 2nd ed. London: Churchill, 1870.

Adams, Ruth M. "The Victorian Woman in Fact and Fiction, 1871-1901." Master's thesis, Radcliffe College, 1951.

Adler, Alfred. The Case of Miss R. London: Allen & Unwin, 1929.

Anderson, James. The Ladies of the Covenant. Memoirs of Distinguished Scottish Female Characters, Embracing the Period of the Covenant and the Persecution. New York: Redfield, 1855.

Anderson, Mary D. British Women at War. London: J. Murray & Pilot Press, 1941.

Anthony, Sylvia. Women's Place in Industry and Home. London: Routledge, 1932.

Arregger, Constance, ed. Graduate Women at Work: A Study of a Working Party of the British Federation of University Women. London: Oriel Press, 1966.

Banks, Joseph Ambrose. Prosperity and Parenthood: A Study of Family Planning among the Victorian Middle Classes. London: Routledge & Kegan Paul, 1954.

___, and Banks, Olive. Feminism and Family Planning in Victorian England. Liverpool: Liverpool University Press, 1964.

Bax, Ernest Belfort. The Fraud of Feminism. London: Grant Richards, 1913.

Beavan, Keith. "Women Demand Equality." Times Educational Supplement 2858 (Feb. 27, 1970):14.

Binyon, Michael. "Girls Shun Engineering 'a National Disgrace.'" Times Educational Supplement 2810 (Mar. 28, 1969):1015.

Birdwell, Russell. Women in Battle Dress. New York: Fine Editions Press, 1942.

Blackburn, Helen. Women's Suffrage: A Record of the Woman's Suffrage Movement in the British Isles. First published, 1902. Reprint, New York: Collectors Editions, Source Book Press, 1970.

Blease, W. Lyon. Emancipation of English Women. London: Constable, 1910.

Bott, Alan John, ed. Our Mothers: A Cavalcade in Pictures, Quotation and Description of Late Victorian Women, 1870-1900. London: Gollancz, 1932.

British Social Biology Council. Women of the Streets:
A Sociological Study of the Common Prostitute, ed.
C. H. Rolph. London: Secker & Warburg, 1955.

Camden, Charles Carroll. The Elizabethan Woman.
Houston: Elsevier Press, 1952.

Chayes, A. H. "Outer and Inner Status of Women."
Educational Record 46 (Fall 1965):435-38.

Chesser, Eustace. Marital and Family Relationships of
English Women. London: Hutchinson, 1956.
     . The Sexual, Marital and Family Relationships of
the English Woman. First published, 1956. Reprint,
New York: Roy, 1957.

Clancey, Richard W. "The Augustan Fair-Sex Debate and
the Novels of Samuel Richardson." Master's thesis,
University of Maryland, 1966.

Clark, Alice. Working Life of Women in the Seventeenth
Century. London: Frank Case, 1968.

Cole, Margaret Postgate. Women of To-day. New York:
T. Nelson, 1938.

"Colleges Must Take Women: Frank's Commission Evidence."
Times Educational Supplement 2577 (Oct. 9, 1964):599.

Collins, S. "The Moslem Family in Britain." Social &
Economic Studies 4 (1955):326-37.

"Corsets to Bridges: Careers for Women." Times Educational Supplement 2575 (Sept. 25, 1964):461.

Courtney, Janet Hogarth. The Adventurous Thirties: A
Chapter in the Women's Movement. London: Oxford
University Press, 1937.

Cuddeford, Gladys M. Women's Society from Victorian
Times to the Present Day. London: H. Hamilton, 1907.

Culhs, Winifred Clara. "What British Women Are Doing in
the War." Lecture, Vassar, 1942.

Cunnington, Cecil Willett. Feminine Attitudes in the
Nineteenth Century. London: W. Heinemann, 1935.

Dangerfield, George. "The Woman's Rebellion." In The
Strange Death of Liberal England, 1910-1914. First
published, 1935. Reprint, New York: Random House,
Capricorn Books, 1961.

Devereaux, Edward, et al. "Child-rearing in England and
the United States: A Cross National Comparison."
Journal of Marriage and Family Living 31 (May 1969):
257-70.

Dunbar, Janet. The Early Victorian Woman: Some Aspects
of Her Life (1837-57). London: G. G. Harrap, 1953.

Dunn, Nell. Talking to Women. New York: Ballantine,
1965.

Earengey, Florence. The Milk-white Lamb: The Legal and
Economic Status of Women, rev. ed. London: National
Council of Women of Great Britain, 1953.

The Education and Training of Girls: A Study by the
Women's Group of Public Welfare. London: National
Council of Social Service, 1962.

Ellis, Sarah Stickney. The Family Monitor. New York:
E. Walker, 1848.
___. The Mothers of England: Their Influence and Re-
sponsibility. London: Fisher, 1843.
___. The Women of England: Their Social Duties, and
Domestic Habits. 13th ed. London: Fisher, 1839.
"Fawcett Library: A London Library Specializing in
Books Concerning the Women's Suffrage Movement."
Times Educational Supplement 2604 (Apr. 16, 1965).
1174-75.
Firth, Raymond. Two Studies of Kinship in London. New
York: Athlone, 1956.
Frost, David, and Jay, Antony. The English. New York:
Stein & Day, 1968.
Fryer, Peter. Mrs. Grundy: Studies in English Prudery.
London: Dennis Dobson, 1963.
Fussell, George E. The English Country Woman: A Farm
House Social History, AD 1500-1900. London: A.
Melrose, 1953.
"Girls Sixth Form College." Times Educational Supplement
2617 (July 16, 1965):113.
"Giving Them Confidence: Back to Work." Times Educa-
tional Supplement 2576 (Oct. 2, 1964):536.
Graham, Maxtome [Jan Struther], ed. Women of Britain:
Letters from England. New York: Harcourt, Brace,
1941.
Green, J. Birds of Britain. New York: Macmillan, 1967.
Greg, William Rathbone. Why Are Women Redundant? London:
N. Trubner, 1869.
Habliekuk, J. "Family Structure and Economic Change in
19th Century Europe." Journal of Economic Theory 15:
1-12.
Hamilton, Cicely Mary. The Englishwoman. New York:
Longmans, Green, 1940.
Harris, Adelaide E. Heroine of the Middle English
Romances. Folcroft, Pa.: Folcroft Press, 1928.
Harris, Frank. Women of Shakespeare. New York: Horizon
Press, 1970.
Heidensohn, Frances. "The Deviance of Women: A Critique
and an Enquiry." British Journal of Sociology 19
(June 1968):160-75.
Heinrich, Joachim. Die Frauenfrage bei Steele und
Addison. Eine Untersuchung zur englischen Litera-
tur und Kulturgeschichte im 17./18. Jahrhundert.
Leipzig: Mayer & Muller, 1930.
Hewitt, Margaret. "The Effect of Married Women's Employ-
ment in the Cotton Textile Districts on the
Organization and Structure of the Home in Lancashire,
1840-1880." Ph.D. dissertation, London University,
1953.
___. Wives and Mothers in Victorian Industry. London:
Rockliff, 1958.

Hole, Christina. The English Housewife in the Seventeenth Century. London: Chatto & Windus, 1953.

Howard, G. E. A History of Matrimonial Institutions. 3 vols. New York: Humanities Press, 1964.

Hudson, Kenneth. Men and Women: Feminism and Antifeminism Today. New York: Transatlantic Arts, 1968.

"Is Science Unfeminine? Women in Industry." Times Educational Supplement 2574 (Sept. 18, 1964):404.

James, Thomas Egbert. Prostitution and the Law. London: W. Heinemann, 1951.

Jephcott, Pearl. Married Women Working. London: Allen & Unwin, 1962.

Joseph, Joyce. "A Research Note on Attitudes toward Work and Marriage of Six Hundred Adolescent Girls." British Journal of Sociology 12 (1961):176-83.

Kamm, Josephine. Rapiers and Battleaxes: The Women's Movement and Its Aftermath. London: Allen & Unwin, 1966.

Kazantzis, Judith. Women in Revolt: The Fight for Emancipation. New York: Grossman, 1968.

Klein, Viola. Britain's Married Women Workers. New York: Humanities Press, 1965.

_____. "The Demand for Professional Woman Power." British Journal of Sociology 12 (1961):1-11.

_____. The Feminine Character. First published, 1946. Reprint. Urbana: University of Illinois Press, 1972.

Knowlson, H. "Married Women Returners: Popular Courses at Bristol." Times Educational Supplement 2592 (Jan. 22, 1965):193.

Labram, G. W. "Swindon Ladies: Training Project to Increase the Supply of Teachers." Times Educational Supplement 2615 (July 2, 1965):16-17.

Lamb, Felicia, and Pickthorn, Helen. Locked-up Daughters. London: Hodder-Stoughton, 1968.

Lang, Elsie M. British Women in the Twentieth Century. London: Laurie, 1929.

LeGros, Clark F. Women, Work and Age. London: Nuffield Foundation, 1962.

Lessing, Doris. The Golden Notebook. New York: Simon & Schuster, 1962.

_____. In Pursuit of the English. London: MacGibbon & Kee, 1960.

Logan, William. An Exposure from Personal Observation, of Female Prostitution in London, Leeds and Rochdale, and Especially in the City of Glasgow, with Remarks on the Cause, Extent, Results, and Remedy of the Evil, 2nd ed. Glasgow: G. Grallie & R. Fleckfield, 1843.

"Low-stream Girls." Times Educational Supplement 2640 (Dec. 24, 1965):1367.

MacCarthy, B. G. Woman Writers: Their Contribution to the English Novel, vol. 1. Later Women Writers, 1744-1818, vol. 2. London: Verry, 1947.

McGregor, O. R. "The Social Position of Women in England: A Bibliography 1850-1914." British Journal of Sociology 6 (1955):48-60.

Marris, Peter. Widows and Their Families. New York: Humanities Press, 1958.

Mayhew, Henry. London Labour and London Poor, 1861-67. 4 vols. Reprint, Clifton, N.J.: Augustus M. Kelley, 1967.

Meikle, Wilma. Towards a Sane Feminism. New York: R. M. McBride, 1917.

Morris, Homer L. Parliamentary Franchise Reform in England 1885-1918. New York: AMS Press, 1921.

Morrison, A. "Perception of Peer Personality by Adolescent Girls." British Journal of Educational Psychology 36 (Nov. 1966):241-47.

Morrison, M. "The British Isles." In Women of All Nations, vol. 4, ed. T. A. Joyce, pp. 756-62. New York: Funk & Wagnalls, 1915.

"Moves towards Integration: Girls' Public Day School Trust Plans." Times Educational Supplement 2703 (Mar. 10, 1967):809.

Norton, Caroline Sheridan. English Laws for Women in the Nineteenth Century. London: privately published, 1854.

Oliphant, Mrs. Alexander, and Linton, Mrs. Lynn. Women Novelists of Queen Victoria's Reign: A Book of Appreciations. London: Hurst & Blackett, 1897.

"Part-time Studies for Young Wives." Times Educational Supplement 2792 (Nov. 22, 1968):1148.

Poppleton, P. K., and Brown, P. E. "Secular Trend in Puberty: Has Stability Been Achieved." British Journal of Educational Psychology 36 (Feb. 1966): 95-100.

The Position of the Woman Graduate Today: A Survey, 1956-1965. London: International Federation of University Women, 1966.

Pratt, Edwin A. Pioneer Women in Victoria's Reign: Being Short Histories of Great Movements. London: G. Newnes, 1897.

"Professional Come Back: Housewives' Choice." Times Educational Supplement 2574 (Sept. 8, 1964):404.

Rendel, Margherita N. Equality for Women. London: Fabian Society, 1968.

Reynolds, Myra. The Learned Lady in England, 1650-1760. New York: Houghton Mifflin, 1920.

Rice, Margery Spring. Working Class Wives. Harmondsworth, Middlesex: Penguin Books, 1939.

Rorabacher, Louise Elizabeth. "Victorian Women in Life and Fiction." Ph.D. dissertation, University of Illinois, 1942.

Rubenius, Anna. The Woman Question in Mrs. Gaskell's Life and Works. Cambridge: Harvard University Press, 1950.

Salomon, Louis. Devil Take Her: A Study of the Rebellious Lover in English Poetry. Cranbury, N.J.: A. S. Barnes, 1961.

Scott, Benjamin. A State Iniquity: Its Rise, Extension, and Overthrow. Clifton, N.J.: Augustus M. Kelley, 1968.

Scott, Peter. "Prejudiced against Women." Times Educational Supplement 2833 (Sept. 5, 1969):18.

Slater, Eliot, and Woodwide, Moya. Patterns of Marriage: A Study of Marriage Relationships in the Urban Working Classes. London: Casswell, 1951.

Smelser, Neil. Social Change in the Industrial Revolution. Chicago: University of Chicago Press, 1959.

Staars, David. The English Woman: Studies in Her Psychic Evolution, trans. J. M. E. Brownlow. London: Smith, Elder, 1909.

"State Home for Women [in Boroda]." Social Welfare 16 (Sept. 1969):24.

Stebbins, Lucy P. London Ladies. New York: AMS Press, 1952.

Stenton, Doris Parsons. The English Woman in History. London: Allen & Unwin, 1957.

Stenton, Frank Merry. "The Historical Bearing of Place-name Studies: The Place of Women in Anglo-Saxon Society." London Royal Historical Society. Transactions 25 (1942):1-13.

Stewart, C. M. "Future Trends in the Employment of Married Women." British Journal of Sociology 12 (1961):1-11.

Stopes, Charlotte. British Freewomen: Their Historical Privilege. London: Sonneschein, 1894.

Strachey, Rachel. "The Cause," a Short History of the Women's Movement in Great Britain. First published, 1928. Reprint, Port Washington, N.Y.: Kennikat Press, 1969.

_____. Our Freedom and Its Results, by Five Women. London: Hogarth Press, 1936.

Teacher Education and Training: A Report by a Committee of Inquiry Appointed by the Secretary of State for Education and Science, under the Chairmanship of Lord James of Rusholme. London: Her Majesty's Stationery Office, Department of Education and Science, n.d.

Thompson, Barbara, and Finlayson, Angela. "Married Women Who Work in Early Motherhood." British Journal of Sociology 14 (June 1963):150-68.

Thompson, Margaret Patricia N. "The Changing Ideal of Womanhood in the Novel and Its Relation to the Feminist Movement, 1837-73." Master's thesis, Cambridge University, 1946.

Thomson, Patricia. The Victorian Heroine: A Changing Ideal, 1837-1873. New York: Oxford University Press, 1956.

Tickner, Frederick Windham. Women in English Economic History. New York: E. P. Dutton, 1923.

Titmyss, Richard. "The Position of Women in the Welfare State." In Comparative Social Problems and Essays on "The Welfare State," ed. S. N. Eisenstadt. New York: Free Press, 1964.

Truefitt, Alison. "Too Few Girl Engineers." Times Educational Supplement 2801 (Jan. 24, 1969):232.

Uberoi, N. "Sikh Women in Southall." Race 6 (July 1964):34-40.

"The Victorian Woman." Victorian Studies 14 (Sept. 1970):7-91.

Villard, Leonie. La femme anglaise au XIXe siècle et son évolution d'après le roman anglais contemporain. Paris, 1920.

Walker, Martha Anne. "The Elizabethan Woman and Her Shakespearean Counterpart." Master's thesis, University of Illinois, 1957.

Warwick, Frances Evelyn Maynard, ed. Progress in Women's Education in the British Empire, Being the Report of the Education Section, Victorian Era Exhibition, 1897. New York: Longmans, Green, 1898.

Watt, Ian. "The New Woman: Samuel Richardson's 'Pamela.'" In The Family: Its Structure and Functions, ed. Rose Coser. New York: St. Martin's Press, 1969.

"Where the Young Girl Is Supreme." Times Educational Supplement 2578 (Oct. 16, 1964):652.

Whiting, Gerald. "Buyer's Mecca: The Retail Business Offers Equality to Women." Times Educational Supplement 2808 (Mar. 14, 1969):839.

Williams, Barbara Ruth. "The Status of Women in England 1832-1850." Master's thesis, University of Illinois, 1957.

Willmott, Peter, and Young, Michael. Family and Class in a London Suburb. London: Routledge & Kegan Paul, 1960.

Wilson, Mona. Jane Austen and Some Contemporaries. Port Washington, N.Y.: Kennikat Press, 1938.

Women's Advisory Committee, Labour Party. Discrimination against Women: A Report on the Position of Women Today to Be Presented to the 45th National Conference of Labour Women, Llandudno, Apr. 2-4, 1968.

Woodham-Smith, Cecil. Lonely Crusader. New York: McGraw-Hill, 1951.

Work among Women. London: Communist Party of Great Britain, 1924.

Young, Michael, and Willmott, Peter. Family and Kinship in East London. New York: Humanities Press, 1957.

Zucconi, Angela. The Responsibilities of Women in Social Life: A Study. Strasbourg: Council of Europe, Council for Cultural Cooperation, 1968.

Ireland

Arensberg, C. M. The Irish Countryman. Gloucester, Mass.: Peter Smith, 1950.
___, and Kimball, S. T. Family and Community in Ireland. Cambridge: Harvard University Press, 1945.
Connery, Donald S. The Irish. New York: Simon & Schuster, 1968.
Coxhead, Elizabeth. Daughters of Erin: Five Women of the Irish Renascence. London: Secker & Warburg, 1965.
Fox, Richard M. Rebel Irishwomen. Dublin: Talbot, 1935.
Freeman, T. W. Ireland. London: Methuen, 1950.
Humphreys, Alexander. New Dubliners: Urbanization and the Irish Family. London: Routledge & Kegan Paul, 1966.
Jones, Emrys. Belfast. London: Oxford University Press, 1960.
Messenger, John C. Isle of Ireland. New York: Holt, Rinehart & Winston, 1969.
Sayers, P. An Old Woman's Reflections. London: Oxford University Press, 1962.

France

Abensour, Leon. Le féminisme sous le règne de Louis-Philippe et en 1848. Paris: Plon-Nourrit, 1913.
___. La femme et le féminisme avant la revolution. Paris: E. Leroux, 1923.
___. Histoire générale du féminisme des origines à nos jours. Paris: Delagrave, 1921.
___. Les vaillantes: heroines, martyres et remplacantes. Paris: Chapelot, 1917.
Anderson, Barbara Jean. "The Working Class Women of Paris during the French Revolution, 1789-1793." Master's thesis, University of Illinois, 1953.
Andrews, John. Remarks on the French and English Ladies, in a Series of Letters; Interspersed with Various Anecdotes, and Additional Matter, Arising from the Subject. London: T. Longman & A. Robinson, 1783.
Auclert, Habertine. Les femmes au gouvernail. Paris: M. Giard, 1923.
Barbey d'Aurevilly, Jules Amédée. Femmes et moralistes. Paris: A. Lemerre, 1906.
Bearne, Catherine Mary Charlton. Heroines of French Society in the Court, the Revolution, the Empire, and the Restoration. London: E. P. Dutton, 1907.
Bordeaux, Henry. Portraits de femmes et d'enfants. Paris: Plon-Mourrit, 1919.

Brantôme, Pierre de Bourdeille. Vues des dames illustres françoises et etrangères. Paris: Gannier Freres, 1873.

Brooks, Geraldine. Dames and Daughters of the French Court. Freeport, N.Y.: Books for Libraries, 1904.

Burniaux, Jeanne. L'éducation des filles; problèmes de l'adolescence. 2nd ed. Paris: Editions Universitaires, 1965.

Cary, Alice, ed. The Josephine Gallery. Philadelphia: J. B. Lippincott, 1869.

Cerati, Marie. Le club des citoyennes républicaines révolutionnaires. Paris: Editions Sociales, 1966.

Chombart de Lauwe. "Status of French Women." International Social Science Journal 14 (1962):26-65.

___. "The Status of Women in French Urban Society." In Comparative Social Problems & Essays on "The Welfare State," ed. S. N. Eisenstadt. New York: Free Press, 1964.

Clark, Frances Ida. The Position of Women in Contemporary France. London: P. S. King, 1937.

Cocteau, Jean. Reines de la France. Paris: Bernard Grasset, 1952.

Courson, Barbara Frances Mary Neave. La femme française pendant la guerre, 2nd ed. Paris: P. Lethielleux, 1916.

Crozier, Michel. Petits fonctionnaires au travail. Compte rendu d'une enquête sociologique effectives dans une grande administration publique parisienne. Paris: Centre National de la Recherche Scientifique, 1955.

DuBroca, Louis, trans. Heroic Women of France, Comprising Examples of the Noble Conduct of Women during the French Revolution. Cincinnati: U. P. James, 1846.

Duche, Natacha. Des jeunes filles parlent. Paris: Flammarion, 1965.

Duval, Paul Alexandre Martin. Femmes de 1900. Paris: Editions de la Madeleine, 1932.

Faguet, Emile. Le féminisme. Paris: Société Française d'imprimerie et de Librairie, 1910.

Farnsworth, William Oliver. Uncle and Nephew in the Old French Chansons De Geste: A Study in the Survival of Matriarchy. New York: Columbia University Press, 1913.

Fitch, Charles Luther. Some Women of France: Agricultural and Commercial Ideas and Photographs of France. Ames, Iowa: Allerey Press, 1920.

Gab [pseud.]. La femme devant la loi. Paris: E. Figuière, 1921.

Gheusi, Pierre Barthélemy. Cinquante ans de Paris, memoires d'un témoin. Paris: Plon, 1939.

57

Goncourt, Edmond Louis Antoine Huot de. L'amour au dix-huitième siècle. Paris: G. Charpentier et E. Fasquelle, 1893.

___. The Woman of the Eighteenth Century: Her Life, from Birth to Death: Her Love and Her Philosophy in the Worlds of Salon, Shop and Street, trans. Jacques Le Clercq and Ralph Roeder. New York: Minton, Balch, 1927.

Gueland-Leridon, Françoise. Recherches sur la condition féminine dans la société d'aujourd'hui. Paris: Presses Universitaires de France, 1967.

Hall, Evelyn Beatrice. The Women of the Salons. New York: G. P. Putnam's Sons, 1926.

Hall, Geoffrey F. Moths Round the Flame: Studies of Charmers and Intriguers. Freeport, N.Y.: Books for Libraries, 1935.

Holland, Clive. "France." In Women of All Nations, vol. 4, ed. T. A. Joyce, pp. 725-31. New York: Funk & Wagnalls, 1915.

Huzard, Antoinette de Bergevin. Femmes d'aujourd'hui, enquête sur les nouvelles carrières féminines. Paris: Calmann-Levy, 1929.

Imbert de Saint-Amand, Arthur Léon. Women of the Valois Court, trans. Elizabeth Gilbert Martin. New York: Charles Scribner's Sons, 1893.

___. Women of Versailles: The Court of Louis XV, trans. E. G. Martin. New York: Charles Scribner's Sons, 1893.

Institut Français d'opinion Publique. Patterns of Sex and Love: A Study of the French Woman and Her Morals. London: Panther Books, 1964.

Joran, Theodore. Les féministes avant le féminisme. Paris: A. Salvaete, 1910.

LaHire, Marie Weyrich de. La femme française, son activité pendant la guerre. Paris: J. Tallandier, 1917.

Lanoux, Armand. "Physiologie du demi-monde en 1900." In Les Ouvres Libres 179 (Nov. 1961):131-62.

Lefevre, Maurice. La femme à travers l'histoire. . . Les courtisanes.--Les amoureuses.--L'emancipatrice. --Les éducatrices.--Précieuse et demoniaque.-- Courtisane et grisette.--Martyrs et bourreaux.--Les saturnales.--L'empire.--Le romantisme.--Le second empire. Paris: A. Fontemoine, 1902.

Legouve, Joseph Wilfred Ernest Gabriel. Histoire morale des femmes, 4th ed. Paris: G. Sandre, 1864.

Lescure, Mathurin Francois Adolphe de. La société française au dix-huitième siècle. Les femmes philosophes. Paris: E. Dentu, 1881.

Mandach, Laure de. Portraits de femmes: Renaissance et Reforme. Geneva: Labor et Filles, 1952.

Martin, Marie Adele. La jeune fille française dans la littérature et la société, 1850-1914. Rennes: Maurice Simon, 1938.

Mason, Amelia Ruth Gere. The Women of the French Salons. New York: Century, 1891.

Maurois, Andre. Femmes de Paris. Paris: Plon, 1954.

Pestalozza, U. "Le matriarcat mediterranée. Son caractère primordial dans l'ambiance religieuse du paleolithique." Diogène 12 (Oct.1955):58-71.

Picard, Roger. Les salons littéraires et la société française, 1610-1789. New York: Brentano's, 1943.

Prevost, Marcel. Lettres à Françoise. Paris: F. Juven, 1902.

_____. Nouvelles lettres à Françoise; ou, La jeune fille d'après guerre. Paris: E. Flammarion, 1924.

Rat, Maurice. Dames et bourgeoises, amoureuses ou galantes du XVI siècle. Paris: Editions d'Histoire et d'Art, Plon, 1955.

Ravenel, Florence Leftwich. Women and the French Tradition. New York: Macmillan, 1918.

Richardson, Joanna. The Courtesans: The Demi-monde in Nineteenth Century France. Cleveland: World, 1967.

Richardson, Lula McDowell. The Forerunners of Feminism in French Literature of the Renaissance from Christine of Pisa to Marie de Gournay. Baltimore: Johns Hopkins Press, 1929.

Seekel, Friedrich. Frankreich, Zentrale des internationalen Mädchenhandels. Berlin: Junker & Dünnhaupt, 1940.

Semaines de la Pensée Marxiste. Femmes du XXe Siècle. Paris: Presses Universitaires de France, 1965.

Sichel, Edith. Women and Men of the French Renaissance. Port Washington, N.Y.: Kennikat Press, 1970.

Simenon, Georges. La femme en France. Paris: Presses de la Cité, 1959.

Sourgen, H. L'éducation civique des femmes: quelques suggestions pratiques. Paris: UNESCO Publications, 1954.

Spont, Henry. La femme dans la France de demain. Paris: Jouve, 1917.

Thomas, Edith. Les femmes de 1848. Paris: Presses Universitaires de France, 1948.

_____. Les pétroleuses. Paris: Gallimard, 1963.

Turgeon, Charles Marie Joseph. Le féminisme français. Paris: L. Lorose, 1902.

Uzanne, Louis Octave. Son altesse la femme. Paris: A. Quantin, 1885.

Watson, Paul Barron. Some Women of France. New York: Coward-McCann, 1936.

Whale, Winifred Stephens. Women of the French Revolution. London: Chapman & Hall, 1922.

Wilson, R. McNair. *Women of the French Revolution*. Port Washington, N.Y.: Kennikat Press, 1970.

Belgium, Germany, the Netherlands, Switzerland

Anthony, Katharine Susan. *Feminism in Germany and Scandinavia*. New York: Henry Holt, 1915.

Arens, Hanns. *Die schöne Münchnerin*. Munich: Kurt Desch Verlag, 1969.

Aron, Albert William. *Traces of Matriarchy in Germanic Hero-Lore. University of Wisconsin Studies in Language and Literature* 9 (1920).

Bainton, Roland H. *Women of the Reformation in Germany and Italy*. Minneapolis: Augsburg, 1971.

Barton, Margaret Ruby. "Women in the National Socialist State, January 1933 - March 1936." Master's thesis, University of Illinois, 1942.

Bauer, Max. *Die deutsche Frau in der Vergangenheit*. Berlin: A. Schall, 1907.

Baumer, Gertrud. *Die Frauengestalt der deutschen Fruhe*. Berlin: F. A. Herbig, 1929.

———. *Männer und Frauen im geistigen werden des deutschen Volkes*. Tübingen: Rainer Wunderlich Verlag, n.d.

Baxter, Richard. *Women of the Gestapo*. London: Quahly Press, 1943.

Bebel, August. *Women under Socialism*, trans. Daniel DeLeon. New York: Schocken, 1971.

Bell, Clair Hayden. *The Sister's Son in the Medieval German Epic: A Study in the Survival of Matriliny*. Berkeley: University of California Press, 1922.

Bianquis, G. *Love in Germany*. New York: Humanities Press, 1964.

Bremme, Gabriele. *Die politische Rolle der Frau in Deutschland; eine Untersuchung über den Einfluss der Frauen bei Wahlen und ihre Teilnahme in Partei und Parliament*. Göttingen: Vandenhoeck & Ruprecht, 1956.

Brüning, Elfriede. *Wege und Schicksale; Frauen unserer Zeit*. Berlin: Kongress-Verlag, 1962.

Bührig, Marga. *Die Frau in der Schweiz*. Bern: Haupt, 1969.

Buresch-Riebe, Ilse. *Frauenleistung im Kriege*. Berlin: F. Eher Nachf, 1941.

Bussman, Hanna. "Die frau im landwirtschaftlichen betrieb." *Archiv der Deutschen Landwirtschaft* 24 (1960):35-48.

Commandeur, Werner, and Sterzel, Alfred. *Das Wunder drüben sind die Frauen; Begegnungen zwischen dresden und Rügen*. Bergisch Gladbach: G. Lübbe, 1965.

"Employment of Women in the Federal Republic of Germany." *International Labour Review* 95 (May 1967):482-87.

Gersdorff, Ursula von, ed. Frauen im Kriegsdienst, 1914-1945. Stuttgart: Deutsche Verlags-Anstalt, 1969.

Groenman, S. "Women's Opinion about Size of Family in the Netherlands." Eugenic Quarterly 2 (1955):224-28.

Haberland, Helga, ed. Frauen der Goethezeit in Briefen, Dokumenter und Bildern, von der Gottschedin bis zu Bettina von Arnim; eine Anthologie. Stuttgart: Reclam, 1960.

Hahn, I. "Dauernahrung und Frauenarbeit." In Zeitschrift fur Ethnologie 51 (1919):243-59.

Hanstein, Adalbert von. Die Frauen in der Geschichte des deutschen Gersteslebens des 18 und 19 Jahrhunderts. Leipzig: Freund & Wittig, 1900.

Hargrave, Mary. Some German Women and Their Salons. London: T. W. Laurie, 1912.

Heller, Otto. Studies in Modern German Literature. Freeport, N.Y.: Books for Libraries, 1905.

Holland, Clive. "Belgium." In Women of All Nations, vol. 4, ed. T. A. Joyce, pp. 735-39. New York: Funk & Wagnalls, 1915.

Ishwaran, K. Family Life in the Netherlands. The Hague: Vitger, 1959.

Jünger, Karl, ed. Deutschlands Frauen und Deutschlands Krieg, ein Rat-, Tat- und Trostbuch; gesammelte Blätter aus Frauenhand. Stuttgart: R. Lutz, 1916.

Kaps, Johannes, ed. The Martyrdom and Heroism of the Women of East Germany: An Excerpt from the Silesian Passion, 1945-1946, trans. Gladys H. Hartinger. Munich: Christ Unterwegs, 1955.

Kellogg, Charlotte Hoffman. Women of Belgium: Turning Tragedy to Triumph. New York: Funk & Wagnalls, 1917.

Kirkpatrick, Clifford. Nazi Germany: Its Women and Family Life. Indianapolis: Bobbs-Merrill, 1938.

Kloos, Werner. Die Bremerin: Ein Almarach, Porträts und Illustrationen aus den Sammlungen des Volke-Museums. Bremen: Schüremann, 1965.

Krauss, F. S. "Frauen-Kauf." Anthropologische Gesellschaft in Wien, Verhandlungen 10, 15 (1885):123.

Lechner and Korbinian. Die Münchnerin, herausgegeben. Stuttgart: Franckh, 1940.

Locke, Amy. "Germany." In Women of All Nations, vol. 4, ed. T. A. Joyce, pp. 698-703. New York: Funk & Wagnalls, 1915.

National Sozialistische Gemeinschaft "Kraft durch Freude." Amt "Schönheit der Arbeit." Frauen im Werk, Schönheit der Arbeit erleichtert der Frau das Einleben im Betrieb. Berlin: Verlag der Deutschen Arbeitsfront, 1940.

Naumann, Ida Blum. Germanische Frauer der Völkerwanderungszeit. Berlin: F. A. Herbig Verlagsbuchhandlung, 1930.

Peacock, N. "Holland." In Women of All Nations, vol. 4, ed. T. A. Joyce, pp. 704-10. New York: Funk & Wagnalls, 1915.

Poehlmann, Christ of Ludwig. Die deutsche Frau nach 1914. Munich: H. Schmidt, 1914.

Puckett, Hugh Wiley. Germany's Women Go Forward. First published, 1930. Reprint, New York: AMS Press, 1967.

Richter, Lina Spiess. Family Life in Germany under the Blockade. London: National Labour Press, 1919.

Semmelroth, Ellen, ed. N. S. Frauenbuch; herausgegeben im Auftrage der obersten Leitung der P.O., N.S. Frauenschaft. Munich: J. F. Lehmann, 1934.

Škerlj, Božo. "Die Liebesübungen der Frau als bevölkerungs-politisches Problem." In Zeitschrift für Rassenkunde und ihre Nachbargebeite, II, 3:178-85. Stuttgart: Ferdinand Enke Verlag, 1935.

Susman, Margarete. Frauen der Romantik. Jena: E. Diederichs, 1929.

"Vrouwenarbeid; Orgaan van de Vereeniging Nationale Tentoon Stelling van Vrouwenarbeid." Uitgave der Afdeeling "Letteren en Wetenschap." Amsterdam: H. J. Poutsma, 1898.

Weinhold, Karl. Die deutschen Frauen in dem Mittelalter. Vienna: C. Gerold's Son, 1897.

Zapp, Eduard. Geschichte der Deutschenfrauen. Berlin: F. Henschel, 1870.

Italy

Altheim, Franz. Epochen der Römischengeschichte. Frankfurt am Main: V. Klostermann, 1934-35.

Andrews, Marian. The Most Illustrious Ladies of the Italian Renaissance. New York: Charles Scribner's Sons, 1904.

Assa, Janine. The Great Roman Ladies, trans. Anne Hollander. New York: Grove Press, 1960.

Balsdon, John Perry. Roman Women: Their History and Habits. New York: John Day, 1963.

Boulting, William. Woman in Italy, from the Introduction of the Chivalrous Service of Love to the Appearance of the Professional Actress. London: Methuen, 1910.

Bruno, Emilio, ed. La donna nella beneficenza in Italia. Turin: Botta, 1910-13.

Carpi, Leone. L'Italia vivente: aristocrazia di nascita e del denaro--borghesia--clero--burocrazia; studi sociali. Milan: F. Vallardi, 1878.

Casagrande di Villaviera, Rita. Le cortigiane veneziane nel cinquecento. Milan: Longanesi, 1968.

Castellani, Maria. Donne italiane di ieri e di oggi. Florence: R-Bemporad, 1937.

Cooper, John M. "Preferential Marriage in Italy."
  Primitive Man 10 (1937):10-11.
Espinosa, Juan de. Diálogo en laude de las muyeres, ed.
  Angela González Simon. Madrid: Consejo Superior de
  Investigaciones Gentíficas, Instituto Nicolás
  Antonio, 1946.
Ferrero, Guglielmo. The Women of the Caesars. New York:
  Century, 1911.
Fortsch, Barbara. Die politische Rolle der Frau in der
  Römischen Republik. Stuttgart: W. Kohlhammer, 1935.
Gage, J. Matronalia. Essai sur les déviations et les
  organisations culturelles des femmes dans l'ancienne
  Rome. Brussels: Latomus, Revue d'Etudes Latines,
  1963.
Garofalo, Anna. L'italiana in Italia. Bari: Laterza,
  1956.
Gini, Corrado, and Carant, Elio. "The Family in Italy."
  Marriage and Family Living 16 (1954):354-61.
Greco, Oscar. Bibliobiografia femminile italiana del
  XIX Secolo. Venice: Presso i principali librai
  d'Italia, 1875.
Grenett, Lucy M. J. "Italy." In Women of All Nations,
  vol. 4, ed. T. A. Joyce. New York: Funk & Wagnalls,
  1915.
Hoffsten, Ruth Bertha. "Roman Women of Rank of the Early
  Empire in Public Life as Portrayed by Dio,
  Paterculus, Suetonius, and Tacitus." Master's thesis,
  University of Pennsylvania, 1939.
Kahn, Franz. Zur Geschichte des römischen Frauen-
  Erbrechts. Leipzig: Breitkopf & Härtel, 1884.
Lougee, Dora Aileen. "The Status of Women as Seen in the
  Earlier Latin Patristic Writers." Master's thesis,
  University of Illinois, 1923.
Lungo, Isidoro del. Women of Florence, trans. Mary C.
  Steagmann. London: Chatto & Windus, 1907.
Monti, Antonio. Donne e passioni del risorgimento.
  Milan: A. Corticelli, 1935.
Moss, Leonard W., and Thomson, Walter H. "The South
  Italian Family: Literature and Observation." Human
  Organization 18 (1959):35-41.
Parca, Gabriella, ed. Italian Women Confess, trans.
  Carolyn Gaiser. New York: Farrar, Straus & Giroux,
  1963.
Pecchiai, Pio. Donne del Rinascimento in Roma: Imperia,
  Lucrezia, figlia d'imperia, lamisteriosa Flammetta.
  Padua: CEDAM, 1958.
Petrullo, Vincenzo M. "A Note on Sicilian Cross-Cousin
  Marriage." Primitive Man 10 (1937):8-9.
Pieroni Bortolotti, Franca. Alle origini del movimento
  femminile in Italia, 1848-1892. Turin: A. Einaudi,
  1963.

Pitkin, Donald S. "Marital Property Considerations among
Peasants: An Italian Example." Anthropological
Quarterly 33 (1960):33-39.
Possenti, Eligio. Milano amorosa. Milan: Baldini &
Castoldi, 1964.
Seeck, Otto. Die Entwicklung der antiken Geschicht-
schreibung und andere populare Schriften. Berlin:
Siemenroth & Troschel, 1898.

Soviet Union

Aalto, P. "Über die jakmuckische Frauensprache" [The
Kalmykh women's language]. Studia mongol 1 (1960):
1-9.
Adams, Marjorie Anne. "The Economic and Social Status of
Women in Russia since 1917." Master's thesis,
Univessity of Illinois, 1971.
Akopian, G. S., ed. Zhenshchiny strany sotsializma.
Moscow: OGIZ, Gosudarstvennoe Izdatelstvo
Politicheskei Literaturi, 1939.
Alt, Hershel, and Alt, Edith. The New Soviet Man: His
Upbringing and Character Development. New York:
Twayne, 1964.
Amfiteatrov, Aleksandr Valentinovich. Zaría russkoí
zhenshchiny. Belgrade: Izdatel'skaía Komissiía,
Palata Akademije Nauka, 1929.
Antin, Mary. The Promised Land. Boston: Houghton
Mifflin, 1969.
Apysheva, Apal. Doroga schast'ía zhenshchin Kirgizstana.
Frunze, Kirgiz SSR, 1969.
Avsarova, M. P. Uzbekskaia zhenshchina v proslom i nasto-
íashchem. Bibliograficheskii ukazatel' literatury
[The Uzbek woman in past and present times. Biblio-
graphical guide to literature]. Tashkent: Gosizdat
UzSSR, 1959.
Azizbekova, P. A. "Ob odnom neopublikovannom dokumente.
Kharakteristike polozheniía azerbaídzhanskoí
zhenshchiny do revoliútsii" [On one unpublished
document. On the characteristics of the condition of
Azerbaijan woman before the Revolution]. Doklady
Akademii Naukov Azerbaídzhanskago SSR 18 (1962):89-92.
Balabanoff, Angelica. Impressions of Lenin. Ann Arbor:
University of Michigan Press, 1964.
Baskakov, N. A. "Altaískaía zhenshchina v dorevoliutsion-
nom proslom" [The Altai woman in the pre-revolutionary
past]. Ist. Faz. Lit. 6 (1964):140-41.
Belfrage, Sally. A Room in Moscow. New York: Reynal,
1963.
Bennigsen, A. "La famille musulmane en Union Sovietique."
Cahiers du Monde Russe et Sovietique 1 (1959-60):
83-108.

Bestuzhevki v riadakh stroitelei sotsializma. Moscow: MYSL', 1969.

Bil'shai-Pilipenko, Vera L'vovna. Reshenie zhenskogo voprosa v SSSR. Moscow: Gosudarstvennoe Izdatel'stvo Politicheskei Literaturi, 1956.

____. The Status of Women in the Soviet Union. Moscow: Foreign Languages Publishing House, 1959.

Black, C. E., ed. The Transformation of Russian Society. Cambridge: Harvard University Press, 1960.

Bloor, Ella Reeve. Women in the Soviet Union. New York: Workers' Library, 1938.

Bobr'onok, Serhii Tykhonovych. Pisnia pro boiovykh podruh. Kiev: Molod, 1964.

Bochkareva, Ekaterina Ivanovna. Svetlyi put'. Moscow: Gosudarst-Vennoe Izdatel'stvo Politicheskei Literaturi, 1967.

Bronfenbrenner, Urie. "Soviet Methods of Character Education: Some Implications for Research." American Psychologist 17 (1962):550-64.

Brown, Donald R. The Role and Status of Women in the Soviet Union. New York: Columbia University, Teachers College Press, 1968.

Buniatov, Grigorii. "Domashnee vospitanie zhenshchiny u Armian Erivanskoi Gubernii" [Home education for Armenian women in the district of Erivan]. Etnograficheskoe obozrenie (1896):124-33.

Central Statistical Board of the Council of Ministers of the USSR. Women in the USSR. Moscow: Foreign Languages Publishing House, 1960.

Chepurkovskii, E. M. "K antropologii russkikh zhenshchin. [Anthropology of Russian women]. Russkii anthropologicheskii zhurnal 4 (1903):13-23.

Chudinov, Aleksandr Nikolaevich. Ocherk istorii russkoi zhenshchiny. St. Petersburg, 1889.

Claus, Claire. Die Stellung der russischen Frau von der Einführung des Christentums bei den Russen bis zu den Reformen Peter des Grossen. Ph.D. dissertation, Basel University, Munich, 1959.

Danilina, K. "Izuchenie truda byta Adzhorok." Sovetskaia etnografiia 56 (1932):228-31.

Danilova, Ekaterina Zakharovna. Sotsial'nye problemy truda zhenshchiny-rabotnitsy. Moscow: MYSL', 1968.

Denich, Bette S. "Sex and Power in the Balkans." A paper presented at the 70th Annual Meeting of the American Anthropological Association, New York, 1971. Mimeo. Barnard College.

DeWitt, Nicholas. "Education and Professional Employment in the USSR." Washington, D.C.: National Science Foundation, 1961.

Dieks, Henry. "Observations on Contemporary Russian Behavior." Human Relations 5 (1952):111-75.

Dodge, Norton T. Women in the Soviet Economy: Their Role in Economic, Scientific, and Technical Development. Baltimore: Johns Hopkins Press, 1966.

Durham, M. Edith. "The Western Balkan Peninsula." In
    Women of All Nations, vol. 4, ed. T. A. Joyce. New
    York: Funk & Wagnalls, 1915.
Elnett, Elaine. Historic Origin and Social Development
    of Family Life in Russia. New York: Columbia
    University Press, 1926.
Field, Alice. Protection of Women and Children in Soviet
    Russia. London: Gollancz, 1932.
Gafarova, M. K. Dukhovnyĭ oblik zhenshchiny Sovetskogo
    Vostoka. 1969.
Gasiorowska, Zenia. Women in Soviet Fiction 1917-1964.
    Madison: University of Wisconsin Press, 1968.
Geiger, H. Kent. The Family in Soviet Russia. Cambridge:
    Harvard University Press, 1968.
___, and Inkeles, Alex. "The Family in the USSR."
    Journal of Marriage and the Family 41 (1956):397-404.
Gromova, Galina Mikhaĭlovna. Sovetskaia zhenshchina-
    truzhenitsa, mat'. Moscow: Profizdat, 1963.
Halle, Fannina W. Die frau in Sowjetrussland. Berlin:
    P. Zsolnay, 1932.
___. Woman in Soviet Russia. London: Routledge, 1933.
___. Women in the Soviet East, trans. Margaret M. Green.
    New York: E. P. Dutton, 1938.
Hodzaeva, R. D. "Obshchestvennoe polozhenie i semeĭny ĭ
    byt uĭgurskoĭ zenshchiny Kazakhstana" [The social
    position and family life of the Uigur woman of
    Kazakhstan]. Trudy Instituta Istoricheskogo,
    Arkheologicheskogo, Etnograficheskogo, Akademii Nauka,
    Kazakhstana SSR 3 (1956):231-84.
Igumnova, Zoia Petrovna. Zhenshchiny Moskvy v gody
    grazhdanskoĭ voĭny. Moscow: Moskovskii Rabochii,
    1958.
Inkeles, Alex. Social Change in Soviet Russia. Cambridge:
    Harvard University Press, 1968.
___, and Geiger, Kent, eds. Soviet Society: A Book of
    Readings. Boston: Houghton Mifflin, 1961.
Iokhel'son-Brodskaia, D. L. "K antropologii zhenshchin
    plemen kraĭnogo severo-vostoka Sibiri" [On the
    anthropology of native women in the extreme northeast
    of Siberia]. Russkiĭ antropologicheskiĭ zhurnal 7
    (1908):1-87.
Jacoby, Susan. "Women in Russia." New Republic 4, 11
    (Apr. 4, 1970):16-18.
Katasheva, L. Natasha, a Bolshevik Women Organizer: A
    Short Bibliography. New York: Workers' Library, 1934.
Khoreva, G. At the Factory in Tiraspol. Moscow:
    Novosti Press, 1965.
Kimpins'ka-Tat siun, Oleksandra. Rik v zhytti ukraïns'koĭ
    zhinky-hospodyni. Winnipeg, Z Peredmovou Ireny
    Kinsch, 1967.
Kingsbury, Susan Myra. Factory, Family and Woman in the
    Soviet Union. New York: G. P. Putnam's Sons, 1935.

Knysh, Irena. Zhinka v choru i s'ohodni. Winnipeg: Nakladom Artorki, 1958.
Kollontai, Alexandra Mikhailovna. Autobiography of a Sexually Emancipated Communist Woman. New York: Herder & Herder, 1971.
____. Trud zhenshchiny v evoliutsii khoziaistva. First published, 1923. Microfilm. Ann Arbor: University of Michigan Press, 1964.
Korevanova, Agrippina Gavrilovna. Moia zhizn. Moscow: Istoriia Zavodov, 1936.
Korshunova, Ekaterina Nikolaevna. Prava sovetskikh zhenshchin. Moscow: Profizdat, 1960.
Kurganov, Ivan Alekseevich. Zhenshchiny i kommunizm. New York, 1968.
Lenin, Vladimir Ilich. On the Emancipation of Women. Moscow: Progress Publishers, 1968.
____. What Is to Be Done? New York: International Publishers, 1929.
Leong, Stephen Mun-Yoon. The Equality of Soviet Women in the Stalin Era, 1928-1953. Master's thesis, University of Illinois, 1960.
Leonov, N. "Nizov'iakh Amura" [On the lower Amur River in Siberia. An essay on the position of native women]. Sovetskii sever 2 (1930):94-98.
Levine, Irving R. The Real Russians. London: W. H. Allen, 1959.
Liubimova, Serafima Timofeevna. Piatidesiatiletie mezhdunarodnogo zhenskogo dnia. Moscow: Znanie, 1960.
Luzbetak, Louis. Marriage and Family in Caucasia. Vienna: St. Gabriel's Mission Press, 1951.
Madison, Bernice G. Social Welfare in the Soviet Union. Stanford: Stanford University Press, 1968.
Maillart, Ella K. Turkestan Solo: One Woman's Expedition from Tien Shan to the Kizil Kum. New York: G. P. Putnam's Sons, 1935.
Mandel, William. Soviet Women and Their Self-Image. Berkeley: W. Mandel, 233 Lake Dr., Calif. 94708.
Marestan, Jean. L'émancipation sexuelle en URSS; impressions de voyage et documents. Paris: G. Mignolet et Storz, 1936.
Maurer, Rose. Soviet Women. New York: National Council of American-Soviet Friendship, 1944.
Meakin, Annette. "Russia." In Women of All Nations, vol. 4, ed. T. A. Joyce, pp. 606-90. New York: Funk & Wagnalls, 1915.
Mez'er, Augusta Vladimirovna. Ukazatel' istoricheskikh romanov. St. Petersburg: Tipografiia. I. N. Storokhopova, 1902.
Moldavian SSR. Tsentral noe statisticheskoe upravlenie. Zhenshchina Moldavii. Kishinev: Gosstatizdat, 1961.

Nash, E. "Recent Trends in Labor Controls in the Soviet
    Union." In Dimensions of Soviet Economic Power.
    Washington, D.C.: Joint Economic Committee of the
    Congress of the United States, 1962.
Nil'skii, Ivan Fedorovich. Semeinaia zhizn' v russkom
    raskolie. St. Petersburg: Departamenta Udflov, 1869.
Nurina, F. Women in the Soviet Union: The Role of
    Women in Socialist Construction. New York: Inter-
    national Publishers, 1934.
O'Brien, Denise. "Women's Warfare: Sorcery among the
    Konda Valley Dani." A paper presented at the 68th
    Annual Meeting of the American Anthropological
    Association, New Orleans, 1969. Mimeo. Temple
    University.
O-Chev. "Zhenshchina Turkestana po narodnym poslovitsam
    i pogovorkam (Opyt sistematsii poslovits i pogovork)"
    [Turkestan women in popular legends and proverbs (an
    attempt of systematization of proverbs and adages)].
    Etnograficheskoe obozrenie 9 (1897):44-58.
Ovsiannikova, Mariia Dmitrievna. Osushchestvlenie
    mechty. Moscow: Gosudarstvennoe Izdatel'stvo
    Politicheskei Literaturi, 1957.
Pachmuss, Temira, trans. and ed. The Selected Works of
    Zinaida Hippius. Urbana: University of Illinois
    Press, 1972.
Pal'vanova, Bibi Pal'vanovna. Oktiabr' i zhenshchiny
    Turkmenistana. Ashkhabad, Turkmen SSR, 1967.
Petrova, L. I., and Gilevskaya, S., eds. Equality of
    Women in the USSR: Materials of [an] International
    Seminar, Moscow, September 15-October 1, 1956.
    Moscow: Foreign Languages Publishing House, 1957.
Pierre, Andre. Les femmes en Union Sovetique, leur rôle
    dans la vie nationale. Paris: Institut Catholique de
    Paris, Institut d'Etudes sociales. Action populaire.
    Bibliothèque de la Recherche sociale, 1960.
Polons'ka-Vasylenko, Nataliia Dmitriyna. Vydatni
    zhinky Ukrainy. Winnipeg: Souzu Ukrainok Kanady,
    1969.
Pomelova, Anotonina Nikolaevna. Slovo o zhenshchinakh
    severa. Arkhangel'sk: Sev.-Zap. Kn. Izdat., 1968.
Poole, Ernest. Katherine Breskovsky "For Russia's
    Freedom." Chicago: C. H. Kerr, 1905.
Popova, Nina Vasil'evna. Sovetskaia zhenshchina. Moscow:
    Profizdat, 1945.
_____. Zhenshchiny strany sotsializma. Moscow:
    Profizdat, 1948.
Pritchina, Efrosiniia Akimovna. Zhenshchina i religiia.
    Moscow: Sovetskaia Rossia, 1960.
Rubenstein, Dale Ross. How the Russian Revolution Failed
    Women. Boston: New England Free Press.
Rumiantseva, Mariia Stepanovna. Spravochnik zhenshchiny-
    rabotnitsy. Moscow: Profizdat, 1963.

Rusova, Sofiïa Fedorivna. Nashi vyznachni zhinky. Winnipeg: Souzu Ukrainok Kanady, 1945.

Schlesinger, Rudolf. Changing Attitudes in Soviet Russia: Documents and Readings. London: Routledge & Kegan Paul, 1956.

Selivanova, Nina Nikolaevna. Russia's Women. New York: E. P. Dutton, 1923.

Serebrennikov, George N. Position of Women in the USSR. Freeport, N.Y.: Books for Libraries, 1937.

Shaffer, Harry G., ed. The Soviet System in Theory and Practice: Selected Western and Soviet Views. New York: Appleton-Century-Crofts, 1965.

Shevliakov, Mikhail Viktorovich. Russkie pisateli o russkoi zhenshchine. St. Petersburg: Izdatel'stvo Ivana Ivanova, 1899.

Shimigorskiĭ, Evgeniĭ Sevast'ĭanovich. Imperatorskoe zhenskoe patrioticheskoe obshchestvo, 1818-1912: istoricheski ocherk. St. Petersburg: Gosudarstvennaïa Tipografiïa, 1912.

Shorish, M. Mobin. "The Employment Opportunities of the Local Women of the Soviet Central Asian Republics." University of Illinois, Comparative Education Division, Department of History and Philosophy of Education, 1970.

_____. "The Place of Local Women in the 'Multi-tiered' Culture of the Soviet Central Asia." A paper presented at the Interdisciplinary Conference on the Process of Change in Contemporary Asian Society, Urbana, 1970. College of Education, University of Illinois.

Shteĭnberg, Evgenii. "Pravovoe polozhenie zhenshchiny v Dagestane." Novyi Vostok 26, 27 (1929):182-99.

Smith, Jessica. Women in Soviet Russia. New York: Vanguard, 1928.

Smulevich, Boleslav Ĭakovlevich. Materinstvo pri kapitalizme i sotsializme. Moscow: Gosudarstvennoe Sotsial'no-ekonomicheskoe Izdatel'stvo, 1936.

Soviet Woman: A Magazine Devoted to Social and Political Problems, Literature and Art. Moscow: Soviet Women's Anti-Fascist Committee and the Central Council of Trade Unions of the USSR, 1945.

Soviet Women to the Women of the World: The Moscow Women's Anti-Nazi Meeting and American Women's Response. New York: American Council on Soviet Relations, n.d.

Storey, Robert G. "USSR People's Court and Woman Lawyers." Women Lawyers Journal 48 (1962):21-23.

_____. "Women Lawyers in the Soviet Union." Women Lawyers Journal 44 (Fall 1956):9-12.

Strasser, Nadja. Die Russin. Berlin: S. Fischer Verlag, 1917.

Sverdlov, G. M. Legal Rights of the Soviet Family: Marriage, Motherhood and the Family in the Soviet Law. London: Soviet News, 1945.

Tatarinova, Nadazhda. Women in the USSR: At Home, at Work, in Society. Moscow: Novosti Press Agency, 1966.

Tatybekova, Zhanetta Saĭmasaevna. Raskreposhchenie zhenshchiny kirgizki velikoĭ oktīabrʹskoĭ sotsialisticheskoĭ revolīūtsieĭ, 1917-1936. Frunze: Izdatelʹstvo Akademii Nauk Kirgizskoi SSR, 1963.

Tchernavin, Tatiana. Nous femmes soviétiques. Trans. S. Campaux. Paris: Payot, 1936.

___. We Soviet Women. New York: E. P. Dutton, 1936.

Toshchakova, E. M. "Altaĭskaĭa zhenshchina v dorevolīūtsionnom proslom" [The woman of the Altai in the pre-revolutionary past]. Uchen. zap. gornoalt. nauchno-issled. Inst. Istor. Iaz. Liter. 2 (1958):108-50.

Tsentralʹnoe Statisticheskoe Upravlenie Narodno-khozīaĭstvennogo Ucheta. Zhenshchina v SSSR. First published, 1937. Reprint, Boston: Foreign Languages Publishing House, 1960.

Tsentralʹnoe Statisticheskoe Upravlenie. Zhenshchiny i deti v SSSR. Moscow: Gosstatizdat, 1963.

Turkmen SSR Statisticheskoe Upravlenie. Zhenshchina v Turkmenskoĭ SSR. Ashkhabad: Gosstatizdat, 1960.

Tymchenko, Zhanaa Pavlivna. Trudīashchi zhinky v borotʹbi za viadei rad na ukraĭn. Kiev: Nachkova Dumka, 1966.

Vagabov, Mustafa Vagabovich. Islam i zhenshchina. Moscow, 1968.

Vasilgevna, G. P. Voprosy semʹi i byta u narodov sredneĭ Azii. Moscow, 1962. Microfilm. Washington, D.C.: Library of Congress, 1966.

Viirsalu, Erika. Women and Youth in Soviet-Occupied Estonia. London: Boreas, 1955.

Vladimirov, Leonid. The Russians. New York: Frederick A. Praeger, 1968.

Waliszewski, Kazimierzi. La femme russe. Paris: Plon, 1926.

Weitzman, S.; Feshback, M.; and Kalchycka, Lydia. "Employment in the USSR: Comparative USSR-US Data." In Dimensions of Soviet Economic Power. Washington, D.C.: Joint Economic Committee of the Congress of the United States, 1962.

Wheeler, Susan Anna Brookings. Daughters of Armenia. New York: American Tract Society, 1877.

Woman of Ukraine: Her Part on the Scene of History, in Literature, Arts and Struggle for Freedom. Philadelphia: Ukrainian National Women's League of America, 1955.

Zabelin, Ivan Egorovich. Domashnii byt russkogo naroda. Moscow: Tipografiia A. I. Mamoitova, 1872.

Greece

Blum, Richard, and Blum, Eva. Health and Healing in Rural Greece: A Study of Three Communities. Stanford: Stanford University Press, 1965.

Braunstein, Otto. Die politische Wirksamkeit der griechischen Frau. Eine Nachwirkung vorgriechischen mutterechtes. Leipzig: Druck von A. Hoffman in Kommission bei G. Fock, 1911.

Bruns, Ivo. Frauenemancipation in Athen, ein Beitrag zur attischen Kulturgeschichte des fünften und vierten Jahrhunderts. Kiliac: Schmidtii et Klaunigii, 1900.

Dubisch, Jill. "Dowry and the Domestic Power of Women in a Greek Island Village." A paper presented at the 70th Annual Meeting of the American Anthropological Association, New York, 1971. Mimeo. Trinity College.

Erdmann, Walter. Die Ehe im alten Griechenland. Munich: Beck, 1934.

Friedl, Ernestine. "The Position of Women: Appearance and Reality." Anthropological Quarterly 40 (1967):97-108.
___. Vasilika, a Village in Modern Greece. New York: Holt, Rinehart and Winston, 1962.

Gorman, Mary Rosaria. The Nurse in Greek Life. Boston: Foreign Languages Publishing House, 1917.

Hoffman, Susannah. "Social Structure, Women and the Occult: An Example from Greece." A paper presented at the 70th Annual Meeting of the American Anthropological Association, New York, 1971. Mimeo. University of California, Berkeley.

Jenzer, Annemarie. Wandlungen in der Auffassung der Frau im ionischen Epos und in der attischen Tragödie bis auf Sophokles. Zurich: Leeman, 1933.

Lallier, Roger. De la condition de la femme dans la famille athénienne au V et au IV siècle. Paris: E. Thorin, 1875.

Lambin, Jane. "The Impact of Industrial Employment on the Position of Women in a Greek Country Town." British Journal of Sociology 14 (Sept. 1963):240-47.

Lambiri, Ioanna. Social Change in a Greek Country Town: The Impact of Factory Work on the Position of Women. Research Monograph Series, 13. Athens: Center of Planning and Economic Research, 1965.

Mabille, Paul. Le communisme & le féminisme a Athens, 1900.

Nortor, G. La femme dans l'antiquité grecque. Paris: H. Laurens, 1901.

Paoli, U. E. La donna greca nell'antichita [The Greek
    woman in antiquity]. 2nd ed. Florence: F. Le
    Monnier, 1955.
Schein, Muriel. "Only on Sundays." Natural History 80
    (1971):52-61.
Slater, Philip Elliot. The Glory of Hera: Greek
    Mythology and the Greek Family. Boston: Beacon
    Press, 1968.
Zevi, Elena. Scene di gineceo e scene di idillio nei
    vasi greci della seconda metà del secoloquinto.
    Rome: Giovanni Bardi, 1938.

Portugal, Spain

Alberti, A. de. "Spain and Portugal." In Women of All
    Nations, vol. 4, ed. T. A. Joyce, pp. 717-24. New
    York: Funk & Wagnalls, 1915.
Bomli, P. W. La femme dans l'Espagne du siècle d'or.
    La Haye: M. Nijhoff, 1950.
Calera, Ana Maria. El libro de la recién casada.
    Barcelona: Ed. Maucci, 1959.
Campo de Alange, Maria. La mujer en España. Madrid:
    Aguilar, 1962.
Carboneres, Manuel. Picaronas y alcahuetes; ó, La
    mancebía de Valencia. Apuntes para la historia de la
    prostitución desde principios del siglo XIV hasta
    poco antes de la abolición de los fueros, con
    profusion de notas y copias de varios documentos
    oficiales. Valencia: Imp. del Mercantil, 1876.
Catalina del Amo, Severo. La mujer: apuntes para un
    libro, 4th ed. Madrid: A. de San Martin (y) A.
    Jubera, 1870.
Deleito y Piñuela, José. La mujer, la casa y la moda
    (en la España del rey poeta). Madrid: Espasa-Calpe,
    1946.
Francos Rodríguez, José. La mujer y la política
    españolas. Madrid: Ed. Pueyo, 1920.
Riegelhaupt, Joyce F. "Saloio Women: An Analysis of
    Informal and Formal Political and Economic Roles of
    Portuguese Peasant Women." Anthropological Quarterly
    40 (1967):109-26.
Selgas y Carrasco, José. Un retrato de mujer. Seville:
    F. Alvarez, 1876.

Scandinavia: Denmark, Finland, Iceland, Norway, Sweden

Anderson, Robert T., and Anderson, Barbara Gallatin.
    "Sexual Behavior and Urbanization in a Danish Village."
    Southwestern Journal of Anthropology 16 (1960):93-109.

Aner, Kerstin. Swedish Women Today: A Personal Appraisal. Stockholm: Swedish Institute, 1966.
Anthony, Katherine Susan. Feminism in Germany and Scandinavia. New York: Henry Holt, 1915.
Burke, P. E., and Marshall, Eva. Social Benefits in Sweden. Stockholm: Swedish Institute, 1966.
Christenson, Harold T. "Cultural Relativism and Premarital Sex Norms." American Sociological Review 25 (Feb. 1960):31-39.
Dahlstrom, Edmund, ed. The Changing Roles of Men and Women. Boston: Beacon Press, 1971.
Drachmann, Emmy. "Denmark." In Women of All Nations, vol. 4, ed. T. A. Joyce. New York: Funk & Wagnalls, 1915.
———. "Iceland." In Women of All Nations, vol. 4, ed. T. A. Joyce. New York: Funk & Wagnalls, 1915.
Eliot, Thomas O. Norway's Families: Trends, Problems, Programs. Philadelphia: University of Pennsylvania Press, 1960.
"Enquiry on Equal Pay in Sweden." International Labour Review 64 (July 1951):90-96.
Fleisher, Frederic. The New Sweden. New York: David McKay, 1967.
Gendall, Murray. Swedish Working Wives: A Study of Determinants and Consequences. Trenton, N.J.: Bedminster Press, 1963.
Haavio-Mannila, Elina. "The Position of Finnish Women: Regional and Cross-National Comparisons." Journal of Marriage and Family Living 31 (May 1969):2.
———. "Sex Differentiation in Role Expectations and Performance." Journal of Marriage and Family Living 29 (August 1967):568-77.
Hegeler, Inge, and Hegeler, Sten. An ABZ of Love. New York: Medical Press, 1963.
Herredsvela, K. Sex Role Pattern and Political Level of Aspiration. Oslo: Mackinskrevet, 1954.
Jenkins, David. Sweden and the Price of Progress. New York: Coward-McCann, 1968.
Kalvesten, Ana-Lisa. Social Structure of Sweden. Stockholm: Swedish Institute, 1966.
Karlsson, Georg. "Sociological Studies of the Family in Scandinavia." Sociological Inquiry 31 (Winter 1961): 47-59.
Krause, Wolfgang. Die Frau in der Sprache der altisländischen Familiengeschichten. Göttingen: Vandenhoeck & Ruprecht, 1926.
Krog, Gina. "Norway." In Women of All Nations, vol. 4, ed. T. A. Joyce, pp. 748-53. New York: Funk & Wagnalls, 1915.
Leijon, Anna-Greta. Swedish Women--Swedish Men. Stockholm: Swedish Institute, 1968.

Linnér, Birgitta. Sex and Society in Sweden. New York: Pantheon Books, 1967.
Lynn, D. B., and Sawrey, W. I. "The Effects of Father Absence on Norwegian Boys and Girls." Journal of Abnormal and Social Psychology 59 (1959):258-62.
Myrdal, Alva. Nation and Family. Cambridge: M.I.T. Press, 1968.
_____. "Swedish Women in Industry and at Home." Annals of the American Academy of Political and Social Science 197 (1938):216-31.
Reports from the Swedish Ladies' Committee to the World's Columbian Exposition at Chicago, 1893. Stockholm: Central-Tryckereit, 1893.
Rossel, Agda. "The Employment of Women in Sweden." International Labour Review 71 (1955):273-90.
Rossel, James. Women in Sweden. Stockholm: Swedish Institute, 1965.
Segerstedt, Torgny T., and Weintraub, Philipp. "Marriage and Divorce in Sweden." Annals of the American Academy of Political and Social Science 272 (1950): 185-94.
Seip, Ellen. Facts about Women in Norway. Madison: University of Wisconsin Press, 1960.
The Status of Women in Norway Today. Oslo: Norwegian Joint Committee on International Social Policy, 1953.
The Status of Women in Sweden: Report to the United Nations. Stockholm: Swedish Institute, 1968.
Strange, Helene. I mødrenes spor, nordfalsterske kvinders arbejde gennem halvardet hundrede aar. Copenhagen: Munksgaard, 1945.
Svalastoga, Kaare. "The Family in Scandinavia." Marriage and Family Living 16 (1954):374-80.
Swedish Divorce Laws. Stockholm: Swedish Institute, 1965.
Sysiharja, Anna-Liisa. "Equality, Home and Work: A Socio-psychological Study on Finnish Student Women's Attitudes towards the Woman's Role in Society." Master's thesis, University of Helsinki, 1960.
Therapeutic Abortion and the Law in Sweden. Stockholm: Swedish Institute, 1964.
Voipio-Juvas, Anni, ed. The Finnish Woman. Helsinki: W. Söderstrom, 1949.

Austria, Bulgaria, Czechoslovakia, Hungary, Poland, Romania, Yugoslavia

Beoković, Mila. Žene heroji <Dušanka Kovačević: Predgovor>. Sarajevo: Svjetlost, 1967.
Bradinska, Radka N. Vŭznikvane i oformiâvane na zhenskoto sotsiâldemok ratichesko dvizhenie. Sofia: NSOF, 1969.

Commission for International Relations of the Federation
of Women's Associations of Yugoslavia. Women's
Rights in Yugoslavia. Belgrade: Publicisticko-
Izdavack Zavod Jugoslavije, 1961.
Dvorský, František, ed. Staré písemné pamatky žen a
deer českých. The Hague: V. Komisi F. Rivnáče, 1869.
Hammel, Eugene A. "The Jewish Mother in Serbia." In
Essays in Balkan Ethnology, ed. William Lockwood.
Berkeley: Kroeber Anthropological Society Special
Publication 1, 1967.
Klemensiewiczowa, Jadwiga Sikorska. Przebojem ku wiedzy;
wspomnienia jednej z pierwszych studentek krakowskich
z XIX wieku. Warsaw: Zakl ad Narodowy im Ossolińskich,
1961.
Kloskowska, Antonina. "Attitudes toward the Status of
Women in Polish Working Class Families, General
Attitudes toward the Respective Roles and the Equality
of the Two Sexes, and towards Children." In Inter-
national Social Science Journal. Paris: UNESCO
Publications, 1962.
Konopczynski, Wladyslaw. Kiedy nami rzadzily kobiety.
London: Veritas, 1960.
Krauss, F. S. "Brautkauf bei den Bulgaren." Anthro-
pologische Gesellschaft in Wien. Mitteilungen 17
(1887):68.
Locke, Amy. "Austria." In Women of All Nations, vol. 4,
ed. T. A. Joyce, pp. 691-97. New York: Funk &
Wagnalls, 1915.
Markovič, Tomislav. Prostitucija: Skripta iz socijalne
patologije. Zagreb: Visoka defektološka škola, 1965.
Matl, J. "Die Frau am Balkan" [The woman in the Balkans].
In Sudslawische Studien, ed. M. Bernath, pp. 191-204.
Munich: Oldenburg, 1965.
Morvay, J. "Asazonyok a nagyscaladban" [Women in the
joint family]. Acta Ethnographica 6 (1957):257-58.
Pachucka, Romana. Pamietniki z lat 1886-1914. Warsaw:
Zaklad Narodowy im Ossolinskich, 1958.
Paskaleva, Virzhinia. Bulgarkata prez vuzrazhdaneto.
Bulgarska Komunisticheska Partia, 1964.
Poland--Glówny Urzad Statystyczny. Kobieta w Polsce;
dane statystyczne. Warsaw, 1968.
Proft, Gabriele. Der Weg zu uns! Die Frauenfrage im
neuen Österreich. Vienna: Sozialistische Partei
Österreichs, 1945.
Prohaska, Dragutin. Ženska lica u hrvatskoj književrosti.
Zagreb: Nakl. Knjizare Mirka Breyera, 1916.
Simic, Andre. "Management of the Male Image in
Yugoslavia." Anthropological Quarterly 42 (1969):
89-101.
Tkadlecková-Vantuchová, Jarmila. Živena--spolok
slovenských žien. Bratislava: Epocha, T. Pravda.

Vukanovic, T. P. "The Position of Women among Gypsies
    in the Kosovo-metohija Region." Journal of Gypsy Lore
    Society 40 (July-Oct. 1961):81-100.
Wasylewski, Stanislaw. Twarz i Kobieta. Krakow:
    Wydawn Literachie, 1960.
Wrochno, Krystyna. Woman in Poland. Warsaw: Inter-
    press, 1969.

OCEANIA

General References

Goodale, Jane C., and Chowning, Ann. "The Contaminating
    Woman." A paper presented at the 70th Annual Meeting
    of the American Anthropological Association, New
    York, 1971. Mimeo. Bryn Mawr College.
Langness, L. L., and Gladwin, Thomas. "Oceania." In
    Psychological Anthropology, ed. Francis L. K. Hsu,
    pp. 167-200. Cambridge, Mass. Schenkman, 1972.
Mead, Margaret. From the South Seas: Studies of
    Adolescence and Sex in Primitive Societies. New York:
    William Morrow, 1939.
Women of the Pacific: A Record of the Proceedings of the
    Eighth Conference. Tokyo: Pan-Pacific and Southwest
    Asia Women's Association, 1958.
Women of the Pacific and Southeast Asia: A Record of the
    Proceedings of the Ninth Conference. Canberra: Pan-
    Pacific and Southeast Asia Women's Association, 1961.

Australia

Berndt, Catherine H. Women's Changing Ceremonies in
    Northern Australia. Paris: Libraire Scientifique,
    Hermann, 1950.
Dawson, M. "The Australian Woman's Changing Image."
    Education Gazette 60 (Nov. 1966):279-84.
DeVidas, J. "Childbirth among the Aranda, Central
    Australia." Oceania 18 (1947):117-19.
Gale, Fay, ed. Women's Role in Aboriginal Society.
    Australian Aboriginal Studies No. 36. Canberra:
    Australian Institute of Aboriginal Studies, 1970.
Goodale, Jane C. Tiwi Wives: A Study of the Women of
    Melville Island, Australia. Seattle: University of
    Washington Press, 1970.
Hart, Charles W. The Tiwi of North Australia. New York:
    Henry Holt, 1960.
Kaberry, Phyllis M. Aboriginal Woman, Sacred and Profane.
    London: Routledge, 1939.

Lockwood, Douglas. I, the Aboriginal. Adelaide:
    Rigby, 1962.
_____. We, the Aboriginals. Melbourne: Cassell, 1963.
MacKenzie, Norman. Women in Australia. London: Angus
    & Robertson, 1963.
Malinowski, Bronislaw. The Family among the Australian
    Aborigines: Sociological Study. London: University
    of London Press, 1913.
Meggitt, J. J. Desert People: A Study of the Walbiri
    Aborigines of Central Australia. Chicago: University
    of Chicago Press, 1962.
Mountfard, Charles P. The Tiwi: Their Art, Myth, and
    Ceremony. London: Phoenix House, 1958.
Pilling, Arnold A., and Pilling, Richard A., eds.
    Diprotodon to Detribalization: Studies of Change
    among Australian Aborigines. East Lansing: Michigan
    State University Press, 1970.
Rischbieth, Bessie Mabel. March of Australian Women: A
    Record of Fifty Years' Struggle for Equal Citizenship.
    Perth: Paterson Brokensha, 1969.
Roheim, G. "Aphrodite or the Woman with a Penis."
    Psychoanalytic Quarterly 14 (1945):350-90.
_____. "Women and Their Life in Central Australia."
    Royal Anthropological Institute of Great Britain and
    Ireland Journal 68 (1933):207-65.
Stanner, W. E. H., and Shells, Helen. Australian
    Aboriginal Studies: Conference on Aboriginal Studies,
    Australian National University, 1961. New York:
    Oxford University Press, 1961.

Indonesia: Indonesia, Malaysia, Philippines, Singapore

Access of Girls and Women to Education in Rural Areas in
    Indonesia. A Contribution to the UNESCO Asian Con-
    ference, Bangkok, 1962. Djakarta: Ministry of
    Education, 1962.
Atienza, Maria Fe G. "The Philippine Women's University
    and Extra-Mural Education for Women." Indian Journal
    of Education 27 (July 1966):11-16.
Belo, Jane. Trance in Bali. New York: Columbia
    University Press, 1960.
Beran, Janice Ann. "Growth and Development of Physical
    Education for Women in the Philippines." Silliman
    Journal 15 (1968):427-38.
Buck, H. H. "Capitana Vicenta." Journal of East Asian
    Studies 4 (Jan. 1955):79-84.
Conklin, Harold C. "Maling, a Manunoo Girl from the
    Philippines: A Day in Pariwa." In The Company of Man,
    ed. J. B. Casagrande, pp. 101-19. New York: Harper
    & Row, 1960.

deMoubray, George Alexander de Chazal. Matriarchy in
the Malay Peninsula and Neighbouring Countries.
London: Routledge, 1931.
Dewey, Alice G. Peasant Marketing in Java. New York:
Free Press, 1962.
DuBois, Cora. The People of Alor: A Social-Psychological
Study of an East Indian Island. New York: Harper &
Row, 1960.
Firth, Rosemary. Housekeeping among Malay Peasants.
First published, 1943. Reprint, Monographs on Social
Anthropology. London: London School of Economics,
1966.
Freeman, J. D. "The Family System of the Iban of Borneo."
In The Developmental Cycle in Domestic Groups, ed.
Jack Goody, pp. 15-52. Cambridge: Cambridge Uni-
versity Press, 1958.
Geertz, Clifford. The Religion of Java. Glencoe,
Ill.: Free Press, 1960.
Geertz, Hildred. The Javanese Family: A Study of Kin-
ship and Socialization. New York: Free Press, 1961.
___, and Geertz, Clifford. "Teknonymy in Bali:
Parenthood, Age-grading and Genealogical Amnesia."
First published, 1904. Reprinted in Marriage, Family
and Residence, ed. P. Bohannan and J. Middleton,
pp. 355-76. Garden City, N.Y.: Natural History
Press, 1968.
Haar, B. Adat Law in Indonesia, trans. George Haas and
Margaret Hordyk. New York: Institute of Pacific
Relations, 1948.
History, Objects and Functions of the National As-
sociation of Women's Institutes Federation of Malaya.
Kuala Lumpur: National Association of Women's
Institutes, n.d.
Hunt, Chester L. "Female Occupational Roles and the
Urban Sex Ratios in the United States, Japan and the
Philippines." Social Forces 43 (Mar. 1965):407-16.
Kartini, Raden Adjeng. Door duisternis tot licht;
gedachten over en voor het javaansche volk. The
Hague: Electrische Drukkerij Luctor et Emergo, 1912.
___. Letters of a Javanese Princess, trans. Agnes Louise
Symmers. First published, 1920. Reprint, New York:
W. W. Norton, 1964.
Kennedy, Raymond. Field Notes on Indonesia. Flores,
1949-50, ed. Harold C. Conklin. New Haven: Human
Relations Area Files Press, 1953.
Kong, Y. S. "The Participation of Women in Public Life
in Sarawak." African Women 3 (Dec. 1958):16-19.
Lardizabal, A. S. "The Filipino Woman." In The Grade
School 14 (Feb. 1967):576-78.
Mead, Margaret, and Bateson, Gregory. Balinese Character.
First published, 1942. Reprint, New York: Academy of
Sciences, 1962.

Nefertiti [pseud.]. Between You and Me. Djakarta:
Gunung Agurg, 1960.
Nimmo, H. Arlo. "Bajau Sex and Reproduction."
Ethnology 9 (1970):251-62.
Nurge, Ethel. Life in a Leyte Village. Seattle:
University of Washington Press, 1965.
Pecson, Geronima T. "The Role of Women in Preserving
Cultural Heritage." UNESCO Philippines 3 (July 1964):
144-47.
Pownall, Evelyn. Mary of Maranao. New York: Cambridge
University Press, 1965.
Prawirodihardjo, Tartib. Women and Their Families in
Community Education. Djakarta: Ministry of Education
and Culture, Department of Community Education, 1960.
Reyes, Felina. Filipino Women, Their Role in the Progress
of Their Nation. Washington: U.S. Department of
Labor, Women's Bureau, 1951.
Rizal y Alonso, Jose. A Letter to the Young Women of
Malolos. Manila: Bureau of Printing, 1932.
Shelford, R. "Women of the Non-Malay Tribes of the
Sunda Islands and Celebes." In Women of All Nations,
vol. 1, ed. T. A. Joyce, pp. 161-85. New York: Funk
& Wagnalls, 1915.
Siraj, M. "The Status of Muslim Women in Family Law in
Singapore." World Muslim League Monthly Magazine 1
(Dec. 1963):40-52.
Sison, P. S. "La place des femmes dans la vue économique
aux Philippines." Révue Internationale du Travail
87 (Feb. 1963):133-49.
Skeat, Walter W. "The Malay Peninsula." In Women of
All Nations, vol. 1, ed. T. A. Joyce, pp. 186-201.
New York: Funk & Wagnalls, 1915.
Steinmann, A. "Zur Verbreitung der 'Couvade' in West-
indonesien" [The diffusion of the "Couvade" in
western Indonesia]. Anthropos 51 (1956):309-11.
Stoodley, Bartlett H. "Some Aspects of Tagalog Family
Structure." In You and Others: Readings in Intro-
ductory Anthropology, ed. A. Kimball Romney and Paul
L. DeVore, pp. 212-23. Cambridge, Mass.: Winthrop,
1973.
Suyin, Han. "The Women of Malaya." African Women 2
(June 1957):63-65.
Tanner, Nancy. "Matrifocality in Indonesia and among
Black Americans." A paper presented at the 70th
Annual Meeting of the American Anthropological
Association, New York, 1971. Mimeo. University of
California, Santa Cruz.
Thomas, Northcote Whitridge. "The Philippine Islands."
In Women of All Nations, vol. 1, ed. T. A. Joyce,
pp. 202-8. New York: Funk & Wagnalls, 1915.

United Nations. Seminar on Measures Required for the
    Advancement of Women with Special Reference to the
    Establishment of a Long Term Programme. Manila,
    1966. Report. New York: United Nations, 1966.
Vreede de Stuers, Cora. The Indonesian Female. The
    Hague: Mouton, 1960.
    . L'emancipation de la femme indonesienne. The
    Hague: Mouton, 1960.
Wallace, Ben J. "Pagan Gaddang Spouse Exchange."
    Ethnology 8 (1969):183-88.
Wynne, Mervyn L. Triad and Tabut: A Survey of the
    Origin and Diffusion of Chinese and Mohammedan Secret
    Societies in the Malay Peninsula, A.D. 1800-1935.
    Singapore: Government Printing Office, 1941.

Melanesia

Cochrane, D. G. "Conflict between Law and Sexual Mores
    on San Cristobal." Oceania 39 (1969):281-89.
Hingston, A. "Melanesia." In Women of All Nations,
    vol. 1, ed. T. A. Joyce, pp. 84-120. New York: Funk
    & Wagnalls, 1915.
Laufer, P. C. "Die Frau und Mutter im melanesischen
    Raum" [The wife and mother in the region of
    Melanesia]. Zeitschrift Missionswissenschaft und
    Religion 47 (1963):47-59.
Robertson, Ruth. "Fiji Women Find New Interests."
    South Pacific Bulletin 11 (Oct. 1961):54-55.
Sebbelov, G. "The Social Position of Men and Women
    among the Natives of East Malekula: New Hebrides."
    American Anthropologist 15 (1913):273-80.
Stewart, Marjorie. "Training Women for Leadership in
    Fiji." South Pacific Bulletin 10 (July 1960):44-45.
Thurnwald, H. "Woman's Status in Buin Society."
    Oceania 5 (1934):142-70.

Micronesia

Erdland, August. "Die Stellung der Frauen in den
    Häuptlingsfamilien der Marshallinseln (Sudsee)."
    Anthropos 4 (1909):106-12.
Fischer, Ann. "Reproduction in Truk." Ethnology 2
    (1963):526-40.
Fischer, John L. "The Position of Men and Women in Truk
    and Ponape: A Comparative Analysis of Kinship
    Terminology and Folktales." Journal of American
    Folklore 69 (1956):55-62.
Gladwin, Thomas. "The Role of Man and Woman on Truk:
    A Problem in Personality and Culture." Transactions
    of the New York Academy of Sciences 15 (1953):305-9.

Goodenough, Ward. "Premarital Freedom on Truk: Theory and Practice." American Anthropologist 51 (1949): 615-20.

Hingston, A. "Micronesia." In Women of All Nations, vol. 1, ed. T. A. Joyce, pp. 127-29. New York: Funk & Wagnalls, 1915.

Swartz, Marc J. "Sexuality and Aggression on Tomonum, Truk." American Anthropologist 60 (1958):467-87.

New Guinea

Aufenanger, H. "Women's Lives in the Highlands of New Guinea." Anthropos 57 (1964):218-66.

Bateson, Gregory. "Sex Ethos and the Itamul Naven Ceremony." In Bateson, Naven, 2nd ed. Stanford: Stanford University Press, 1958.

Berndt, Ronald Murray. Excess and Restraint: Social Control among a New Guinea Mountain People. Chicago: University of Chicago Press, 1962.

Buchbinder, Georgeda. "Explanation of Low Fertility in the New Guinea Highlands." A paper presented at the 69th Annual Meeting of the American Anthropological Association, San Diego, 1970. Mimeo. Columbia University.

Clancy, Elizabeth Durack. "Women of Papua and New Guinea." Australian External Territories 9 (Aug. 1969):18-23.

Couvee, L. M. J. "Marriage, Obstetrics, and Infant Mortality among the Kapauku in the Central Highlands, West New Guinea." Tropical and Geographical Medicine 14 (1962):325-33.

Dornstreich, Mark D., and Buchbinder, Georgeda. "Differential Female Mortality in New Guinea as a Factor in Population Regulation." A paper presented at the 69th Annual Meeting of the American Anthropological Association, San Diego, 1970. Mimeo. Rutgers University.

Essai, Brian. Papua and New Guinea: A Contemporary Survey. Melbourne: Oxford University Press, 1961.

Ford, Edward. "Notes on Pregnancy and Parturition in the D'Entrecasteaux Islands." Medical Journal of Australia 27 (1940):498-501.

Glasse, R. M., and Meggitt, M. J., eds. Pigs, Pearlshells and Women: Marriage in the New Guinea Highlands. Englewood Cliffs, N.J.: Prentice-Hall, 1969.

Glasse, Robert. "Mask of Venery: Ideology and Sex in the New Guinea Highlands." A paper presented at the 70th Annual Meeting of the American Anthropological Association, New York, 1971. Mimeo. CUNY, Queens.

Held, J. L. Papuas of Waropen. The Hague: Martinus
    Nijhoff, 1957.
Hogbin, Ian H. Transformation Scene. The Changing
    Culture of a New Guinea Village. London: Routledge
    & Kegan Paul, 1951.
Hunt, Robert. Personalities and Cultures: Readings in
    Psychological Anthropology. New York: Natural
    History Press, 1967.
Langness, Lewis L. "Sexual Antagonism in the New Guinea
    Highlands: A Bena Bena Example." Oceania 37 (1967):
    161-77.
Lehner, Stephan. "Die soziale Stellung der Frau bei
    der papuavisch-melanesischen Bevölkerung von
    Nordost-Neuguinea." Gesellschaft für Völkerkunde
    mitteilungsblatt 3 (1934):12-18.
Mead, Margaret. Growing Up in New Guinea. New York:
    Mentor, 1961.
    . The Mountain Arapesh. Garden City, N.Y.: Natural
    History Press, 1968.
    . Sex and Temperament in Three Primitive Societies.
    New York: Dell, 1963.
Meggitt, M. J. "Male-female Relationships in the High-
    lands of Australian New Guinea." American Anthro-
    pologist 66 (Aug. 1964):204-24.
Newman, Philip L. Knowing the Gurumba. San Francisco:
    Holt, Rinehart & Winston, 1965.
Read, Kenneth E. The High Valley. New York: Charles
    Scribner's Sons, 1965.
Reay, Marie. The Kuma. Melbourne: Melbourne University
    Press, 1956.
Ross, J. A. "The Puberty Ceremony of the Chimbu Girl in
    the Eastern Highlands of New Guinea." Anthropos 60
    (1965):423-32.
Seligmann, Charles Gabriel. "Torres Strait and New
    Guinea." In Women of All Nations, vol. 1, ed. T. A.
    Joyce, pp. 151-60. New York: Funk & Wagnalls, 1915.
Stewart, Marjorie. "Women's Clubs in Netherlands New
    Guinea." South Pacific Bulletin 11 (July 1961):56-57.
Strathern, Andrew. "The Female and Male Spirit Cults in
    Mount Hagen." Man 5 (Dec. 1970):571-85.
    . "Male Initiation Cults in New Guinea Highlands
    Societies." Ethnology 9 (1970):373-88.
Strathern, Marilyn. Women in Between: Female Roles in a
    Male World, Mount Hagen, New Guinea. New York:
    Seminar Press, 1972.
Wedgwood, Camilla H. "Girls' Puberty Rites in Manam
    Islands, New Guinea." Oceania 4 (1933-1934):132-55.
    . "Woman in Manam." Oceania 7 (1937):401-28; 8 (1937):
    170-92.
Whiteman, J. "Girls' Puberty Ceremonies amongst the
    Chimbu." Anthropos 60 (1965):410-22.

Polynesia

Barrow, Tui Terence. Women of Polynesia: Polynesian
Studies by H. Sieben. Wellington: Seven Seas, 1967.

Best, Elsdon. "Maori Customs Pertaining to Birth and
Baptism." Journal of the Polynesian Society 38
(1929):241-69.

Curson, Peter. "Birth and Illegitimacy in Rarotonga."
Journal of the Polynesian Society 78 (1969):112-23.

Deihi, Joseph. "The Position of Woman in Samoan
Culture." Primitive Man 5 (1932):21-26.

Gunson, N. "Great Women and Friendship Contract Rites
in Pre-Christian Tahiti." Journal of Polynesian
Society 73 (Mar. 1964):53-69.

Hanson, F. Allan. "The Rapan Theory of Conception."
American Anthropologist 72 (1970):1444-47.

Heuer, Berys N. "Maori Women in Traditional Family and
Tribal Life." Journal of Polynesian Society 78
(1969):448-94.

Hingston, A. "Polynesia." In Women of All Nations,
vol. 1, ed. T. A. Joyce, pp. 36-69. New York: Funk
& Wagnalls, 1915.

Holland, Beverley. "New Interests for Aitutaki Women."
South Pacific Bulletin 11 (Jan. 1961):44-62.

Joyce, Thomas Athol. "New Zealand." In Women of All
Nations, vol. 1, ed. T. A. Joyce, pp. 70-83. New
York: Funk & Wagnalls, 1915.

Mead, Margaret. Coming of Age in Samoa: A Psychological
Study of Primitive Youth for Western Civilization.
Foreword by F. Boas. New York: Morrow, 1928.

___. Coming of Age in Samoa: A Study of Adolescence
and Sex in Primitive Society. New York: Mentor, 1949.

Mulligan, D. G. Maori Adolescence in Rakau. Victoria
University Publications in Psychology, 9. Wellington:
Victoria University College, 1957.

Ritchie, Jane. Childhood in Rakau: The First Five Years
of Life. Victoria University Publications in
Psychology, 10. Wellington: Victoria University
College, 1957.

Simpson, Helen. The Women of New Zealand. Reprint,
New York: Humanities Press, 1962; Fernhill House,
1962.

Suggs, Robert C. Marquesan Sexual Behavior: An Anthropological Study of Polynesian Practices. New York:
Harcourt, Brace & World, 1966.

Vayda, A. P. "Maori Women and Maori Cannibalism." Man
60 (1960):70-71.

SOUTH AMERICA

Introductory Texts and General References

Anzoategui, Yderla G. La mujer y la política; historia del femenismo mundial. Buenos Aires: Ed. Mendoza, 1953.

Carluci, M. A. "La 'couvade' en Sudamerica" [The "couvade" in South America]. Runa 6 (June 1957):53.

de la Torre Mulhare, Mirta. "The Cult of Virginity and the Double Standard: Latin American Models." A paper presented at the 70th Annual Meeting of the American Anthropological Association, New York, 1971. Mimeo. University of Pittsburgh.

Fock, Niels. "South American Birth Customs in Theory and Practice." In Cross-cultural Approaches: Readings in Comparative Research, ed. Clellan S. Ford, pp. 126-44. New Haven: Human Relations Area Files Press, 1967.

Illustres Americanas. Paris: Librería de la Viuda de Wincop, 1825.

Koch-Grunberg, Theodor. "South America." In Women of All Nations, vol. 2, ed. T. A. Joyce. New York: Funk & Wagnalls, 1915.

O'Leary, Timothy J. Ethnographic Bibliography of South America. New Haven: Human Relations Area Files Press, 1963.

Secretaria General de OEA, ed. Convención Interamericana sobre Concesión de los Derechos Civiles a la Mujer. Washington, D.C.: Pan American Union, Publishing Division, 1948.

Steward, Julian H., and Faron, Louis C. Native Peoples of South America. New York: McGraw-Hill, 1959.

Weiler, Ludwig. Die Südamerikanerin. Düsseldorf: Hellas Verlag, 1959.

Amazonia: Brazil, French Guiana, Guyana, Surinam, Uruguay

Amora, Paulo. Rebelião das mulheres em Minas Gerais. Rio de Janeiro: Ed. GRD, 1968.

Austregesilo, Antonio. Perfit da mulher brasileira (esboço a cerca do feminismo no Brasil). Rio de Janeiro: Ed. Guanabara, Waissman Koogan, 1938.

Biocca, Ettore. Yanoama: The Narrative of a White Girl Kidnapped by Amazonian Indians, as told to Ettore Biocca, trans. Dennis Rhodes. New York: E. P. Dutton, 1970.

Bittencourt, Adalzira. A mulher paulista na história. Rio de Janeiro: Livros de Portugal, 1954.

Cannon, Mary Minerva. Women Workers in Brazil. Washington, D.C.: U.S. Department of Labor, Women's Bureau, 1946.

Chagnon, Napoleon. Yanomamo: The Fierce People. New York: Holt, Rinehart & Winston, 1968.

de Jesus, Carolina Maria. Child of the Dark: The Diary of Carolina Maria de Jesus. New York: Signet, 1962.

Expilly, Charles. Mulheres e costumes do Brasil; tradução prefácio e notas de Gastão Penalva. São Paulo: Ed. Nacional, 1935.

Gleason, Judith. Agotime: Her Legend. New York: Grossman, 1970.

Gregor, Thomas. "Exposure and Seclusion: A Study of Institutionalized Isolation among the Mehinacu Indians of Brazil." Ethnology 9 (1970):234-50.

Kloos, Peter. "Female Initiation among the Maroni River Caribs." American Anthropologist 71 (1969):898-905.

Koch-Grünberg, Theodor. "Frauenarbeit bei den Indianern Nordwestbrasiliens." Anthropologische Gesellshaft in Wien. Mittelungen 38 (1908):172-81.

Kuznets, Simon; Moore, Wilbert; and Spengler, Joseph. Economic Growth: Brazil, India, Japan. Durham, N.C.: Duke University Press, 1955.

Landes, Ruth. The City of Women. New York: Macmillan, 1947.

Morais, Vamberto. A emancipação da mulher; as raízes do preconceito antifeminino e seu declínio. Brazil: Ed. Cital, 1968.

Muraro, Rose Marie. A mulher na construção do mundo futuro. Petropolis: Vozes, 1967.

Murphy, R. F. "Matrilocality and Patrilineality in Mundurucu Society." American Anthropologist 58 (1956): 414-34.

Nicolas, Maria. Vultos paranaenses. Brazil: Curitiba, 1966.

Pereira, Armando. Mulheres deitadas. Rio de Janeiro: Grafica Record. Ed., 1969.

____. Sexo e prostituição. Rio de Janeiro: Grafica Record. Ed., 1967.

Rodriguez, João Batista Cascudo. A mulher brasileira: direitos políticos e civís. Fortaleza: Imp. Universitaria do Ceara, 1962.

Sabino, Ignez. Mulheres illustres do Brazil. Rio de Janeiro: H. Garrier, 1899.

Saffioti, Heleieth lara Bongiovani. A mulher na sociedade de classes; mito e realidade. São Paulo: Quatro Artes, 1969.

Shapiro, Judith. "Male Bonds and Female Bonds: An Illustrative Comparison." A paper presented at the 70th Annual Meeting of the American Anthropological Association, New York, 1971. Mimeo. University of Chicago.

____. "Yanomamo Women: How the Other Half Lives." A
   paper presented at the 69th Annual Meeting of the
   American Anthropological Association, San Diego,
   1970. Mimeo. University of Chicago.
Smith, Raymond Thomas. The Negro Family in British
   Guiana: Family Structure and Social Status in the
   Villages. New York: Humanities Press, 1957.
Terra, Stuart. Rio after Dark. New York: Macfadden
   Bartell, 1970.
Tovar, Beatriz. Mulheres portuguêsas no Brazil. Rio
   de Janeiro: Grafica Ed. Helios, 1966.
Vorcarottorta, Elisabeth. A mulher de heje e a de
   sempre censaio social. Belo Horizonte, Brazil: Ed.
   Itatiaia, 1958.
Yde, J. "Agriculture and Division of Work among the
   Waiwai." Folk 2 (1960):83-97.

Chaco: Bolivia, Paraguay

Metraux, Alfred. "La mujer en la vida social y religiosa
   de los indios chiriguano." Tucumán Universidad
   Nacional Instituto de Etnología Revista 4 (1935):
   145-68.
Paredes de Salazar, Elssa. Diccionario biográfico de la
   mujer boliviana. La Paz: Ediciones Isla, 1965.
Rico, Heidi K. de. Páginas íntimas de la mujer
   boliviana. Tupiza: Ediciones Rico, 1970.
Urbieta Rojas, Pastor. La mujer paraguaya: esquema
   historiográfico. Asunción: Colección Paraguay, 1962.
Urquida, José Macedonio. Bolivianas ilustres; heroinas,
   escritoras, artistas; estudios biográficos y críticos.
   La Paz: Escuela Tipográfica Salesiana, 1918.
____. Bolivianas ilustres; las guerrilleras de la in-
   dependencia; estudios biográficos y críticos. La
   Paz: J. Camarlinghi, 1967.
Vittone, Luis. La mujer paraguaya en la vida nacional.
   Asunción, 1968.

Patagonia: Argentina

Blomberg, Hector Pedro. Mujeres de la historia
   Americana. Buenos Aires: Librerias Anaconda, 1933.
Fúrlong Cardiff, Guillermo. La cultura femenina en la
   época colonial. Buenos Aires: Ed. Kapelusz, 1951.
Henry, Jules. "The Social Function of Child Sexuality
   in Pilaga Indian Culture." In Psychosexual Develop-
   ment in Health and Disease, ed. Paul H. Hoch and
   Joseph Zubin. New York: Grune and Stratton, 1949.
Landres, Albert. El camino a Buenos Aires; la strata
   de blancas. Buenos Aires: Ediciones Aga-Taura, 1967.
____. The Road to Buenos Aires, trans. Eric Sutton.
   London: Constable, 1928.

Mafud, Julio. La revolución sexual Argentina. Buenos
Aires: Ed. Américalee, 1966.
Pichel, Vera. Mi país y sus mujeres. Buenos Aires: Ed.
Sudestade, 1968.
Sosa de Newton, Lily. Las Argentinas, de ayer a hoy.
Buenos Aires: Librería y Editorial L. V. Zanetti, 1967.
Villafañe Casal, María Teresa. La mujer en la pampa
(siglos VIII y XIX). La Plata: A. Domínguez, 1958.

Araucanian: Chile

Anderson, C. Arnold, and Bowman, Mary Jean, eds.
Education and Economic Development. Chicago: Aldine,
1965.
Grez, Vicente. Las mujeres de la independencia.
Santiago: Zig-Zag, 1966.
Hilger, M. Inez. Araucanian Child Life and Its Cultural
Background. Smithsonian Miscellaneous Collections,
133. Washington, D.C.: Smithsonian Institution, 1957.
Klimpel Alvarado, Felícitas. La mujer chilena: el
aporte femenino al progreso de Chile. Santiago: Ed.
Andrés Bello, 1962.
Toro Goday, Julia. Presencia y destino de la mujer en
nuestro pueblo. Santiago: Ediciones Maipo, 1967.

Andean: Peru

Buitron, A. "Situación económica, social y cultural de
la mujer en los paises andionos." América Indígena
16 (Apr. 1956):83-92.
Cannon, Mary Minerva. Women Workers in Peru. Washington,
D.C.: U.S. Department of Labor, Women's Bureau, 1947.
Cornejo Bouroncle, Jorge. Sangre andina; diez mujeres
cuzqueñas. Cuzco: H. G. Rozas Sucesores, 1949.
García y García, Elvira. La mujer peruana a través de
los siglos; serie historiada de estudios y obser-
vaciones. Lima: Imp. Americana, 1924-25.
McClung, Jean. Effects of High Altitude on Human Birth:
Observations on Mothers, Placentas, and the Newborn
in Two Peruvian Populations. Cambridge: Harvard
University Press, 1969.
Portal, Magda. El aprismo y la mujer. Lima: Ed.
Cooperativa Apista Atahualpa, 1934.
Price, Richard. "Trial Marriage in the Andes." Ethnology
4 (1965):310-32.
Wellin, E. "Pregnancy, Childbirth, and Midwifery in the
Valley of Ica, Peru." Health Information Digest for
Hot Countries 3 (1956):1-15.

Chibcha: Colombia, Ecuador

Andrade Coello, Alejandra. Cultura femenina; floración intelectual de la mujer ecuatoriana en el siglo XX. Quito: Talleres Gráficos del Ministerio de Educación, 1942.

Arroyo, Cesar Emilio. Siete medallas. Quito: Ed. Casa de la Cultura Ecuatoriana, 1962.

Chavarriaga Meyer, Jose Luis. Derechos y reivindicaciones de la mujer colombiana; tesis de grado para obtener el titulo de doctor en derecho y crencias politicas, presentaden la facultad de derecho y credencias politicas de la Universidad nacional. Bogotá: Ed. ABC, 1940.

Cohen, Lucy M. Las Colombianas ante la renovación universitaria. Bogotá: Ediciones Tercer Mundo, 1971.
_____. "Patrones de práctica profesional en mujeres." Educación Médica y Salud 2 (1968):1-22.

Melo Lancheros, Livia Stella. Valores femeninos de Colombia. Bogotá, 1966.

Monsalve, José Delores. Mujeres de la independencia. Bogotá: Imp. Nacional, 1926.

Schrimshaw, Susan C. "A Description of Non-coresidential Polygyny in Spanish Ecuador." A paper presented at the 70th Annual Meeting of the American Anthropological Association, New York, 1971. Mimeo. Columbia University.

Seijas, Haydee. Review of Las Colombianas ante la Renovacion Universitaria by Lucy Cohen. American Anthropologist 75 (1973):1012-13.

Sepúlveda Niño, Saturnino. La prostitución en Colombia; una quiebra de las estructuras sociales. Bogotá: Ed. Andes, 1970.

Seminar on the Status of Women in Family Law, Bogota, 1963. United Nations. Report. New York: United Nations, 1964.

Uribe de Acosta, Ofelia. Una voz insurgente. Bogotá: Ed. Guadalupe, 1963.

Vaca, Victor Hugo. La prostitución en el Ecuador. Quito: Ed. Universitaria, 1954.

Watson, Lawrence C. "Sexual Socialization in Guajiro Society." Ethnology 11 (1972):150-56.

Whitten, Norman E., Jr. "Personal Networks and Musical Contexts in the Pacific Lowlands of Colombia and Ecuador." In Afro-American Anthropology: Contemporary Perspectives, ed. Norman E. Whitten, Jr., and John F. Szwed, pp. 203-18. New York: Free Press, 1970.
_____. "Ritual Enactment of Sex Roles in the Pacific Lowlands of Ecuador-Colombia." A paper presented at the 70th Annual Meeting of the American Anthropological Association, New York, 1971. Mimeo. University of Illinois.

Whittington, James. "Polygyny in an Afro-American
    Society in the Choco of Northwestern Colombia." A
    paper presented at the 70th Annual Meeting of the
    American Anthropological Association, New York,
    1971. Mimeo. University of Florida.

Antilles: Cuba, Dominican Republic, Haiti,
Jamaica, Puerto Rico, Venezuela, West Indies

Berman, Joan. "Women in Cuba." Woman: A Journal of
    Liberation 1 (Summer 1970):10.
Blake, Judith. Family Structure in Jamaica: The Social
    Context of Reproduction. New York: Free Press,
    1961.
Bouchereau, M. G. Haiti et ses femmes; une étude d'évolu-
    tion culturelle. Port-au-Prince: Presses Libres,
    1957.
Briceno Vasquez, Ramón María. Estudios sociológicos.
    Trujillo, Venezuela: Ediciones del Ejecutivo del
    Estado Trujillo, 1963.
Camarano, Chris. "On Cuban Women." Leviathan 21
    (May 1970):39-42.
Castro, Fidel. Discurso de clausura ante el congres de
    mujeres de toda América. Peking: Ediciones en
    Lenguas Extranjeras, 1963.
___, and Jenness, Linda. Women and the Cuban Revolution.
    New York: Pathfinder Press, 1970.
Clarke, Edith. My Mother Who Fathered Me. London:
    Allen & Unwin, 1957.
Clemente Travieso, Carmen. Mujeres de la independencia;
    seis biografias de mujeres venezolanas. Mexico City,
    1964.
Cohen, Yehudi A. "Structure and Function: Family Or-
    ganization and Socialization in a Jamaican Community."
    American Anthropologist 58 (1956):664-86.
de Carmenes, N. "Some Aspects of the Guayguiri Indian
    Woman's Life." Boletín Indigenista 17 (June 1957):
    185-89.
de la Torre Mulhare, Mirta. "Sexual Ideology in Pre-
    Castro Cuba: A Cultural Analysis." Ph.D. dissertation,
    University of Pittsburgh, 1969.
Dolz y Arango, María Luisa. La liberación de la mujer
    cubana por la educación. Homenaje de la ciudad de la
    Havana en el centenario de su nacimiento, 1854-4 de
    octubre-1954. Havana: Oficina del Historiador de la
    Ciudad, 1955.
Gordon, Linda. "Speculations on Women's Liberation in
    Cuba." Women: A Journal of Liberation 1 (Summer
    1970):14.
Hellerman, Marcia. "Aruban Mating Patterns." A paper pre-
    sented at the 70th Annual Meeting of the American
    Anthropological Association, New York, 1971. Mimeo.
    CUNY.

Kaplan, M. R. "Sex and Death in Piaroa World Ordering."
A paper presented at the 69th Annual Meeting of the
American Anthropological Association, San Diego, 1970.
Mimeo. Vanderbilt University.
Kennedy, Raymond. The Ageless Indies. New York: John
Day, 1942.
Lewis, Oscar. La Vida. New York: Random House,
Vintage Books, 1965.
Mintz, Sidney. "The Employment of Capital by Market
Women in Haiti." In Capital, Saving and Credit in
Peasant Societies, ed. R. Firth and B. S. Yamey.
Chicago: Aldine, 1964.
Ottorbein, Keith F. "Caribbean Family Organization: A
Comparative Analysis." American Anthropologist 67
(1965):66-79.
Pollock, Nancy J. "Women and the Division of Labor: A
Jamaican Example." American Anthropologist 74 (1972):
689-92.
Reyes, Antonio. "Presidentas" de Venezuela (Primeras
damas de la República en el siglo XIX). Matronas que
fueron honor para la patria y blasón de la República.
Caracas: Imp. Nacional, 1955.
Smith, Raymond T. "The Family in the Caribbean." In
Caribbean Studies: A Symposium, ed. Vera Rubin.
Seattle: University of Washington Press, 1960.
Stern, Judith. "Men Are Like That: The Definition of
Manhood in Puerto Rico." A paper presented at the
69th Annual Meeting of the American Anthropological
Association, San Diego, 1970. Mimeo. University of
Pennsylvania.
Sutherland, Elizabeth. The Youngest Revolution: A
Personal Report on Cuba. New York: Dial Press, 1969.
Trouillot, H. "La condition de la femme de couleur à
Saint-Domingue." Société Haitienne d'Histoire de
Geographie et de Géologie, Revue 30 (Jan.-Apr. 1957):
21-54.
Vinelas, Estrella. Cuban Madam. New York: Paperback
Library, 1969.
Zavalloni, M. Adolescent Values in a Changing Society:
A Study of Trinidad Youth. New York: Humanities
Press, 1968.

NORTH AMERICA

General References

Honigmann, John J. "North America." In Psychological
Anthropology, ed. Francis L. K. Hsu, pp. 121-66.
Cambridge, Mass.: Schenkman, 1972.

Murdock, George Peter. Ethnographic Bibliography of North America. 3rd ed. New Haven: Human Relations Area Files Press, 1960.

Native Americans

Benedict, Ruth. Patterns of Culture. New York: Mentor, 1934.
Driver, Harold E. "Geographical-historical versus Psycho-functional Explanations of Kin Avoidances." Current Anthropology 7 (1966):131-60, 176-82.
___. "Girls' Puberty Rites and Matrilocal Residence." American Anthropologist 71 (1969):905-8.
___. "Girls' Puberty Rites in Western North America." University of California Anthropological Records 6 (1941):21-90.
___. Indians of North America, 2nd ed. Chicago: University of Chicago Press, 1964.
___, and Riesenberg, Saul H. Hoof Rattles and Girls' Puberty Rites in North and South America. Indiana University Publications in Anthropology and Linguistics. Memoir 4, 1950.
Driver, Harold E., and Sanday, Peggy R. "Factors and Clusters in Kin Avoidances and Related Variables." Current Anthropology 7 (1966):169-76.
Foreman, Carolyn Thomas. Indian Women Chiefs. Muskogee, Okla.: Hoffman, 1966.
Hallowell, A. I. "Shabwan: A Dissocial Indian Girl." American Journal of Orthopsychiatry 8 (1938):329-40.
Jacobs, Sue-Ellen. "Berdache: A Brief Review of the Literature." Colorado Anthropologist 1 (1968): 25-40.
Josephy, Alvin M., Jr. The Indian Heritage of America. New York: Bantam Books, 1969.
Leacock, Eleanor Burke, and Lurie, Nancy Oestreich, eds. North American Indians in Historical Perspective. New York: Random House, 1971.
Marriott, Alice. Greener Fields: Experiences among the American Indians, First published, 1952. Reprint, Garden City, N.Y.: Doubleday, Dolphin Books, 1962.
Meachem, A. B. Wi-ne-ma and Her People. Hartford: American Publishing, 1876.
Roark, Sue. "Domestic Politics and the Division of Labor and Management by Sex." A paper presented at the 70th Annual Meeting of the American Anthropological Association, New York, 1971. Mimeo. SUNY, Geneseo.
Spencer, Robert F., and Jennings, Jesse. The Native Americans. New York: Harper & Row, 1965.
Tiffany, Warren I. Old Ways for New. Washington, D.C.: Bureau of Indian Affairs, 1966.

Waddell, Jack O., and Watson, O. Michael. The American
    Indian in Urban Society. Boston: Little, Brown,
    1971.
Wax, Murray L. Indian Americans: Unity and Diversity.
    Englewood Cliffs, N.J.: Prentice-Hall, 1971.

Eskimo and Northwest Coast

Briggs, Jean L. "Kaplunga Daughter: Living with
    Eskimos." Transaction 7 (1970):12-24.
____. Never in Anger: Portrait of an Eskimo Family.
    Cambridge: Harvard University Press, 1970.
Chance, Norman A. "Culture Change and Integration: An
    Eskimo Example." American Anthropologist 62 (1960):
    1028-44.
____. The Eskimo of North Alaska. New York: Holt,
    Rinehart & Winston, 1966.
Griffin, Naomi Musmaker. The Roles of Men and Women in
    Eskimo Culture. Chicago: University of Chicago
    Press, 1930.
Gubser, Nicholas J. The Nunamiut Eskimos: Hunter of
    Caribou. New Haven: Yale University Press, 1965.
Guemple, D. L. "Inuit Spouse Exchange." Chicago:
    University of Chicago, Department of Anthropology,
    1961. Mimeo.
Hippler, Arthur E. "Additional Perspective on Eskimo
    Female Infanticide." American Anthropologist 74
    (1972):1318-19.
Honigmann, Irma, and Honigmann, John. "Child Rearing
    Patterns among the Great Whale River Eskimo."
    Anthropological Papers of the University of Alaska 2
    (1953):31-50.
Lantis, Margaret. Eskimo Childhood and Interpersonal
    Relationships. Nunivak Bibliographies and
    Genealogies. Seattle: University of Washington
    Press, 1960.
Lewis, Claudia. Indian Families of the Northwest Coast:
    The Impact of Change. Chicago: University of
    Chicago Press, 1970.
McElroy, Ann. "The Influence of Modernization on Female
    Eskimo Role Identification." A paper presented at
    the 70th Annual Meeting of the American Anthro-
    pological Association, New York, 1971. Mimeo. SUNY,
    Buffalo.
Nakayama, Eiji. "Some Notes on a Woman of Aleut."
    Anthropological Society of Tokyo Journal 49 (1934):
    23-29.
Washburne, Heluiz Chandler. Land of the Good Shadows.
    The Life Story of Anauta, an Eskimo Woman. New York:
    John Day, 1940.

Eastern Subarctic

Barnouw, Victor. "The Phantasy World of the Chippewa
    Woman." Psychiatry: Journal for the Study of
    Interpersonal Relations 12 (1949):67-76.
Bouginnan, Erika. "A Life History of an Ojibwa Young
    Woman." In Primary Records in Culture and Personality,
    vol. 1, ed. Bert Kaplan. Madison: Microcard
    Foundation, n.d.
Hallowell, A. Irving. "Sin, Sex and Sickness in
    Saulteaux Belief." British Journal of Medical
    Psychology 18 (1939):191-97.
Hilger, M. Inez. Chippewa Child Life and Its Culture
    Background. Bulletin 146. Washington, D.C.: Bureau
    of American Ethnology, 1952.
____. "Chippewa Pre-natal Food and Conduct Taboos."
    Primitive Man 9 (1936):46-48.
Landes, Ruth. The Ojibwa Woman. New York: W. W.
    Norton, 1971.
Leacock, Eleanor. "Matrilocality in a Simple Hunting
    Economy (Montagnais-Naskapi)." Southwestern Journal
    of Anthropology 11 (1955):31-47.

Iroquois and Other Eastern Tribes

Anderson, Rufus. Memoir of Catherine Brown, Christian
    Indian of the Cherokee Nation, 2nd ed. Boston:
    Croker & Brewster, 1825.
Carr, L. "On the Position of Women among the Huron-
    Iroquois Tribes." In Sixteenth Annual Report of
    Peabody Museum of American Archeology and Ethnology,
    p. 3. Cambridge: Harvard University, 1884.
Foster, Anna. The Mohawk Princess: Being Some Account
    of the Life of Tekahion-Wake (E. Pauline Johnson).
    Vancouver: Lion's Gate, 1931.
Goggin, John M., and Sturtevant, William C. "The
    Calusa: A Stratified, Non-agricultural Society (With
    Notes on Sibling Marriage)." In Explorations in
    Cultural Anthropology: Essays in Honor of George
    Peter Murdock, ed. Ward H. Goodenough, pp. 179-219.
    New York: McGraw-Hill, 1964.
Goldenweiser, A. A. "Functions of Women in Iroquois
    Society." American Anthropologist 17 (1915):376.
Haas, Mary. "Men's and Women's Speech in Koasati." In
    Language in Culture and Society, ed. Dell Hymes, pp.
    228-34. New York: Harper & Row, 1964.
Hewitt, J. N. B. "Status of Woman in Iroquois Polity."
    Smithsonian Annual Reports for the Year Ending 30 June
    1932, pp. 475-88. Washington, D.C.: Smithsonian
    Institution, 1933.
Howell, Norma A. "Potawatomi Pregnancy and Child Birth."
    Master's thesis, University of Kansas, 1970.
Lurie, Nancy O., ed. Mountain Wolf Woman, Sister of
    Crashing Thunder: The Autobiography of a Winnebago
    Indian. Ann Arbor: University of Michigan Press, 1966.

Richards, Cara E. "Matriarchy or Mistake: The Role of
    Iroquois Women through Time." In Cultural Stability
    and Cultural Change, ed. Verne F. Ray, pp. 36-45.
    Seattle: University of Washington Press, 1957.
____. "The Role of Iroquois Women." Ph.D. dissertation,
    Cornell University, 1957.
Watson, Virginia. The Princess Pocahontas. Philadelphia:
    Penn, 1916.

Southwest, Plains, Basin, Prairie,
Central U.S., California

Aberle, S. B. D. "Child Mortality among Pueblo Indians."
    American Journal of Physical Anthropology 16 (1932):
    339-51.
____. "Maternal Mortality among the Pueblos." American
    Journal of Physical Anthropology 18 (1934):431-57.
Aswad, Barbara C. "Key and Peripheral Roles of Noble
    Women in a Middle Eastern Plains Village." Anthropo-
    logy Quarterly 40 (1967):139-52.
Bailey, Garrick. "Patrilineality and Matrilocality among
    the Osage." A paper presented at the 70th Annual
    Meeting of the American Anthropological Association,
    New York, 1971. Mimeo. University of Tulsa.
Bell, Willis H., and Castetter, Edward F. Pima and
    Papago Indian Agriculture. Albuquerque: University
    of New Mexico Press, 1942.
Bennett, Kay. Kiabah: Recollection of a Navajo Girl-
    hood. Great West and Indian Series. Los Angeles:
    Westernlore Press, 1964.
Blanchard, Kendall. "The Protestant Mission in Ramah
    and the 'Liberation' of the Navajo Woman." A paper
    presented at the 70th Annual Meeting of the American
    Anthropological Association, New York, 1971. Mimeo.
    Middle Tennessee State University.
Colson, Elizabeth. "Autobiograhies of Three Pomo Women."
    In Primary Records in Culture and Personality, vol. 1,
    ed. Bert Kaplan. Madison: Microcard Foundation, n.d.
Driver, Harold E. "Reply to Opler on Apachean Sub-
    sistence, Residence, and Girls' Puberty Rites."
    American Anthropologist 74 (1972):1147-51.
Eyman, Francis. "The Teshoa, a Shoshonean Woman's
    Knife: A Study of American Indian Chopper Industries."
    Pennsylvania Archaeologist 34 (1968):9-52.
Flannery, Regina. "The Position of Women among the
    Mescalero Apache." Primitive Man 5 (1932):26-32.
Freed, Stanley A., and Freed, Ruth S. "A Note on
    Regional Variation in Navajo Kinship Terminology."
    American Anthropologist 72 (1970):1439-44.
Gilmore, M. R. "Notes on Gynecology and Obstetrics of
    the Arikara Tribe." Michigan Academy of Science,
    Arts and Letters, Papers 14 (1930):71-81.

Hammsy, Laila Shukry. "The Role of Women in a Changing Navaho Society." American Anthropologist 59 (1957): 101.

Hebard, Grace Raymond. Sacajawea. Glendale, Calif.: Arthur H. Clark, 1933.

Hilger, M. Inez. Arapaho Child Life and Its Cultural Background. Bulletin 148. Washington, D.C.: Bureau of American Ethnology, 1952.

Joseph, Alice. The Desert People: A Study of the Papago Indians. Chicago: University of Chicago Press, 1949.

Kelly, I. Review of The Autobiography of Delfina Cuero. A Diegueno Indian [woman]. American Anthropologist 71 (1969):111.

Kluckhohn, Clyde. Navaho Witchcraft. Boston: Beacon Press, 1944.
____. "Navaho Women's Knowledge of Their Song Ceremonials." El Palacio 45 (1938):87-92.
____. "Some Aspects of Navaho Infancy and Early Childhood." In Psychoanalysis and the Social Sciences, vol. 1, ed. G. Roheim. New York: International Universities Press, 1947.
____, and Leighton, Dorothea. The Navaho, rev. ed. Garden City, N.Y.: Doubleday, 1962.

Kluckhohn, Clyde, and Rosenzweig, J. "Two Navaho Children over a Five Year Period." American Journal of Orthopsychiatry 19 (1947):266-78.

Lampman, E. S. Navaho Sister. Garden City, N.Y.: Doubleday, 1956.

Leighton, Dorothea C., and Adair, John. People of the Middle Place: A Study of the Zuni Indians. New Haven: Human Relations Area Files Press, 1966.

Lewis, Oscar. "Manly-hearted Women among the North Piegan." American Anthropologist 43 (1941):173-87.

Lowie, Robert H. The Crow Indians. New York: J. J. Little, 1935.

Marriott, Alice. Maria: The Potter of San Ildefonso. Norman: University of Oklahoma Press, 1948.
____. Ten Grandmothers. Norman: University of Oklahoma Press, 1945.

Matthews, W. Navaho Legends. First published, 1897. Reprint, New York: Kraus Reprint, n.d.

Mead, Margaret. The Changing Culture of an Indian Tribe. New York: Columbia University Press, 1932.

Michelson, Truman. "The Autobiography of a Fox Indian Woman" (1918-19). Bureau of American Ethnology, Annual Report 40 (1925):295-349.
____. The Narrative of a Southern Cheyenne Woman. Smithsonian Institution, Miscellaneous Collections, 87. Washington, D.C.: Smithsonian Institution, 1932.
____. "Narrative of an Arapaho Woman." American Anthropologist 35 (1933):595-610.

O'Meara, Walter. Daughters of the Country: The Women of the Fur Traders and Mountain Men. New York: Harcourt, Brace & World, 1968.

Opler, Morris E. "Cause and Effect in Apachean Agriculture, Division of Labor, and Girls' Puberty Rites." American Anthropologist 74 (1972):1133-46.

Parsons, Elsie Clews. "Mothers and Children at Zuni, New Mexico." Man 19 (1919):168-73.

___. "A Pueblo Indian Journal." American Anthropological Association Memoir 32 (1925):6.

___. "Tewa Mothers and Children." Man 24 (1924): 148-51.

___. "Waiyoutitsa of Zuni, New Mexico." Scientific Monthly 9 (1919):443-57.

Qoyawagma, Polingaysi [Elizabeth White]. No Turning Back: A True Account of a Hopi Indian Girl's Struggle to Bridge the Gap between the World of the People and the World of the White Man. As told to Vada F. Carlson. Albuquerque: University of New Mexico Press, 1964.

Reichard, G. Dezba: Woman of the Desert. New York: J. J. Augustin, 1939.

___. Navaho Religion: A Study of Symbolism. New York: Bollingen Foundation, 1950.

___. Social Life of the Navaho Indians: With Some Attention to Minor Ceremonies. New York: AMS Press, 1928.

___. Spider Woman: A Story of Navajo Weavers and Chanters. New York: Macmillan, 1934.

Sandoz, Mari. Old Jules. Boston: Little, Brown, 1935.

Schlegel, Alice. "The Socialization of the Hopi Girl." Ethnology 12 (1973):449-62.

Searcy, Ann McElroy. Contemporary and Traditional Prairie Potawatomi Child Life. Potawatomi Study Research Report 7. Lawrence: University of Kansas, 1965.

Smithson, Carma L. The Havasupai Woman. University of Utah Anthropological Papers, Apr. 1959. New York: Johnson Reprint, 1959.

Spencer, K. Reflection of Social Life in the Navaho Origin Myth. Albuquerque: University of New Mexico Press, 1947.

Spindler, Louise S. "Menomini Women and Culture Change." American Anthropological Association Memoir 91 (1962).

___. "Sixty-one Rorschachs and Fifteen Expressive Autobiographic Interviews of Menomini Indian Women." In Primary Records in Culture and Personality, vol. 2, ed. Bert Kaplan. Madison: Microcard Foundation, 1957.

___. "Women and Culture Change: A Case Study of the Menomini Indians." Ph.D. dissertation, Stanford University, 1956.

Underhill, Ruth M. The Autobiography of a Papago Woman. Washington, D.C.: American Anthropological Association, 1936.

___. Papago Indian Religion. New York: Columbia
    University Press, 1946.
___. Papago Indians of Arizona and Their Relatives, the
    Pima. Kansas: Haskell Institute, 1941.
___. Singing for Power. Berkeley: University of⦿
    California Press, 1938.
Voegelin, C. F. The Shawnee Female Diety. First pub-
    lished, 1936. Reprint, New Haven: Human Relations
    Area Files Press, 1970.
Wright, Harold Bell. Long Ago Told. New York: D.
    Appleton, 1929.

Canada

Canadian Women's Education Press. Women Unite! An
    Anthology of the Canadian Women's Movement. Toronto:
    Canadian Women's Educational Press, 1972.
Changing Patterns in Women's Employment. Ottawa:
    Canada Department of Labour, Women's Bureau, 1966.
Cleverdon, Catherine L. The Woman Suffrage Movement in
    Canada. Toronto: University of Toronto Press, 1950.
Douglas, James. The Status of Women in New England &
    New France. Kingston: Jackson Press, 1912.
Hall, Oswald. Gender and the Division of Labour:
    Implications of Traditional Divisions Between Men's
    Work and Women's Work in Our Society. Ottawa:
    Canada Department of Labour, 1964.
Healy, William J. Women of Red River: Being a Book
    Written from the Recollections of Women Surviving
    from the Red River Era. Centennial ed. Minneapolis:
    Ross & Haines, 1967.
Innis, Mary Quayle. The Clear Spirit: Twenty Canadian
    Women and Their Times. Toronto: Published for the
    Canadian Federation of University Women by University
    of Toronto Press, 1966.
Lugrin, N. de Bertrand. The Pioneer Women of Vancouver
    Island, 1843-1866. Vancouver: Women's Canadian Club
    of Victoria, 1928.
Nielsen, Dorise Winnifred Webber. New Worlds for Women.
    Toronto: Progress Books, 1944.
Ramos, Maria. Mulheres da América. Rio de Janeiro: J.
    Alvaro, 1964.
Rocher, Guy. "Pattern and Status of French Canadian
    Women." International Social Science Journal 14
    (1962):131-37.
Woodsworth, Sheila. Maternity Protection for Women
    Workers in Canada. Ottawa: Canada Department of
    Labour, Women's Bureau, 1967.

Mexico and Central America

97

Adams, Richard N. "A Survival of the Meso-American Bachelor House." American Anthropologist 54 (1952): 589-93.

Arnaíz Amigo, Aurora. Femenismo y femenidad. Mexico City, 1965.

Beals, Ralph L. "The Tarascans." In Handbook of Middle American Indians, vol. 8, ed. Robert Wauchope, pp. 725-73. Austin: University of Texas Press, 1969.

Bernídez, María Elvira. La vida familiar del mexicano. Mexico City: Antigua Librería Robredo, 1955.

Brown, Judith K. "Sex Division of Labor among the San Blas Cuna." Anthropological Quarterly 43 (1970): 57-63.

Carrasco Puente, Rafael. Bibliografía de Catarinra de San Juan y de la China poblana. Mexico City: Secretaría de Relaciones Exteriores, Departamento de Información para el Extranjero, 1950.

Cházaro, Gabriel. De la mujer; ensayo. Mexico City: Ed. Citlaltépetl, 1964.

Chiñas, Beverly L. "A Role Model for Explaining Women's Roles in Isthmus Zapotec Culture." In The Isthmus Zapotecs, Ch. 8. New York: Holt, Rinehart & Winston, 1972.

———. "Women as Ethnographic Subjects." A paper presented at the 1970 Meeting of the Southwestern Anthropological Association, Asilomar, Calif., 1970.

Chumacero, Rosalia de. Perfil y pensaminento de la mujer mexicana. Mexico City, 1961.

Colón Ramírez, Consuelo. Mujeres de Mexico. Mexico City: Imp. Gallarcta, 1944.

Congreso Femenista de Yucatán. "El primer congreso femenista de Yucatán, convocado por el c. gobernador y comandante militar del estado, gral. d. Salvador Alvarado, y reunido en el teatro 'peon contreras' de esta ciudad, del 15 al 16 de enero de 1916," Andes de esa Memorable Asamblea. Merida, 1916.

Covarrubias, Miguel. Mexico South: The Isthmus of Tehuantepec. New York: Alfred A. Knopf, 1946.

Diebold, A. R., Jr. "The Huave." In Handbook of Middle American Indians, vol. 7, ed. Robert Wauchope, pp. 478-88. Austin: University of Texas Press, 1969.

Driver, Harold E., and Driver, Wilhelmine. Ethnography and Acculturation of the Chichimeca-Jonaz of Northeast Mexico. Bloomington: Indiana University Research Center, 1963.

Elmendorf, Mary Lindsay. The Mayan Woman and Change. Cuaderno 81. Cuernavaca: Centro Intercultural de Documentación, 1972.

———. "Role of Women as Agents for Peaceful Social Change." A paper presented at the 1971 Meeting of the Society for International Development, Ottawa. Mimeo. University of Florida.

Escobedo, Raquel. Galería de mujeres ilustres. Mexico
City: Editores Mexicanas Unidas, 1967.
Gamio de Alba, Ana Margarita. La mujer indígena de
Centro América. Mexico City: Ediciones Especiales
del Instituto Indigenista Interamericano, 1957.
____. La mujer indígena de Centro América, sumaria
recopilación acerca de sus condiciones de vida.
Ediciones Especiales, 31. Mexico City: Instituto
Indigenista Interamericano, 1967.
Gruening, Ernest. "Women." In Gruening, Mexico and Its
Heritage. New York: Greenwood Press, 1968.
Guiteras-Holmes, Colexe. Perils of the Soul. New York:
Free Press, 1961.
Hansen, Edward. "Idioms of Male-Female Conflict in the
Hispanic World." A paper presented at the 70th Annual
Meeting of the American Anthropological Association,
New York, 1971. Mimeo. CUNY, Queens.
Hayner, Norman S. "The Family in Mexico." Marriage and
Family Living 16 (Nov. 1954):369-73.
____. "Notes on the Changing Mexican Family." American
Sociological Review 7 (Aug. 1942):489-97.
Hellbon, Anna-Britta. La participacion cultural de las
mujeres indias y mestizas en el México precortesano y
postrevolucionario. Monograph Series, 10. Stockholm:
Ethnographical Museum, 1967.
Hinshaw, Robert; Pyeatt, Patrick; and Habicht, Jean-
Pierre. "Environmental Effects on Child-spacing and
Population Increase in Highland Guatemala." Current
Anthropology 13 (Apr. 1972):216-30.
Hotchkiss, John C. "Children and Conduct in a Ladino
Community of Chiapas." In You and Others: Readings
in Introductory Anthropology, ed. A. Kimball Romney
and Paul L. DeVore, pp. 174-83. Cambridge, Mass.:
Winthrop, 1973.
Hubbell, Linda J. "The Network of Kinship, Friendship
and Compadrazgo among Middle-class Mexican Women."
A paper presented at the 70th Annual Meeting of the
American Anthropological Association, New York, 1971.
Mimeo. University of California, Berkeley.
Kelly, Isabel. "El adiestramiento de parteras en
México, desde el punto de vista anthopológico" [The
training of midwives in Mexico, from anthropological
point of view]. América Indígena 15 (Apr. 1955):
109-17.
____. "An Anthropological Approach to Midwifery Training
in Mexico." Journal of Tropical Pediatrics 1 (1956):
200-205.
Langner, T. S. "Psychophysiological Symptoms and the
Status of Women in Two Mexican Communities." In
Approaches to Cross-cultural Psychiatry, ed. J. M.
Murphy and A. Leighton. Ithaca: Cornell University
Press, 1965.

LEWIS AND CLARK COLLEGE LIBRARY
PORTLAND, OREGON 97219

Leslie, C. M. Now We Are Civilized: A Study of the World View of the Zapotec Indians of Mitla, Oaxaca. Detroit: Wayne State University Press, 1960.

Lewis, José Guillermo. Por las generaciones futuras. Antecedentes, documentos y discusiones sobre las leyes de examen pre-nupcial y profilaxis social. Panama City: Imp. Nacional, 1929.

Lewis, Oscar. The Children of Sanchez. New York: Random House, 1961.

———. "A Day in the Life of a Mexican Peasant Family." Marriage and Family Living 18 (Feb. 1956):3-13.

———. "Husbands and Wives in a Mexican Village: A Study of Role Conflict." American Anthropologist 51 (Oct.-Dec. 1949):602-10.

———. Pedro Martinez, a Mexican Peasant and His Family. New York: Random House, 1964.

Litzler, Beverly N. "Role Perception and Marketing among Isthmus Zapotecs." A paper presented at the 68th Annual Meeting of the American Anthropological Association, New Orleans, 1969. Mimeo. Chico State College.

———. "Women of San Blas Atempa: An Analysis of the Economic Role of Isthmus Zapotec Women in Relation to Family and Community." Ph.D. dissertation, University of California, 1968.

Lombardo Otero de Soto, Rosa Maria. La mujer Tzeltal. Mexico City, 1944.

Madsen, William. "The Nahua." In Handbook of Middle American Indians, vol. 8, ed. Robert Wauchope, pp. 602-37. Austin: University of Texas Press, 1969.

———. The Virgin's Children: Life in an Aztec Village Today. Austin: University of Texas Press, 1960.

Magner, James A. Men of Mexico. Freeport, N.Y.: Books for Libraries, 1968.

Millan, Verna Carleton. "Freedom for Mexican Women." In Mexico Reborn. Boston: Houghton Mifflin, 1939.

Modiano, Nancy. "A Chamula Life." Natural History 77 (1968):58-63.

Montalban, L. "La prostitucion aborígen en Nicaragua" [Native prostitution in Nicaragua]. Nicaragua Indígena 3 (1968):34-39.

Morton, Ward M. Woman Suffrage in Mexico. Gainesville: University of Florida Press, 1962.

Nader, Laura. "An Analysis of Zapotec Law Cases." Ethnology 3 (1964):404-19.

———. "The Trique of Oaxaca." In Handbook of Middle American Indians, vol. 7, ed. Robert Wauchope, pp. 400-416. Austin: University of Texas Press, 1969.

Olmsted, D. L. "The Tequistlatec and Tlapanec." In Handbook of Middle American Indians, vol. 7, ed. Robert Wauchope, pp. 553-64. Austin: University of Texas Press, 1969.

O'Nell, Carl. "Male and Female Dreamworlds in a Zapotec Community." A paper presented at the 68th Annual

Meeting of the American Anthropological Association,
New Orleans, 1969. Mimeo. Notre Dame University.
___, and Selby, Henry A. "Sex Differences in the
Incidence of Susto in Two Zapotec Pueblos: An
Analysis of the Relationship between Sex Role Ex-
pectations and a Folk Illness." Ethnology 7 (1968):
95-105.
O'Sullivan-Beare, Nancy. Las mujeres de los conquis-
tadores; la mujer española en los comienzos de la
colonización Americana (aportaciones para el
estudio de la transculturación). Madrid: Biblio-
gráfica. Española, 1956.
Paz, Octavio. The Labyrinth of Solitude. New York:
Grove Press, 1961.
Plattner, Stuart. "Occupation and Marriage in a Mexican
Trading Community." A paper presented at the 69th
Annual Meeting of the American Anthropological As-
sociation, San Diego, 1970. Mimeo. Stanford
University.
Pozas, I. H. de. "La posicion de la mujer dentro de la
estructura social Tzotzil" [The status of women
within Tzotzil social structure]. Ciencas politicas
y sociales 5 (1959):565-75.
Pozas, Ricardo Arciniega. Chamula, un pueblo indio de
los altos de Chiapas. Vol. 8. Mexico City:
Ediciones del Instituto Nacional Indigenista, 1959.
___. Juan Perez Jolete. Mexico City: Fondo de
Cultura Economica, 1952.
___. Juan the Chamula. Berkeley: University of
California Press, 1962.
Reina, Ruben. "Eastern Guatemalan Highlands: The
Pokomames and Chorti." In Handbook of Middle
American Indians, vol. 7, ed. Robert Wauchope, pp.
101-32. Austin: University of Texas Press, 1969.
Romero de Terreros y Vinent, Manuel. Ex antiquis:
bocetos de la vida social en la Nueva España.
Guadalajara: Ediciones Jaime, 1919.
Romero de Valle, Emilia, ed. Mujeres de América. Mexico
City: Secretaría de Educación Pública, 1948.
Romney, A. Kimball, and Romney, Romaine. "The Mixtecans
of Juxtlahuaca, Mexico." In Six Cultures, ed. Beatrice
B. Whiting. New York: John Wiley & Sons, 1963.
Rubel, Arthur J. "Meso-American Bachelor Houses Re-
visited." Anthropological Quarterly 40 (1967):217-25.
Salovesh, Michael. "Living with the Wife's Father under
a Rule of Patrilocal Residence: Obligatory Alter-
natives Meet the Ethnographic Atlas." A paper
presented at the 68th Annual Meeting of the American
Anthropological Association, New Orleans, 1969.
Mimeo. Purdue University.
Schwerin, Karl H., and Schwerin, Judith D. A. "A Menstruation Sash from Tlaxcala, Mexico." Man 61 (1961):
208-9.

Service, Elman. "The Northern Tepehuan." In Handbook of Middle American Indians, vol. 8, ed. Robert Wauchope, pp. 822-28. Austin: University of Texas Press, 1969.

Soustelle, Jacques. "Un rite de fertilité des femmes Mazahua (Mexique)." Bulletin de la Société Suisse des Americanistes 30 (1966):3-6.

Tax, Sol, and Hinshaw, Robert. "The Maya of the Midwestern Highlands." In Handbook of Middle American Indians, vol. 7, ed. Robert Wauchope, pp. 69-100. Austin: University of Texas Press, 1969.

Torres de Ianello, Reina. La mujer Cuna de Panamá. Mexico City: Ediciones Especiales del Instituto Indigenista Interamericano, 1957.

Villa Rojas, Alfonso. "The Maya of Yucatan." In Handbook of Middle American Indians, vol. 7, ed. Robert Wauchope, pp. 244-75. Austin: University of Texas Press, 1969.

Wattles, J. D. "Jalacingo Woman: An Individual and Her Society." Phylon 16 (1955):41-55.

Wright, Norman Pelham. Mexican Kaleidoscope. London: Heinemann, 1947.

Zendejas, Adelina. La mujer en la Intervención Francesa. Mexico City: Sociedad Mexicana de Geografía y Estadística, Sección de Historia, 1962.

United States

Afro-American

Angelou, Mary. I Know Why the Caged Bird Sings. New York: Random House, 1970.

Appeal to the Women of the Nominally Free States. Freeport, N.Y.: Books for Libraries, 1883.

Beal, Frances M. "Double Jeopardy: To Be Black and Female." New Generation 51 (Fall 1969):23-28.

Bell, R. R. "Lower Class Negro Mothers' Aspirations for Their Children." Social Forces 43 (May 1965):493-500.

Billingsley, Andrew, and Billingsley, Amy Tate. "Negro Family Life in America." Social Service Review 39 (Sept. 1965):310-19.

Brody, Eugene B. "Color and Identity Conflict in Young Boys: Observations of Negro Mothers and Sons in Urban Baltimore." Psychiatry, May 1963.

Brown, Hallie Guinn, ed. Homespun Heroines and Other Women of Distinction. Xenia, Ohio: Aldine, 1926.

Burton, R. V., and Whiting, J. W. M. "The Absent Father and Cross-Sex Identity." Merrill-Palmer Quarterly 7 (Apr. 1961):85-95.

Cade, Toni, ed. The Black Woman: An Anthology. New York: New American Library, 1970.

Carson, Josephine. Silent Voices: The Southern Negro Woman Today. New York: Dell, Delacorte Press, 1969.

Chisholm, Shirley. Unbought and Unbossed. Boston: Houghton Mifflin, 1970.

Cleaver, Eldridge. Soul on Ice. New York: McGraw-Hill, 1968.

Cole, Johnette B. "Black Women in America: An Annotated Bibliography." Black Scholar, Dec. 1971.

Cooper, Anna J. Voice from the South, by a Black Woman of the South. First published, 1892. Reprint, New York: Negro Universities Press, 1969.

Cummings, Gwenna. "Black Women: Often Discussed but Never Understood." In The Black Power Revolt, ed. F. B. Barbour. Boston: Extending Horizons Books, 1968.

D'Andrade, R. G. "Father Absence and Cross-Sex Identification." Ph.D. dissertation, Harvard University, 1962.

Dandridge, Dorothy, and Conrad, Earl. Everything and Nothing: The Dorothy Dandridge Tragedy. New York: Abelard-Schuman, 1970.

Dannett, Sylvia G. L. Profiles of Negro Womanhood. Yonkers, New York: Educational Heritage, 1969.

David, Jay, and Watkins, Mel, eds. Black Woman: Portraits in Fact and Fiction. New York: William Morrow, 1970.

Deasy, Leila, and Quinn, Olive. "The Urban Negro and Adoption of Children." Child Welfare, Nov. 1962.

Douglass, Joseph H. "The Urban Negro Family." In The American Negro Reference Book, ed. John R. Davis, pp. 522-47. Englewood Cliffs, N.J.: Prentice-Hall, 1966.

Epstein, Cynthia Fuchs. "Black and Female: the Double Whammy." Psychology Today 7 (1973):57-61, 89.

Fauset, Arthur. Sojourner Truth: God's Faithful Pilgrim. Chapel Hill: University of North Carolina Press, 1938.

Fichter, Joseph Henry. Negro Women Bachelors: A Comparative Exploration of the Experiences and Expectations of College Graduates of the Class of June, 1961. Chicago: University of Chicago, Chicago National Opinion Research Center, 1965.

Frazier, Franklin. The Negro Family in the United States. New York: Dryden Press, 1948.

Gipson, Theodore H. "Education Status of the Negro Family in Louisiana." Journal of Educational Sociology 32 (Oct. 1958):83-89.

Gollock, Georgina A. Daughters of Africa. Westport, Conn.: Negro Universities Press, 1932.

Gonzalez, Nancie L. "Toward a Definition of Matrifocality." In Afro-American Anthropology: Contemporary Perspectives, ed. Norman E. Whitten, Jr., and John F. Szwed, pp. 231-44. New York: Free Press, 1970.

Gordon, Eugene. The Position of Negro Women. New York: Workers' Library, 1935.

Gould, Flo, and Kerekhoff, Richard. "Family Life Education for the Biracial Community." Journal of Negro Education 29 (Spring 1960):187-90.

Hannerz, Ulf. "Roots of Black Manhood." Transaction 10 (Oct. 1969):12-21.

_____. Soulside: Inquiries into Ghetto Culture and Community. New York: Columbia University Press, 1970.

Harding, Nina. "Interrelationship of the Black Struggle with the Woman Question." Seattle: Seattle Radical Women, 2940 36th Ave. S., Wash. 98144.

Hare, Nathan, and Hare, Julia. "Black Women 1970." Transaction 8 (Nov.-Dec. 1970):65-69.

Haviland, Laura S. Woman's Life-Work: Labors and Experiences. Freeport, N.Y.: Books for Libraries, 1887.

Higgins, Chester. Black Woman. New York: McCall, 1970.

Himes, Joseph S. "Interrelation of Occupational and Spousal Roles in a Middle Class Negro Neighborhood." Marriage and Family Living 22 (Nov. 1960):362.

Jones, Bessie, and Hawes, Bess Lomax. Step It Down: Games, Plays, Songs, and Stories from the Afro-American Heritage. New York: Harper & Row, 1973.

Kearney, Belle. Slaveholder's Daughter. Westport, Conn.: Negro Universities Press, 1900.

Knebel, Fletcher. "Identity: The Black Woman's Burden." Look 23 (Sept. 1969):77-79.

Kunstadter, Peter. "A Survey of the Consanguine or Matrifocal Family." American Anthropologist 65 (Feb. 1963):56-66.

Ladner, Joyce A. Tomorrow's Tomorrow: The Black Woman. New York: Doubleday, 1971.

Landes, Ruth. "Negro Slavery and Female Status." Les Afro-Américains: Mémoires de l'Institut Français d'Afrique Noire 27 (1953):265-68.

LaRue, Linda J. M. "Black Liberation and Women's Liberation." Transaction 8 (Nov.-Dec. 1970):59-64.

Lewis, Hylan. "The Changing Negro Family." In The Nation's Children, ed. Eli Ginzberg. New York: Columbia University Press, 1960.

Liebow, Elliot. Tally's Corner. Boston: Little, Brown, 1967.

McCord, William, et al. Life Styles in the Black Ghetto. New York: W. W. Norton, 1969.

McDougall, Harold. Black Woman. New York: Saturday Review Press, McCall Books, 1970.

Mack, Dolores. "Where the Black Matriarchy Theorists Went Wrong." Psychology Today 4 (Jan. 1971):24, 86-87.

Majors, Monroe A. Noted Negro Women. Freeport, N.Y.: Books for Libraries, 1893.

Malcolm X [Little]. The Autobiography of Malcolm X.
New York: Grove Press, 1966.
____. Malcolm X Speaks, ed. G. Breitman. New York:
Grove Press, 1965.
Marvick, Dwaine. "The Political Socialization of the
American Negro." Annals of the American Academy of
Political and Social Science 361 (Sept. 1965):112-27.
Middleton, Russell, and Putney, Snell. "Dominance in
Decisions in the Family: Race and Class Differences."
American Journal of Sociology 65 (May 1960):605-9.
Moody, Anne. Coming of Age in Mississippi. New York:
Dell, 1968.
Moynihan, Daniel Patrick. The Negro Family: The Case
for National Action. Washington, D.C.: U.S.
Department of Labor, 1965.
Negro Families in Rural Wisconsin: A Study of Their
Community Life. Madison: Governor's Commission on
Human Rights, 1959.
Noble, Jeanne L. "The American Negro Women." In The
American Negro Reference Book, ed. Jon P. Davis, pp.
522-47. Englewood Cliffs, N.J.: Prentice-Hall, 1966.
Opler, Marvin K. "The Influence of Ethnic and Class
Structures on Child Care." Social Problems 3 (July
1955):12-21.
Orshansky, Mollie. "Children of the Poor." Social
Science Research Council Bulletin, July 1963.
Raden, Norma, and Kamii, Constance K. "The Child-
rearing Attitudes of Disadvantaged Negro Mothers and
Some Educational Implications." Journal of Negro
Education 34 (Spring 1965):138-46.
Rainwater, Lee. "Crucible of Identity: The Negro
Lower-class Family." Daedalus 95 (Winter 1966):
172-216.
Rosen, Lawrence. "Matriarchy and Lower-class Negro Male
Delinquency." Social Problems 17 (1969):175-88.
Schwartz, M. "Northern United States Negro Matriarchy:
Status versus Authority." Phylon 26 (Spring 1965):
18-24.
Shimkin, Dimitri, ed. The Family Structure of Black
America. The Hague: Mouton, in press.
Slaughter, Diana T. "Becoming an Afro-American Woman."
Special issue, Women in Education, School Review 80
(1972):299-318.
Stack, Carol B. "The Kindred of Viola Jackson: Residence
and Family Organization of an Urban Black American
Family." In Afro-American Anthropology: Contemporary
Perspectives, ed. Norman E. Whitten, Jr., and John F.
Szwed, pp. 303-12. New York: Free Press, 1970.
____. "Parenthood, Kindreds and Domestic Networks of Urban
Blacks." A paper presented at the 70th Annual Meeting
of the American Anthropological Association, New York,
1971. Mimeo. University of Illinois.

105

Stampp, Kenneth M. The Peculiar Institution. New York:
    Alfred A. Knopf, 1956.
Strodtbeck, Fred L. "The Poverty-Dependency Syndrome
    of the ADC Female-Based Negro Family." American
    Journal of Orthopsychiatry 34 (Mar. 1964):216-17.
Tanner, Nancy. "Matrifocality in Indonesia and among
    Black Americans." A paper presented at the 70th
    Annual Meeting of the American Anthropological As-
    sociation, New York, 1971. Mimeo. University of
    South Carolina.
Tcholakian, Arthur. Majesty of the Black Woman. New
    York: Van Nostrand Reinhold, 1971.
Teer, Barbar Ann. "Needed: A New Image." In The Black
    Power Revolt, ed. Floyd B. Barbour, pp. 219-23.
    Boston: Porter Sargent, 1968.
Vincent, Clark. Unmarried Mothers. Glencoe, Ill.: Free
    Press, 1961.
Ware, Celestine. "The Black Family and Feminism: A
    Conversation with Eleanor Holmes Norton." Ms. 1
    (Spring 1972):95-6.
Watkins, Mel, and David, Jay, eds. To Be a Black Woman:
    Portraits in Fact and Fiction. New York: William
    Morrow, 1971.
Williams, Maxine. Black Women's Liberation. New York:
    Pathfinder Press, n.d.
Women's Bureau, U.S. Department of Labor. Negro Women
    in the Population and in the Labor Force. Washington,
    D.C.: U.S. Government Printing Office, n.d.
Woods, Frances Jerome, and Lancaster, Alice Cunningham.
    "Cultural Factors in Negro Adoptive Parenthood."
    Social Work, Oct. 1962.
Young, Virginia H. "Afro-American Mother-Child
    Relationships." A paper presented at the 70th Annual
    Meeting of the American Anthropological Association,
    New York, 1971. Mimeo. Finch College.

Chicana

Allen, Ruth A. "Mexican Peon Women in Texas." Sociology
    and Social Research 16 (Nov.-Dec. 1931):131-42.
Altus, William D. "The American Mexican: The Survival
    of a Culture." Journal of Social Psychiatry 29 (May
    1949):211-20.
Baroni, Albert. "Restraint Perception and Social
    Contact: The Case of the Urban Chicano Female." A
    paper presented at the 69th Annual Meeting of the
    American Anthropological Association, San Diego, 1970.
    Mimeo. UCLA.
Correa, Viola. "La Nueva Chicana." Vocations for Social
    Change 18 (Sept.-Oct. 1970):19.
Grebler, Leo. The Mexican-American People. New York:
    Free Press, 1970.

Hernandez, Isabel. "The Role of the Chicana in the Movement." Paper, Sacramento, California State University Library, 1969.

Humphrey, Norman Daymond. "The Changing Structure of the Detroit Mexican Family: An Index of Acculturation." American Sociological Review 9 (Dec. 1944):622-26.

———. "Some Marriage Problems of Detroit Mexicans." Applied Anthropology 3 (1943-44):13-15.

Jones, Robert C. "Ethnic Family Patterns: The Mexican Family in the United States." American Journal of Sociology 53 (May 1948):450-52.

McWilliams, Carey. North from Mexico. Philadelphia: J. B. Lippincott, 1949.

Madsen, William. The Mexican-Americans of South Texas. New York: Holt, Rinehart & Winston, 1964.

Martinez, Elizabeth Sutherland. "Colonized Women: The Chicana." In Sisterhood Is Powerful, ed. Robin Morgan, pp. 376-79. New York: Random House, Vintage Books, 1970.

Rubel, Arthur. "The Family." In Across the Tracks, pp. 55-100. Austin: University of Texas Press, Hogg Foundation for Mental Health, 1966.

Serrano, Ester. "Barefoot and Pregnant." In Notes on Women's Liberation. Detroit: News & Letters, 1970.

Vasquez, Enriqueta. "La Chicana: Let's Build a New Life." El Grito del Norte 2 (Nov. 15, 1969):11.

———. "Chicana: Slave? Companion? Co-Partner?" Bronze 1 (June 1969):12.

———. "Despierten! Hermanos." El Grito del Norte 3 (Apr. 29, 1970):6.

———. "The Mexican-American Woman." In Sisterhood Is Powerful, ed. Robin Morgan, pp. 379-84. New York: Random House, Vintage Books, 1970.

———. "La Mujer in the Chicano Movement." Bronze 1 (June 1969):13.

"Woman's Question." Venceremos: Colegio de Aztlan (Nov. 1970):30.

Young, Virginia Heyer. "Family and Childhood in a Southern Negro Community." American Anthropologist 75 (1970):1054-55.

General

American Academy of Political and Social Science, Philadelphia. "Woman's Work and Organizations." Annals 28 (1906).

———. "Women in the Modern World," ed. Viva B. Boothe. Annals 143 (May 1929).

———. "Women's Opportunities and Responsibilities," ed. Louise M. Young. Annals 251 (May 1947).

American Woman's Association. Women Workers through the Depression: A Study of White-Collar Employment. New York: Macmillan, 1934.

Amsler, Margaret H. "The Status of Married Women in the Texas Business Association." Texas Law Review 43 (1965):669-79.

Astin, Helen S. The Woman Doctorate in America: Origins, Career and Family. New York: Russell Sage Foundation, 1969.

Ayling, Keith. Calling All Women. New York: Harper, 1942.

Banning, Margaret Culkin. Women for Defense. New York: Duell, Sloan & Pearce, 1942.

Beard, Mary Ritter, ed. America through Women's Eyes. New York: Macmillan, 1933.

Beatty, Jerome, Jr. The Girls We Leave Behind: A Terribly Scientific Study of American Women at Home. Garden City, N.Y.: Doubleday, 1963.

Beecher, Catherine Esther. The Evils Suffered by American Women and American Children: The Causes and the Remedy. New York: Harper, 1847.

Benson, Mary Sumner. Women in Eighteenth-Century America: A Study of Opinion and Social Usage. First published, 1935. Reprint, Port Washington, N.Y.: Kennikat Press, 1966.

Bettelheim, Bruno. The Children of the Dream: Communal Child-rearing and American Education. New York: Macmillan, 1969.

Bier, William C., ed. Woman in Modern Life. New York: Fordham University Press, Institute of Pastoral Psychology, 1968.

Blanc, Marie Therese de Solms. The Condition of Woman in the United States: A Traveler's Notes, trans. Abby Langdon Alger. Boston: Roberts Brothers, 1895.

Blood, Robert O., and Wolfe, Donald M. Husbands and Wives: The Dynamics of Married Living. New York: Free Press, 1960.

Blumenthal, Walter Hart. American Panorama: Pattern of the Past and Womanhood in Its Unfolding. Worcester, Mass.: A. J. St. Onge, 1962.

____. Brides from Bridewell: Female Felons Sent to Colonial America. Rutland, Vt.: C. E. Tuttle, 1962.

Breckinridge, Sophonisba Preston. Women in the Twentieth Century: A Study of Their Political, Social and Economic Activities. New York: McGraw-Hill, 1933.

Bruce, Henry Addington Bayley. Woman in the Making of America, rev. ed. Boston: Little, Brown, 1933.

Calhoun, Arthur. A Social History of the American Family from Colonial Times to the Present. New York: Barnes & Noble, 1945.

California Advisory Commission on the Status of Women. California Women: A Report. Sacramento: State of California, Documents Section, 1967.

____. California Women: A Report, ed. Betty Concannon. Sacramento: State of California, Documents Section, 1969.

Callahan, Sidney Cornelia. The Illusion of Eve: Modern Woman's Quest for Identity. New York: Sheed & Ward, 1965.

Caplow, Theodore, and Bahr, Howard M. Disaffiliation among Urban Women. New York: Columbia University, Bureau of Applied Social Research, 1970.

Cash, W. J. The Mind of the South. New York: Alfred A. Knopf, 1941.

Cassara, Beverly Benner, ed. American Women: The Changing Image. Boston: Beacon Press, 1963.

Caudill, William. "Tiny Dramas: Vocal Communication between Infants and Mothers in Japan and America." A paper presented at the 68th Annual Meeting of the American Anthropological Association, New Orleans, 1969. Mimeo. National Institutes of Mental Health.

___, and Frost, Lois. "A Comparison of Maternal Care and Infant Behavior in Japanese-American, American, and Japanese Families." A paper presented at the 70th Annual Meeting of the American Anthropological Association, New York, 1971. Mimeo. National Institute of Mental Health.

Chesnut, Mary Boykin. A Diary from Dixie. Boston: Houghton Mifflin, 1949.

Christensen, Jean. "The Status of Women in Oregon." Women Lawyers Journal 49 (Spring 1963):11.

Christenson, Harold T. "Cultural Relativism and Premarital Sex Norms." American Sociological Review 25 (Feb. 1960):31-39.

Christy, Howard Chander. The American Girl as Seen and Portrayed by Howard Chandler Christy. New York: Moffat, Yard, 1906.

Citizens' Advisory Council on the Status of Women. Task Force on Health and Welfare. Women and Their Families in Our Rapidly Changing Society: Report. Washington, D.C.: U.S. Government Printing Office, 1968.

___. Task Force on Labor Standards. Report to the Citizens' Advisory Council on the Status of Women. Washington, D.C.: U.S. Government Printing Office, 1968.

Clark, Margaret, and Anderson, Barbara Gallatin. Culture and Aging: Anthropological Study of Older Americans. Springfield, Ill.: Charles C. Thomas, 1967.

Clarke, Ida Gallagher. American Women and the World War. New York: D. Appleton, 1918.

Cohn, David L. Love in America: An Informal Study of Manners and Morals in American Marriage. New York: Simon & Schuster, 1943.

Communist Party of the U.S.A. American Working Women and the Class Struggle. New York: Workers' Library, 1930.

Conference on the American Woman, Her Changing Role as Worker, Homemaker and Citizen. Washington, D.C.: U.S. Department of Labor, 1948.

Conference on "Woman's Destiny--Choice or Chance?"
Washington, D.C.: U.S. Department of Labor, Women's
Bureau, 1963.

Coser, Rose L., ed. Life Cycle and Achievement in
America. New York: Harper & Row, Torch Books, 1969.

Coxe, Margaret. Claims of the Country on American
Females. Columbus, Ohio: I. N. Whiting, 1842.

Cross, Barbara M., ed. The Educated Woman in America:
Selected Writings of Catherine Beecker, Margaret
Fuller, and M. Carey Thomas. New York: Teachers
College Press, 1965.

Das, Sonya R. Sklar. The American Woman in Modern
Marriage. New York: Philosophical Library, 1948.

Davis, Allison W., and Havighurst, Robert J. The Father
of the Man: How Your Child Gets His Personality.
Boston: Houghton Mifflin, 1947.

DeRham, Edith. The Love Fraud: Why the Structure of
the American Family Is Changing and What Women Must
Do to Make It Work. New York: C. N. Potter, 1965.

Dexter, Elizabeth W. Anthony. Colonial Women of
Affairs: A Study of Women in Business and the Pro-
fessions in America Before 1776. Boston: Houghton
Mifflin, 1924.

Dingwall, Eric John, The American Woman: A Historical
Study. London: Duckworth, 1956.

Dollard, John. Caste and Class in a Southern Town.
Garden City, N.Y.: Doubleday, 1957.

Dorr, Rheta Childe. What Eight Million Women Want.
Boston: Small, Maynard, 1910.

Dreiser, Theodore. An American Tragedy. First published, 1926. Reprint, New York: Heritage Press,
1954.

Eaton, Clement. Freedom of Thought in the South. New
York: Peter Smith, 1951.

Eaton, Joseph. "Folk Obstetrics and Pediatrics Meet
the M.D.: A Case Study of Social Anthropology and
Medicine." In Patients, Physicians and Illness, ed.
E. Gartly Jaco, pp. 207-21. Glencoe, Ill.: Free
Press, 1958.

Ellet, Elizabeth Fries. The Women of the American
Revolution. First published, 1849. 3 vols. New
York: Haskell House, 1969.

Farmer, Lydia Hoyt. The National Exposition Souvenir.
What America Owes to Women. Chicago: C. W. Moulton,
1893.

Fetz, Jennifer. "On the Block: Urban Perspectives." A
paper presented at the 69th Annual Meeting of the
American Anthropological Association, San Diego,
1970. Mimeo. Seattle: University of Washington.

Foremost Women in Communications: A Biographical
Reference Work on Accomplished Women in Broadcasting,
Publishing, Advertising, Public Relations, and Allied
Professions. New York: Foremost American Publishing,
1970.

Fowler, William Worthington. Woman on the American
    Frontier: A Valuable and Authentic History of the
    Heroism, Adventures, Privations, Captivities, Trials,
    and Noble Lives and Deaths of the "Pioneer Mothers of
    the Republic." First published, 1879. New York:
    Collectors Editions, Source Book Press, 1970.
Freeman, Julia Deane. Women of the South Distinguished
    in Literature. New York: Derby & Jackson, 1861.
Furman, Lucile. The Status of Women in the United
    States, 1952. Washington, D.C.: U.S. Department of
    Labor, Women's Bureau, 1952.
    . The Status of Women in the United States, 1953.
    Washington, D.C.: U.S. Department of Labor, Women's
    Bureau, 1953.
Gans, Herbert. The Levittowners. New York: Random
    House, Pantheon Books, 1967.
    . The Urban Villagers. Glencoe, Ill.: Free Press,
    1962.
Gaudefroy-Demombynes, Jean. "La femme aux Etats-Unis;
    Choses vues inédetes." Les Ouvres Libres 214 (1939):
    163-224.
Gehman, Richard. "Plainest of Pennsylvania's Plain
    People: Amish Folk." National Geographic 128 (Aug.
    1965):227-53.
Geiss, Anne. "Women in the Subculture of Addiction."
    A paper presented at the 69th Annual Meeting of the
    American Anthropological Association, San Diego,
    1970. Mimeo. University of Kentucky.
Gillin, J. P. "The Old Order Amish of Pennsylvania."
    In Anthropology, ed. Samuel Rapport and Helen Wright.
    New York: New York University Press, 1967.
Graves, A. J. Woman in America: Being an Examination
    into the Moral and Intellectual Condition of American
    Female Society. New York: Harper, 1843.
Greenburg, Dan. How to Be a Jewish Mother. Los Angeles:
    Price, Stern, Sloan, 1964.
Grossman, Edward. "In Pursuit of the American Woman."
    Harper's Magazine 240 (1970):47-69.
Groves, Ernest Rutherford. The American Woman: The
    Feminine Side of a Masculine Civilization. New York:
    Greenberg, 1937.
Gruberg, Martin. Women in American Politics: An
    Assessment and Sourcebook. Oshkosh: Academia Press,
    1968.
Hagood, Margaret. Mothers of the South. Chapel Hill:
    University of North Carolina Press, 1939.
Hanaford, Phebe A. Daughters of America. Boston: B. B.
    Russell, 1883.
Hatcher, Orie Latham. Rural Girls in the City for Work:
    A Study Made for the Southern Woman's Educational
    Alliance. Richmond: Garrett & Massie, 1930.

Hausnecht, E. G. Murray. The Joiners: A Sociological
Description of Voluntary Association Membership in
the United States. New York: Bedminster Press,
1962.
Hawes, Elizabeth. Anything but Love: A Complete Digest
of the Rules for Feminine Behavior from Birth to
Death, Given Out in Print, on Film, and over the Air,
Read, Seen, Listened to Monthly by Some 340,000,000
American Women. New York: Rinehart, 1948.
Hellman, Florence S., ed. List of References Relating to
Notable American Women. Washington, D.C.: Library of
Congress, Division of Bibliography, 1931.
Henkle, Henrietta. Women Who Shaped History. New York:
Crowell-Collier, 1968.
Heron, A. Toward a Quaker View of Sex. Friends Book-
store, 1964.
Herreshoff, David. American Disciples of Marx: From the
Age of Jackson to the Progressive Era. Detroit:
Wayne State University Press, 1967.
Hobson, Elizabeth Kimball. A Report Concerning the
Adored Women of the South. Baltimore: J. Murphy,
1896.
Hollister, Horace Adelbert. The Woman Citizen: A Problem
in Education. New York: D. Appleton, 1918.
Horton, Patricia Marttila. "Television and the American
Woman." Master's thesis, University of Illinois, 1966.
Hosteler, John A. Amish Society. Baltimore: Johns
Hopkins Press, 1968.
____. "Persistence and Change Patterns in Amish Society."
In Beyond the Frontier, ed. Paul Bohannan and Fred
Plog. New York: Natural History Press, 1967.
Humphrey, Grace. Women in American History. Indianapolis:
Bobbs-Merrill, 1919.
Humphrey, Seth. Following the Prairie Frontier.
Minneapolis: University of Minnesota Press, 1931.
Hunt, Chester L. "Female Occupational Roles and the
Urban Sex Roles in the United States, Japan and the
Philippines." Social Forces 43 (Mar. 1965):407-16.
Hunt, Ethel Alice. Wisconsin Women in the War Between the
States. Madison: Wisconsin History Commission, 1911.
Hunt, Morton M. Her Infinite Variety: The American Woman
as Lover, Mate and Rival. New York: Harper & Row, 1962.
Irwin, Inez. Angels and Amazons: A Hundred Years of
American Women. Garden City, N.Y.: Doubleday, Doran,
1933.
Jacobs, Jane. The Death and Life of Great American Cities.
New York: Random House, 1961.
Jensen, Oliver Ormerod. The Revolt of American Women: A
Pictorial History of the Century of Change from Bloomers
to Bikinis--from Feminism to Freud. New York:
Harcourt, Brace, 1952.
Johnson, Dallas. Don't Underestimate Woman Power: A Blue-
print for Intergroup Action. New York: Public Affairs
Committee, 1951.

Kaplan, Bert, and Plant, Thomas A. Personality in a
Communal Society: An Analysis of the Mental Health
of the Hutterites. Lawrence: University of Kansas
Publications, Social Science Studies, 1956.
Kass, Babette. The Economic Strength of Business and
Professional Women. New York: National Federation
of Business and Professional Women's Clubs, 1959.
Kehoe, Alice B. "Freud vs. Mothering: Shifts in
American Interpretation of Mother-Infant Relation-
ships." A paper presented at the 70th Annual Meeting
of the American Anthropological Association, New
York, 1971. Mimeo. Marquette University.
Kemble, Frances. Journal of a Residence on a Georgian
Plantation, 1838-39, ed. J. Scott. New York:
Alfred A. Knopf, 1961.
Kluckhohn, Florence. "The American Family and the
Feminine Role." In Human Relations: Concepts and
Cases in Concrete Social Science, vol. 1, ed. H. Cabot
and J. Kahl, Ch. 9. Cambridge: Harvard University
Press, 1953.
Knudson, Mary. "Sex Differences in Dominance Behavior
of Young Human Primates." A paper presented at the
70th Annual Meeting of the American Anthropological
Association, New York, 1971. Mimeo. University of
Nevada.
Labarca Hubertson, Amanda. Actividades femeninas en
los Estados Unidos. Santiago, Chile: Imp.
Universitaria, 1914.
LaFollette, Cecile Tipton. "A Study of the Problems of
652 Gainfully Employed Married Women Homemakers."
Master's thesis, Columbia University, Teachers
College, 1934.
Lamson, Peggy. Few Are Chosen: American Women in
Political Life Today. Boston: Houghton Mifflin,
1968.
Lebeson, Anita Libman. Recall to Life: The Jewish
Woman in America. South Brunswick, N.J.: Thomas
Yoseloff, 1970.
Lemons, James Stanley. The Woman Citizen: Social
Feminism in the 1920's. Urbana: University of
Illinois Press, 1973.
Leonard, Eugenie A. The Dear-bought Heritage.
Philadelphia: University of Pennsylvania Press, 1965.
Lewis, Helen Matthews. The Woman Movement and the Negro
Movement: Parallel Struggles for Rights.
Charlottesville: University of Virginia, 1949.
Lifton, Robert J., ed. The Woman in America. Boston:
Beacon Press, 1965.
Lilienthal, Meta. From Fireside to Factory. New York:
Rand School of Social Science, 1916.
Longbell, Marjorie R. America and Women: Fictionalized
Biography. Philadelphia: Dorrance, 1962.

Loomis, Charles P. "The Old Order Amish as a Social
    System." In Social Systems, ed. Charles P. Loomis.
    New York: Van Nostrand Reinhold, 1960.
Lopata, Helena Znaniechi. Occupation Housewife. New
    York: Oxford University Press, 1971.
Low, Seth, and Spindler, Pearl. Child Care: Working
    Mothers in U.S. Publication 461. Washington, D.C.:
    Children's Bureau, 1968.
Lutz, Alma. Crusade for Freedom: Women of the Anti-
    slavery Movement. Boston: Beacon Press, 1968.
McClelland, David. "Wanted: A New Self-Image for
    Women." In The Woman in America, vol. 3, ed. Robert
    J. Lifton, pp. 173-92. Boston: Houghton
    Mifflin, Daedalus Library, 1965.
McCracken, Elizabeth. The Woman of America. New York:
    Macmillan, 1904.
Macphail, Andrew. Essays in Fallacy. New York:
    Longmans, Green, 1910.
Marriott, Alice Lee. Hell on Horses and Women. Norman:
    University of Oklahoma Press, 1953.
Mason, Otis Tufton, and Hough, Walter. "North America."
    In Women of All Nations, vol. 3, ed. T. A. Joyce,
    pp. 393-488. New York: Funk & Wagnalls, 1915.
Mead, Kate Campbell. Medical Women of America: A Short
    History of the Pioneer Medical Women of America and
    of a Few of Their Colleagues in England. New York:
    Froben Press, 1933.
Mead, Margaret. And Keep Your Powder Dry. San Diego:
    Morrow, 1943.
___, and Kaplan, Frances B., eds. American Women: The
    Report of the President's Commission on the Status of
    Women. New York: Charles Scribner's Sons, 1965.
Merriam, Eve. After Nora Slammed the Door: American
    Women in the 1960's: The Unfinished Revolution.
    Cleveland: World, 1964.
___, ed. Growing Up Female in America: Ten Lives.
    Garden City, N.Y.: Doubleday, 1971.
Meyer, Annie, ed. Woman's Work in America. New York:
    Henry Holt, 1891.
Milner, Esther. Dialogue on Women. Indianapolis:
    Bobbs-Merrill, 1967.
Morgan, Edmund. The Puritan Family. New York: Harper
    & Row, 1966.
Myrdal, Gunnar. An American Dilemma. 2 vols. New York:
    Harper & Row, 1941-44.
Nag, Moni. "Sex, Culture and Human Fertility: India
    and the United States." Current Anthropology 13
    (Apr. 1972):231-37.
Nearing, Scott. Woman and Social Progress: A Dis-
    cussion of the Biologic, Domestic, Industrial and
    Social Possibilities of American Women. New York:
    Macmillan, 1912.

Newton, Esther, and Walton, Shirley. "The Person Is Political: Consciousness Raising and Personal Change in the Women's Liberation Movement." A paper presented at the 70th Annual Meeting of the American Anthropological Association, New York, 1971. Mimeo. SUNY, Purchase.

Nock, A. J. "Utopia in Pennsylvania: The Amish." In Points of Departure, ed. Arthur J. Carr and William Steinhoff. New York: Harper & Row, 1960.

Parsons, Talcott. "Age and Sex in the Social Structure of the U.S." New York: Bobbs-Merrill, n.d.

Pinckney, Eliza. Journal and Letters of Eliza Lucas. Spartanburg, S.C.: Reprint Co., 1967.

Potter, David. American Women and American Character. DeLand, Fla.: Stetson University Press, 1962.

Rainwater, Lee. Working Man's Wife: Her Personality, World, and Life Style. New York: Oceana Publications, 1959.

Ravenel, Harriott Horry. Eliza Pinckney. First published, 1896. Reprint, Spartanburg, S.C.: Reprint Co., 1967.

Reca, Telma. De la vida norteamericana. Buenos Aires: M. Gleizer, 1932.

Rice, Charles S., and Steinmetz, Rollin C. The Amish Year. New Brunswick, N.J.: Rutgers University Press, 1956.

Riegel, Robert Edgar. American Feminists. Lawrence: University of Kansas Press, 1963.

———. American Women: A Story of Social Change. Rutherford, N.J.: Fairleigh Dickinson University Press, 1970.

Roche, Charles E. "The United States and Canada." In Women of All Nations, vol. 4, ed. T. A. Joyce, pp. 763-68. New York: Funk & Wagnalls, 1915.

Roe, Dorothy. The Trouble with Women Is Men. Englewood Cliffs, N.J.: Prentice-Hall, 1961.

Rogers, Agnes. Women Are Here to Stay: The Durable Sex in Its Infinite Variety through Half a Century of American Life. New York: Harper, 1949.

Roosevelt, Eleanor. It's Up to Women. New York: Frederick A. Stokes, 1933.

Ross, Isabel. Charmers and Cranks: Twelve Famous American Women Who Defied the Conventions. New York: Harper & Row, 1965.

Ross, Mary Steele. American Women in Uniform. Garden City, N.Y.: Garden City, 1943.

Ross, Nancy Wilson. Westward the Women. New York: Alfred A. Knopf, 1944.

Saloutos, Theodore. The Greeks in the United States. Cambridge, Mass.: Harvard University Press, 1964.

Saunders, Louise, ed. Women in National Service: A Report on a National Service Institute. New York: National Council of the Women of the U.S.

Schreiber, William. Our Amish Neighbors. Chicago: University of Chicago Press, 1962.

Schur, Edwin M., ed. The Family and the Sexual Revolution: Selected Readings. Bloomington: Indiana University Press, 1964.

Scofield, N. E. "Some Changing Roles of Women in Suburbia: A Social Anthropological Case Study." Transactions of the New York Academy of Science 22 (Apr. 1960):450-57.

Scott, Ann Firor. "The 'New Woman' in the New South." South Atlantic Quarterly 61 (Autumn 1962):473-83.

_____. Women in American Life: Selected Readings. Boston: Houghton Mifflin, 1970.

Scott-Maxwell, Florida. Women and Sometimes Men. First published, 1957. Reprint, New York: Perennial Library, 1971.

Sickels, Eleanor Maria. Twelve Daughters of Democracy: True Stories of American Women, 1865-1930. New York: Viking, 1941.

Silverman, Irene. Nine to Five and After: The Feminine Art of Living and Working in the Big City. Garden City, N.Y.: Doubleday, 1964.

Sinclair, Andrew. The Better Half: The Emancipation of the American Woman. New York: Harper & Row, 1965.

Smith, Annie S. As Others See Her: One Englishwoman's Impressions of the American Woman in War Time. Boston: Houghton Mifflin, 1919.

Sprague, William Forrest. Women and the West: A Short Social History. Boston: Christopher, 1940.

Stern, Madeleine Bettina. We the Women: Career Firsts of Nineteenth-Century America. New York: Schulte, 1963.

Stoddard, Hope. Famous American Women. New York: Thomas Y. Crowell, 1970.

Streetwalker. New York: Crown, Gramercy Press, 1962.

Sufa, Icken. "The Female-Based Household in Public Housing." Human Organization 24 (1965):135.

Taylor, Susan D.; Wilton, M., and Osnos, R. "The Wives of Drug Addicts." American Journal of Psychiatry 123 (Nov. 1966):5.

Transaction Magazine 8. Special issue on women, Nov.-Dec. 1970.

Underwood, John Levi. The Women of the Confederacy: In Which Is Presented the Heroism of the Women of the Confederacy with Accounts of Their Trials during the War and the Period of Reconstruction, with Their Ultimate Triumph over Adversity. New York: Neale, 1906.

U.S. Office of Education. Gallant American Women. New York: Columbia University Press, 1939-40.

U.S. Office of War Information. Women in the War Campaign. Washington, D.C.: U.S. Army, Recruiting Publicity Bureau, 1943.

U.S. Women's Bureau. College Women Seven Years after Graduation: Resurvey of Women Graduates, Class of 1957. Washington, D.C.: U.S. Government Printing Office, 1966.

___. Handbook on Women Workers. Washington, D.C.: U.S. Government Printing Office, n.d.

___. Highlights 1920-1960. Washington, D.C.: U.S. Government Printing Office, n.d.

___. Spotlight on Women in the United States, 1956-57. Washington, D.C.: U.S. Government Printing Office, 1957.

___. Today's Woman in Tomorrow's World: Report of a Conference Commemorating the 40th Anniversary of the Women's Bureau, June 2-3, 1960. Washington, D.C.: U.S. Government Printing Office, 1960.

Utah Women: Opportunities, Responsibilities: Report. Salt Lake City: Governor's Committee on the Status of Women in Utah, 1966.

Varigny, Charles Victor Crosnier de. La femme aux Etats-Unis. Paris: A. Colin, 1893.

Warner, James A. The Quiet Land. New York: Grossman, 1970.

Wasserstrom, William. Heiress of All the Ages: Sex and Sentiment in the Genteel Tradition. Minneapolis: University of Minnesota Press, 1959.

Wilson, Jeannie Lansley. The Legal and Political Status of Women in the United States. Cedar Rapids: Torch Press, 1912.

Wolff, Janet L. What Makes Women Buy: A Guide to Understanding and Influencing the New Woman of Today. New York: McGraw-Hill, 1958.

"Women in America." Daedalus 93 (Spring 1964).

Women Workers in Illinois. Springfield, Ill.: Bureau of Employment Security, 1964.

Woodward, Helen Beal. The Bold Women. New York: Farrar, Straus & Young, 1953.

Woolson, Abba Louisa. Woman in American Society. Boston: Roberts Bros., 1873.

Yoors, Jan. The Gypsies. New York: Simon & Schuster, 1967.

PART TWO: SUBJECT TOPICS

GENERAL REFERENCES

Beauvoir, Simone de. Force of Circumstance. New York: G. P. Putnam, 1965.

____. The Second Sex. First published, 1953. New York: Bantam Books, 1970.

Brophy, Brigid. "Speaking Out: Woman Is a Prisoner of Her Sex." Saturday Evening Post, Nov. 1963.

Brown, J. K. "W. Schmidt's 'Mutterrecht' and Cross-cultural Research." Anthropos 63 (1968-69):3-6.

Bruère, Martha S. Laughing Their Way: Women's Humor in America. New York: Macmillan, 1934.

Callahan, Sidney. The Illusion of Eve. New York: Sheed & Ward, 1965.

Chiñas, Beverly Litzler. "Women as Ethnographic Subjects." In Women in Cross-cultural Perspective: A Preliminary Sourcebook, ed. Sue-Ellen Jacobs. Urbana: University of Illinois, Department of Urban & Regional Planning, 1971, pp. 22-31.

Chombart de Lauwe, Marie-Jose, and Chombart de Lauwe, Paul Henry. La femme dans la société: Son image dans differents milieux sociaux. Paris: Centre National de la Recherche Scientifique, 1963.

Chombart de Lauwe, P. "Introduction: Images of Women in Society." International Social Science Journal 14 (1962):7-25.

Clarke, E. My Mother, Who Fathered Me. First published, 1957. Reprint, New York: Humanities Press, 1966.

Cole, William. Women Are Wonderful. Boston: Houghton Mifflin, 1956.

Cutler, John H. What about Women? New York: Ives Washburn, 1961.

Davis, Elizabeth Gould. The First Sex. Baltimore: Penguin, 1972.

Degler, Carl. "Revolution without Ideology: The Changing Place of Women in America." In The Woman in America, vol. 3, ed. Robert J. Lifton, pp. 193-210. Boston: Houghton Mifflin, Daedalus Library, 1965.

DeLeeuw, Hendrick. Women: The Dominant Sex. New York: A. S. Barnes. Thomas Yoseloff, 1957.

DeVries, H. Das Weib bei den Naturvolkern. Die Asiatin. Die Slawin [The woman among primitive peoples. The Asiatic woman. The Slav woman]. Dusseldorf: Hellas, 1960.

Durkheim, Emile. Suicide: A Study in Sociology. Glencoe, Ill.: Free Press, 1951.

Efimenko, P. P. "Znachenie zhenshchiny v oriniǎkskuiǔ spokbu." In Izvestiia Gosudarstvennoǐ Akademii Material'noǐ kul'tur y 11 (1931):3-4.

Evans-Pritchard, Edward E. The Position of Women in Primitive Societies and Other Essays in Social Anthropology. New York: Free Press, 1963.

Fanon, Frantz. The Wretched of the Earth. First published, 1963. Reprint, New York: Grove Press, 1965.

Fischer, Ann. "The Position of Women in Anthropology." American Anthropologist 70 (1968):2.

Fitzsimons, John. Women Today. New York: Sheed & Ward, 1952.

Friedl, Ernestine. "The Position of Women: Appearance and Reality." Anthropological Quarterly 40 (1967): 97-108.

Garandy, Roger. Femmes du xx° siècle: Semaine de la Pensée Marxiste. Paris: Presses Universitaires de France, 1965.

Goldberg, Steven. The Inevitability of Patriarchy: Why the Biological Difference between Men and Women Always Produces Male Domination. New York: William Morrow, 1973.

Golde, Peggy. Women in the Field: Anthropological Experiences. Chicago: Aldine, 1970.

Guide to Current Female Studies, vol. 2. New York: Feminist Press, 1972.

Hacker, Helen. "Marx, Weber and Pareto on the Status of Women." American Journal of Economics and Sociology 12 (1952):149.

____. "Women as a Minority Group." Social Forces 31 (Oct. 1951):60-69. Reprint, Indianapolis: Bobbs-Merrill, n.d.

Hawes, Elizabeth. Men Can Take It. New York: Random House, 1939.

____. Why Women Cry; or, Wenches with Wrenches. Clifton, N.J.: Reynal & Hitchcock, 1943.

Herschberger, Ruth. Adam's Rib. New York: Pellegrini & Cudahy, 1948.

Hicks, Judy. An Anthropological Approach to the Position of Women. S.C.E.F., 3210 West Broadway, Louisville, Ky. 40211.

Holden, Dronie. "The Theoretical Model as Data Maker, or, Who Took the Women out of Primitive Society." A paper presented at the 71st Annual Meeting of the American Anthropological Association, Toronto, 1972. Mimeo. New School for Social Research.

Huber, Joan, ed. "Changing Women in a Changing Society." American Journal of Sociology 78, 4 (1973):763-1062.

Hunt, Morton. Her Infinite Variety: The American Woman as Lover, Rival, and Mate. New York: Harper & Row, 1962.

Hutchins, Robert M., and Adler, M. J., eds. The Great Ideas Today: The Difference of Women and the Difference It Makes. Chicago: Encyclopaedia Britannica, 1968.

International American Conference. Convencion Inter-americana sobre en le Novena Conferencia Internacional Americana, Bogota, Marzo 30-Mayo 2, 1948 [Inter-American convention on the granting of civil rights to women, signed at the Ninth International Conference of American States, Bogota, March 30-May 2, 1948]. Washington, D.C.: Union Panamericana, 1948.

Jacobs, Sue-Ellen. "Anthropologically Speaking, Women. . . ." Mutha. Sacramento Women's Liberation, 1970.

____. Women in Cross-cultural Perspective: A Preliminary Sourcebook. Urbana: University of Illinois, Department of Urban & Regional Planning, 1971.

Jarnow, Jeannette A., and Judells, Beatrice. Inside the Fashion Business. New York: John Wiley, 1966.

Joyce, Thomas, ed. Women of All Nations: A Record of Their Characteristics, Habits, Manner, Customs and Influence. New York: Funk & Wagnalls, 1912.

Keiiser, J. L. J. de. "De emotionaliteit der vrouw bij de natuurvolken." In Mensch en Maatschappi 4 (1928): 439.

Klein, Grace, and Cooper, Mae Klein [Farewell, Nina]. The Unfair Sex. New York: Simon & Schuster, 1953.

Klein, Viola. The Feminine Character: History of an Ideology. First published, 1948. Reprint, Urbana: University of Illinois Press, 1972.

Landy, Avrom. Marxism and the Woman Question. New York: Workers Library, 1943.

Lazarte, J. "Condición de la mujer en las differentes culturas y pueblos" [The condition of women in different cultures and villages]. Solidaridad obrera (Apr. 1957):629-40.

Leavitt, Ruby, and Sykes, Barbara. "Aboriginal Woman: Female versus Male Approaches." A paper presented at the 71st Annual Meeting of the American Anthropological Association, Toronto, 1972. Mimeo. Manhattan Community College.

Lenski, Gerhard. Power and Privilege: A Theory of Social Stratification. New York: McGraw-Hill, 1966.

Linton, Sally. "Woman the Gatherer: Male Bias in Anthropology." In Women in Cross-cultural Perspective: A Preliminary Sourcebook, ed. Sue-Ellen Jacobs. Urbana: University of Illinois, Department of Urban & Regional Planning, 1971, pp. 9-21.

Lurie, Nancy Oestreich. Review of Women in the Field: Anthropological Experiences, ed. Peggy Golde. Science 171 (1971):1135-36.

____. "Women in Early American Anthropology." In Pioneers of American Anthropologists, ed. June Helm, pp. 31-81. Seattle: University of Washington Press, 1966.

Mason, Otis T. Woman's Share in Primitive Culture. New York: D. Appleton, 1894.

Moderna enciclopedia femminile. La donna e il suo mondo. A cura di Vanna Chirone. Turin: Editrice S.A.I.E., 1956.

Oakley, Ann. Sex, Gender and Society. London: Temple Smith, 1972.

Ortner, Sherry B. "Is Female to Male as Nature to Culture?" A paper presented at the 71st Annual Meeting of the American Anthropological Association, Toronto, 1972. Mimeo. Sarah Lawrence College.

Partorino, Carlos Juliano Torres. Teu lar, tua vida. Rio de Janeiro: J. Ozon, 1962.

Patai, Raphael, ed. Women in the Modern World. New York: Free Press, 1967.

Raphael, Dana, ed. The Status of the Female. The Hague: Mouton, in press.

Raya, Gino. Che cosa e la donna. Rome: Cirrana, 1963.

Révész, Andrés. La mujer ideal. Madrid: A. Aguado, 1945.

Richards, Cara E. Man in Perspective: An Introduction to Cultural Anthropology. New York: Random House, 1972.

_____. "Presumed Behavior: Modification of the Ideal-Real Dichotomy." American Anthropologist 71 (1969): 1115-16.

Safilios-Rothschild, Constantina. Toward a Sociology of Women. Lexington, Md.: Xerox College Publishing, 1972.

Sanday, Peggy R., and Rosen, Daniel. "Toward a Theory of the Status of Women: An Example of the Use of the Ethnographic Atlas in Cross-cultural Theory Construction." A paper presented at the 70th Annual Meeting of the American Anthropological Association, New York, 1971. Mimeo. Carnegie-Mellon University.

Scherer, Alice. Die Frau: Wesen and Aufgaben. Freiburg: Herder, 1951.

Secretaria General de OEA, ed. Convención Interamericana sobre Concesion de los Derechos Civiles a la mujer. Pan American Union, 1948.

Stern, Karl. The Flight from Women. New York: Farrar, Straus & Giroux, Noonday Press, 1965.

Stern, Paula. "The Womanly Image: Character Assassination through the Ages." Atlantic 225 (Mar. 1970): 87-90.

Sullero, Evelyne. Women, Society and Change, trans. Margaret Archer. New York: McGraw-Hill, 1971.

Theobald, Robert. Dialogue on Women. Indianapolis: Bobbs-Merrill, 1967.

Thomas, W. I. "Why Women Are So." In The Family, ed. E. B. Renter and J. R. Runner, pp. 443-49. New York: McGraw-Hill, 1931.

Thomé, Yolanda Bettencourt. A mulher no mundo de hoje. Petrópolis: Editôra Vozes, 1967.

Van Den Berghe, Pierre L. Another Perspective on Man ... and Woman and Child: Age and Sex Differentiation. Belmont, Calif.: Wadsworth, 1973.

Wallin, Paul. "A Guttman Scale for Measuring Woman's Neighborliness." American Journal of Sociology 59 (1953):243-46.

Wartolowska, Z. "Rola kobiety w spoleczenstwie pier-
wotnym" [The role of women in primitive society].
Dawna Kultura 3 (1955):104-9.
Werner, E. "Zur Frauenfrage und zum Frauenkult im
Mittelalter: Robert v. Arbrissel and Fontevrault"
[The Medieval woman-problem and woman cult: Robert
V. Arbrissel and Fontevrault]. Forsch. u. Fortschy.
20 (Sept. 1955):269-76.
"Woman's Place." Special Supplement. Atlantic 225
(Mar. 1970):81-126.
"Women around the World." Annals of the American
Academy of Political and Social Science 375 (Jan.
1968).

PRIMATE STUDIES

Abrams, Patricia S. "Repeated Mother-Infant Separations
in Rhesus Monkeys." A paper presented at the 69th
Annual Meeting of the American Anthropological As-
sociation, San Diego, 1970. Mimeo. University of
California, Davis.
Benfer, Robert A., and Page, John W. "Sexual Dimorphism
and Primate Numerical Taxonomy." A paper presented at
the 70th Annual Meeting of the American Anthropological
Association, New York, 1971. Mimeo. University of
Missouri, Columbia.
Brace, C. Loring. "Sapient Chauvinism and Australopithe-
cine Sexual Recognition." A paper presented at the
70th Annual Meeting of the American Anthropological
Association, New York, 1971. Mimeo. University of
Michigan.
Bramblett, Claud A. "The Subordinate Mother: An
Analysis of Supportive Behaviors." A paper presented
at the 70th Annual Meeting of the American Anthro-
pological Association, New York, 1971. Mimeo.
University of Texas.
___. "Vervet Monkeys and Their Mothers." A paper pre-
sented at the 69th Annual Meeting of the American
Anthropological Association, San Diego, 1970. Mimeo.
University of Texas.
Branscomb, Susan. "Piaget's Concept of the Schema as a
Paradigm for Describing the Ontogeny of Monkey
Behavior." A paper presented at the 70th Annual
Meeting of the American Anthropological Association,
New York, 1971. Mimeo. University of California,
Berkeley.
Burton, Frances. "Evidence for Sexual Antagonism among
Non-human Primates." A paper presented at the 70th
Annual Meeting of the American Anthropological As-
sociation, New York, 1971. Mimeo. University of
Toronto.

Denham, Woodrow. "Energy Relations and Some Basic Pro-
perties of Primate Social Organization." American
Anthropologist 73 (1971):77-95.
DeVore, Irvin, ed. Primate Behavior. New York: Holt,
Rinehart & Winston, 1965.
Goodall, Jane van Lawick. In the Shadow of Man. London:
William Collins, 1971.
___. "Mother-Offspring Relationships in Free-Ranging
Chimpanzees." In Primate Ethology, ed. Desmond
Morris. Chicago: Aldine, 1967.
Kortlandt, Adriaan. "Chimpanzees in the Wild."
Scientific American 206 (1962):128-38.
Kummer, Hans. Primate Societies. New York: Aldine-
Atherton, 1971.
Lancaster, Jane B. "Female Bonding: Social Relations
between Adult Female Vervet Monkeys." A paper pre-
sented at the 69th Annual Meeting of the American
Anthropological Association, San Diego, 1970. Mimeo.
Rutgers University.
___. "In Praise of the Achieving Female Monkey." In
The Female Experience, ed. Carol Tavris, pp. 5-9.
Del Mar, Calif.: CRM, 1973.
___. "Play-mothering of Infants by Juvenile Female
Vervet Monkeys." A paper presented at the 68th
Annual Meeting of the American Anthropological As-
sociation, New Orleans, 1969. Mimeo. University of
California, Berkeley.
Liebowitz, Lila. "Desmond Morris Is Wrong, about
Breasts, Buttocks, and Body Hair." Psychology Today
3 (1970):16-22.
Reynolds, Vernon. "The Man of the Woods." Natural
History 73 (1964):44-51.
Sussman, Robert W. "Addendum: Child Transport, Family
Size, and Increase in Human Population during the
Neolithic." Current Anthropology 13 (Apr. 1972):
258-59.
Van Den Berghe, Pierre L. Another Perspective on Man
... and Woman and Child: Age and Sex Differentiation.
Belmont, Calif.: Wadsworth, 1973.
Weiss, Kenneth M. "Sex and the Single Fossil: A
Comment on the Sex Ratio of Fossil Hominid Remains."
A paper presented at the 70th Annual Meeting of the
American Anthropological Association, New York, 1971.
Mimeo. University of Michigan.
Williams, Sharlotte Neely. "The Limitations of the
Male/Female Activity Distinction among Primates: An
Extension of Judith K. Brown's 'A Note on the
Division of Labor by Sex.'" American Anthropologist
73 (1971):805-6.

ANATOMY AND PHYSIOLOGY

Baker, Roger G., and Stone, Calvin P. "Growth in the

Height and Weight in College and University Women."
Science 83 (1936):59-61.
Beall, Elizabeth. "The Relation of Various Anthro-
pometric Measurements of Selected College Women to
Success in Certain Physical Activities." Master's
thesis, Columbia University, 1939.
Bernstein, Lionel Mandel. "Body Composition as Related
to Heat Regulation in Women." Master's thesis,
University of Illinois, 1959.
Boston Women's Health Course Collective. Our Bodies
Our Selves: A Course by and for Women. Boston: New
England Free Press, 1971.
Erikson, Erik. "Inner and Outer Space: Reflections on
Womanhood." In The Women in America, ed. Robert J.
Lifton, pp. 1-27. Boston: Houghton Mifflin, 1965.
Ford, Clellan Stearns. A Comparative Study of Human
Reproduction. First published, 1945. Reprint, New
Haven: Human Relations Area Files Press, 1964.
Frank, Avis Rae. "The Relationship of Total Body
Agility Reaction Time to the Agility Run among
College Women." Master's thesis, University of Illinois,
1948.
Hamburg, David A., and Lunde, Donald T. "Sex Hormones in
the Development of Sex Differences in Human Beings."
In The Development of Sex Differences, ed. Eleanor E.
Maccoby, pp. 1-24. Stanford: Stanford University
Press, 1966.
Hilliard, Marion. Women and Fatigue. Garden City, N.Y.:
Doubleday, 1960.
Llewellyn-Jones, Derek. Every Woman and Her Body. New
York: Taplinger, 1971.
Macabee, June Marilyn. "The Relationship between Body
Proportions of College Women to Running, Throwing,
and Jumping Activities." Master's thesis, University
of Illinois, 1950.
Montagu, Ashley. The Natural Superiority of Women. Rev.
ed. New York: Macmillan, 1968.
Moore, Lillian Mary. Periodic Variations in Cardio-
vascular Activities and in Respiratory Rate in Women.
Berkeley: University of California Press, 1923.
Novak, Emil. The Woman Asks the Doctor. Baltimore:
Williams & Wilkins, 1949.
Reich, Wilhelm. The Function of the Orgasm. New York:
Orgone Institute Press, 1942.
Ryder, Alice Elizabeth. "Calcium Utilization by Normal
Women on Three Levels of Intake." Ph.D. dissertation,
University of Chicago, 1935.
Schoepf, Brooke Grundfest. "Raging Hormones or Raging
Females? A Biocultural Review." A paper presented at
the 70th Annual Meeting of the American Anthropological
Association, New York, 1971. Mimeo. New York
University.
Trimmer, Eric. Femina: What Every Woman Should Know
about Her Body. New York: Stein & Day, 1966.

PSYCHOLOGICAL STUDIES

Adams, Margaret. "The Compassion Trap, Women Only."
Psychology Today, Nov. 1971, p. 70.

Anastasi, Ann. Differential Psychology. New York:
Macmillan, 1958.

Angrist, Shirley S. Women after Treatment: A Study of
Former Mental Patients and Their Normal Neighbors.
New York: Appleton-Century-Crofts, 1968.

Ansón, Francisco. Mujer y sociedad. Madrid: Ediciones
Rialp, 1966.

Apuleius, Madaurensis. Amor and Psyche; the Psychic
Development of the Feminine; a Commentary on the Tale
by Apuleius, by Erich Neumann, trans. Ralph Manheim.
New York: Random House, Pantheon Books, 1956.

Bandura, Albert, and Walters, Richard H. Social Learning
and Personality Development. New York: Holt, Rinehart
& Winston, 1963.

Bardwick, Judith M. Feminine Personality and Conflict.
Monterey, Calif.: Brooks-Cole, 1970.

____. Psychology of Women: A Study of Bio-Cultural
Conflicts. New York: Harper & Row, 1971.

____, ed. Readings on the Psychology of Women. New York:
Harper & Row, 1972.

Bednarik, Karl. The Male in Crisis. New York: Alfred
A. Knopf, 1970.

Benedict, Ruth. "Continuities and Discontinuities in
Cultural Conditioning." Psychiatry 1 (May 1938):161-
68.

____. Patterns of Culture. New York: New American
Library, Mentor Books, 1934.

Bergler, Edmund. Fashion and the Unconscious. New York:
R. Brunner, 1953.

Bier, William C., ed. Woman in Modern Life. New York:
Fordham University Press, 1968.

Breer, Paul E., and Locke, Edwin A. Task Experience as
a Source of Attitudes. Homewood, Ill.: Dorsey, 1965.

Brim, Orville G. "Family Structure and Sex-role Learning
by Children." Sociometry 21 (1958):1-16.

____. "Personality Development as Role-learning." In
Personality Development in Children, ed. Ira Iscoe
and Harold Stevenson. Austin: University of Texas
Press, 1960.

____, and Wheeler, Stanton. Socialization after Childhood:
Two Essays. New York: John Wiley, 1966.

Bronfenbrenner, Urie. "Some Familial Antecedents of
Responsibility and Leadership in Adolescents." In
Studies in Leadership, ed. L. Petrillo and B. Bass.
New York: Holt, Rinehart & Winston, 1960.

Brown, Daniel. "Sex-Role Development in a Changing
Culture." Psychological Bulletin 54 (May 1958): 232-
42.

Brown, Nona B. "Inquiry into the Feminine Mind." New
York Times Magazine, Apr. 12, 1964, p. 17.
Burton, Roger V., and Whiting, John W. M. "The Absent
Father and Cross-sex Identity." Merrill-Palmer
Quarterly of Behavior and Development 7 (1961):85-95.
Buytendijk, Frederick Jacobus Johannes. La femme, ses
modes d'être, de paraître, d'exister; essai de
psychologie existentielle. First published, 1954.
2nd ed., Bruges: Desclée de Brouwer, 1961.
Chapman, Joseph Dudley. The Feminine Mind and Body: The
Psychosexual and Psychosomatic Reactions of Women.
New York: Philosophical Library, 1967.
Clauson, John A., ed. Socialization and Society. Boston:
Little, Brown, 1968.
Colby, Kenneth M. "Sex Differences in Dreams of
Primitive Tribes." American Anthropologist 65 (1963):
1116-22.
Coleman, James. The Adolescent Society. New York:
Free Press, 1961.
_____. Adolescents and the Schools. New York: Basic
Books, 1965.
Coult, A. D. "Causality and Cross-sex Prohibitions."
American Anthropologist 65 (Apr. 1963):266-77.
Deutsch, Helene. The Psychology of Women. 2 vols. New
York: Grune & Stratton, 1944.
Douvan, Elizabeth. "Independence and Identity in
Adolescents." Children 4 (1957):186-90.
Du Bois, Cora. The People of Alor: A Social-
psychological Study of an East Indian Island. New
York: Harper & Row, 1960.
Erikson, Erik H. Identity, Youth and Crisis. New York:
W. W. Norton, 1968.
Feldman, Harold. Development of the Husband-Wife
Relationship. Ithaca: Cornell University Press, 1965.
Ferguson, Charles W. The Male Attitude. Boston: Little,
Brown, 1966.
Figes, Eva. Patriarchal Attitudes. New York: Fawcett,
Premier Books, 1970.
Firkel, Eva. Mature Woman. Notre Dame, Ind.: Fides,
1968.
Fjeld, Harriet. "A Comparison of Major Groups of College
Women on the Kuder-Preference Record Personality."
Educational and Psychological Measurement 12 (1952):
665-68.
Freud, Sigmund. "Feminity." In New Introductory Lectures
on Psycho-analysis, ed. J. Strachey, pp. 112-35.
New York: W. W. Norton, 1965.
Fromm, Erich. The Art of Loving. New York: Harper &
Row, 1956.
Gavron, Hannah. The Captive Wife: Conflicts of House-
bound Mothers. New York: Humanities Press, 1966.
George, W. L. Intelligence of Woman. Boston: Little,
Brown, 1916.

Goldberg, Philip. "Are Women Prejudiced against Women?"
    Transaction, Apr. 1968, pp. 28-30.
Goode, William J. "The Theoretical Importance of Love."
    American Sociological Review 24 (1959):38-47.
Hallowell, A. Irving. "Acculturation Processes and
    Personality Changes as Indicated by the Rorschach
    Techniques." Rorschach Research Exchange 6 (1942):
    42-50.
Hansson, Laura. The Psychology of Woman. London: G.
    Richards, 1899.
Harding, Mary Esther. The Way of All Women: A Psycho-
    logical Interpretation. New York: Longmans, Green,
    1933.
    . Woman's Mysteries: Ancient and Modern. Intro.
    C. G. Jung. New York: G. P. Putnam's, 1971.
Hartley, Catherine G. "Implications of Changes in Sex
    Role Patterns." In The Family and Change, ed. John
    Edwards, pp. 212-25. New York: Alfred A. Knopf, 1969.
Heymans, Gerardus. Die Psychologie der Frauen.
    Heidelberg: C. Winter, 1910.
Hinkle, Beatrice. "On the Arbitrary Use of the Terms
    'Masculine' and 'Feminine.'" Psycho-Analytic Review
    7 (1920).
Horney, Karen. Feminine Psychology, ed. Harold Kelman.
    New York: W. W. Norton, 1967.
    . New Ways in Psychoanalysis. New York: W. W.
    Norton, 1939.
Hunt, Morton M. The Natural History of Love. New York:
    Alfred A. Knopf, 1959.
Jahoda, G. "Sex Differences in Preferences for Shapes:
    A Cross-cultural Replication." British Journal of
    Psychology 47 (1956):126-32.
Kammeyer, Kenneth. "Birth Order and the Feminine Sex
    Role among College Women." American Sociological
    Review 31 (Aug. 1966):508-15.
    . "Sibling Position and the Feminine Role." Journal
    of Marriage and the Family 29 (1967):494-99.
Kardiner, Abram; Karush, Aaron; and Ovesay, Lionel. "A
    Methodological Study of Freudian Theory: Narcissism,
    Bisexuality, and the Dual Instinct Theory." Journal
    of Nervous and Mental Disease 129 (1959):207-21.
Kennedy, D. "Explorations in the Cross-Cultural Study
    of Mental Disorders." Ph.D. dissertation, Cornell
    University, 1959.
Kirkpatrick, Clifford. "Inconsistency in Attitudinal
    Behaviour with Special Reference to Attitudes toward
    Feminism." Journal of Applied Psychology 20 (1936):
    535-40.
Kohlberg, Lawrence. "A Cognitive-Developmental Analysis
    of Children's Sex-role Concepts and Attitudes." In
    The Development of Sex Differences, ed. Eleanor
    Maccoby, pp. 82-172. Stanford: Stanford University
    Press, 1966.

Konopka, G. The Adolescent Girl in Conflict. Englewood
Cliffs, N.J.: Prentice-Hall, 1966.
Laing, R. D. The Divided Self: An Existential Study in
Sanity and Madness. New York: Barnes & Noble, 1960.
LaPiere, Richard. The Freudian Ethic. Des Moines,
Iowa. Duell, Sloan & Pearce, 1959.
Lausky, Leonard. "The Family Structure also Affects the
Model: Sex-role Identification in Parents of Pre-
school Children." Merrill-Palmer Quarterly 10 (1964):
39-50.
Levi-Strauss, Claude. The Savage Mind. Chicago:
University of Chicago Press, 1967.
Levy, L. H. "Sexual Symbolism: A Validity Study."
Journal of Consulting Psychology 18 (1954):43-46.
Lewis, Edwin C. Developing Woman's Potential. Ames:
Iowa State University Press, 1968.
Maccoby, Eleanor, ed. The Development of Sex Differences.
Stanford: Stanford University Press, 1966.
McElroy, W. A. "A Sex Difference in Preferences for
Shapes." British Journal of Psychology 45 (1954):
209-16.
McKee, John P., and Sheriffs, Alex C. "The Differential
Evaluation of Males and Females." Journal of Person-
ality 25 (1957):356-71.
___. "Men's and Women's Beliefs, Ideals, and Self-
concepts." American Journal of Sociology 54 (Jan.
1954):356-63.
Marion, Henri. Psychologie de la femme. 6th ed. Paris:
A. Colin, 1913.
Maslow, Abraham H. Motivation and Personality. New
York: Harper & Row, 1954.
Mead, Margaret. Coming of Age in Samoa: A Study of
Adolescence and Sex in Primitive Society. New York:
New American Library, Mentor Books, 1949.
___. Growing up in New Guinea. New York: New American
Library, Mentor Books, 1961.
___. The Mountain Arapesh. Garden City, N.Y.:
Doubleday, Natural History Press, 1968.
___. Sex and Temperament in Three Primitive Societies.
First published, 1935. Reprint, New York: Dell, 1963.
___, and Metraux, Rhoda, eds. The Study of Culture at a
Distance. First published, 1953. Reprint, Chicago:
University of Chicago Press, 1971.
Menken, Alice Davis. On the Side of Mercy: Problems in
Social Readjustment. New York: Covici, Friede, 1933.
Meyers, Thomas. "The Clitorid Woman." Psychiatric
Quarterly 40 (1966):248-57.
Miller, Benjamin F. Masculinity and Feminity. Boston:
Houghton Mifflin, 1971.
Minturn, Leigh, and Cambert, William W. "A Cross-
cultural Linguistic Analysis of Freudian Symbols."
Ethnology 4 (1964):336-42.

Mischel, Walter. "Father Absence and Delay of Gratifica-
tion: Cross-cultural Comparisons." Journal of
Abnormal and Social Psychology 63 (1961):116-24.
___. "A Social-learning View of Sex Differences in
Behavior." In The Development of Sex Differences, ed.
Eleanor Maccoby, pp. 56-81. Stanford: Stanford
University Press, 1966.
Moller, H. "The Meaning of Courtly Love." Journal of
American Folklore 73 (1951):39-52.
___. "The Social Causation of the Courtly Love Complex."
Comparative Studies in Society and History 1 (1959):
137-62.
Moustakas, Clark E., ed. The Self: Explorations in
Personal Growth. New York: Harper & Row, 1956.
Murphy, Robert F. "Social Structure and Sex Antagonism."
Southwestern Journal of Anthropology 15 (1959):89-98.
Nelson, E. "Persistence of Attitudes of College
Students Fourteen Years Later." Psychological Mono-
graphs 68 (1954):2.
Neumann, Erich. Amor and Psyche: The Psychic Develop-
ment of the Feminine. New York: Pantheon, 1956.
Newton, Esther, and Walton, Shirley. "The Personal Is
the Political: Consciousness-raising and Personal
Change in the Women's Liberation Movement." A paper
presented at the 70th Annual Meeting of the American
Anthropological Association, New York, 1971. Mimeo.
State University of New York, Stony Brook.
Newton, Niles. Maternal Emotions. New York: Hoeber
Medical Division, Harper, 1955.
___. "Trebly Sensuous Woman." Psychology Today (July
1971):68.
Papanek, Mariam L. "Authority and Sex Roles in the
Family." Journal of Marriage and the Family 31 (Feb.
1969):88-96.
Patrick, G. T. W. "The Psychology of Woman." Popular
Science Monthly 47 (1895):209-24.
Phillip, Derek L., and Segal, Bernard F. "Sexual Status
and Psychiatric Symptoms." American Sociological
Review 34 (Feb. 1969):57-72.
Pressel, Esther J. "Spiritual Dichotomy of Social
Relations between Men and Women." A paper presented
at the 71st Annual Meeting of the American Anthro-
pological Association, Toronto, 1972. Mimeo.
Colorado State University.
Reeves, Nancy. Womankind: Beyond the Stereotypes.
Chicago: Aldine-Atherton, 1971.
Rham, Edith de. The Love Fraud. New York: Clarkson
N. Potter, 1965.
Rheingold, Joseph C. The Fear of Being a Woman: A
Theory of Maternal Destructiveness. New York: Grune
& Stratton, 1967.
___. The Mother, Anxiety, and Death. Boston: Little,
Brown, 1967.

Roheim, Geza. "Aphrodite or the Woman with a Penis." Psychoanalytic Quarterly 14 (1945):350-90.
___. Psychoanalysis and Anthropology: Culture, Personality and the Unconscious. New York: International Universities Press, 1950.
Rosenfels, Paul. Love and Power: The Psychology of Interpersonal Creativity. New York: Libra, 1966.
Rougemont, Denis de. Love in the Western World. New York: Random House, Pantheon Books, 1956.
Sexton, Patricia C. The Feminized Male. New York: Random House, 1970.
Shapiro, Judith. "Male Bonds and Female Bonds: An Illustrative Comparison." A paper presented at the 70th Annual Meeting of the American Anthropological Association, New York, 1971. Mimeo. University of Chicago.
Sherman, Julia A. On the Psychology of Women: A Survey of Empirical Studies. Springfield, Ill.: Charles C. Thomas, 1971.
___. "Problem of Sex Differences in Space Perception and Aspects of Intellectual Functioning." Psychological Review 74 (July 1967):290-99.
Shirley, Robert W., and Romney, A. Kimball. "Love Magic and Socialization Anxiety: A Cross-cultural Study." American Anthropologist 64 (1962):1028-31.
Silverman, Sydel F. "The Life Crisis as a Clue to Social Functions." Anthropological Quarterly 40 (1967): 127-28.
Steinman, Ann. "Self-Conceptions of College Women Compared with Their Concept of Ideal Women and Men's Ideal Woman." Journal of Counseling Psychology 11 (1964):370-74.
___, and Fox, David, J. "Specific Areas of Agreement and Conflict in Women's Self-perception and Their Perception of Men's Ideal Woman in Two South American Urban Communities and an Urban Community in the United States." Journal of Marriage and the Family 31 (1969):281-89.
Stephens, William N. The Oedipus Complex: Cross-cultural Evidence. New York: Free Press, 1962.
Stevens, Barbara C. Marriage and Fertility of Women Suffering from Schizophrenia or Affective Disorders. New York: Oxford University Press, 1969.
Stuart, M., and Lin, W. T. The Changing Woman: The Impact of Family Planning. Boston: Little, Brown, 1969.
Tavris, Carol, ed. The Female Experience. Del Mar, Calif.: CRM Publications, 1973.
Thompson, Clara. "Cultural Pressures in the Psychology of Women." Psychiatry 5 (1942):331-39.
Thompson, Helen Bradford. The Mental Traits of Sex. Chicago: University of Chicago Press, 1903.
Tweker, Sylvia. "Humanness and the Sexes." Adult Leadership 18 (May 1969):14-17.

Van Den Berg, J. H. The Changing Nature of Man. New
    York: W. W. Norton, 1961.
Van Waters, Miriam. "The Adolescent Girl among
    Primitive People." Journal of Religious Psychology
    6 (1913):375; 7 (1914):32.
Weisstein, Naomi. Kinder, Küche, Kirche as Scientific
    Law: Psychology Constructs the Female. Boston:
    New England Free Press, 1968.
_____. "Psychology Constructs the Female; or the Fantasy
    Life of the Male Psychologist (with Some Attention
    to the Fantasies of His Friends, the Male Biologist
    and the Male Anthropologist)." Social Education 35
    (1971):362-73.
Whiting, Beatrice B. "Sex Identity Conflict and Physical
    Violence: A Comparative Study." American Anthro-
    pologist 67 (1965):123-40.
Whiting, John W. M. "The Effects of Climate on Certain
    Cultural Practices." In Explorations in Cultural
    Anthropology: Essays in Honor of George Peter
    Murdock, ed. Ward Goodenough, pp. 511-44. New York:
    McGraw-Hill, 1964.
_____. "Resource Mediation and Learning by Identification."
    In Personality Development in Children, ed. Ira Iscoe
    and Harold W. Stevenson. Austin: University of
    Texas Press, 1960.
Wit, G. A. de. Symbolism of Masculinity and Feminity.
    New York: Springer, 1935.

SEX AND SEXUALITY

Benedek, Therese. Psychosexual Function in Women. New
    York: Ronald Press, 1952.
Bergler, Edmund, and Kroger, William S. Kinsey's Myth
    of Female Sexuality: The Medical Facts. New York:
    Grune & Stratton, 1954.
Bernard, Jessie. The Sex Game. New York: Prentice-
    Hall, 1968.
Bick, Mario. "Blind Man's Bluff: The Anthropologist
    Confronts Sexual Antagonism." A paper presented at
    the 70th Annual Meeting of the American Anthropological
    Association, New York, 1971. Mimeo. Bard College.
Bloch, Iwan. The Sexual Life of Our Time in Its Re-
    lation to Modern Civilization. London: Allied, 1908.
Bonaparte, Marie. Female Sexuality. New York:
    International Universities Press, 1956.
Brecher, Ruth, and Brecher, Edward. An Analysis of
    Human Sexual Response. Boston: Little, Brown, 1966.
Brenton, Myron. The American Male. New York: Coward-
    McCann, 1966.
Brown, Helen Gurley. Sex and the Office. New York:
    Random House, 1964.

___. *Sex and the Single Girl*. New York: Random House, 1962.

Brown, J. S. "A Comparative Study of Deviation from Sexual Mores." *American Sociological Review* 17 (1952):135-46.

Brown, Judith K. "A Cross-cultural Study of Female Initiation Rites." Ph.D. dissertation, Harvard University, 1962.

Bullough, Vern L. *The History of Prostitution*. New Hyde Park, N.Y.: University Books, 1964.

Campbell, Bernard, ed. *Sexual Selection and the Descent of Man, 1871-1971*. Chicago: Aldine, 1972.

Carpenter, Edward. *Sex-love. Woman. Marriage*. Manchester: Labour Press Society, 1894.

Carstairs, G. M. "Cultural Differences in Sexual Deviation." In *The Pathology and Treatment of Sexual Deviation*, ed. Ismond Rosen, pp. 419-34. New York: Oxford University Press, 1964.

Catling, Patrick Skene. *The Experiment*. New York: Trident Press, 1967.

Chartham, Robert. *Mainly for Wives: The Art of Sex for Women*. New York: New American Library, 1969.

Chassequet-Smirgel, J. *Female Sexuality: New Psychoanalytic Views*. Ann Arbor: University of Michigan Press, 1970.

Cohen, Mabel Blake. "Personal Identity and Sexual Identity." *Psychiatry* 29 (1966):1-14.

Cohen, Yehudi. "Ends and Means in Political Control: State Organization and the Punishment of Adultery, Incest, and Violation of Celibacy." *American Anthropologist* 71 (1969):658-87.

Copelan, Rachel. *The Sexually Fulfilled Woman*. New York: Weybright & Talley, 1972.

Davis, Katherine B. *Factors in the Sex Life of Twenty Two Hundred Women*. New York: Harper, 1929.

DeMartino, Manfred F. *The New Female Sexuality*. New York: Julian Press, 1969.

___, ed. *Sexual Behavior and Personality Characteristics*. New York: Grove Press, 1966.

d'Eaubonne, Francoise. *Le complexe de Diane. Erotisme du féminisme*. Paris: R. Julliard, 1951.

Ellis, Albert, and Abarbanel, Albert, eds. *The Encyclopedia of Sexual Behavior*. 2 vols. New York: Hawthorn Books, 1961.

Ellis, Albert, and Sagarin, Edward. *Nymphomania: A Study of the Over-sexed Woman*. New York: MacFadden-Bartell, 1965.

Ellis, Havelock. *The Erotic Rights of Women*. London: British Society for the Study of Sex Psychology, 1918.

___. *Studies in the Psychology of Sex*. New York: Random House, 1937.

Engle, Bernice Attis. "A Study of Castration." *Psychoanalytic Review* 23 (1936).

Fairchild, Johnson E., ed. Women, Society, and Sex. New York: Sheridan House, n.d.

Ford, Clellan Stearns, and Beach, F. Patterns of Sexual Behavior. New York: Harper & Row, 1951.

Fox, Robin. "The Evolution of Human Sexual Behavior." New York Times Magazine, Mar. 24, 1968, pp. 32-33, 79, 82-102.

Freud, Sigmund. Three Essays on the Theory of Sexuality, trans. and ed. James Strachey. New York: Basic Books, 1963.

Gagnon, John H. "Sexuality and Sexual Learning in the Child." Psychiatry 8 (Aug. 1965):212-28.

Giese, Hans, ed. Sexuality of Women. New York: Stein & Day, 1970.

Goldman, George D. Modern Woman: Her Psychology and Sexuality. Springfield, Ill.: Charles C. Thomas, 1969.

Goody, Jack. "A Comparative Approach to Incest and Adultery." In Marriage, Family and Residence, ed. Paul Bohannan and John Middleton, pp. 21-46. New York: Natural History Press, 1968.

Greene, Gael. Sex and the College Girl. New York: Dial Press, 1964.

Hayden, Casey. "Sex and Caste." Liberation 1 (Apr. 1966); 2 (Dec. 1966).

Henriques, Fernando. Love in Action: The Sociology of Sex. New York: E. P. Dutton, 1960.

Herschfeld, Magnus. Women East and West: Impressions of a Sex Expert. London: Heinemann, 1935.

Himmelhock, Jerome, and Fava, Sylvia F., eds. Sexual Behavior in American Society. New York: W. W. Norton, 1955.

James, Jennifer. "Economic Aspects of Sexuality." A paper presented at the 71st Annual Meeting of the American Anthropological Association, Toronto, 1972. Mimeo. University of Washington, Seattle.

Jeanniere, Abel. The Anthropology of Sex. New York: Harper & Row, 1967.

Jones, Ernest. "Mother-Right and the Sexual Ignorance of Savages." International Journal of Psychoanalysis 6 (1925):109-30.

Kinsey, Alfred C.; Pomeroy, Wardell B.; Martin, Clyde E.; and Gebhard, Paul H. Sexual Behavior in the Human Female. Philadelphia: W. A. Saunders, 1953.

Koedt, Anne. The Myth of the Vaginal Orgasm. Rev. ed. Boston: New England Free Press, n.d.

Kreps, Juanita. Sex in the Marketplace: American Women at Work. Baltimore: Johns Hopkins University Press, 1971.

Kronhausen, Phyllis, and Kronhausen, Eberhard. Sexually Responsive Woman. New York: Ballantine, 1965.

McPartland, John. Sex in Our Changing World. Garden City, N.Y.: Blue Ribbon Books, 1947.

Malinowski, B. The Sexual Life of Savages. New York: Harcourt, Brace & World, 1929.

Marcus, Steven. The Other Victorians: A Study of Sexuality and Pornography in Mid-nineteenth Century England. New York: Basic Books, 1966.

Marcuse, Herbert. Eros and Civilization. Boston: Beacon Press, 1955.

Marshall, Donald S., and Suggs, Robert C., eds. Human Sexual Behavior: Variations across the Ethnographic Spectrum. New York: Basic Books, 1970.

Masters, William H., and Johnson, Virginia. Human Sexual Response. Boston: Little, Brown, 1966.

Mead, Margaret. Cultural Determinants of Sexual Behavior in Sex and Internal Secretions. 3d ed., ed. W. C. Young. Baltimore: Williams & Wilkins, 1971.

____. "First Discussion: The Childhood Genesis of Sex Difference in Behavior." In Discussion on Child Development, vol. 3, ed. J. M. Tanner and Barbal Inhelder. London: Tavistock, 1958.

____. Male and Female. New York: William Morrow, 1953.

____. Sex and Temperament in Three Primitive Societies. First published, 1935. Reprint, New York: Dell, 1963.

Money, John, ed. Sex Research, New Developments. New York: Holt, Rinehart & Winston, 1965.

Montagu, Ashley. Sex, Man, and Society. New York: G. P. Putnam, 1969.

Moustakas, Clark E. "Self-Esteem (Dominance Feeling) and Sexuality in Women." Journal of Social Psychology 16 (1942):259-94.

Munroe, Robert L., and Munroe, Ruth H. "A Cross-cultural Study of Sex, Gender and Social Structure." Ethnology 8 (1969):206-11.

Murdock, George Peter. "Cultural Correlates of the Regulation of Premarital Sex Behavior." In Process and Pattern in Culture: Essays in Honor of Julian H. Steward, ed. Robert Manners, pp. 399-410. Chicago: Aldine, 1964.

____. "The Social Regulation of Sexual Behavior." In Psycho-sexual Development in Health and Disease, ed. Paul Hoch and Joseph Zubin. New York: Macmillan, 1949.

Nemecek, Ottokar. Virginity: Pre-nuptial Rites and Rituals. New York: Philosophical Library, 1958.

Newton, Esther. Mother Camp: Female Impersonators in America. Englewood Cliffs, N.J.: Prentice-Hall, 1971.

Palson, Charles, and Palson, Rebecca. "Sex and Sex Roles as a System of Symbols." A paper presented at the 70th Annual Meeting of the American Anthropological Association, New York, 1971. Mimeo. Temple University.

Parsons, Elsie Clews. The Old-fashioned Woman: Primitive Fancies about Sex. New York: G. P. Putnam, 1913.

Subject Topics

Ploss, Herman Heinrich. Woman in the Sexual Relation: An Anthropological and Historical Survey. New York: Medical Press of New York, 1964.

Pollak, Otto, and Friedman, Alfred S., eds. Family Dynamics and Female Sexual Delinquency. Palo Alto, Calif.: Science & Behavior Books, 1969.

Reiss, I. L. "The Double Standard in Premarital Sexual Intercourse: A Neglected Concept." Social Forces 34 (1956):224-30.

Robinson, Marie N. The Power of Sexual Surrender. Garden City, N.Y.: Doubleday, 1959.

Rosenblatt, Paul C.; Fugita, Stephen S.; and McDowell, Kenneth V. "Wealth Transfer and Restrictions on Sexual Relations during Betrothal." Ethnology 8 (1969):319-28.

Ruitenbeek, Hendrik M., ed. Psychoanalysis and Female Sexuality. New Haven: College & University Press, 1966.

Sagarin, Edward, ed. "Sex and the Contemporary American Scene." Annals of the American Academy of Political and Social Science 376 (Special Issue, Mar. 1968).

Seidenberg, Robert. "Is Sex without Sexism Possible?" Sexual Behavior, Jan. 1972, p. 46.

Seward, Georgene H. Sex and the Social Order. New York: McGraw-Hill, 1946.

Sexual Behavior. Periodical. C.R.M. Publication, Boulder, Colo.

"The Sexual Renaissance in America." Journal of Social Issues 22 (Apr. 1966).

Sherfey, Mary Jane. The Nature and Evolution of Female Sexuality. New York: Random House, 1972.

Sorokin, Pitrim. The American Sex Revolution. Boston: Porter Sargent, 1957.

Stannard, Una. "Clothing and Sexuality." Sexual Behavior, May 1971, p. 25.

Stekel, Wilhelm. Frigidity in Women. 2 vols. London: Boni & Liveright, 1926.

Thomas, William Isaac. Sex and Society. Chicago: University of Chicago Press, 1906.

Tobias, R. B. Women as Sex Vendors; or, Why Women Are Conservative. Chicago: C. H. Kerr, 1918.

Vincent, Clark. Unmarried Mothers. New York: Free Press, 1961.

Ward, David A., and Kassebaum, Gene G. Women's Prison: Sex and Social Structure. Chicago: Aldine, 1972.

Weininger, Otto. Sex and Character. London: Heinemann, 1906.

Winick, Charles. "Sex and Advertising." Sexual Behavior, Apr. 1971, p. 36.

Wolf, Deborah. "Female Identity in Male Transvestites." A paper presented at the 70th Annual Meeting of the American Anthropological Association, New York, 1971. Mimeo. University of California, Berkeley.

Young, Wayland. Eros Denied: Sex in Western Society. New York: Grove Press, 1964.

136

SOCIALIZATION: ROLE DEVELOPMENT AND CHILD-REARING PRACTICES

Abernathy, Virginia D. "Social Network and Maternal Response." A paper presented at the 69th Annual Meeting of the American Anthropological Association, San Diego, 1970. Mimeo. Harvard University.

Angrist, Shirley S. "Role Constellation as a Variable in Women's Leisure Activities." Social Forces 45 (1967):423-31.

Baker, Luther G. "The Personal and Social Adjustment of the Never-married Woman." Journal of Marriage and the Family 30 (1968):473.

Barry, Herbert, III; Bacon, Margaret K.; and Child, Irvin L. "A Cross-cultural Survey of Some Sex Differences in Socialization." Journal of Abnormal and Social Psychology 55 (1957):327-32.

———. "Definitions, Ratings and Bibliographic Sources for Child Training Practices of 110 Cultures." In Cross-cultural Approaches: Readings in Comparative Research, ed. Clellan S. Ford, pp. 293-331. New Haven: Human Relations Area Files Press, 1967.

———. "Relation of Child Training to Subsistence Economy." In Cross-cultural Approaches: Readings in Comparative Research, ed. Clellan S. Ford, pp. 246-59. New Haven: Human Relations Area Files Press, 1967.

Bender, Marylin. The Beautiful People. New York: Coward-McCann, 1967.

Bettelheim, Bruno. Symbolic Wounds: Puberty Rites and the Envious Male. Rev. ed. New York: Collier, 1962.

Bleumen, Jean. "A Theoretical Framework for the Analysis of Sex-role Differentiation." A paper presented at the 70th Annual Meeting of the American Anthropological Association, New York, 1971. Mimeo. Carnegie-Mellon University.

Brim, Orville. "Family Structure and Sex Role Learning by Children: A Further Analysis of Helen Koch's Data." Sociometry 21 (1958):1-16.

Brim, Orville G., Jr, and Wheeler, Stanton. Socialization after Childhood: Two Essays. New York: John Wiley, 1966.

Brose, Alberta J. "Some Aspects of Role Change in Women Students over Thirty." A paper presented at the 70th Annual Meeting of the American Anthropological Association, New York, 1971. Mimeo. California State College, Long Beach.

Brown, Daniel. "Sex-role Preferences in Young Children." Psychological Monographs 70 (1956):1-19.

Brown, Judith K. "The Archaic Illusion: A Reexamination of Levi-Strauss's View of the Developing Child." A paper presented at the 70th Annual Meeting of the American Anthropological Association, New York, 1971. Mimeo. Oakland University.

___. "Girls' Puberty Rites: A Reply to Driver."
American Anthropologist 72 (1970):1450-51.
___. "A Note on the Division of Labor by Sex."
American Anthropologist 72 (1970):1073-78.
___. "A Cross-cultural Study of Female Initiation Rites."
American Anthropologist 65 (1963):837-53.
Chabrol, Claude. Le récit féminin: contribution a
l'analyse semiologique du courrier du coeur et des
entrevues ou enquêtes sur la femme dans la presse
féminine actuelle. The Hague: Mouton, 1971.
Chodorow, Nancy. "Psychology and Socialization." A
paper presented at the 71st Annual Meeting of the
American Anthropological Association, Toronto, 1972.
Mimeo. Brandeis University.
Clarkson, Frank E. "Family Size and Sex-role Stereotypes."
Science 167 (1970):390-92.
Cohen, Yehudi A. "The Establishment of Identity in a
Social Nexus: The Special Case of Initiation
Ceremonies and Their Relation to Value and Legal
Systems." American Anthropologist 66 (1964):529-52.
___. The Transition from Childhood to Adolescence:
Cross-cultural Studies of Initiation Ceremonies, Legal
Systems and Incest Taboos. Chicago: Aldine, 1964.
Cottrell, Leonard S. "The Adjustment of the Individual
to His Age and Sex Roles." American Journal of
Sociology 53 (Nov. 1946):184-89.
Cowan, John. The Science of a New Life. First published,
1874. New York: Collectors Editions, Source Book
Press, 1970.
Dahlström, Edmund. The Changing Roles of Men and Women.
Boston: Beacon Press, 1971.
D'Andrade, Roy G. "Sex Differences and Cultural In-
stitutions." In The Development of Sex Differences,
ed. Eleanor Maccoby, pp. 173-203. Stanford: Stanford
University Press, 1966.
Darwin, Charles. The Descent of Men and Selection in
Relation to Sex. London: Murray, 1871.
Densmore, Dana. Sex Roles and Female Oppression. Boston:
New England Free Press, n.d.
Dinitz, S.; Dynes, R.; and Clarke, A. "Preferences for
Male or Female Children: Traditional or Affectional."
Journal of Marriage and Family Living 16 (May 1954):
128-30.
Elder, Glenn, and Bowerman, Charles. "Family Structure
and Child-rearing Patterns: The Effect of Family Size
and Sex Composition." American Sociological Review
28 (1963):891-904.
Ellis, Albert. The American Sexual Tragedy. Rev. ed.
New York: Lyle Stuart, 1962.
Ellis, Havelock. Man and Woman. London: Walter Scott,
1904.
Erikson, Erik. "Sex Differences in the Play Configura-
tions of Pre-Adolescents." American Journal of
Orthopsychiatry 21 (Oct. 1951):4.

Fand, Alexandra Botwinik. Sex Role and Self Concept: A Study of the Feminine Sex Role as Perceived by Eighty-five Women for Themselves, Their Ideal Woman, the Average Woman and Man's Ideal Woman. Ann Arbor: University Microfilms, 1955.

Farber, Seymour M., ed. Man and Civilization: The Potential of Woman: A Symposium. New York: McGraw-Hill, 1963.

___, and Wilson, Roger H. L. The Potential of Woman. New York: McGraw-Hill, 1963.

___, eds. The Challenge to Women. New York: Basic Books, 1966.

Flugel, J. C. Psychology of Clothes. New York: International Universities Press, 1966.

Fogarty, M. P.; Rapoport, R.; and Rapoport, R. N. Sex, Career, and Family: Including an International Review of Women's Roles. London: Allen & Unwin, 1971.

Foote, Nelson. "Change in American Marriage Patterns and the Role of Women." Eugenics Quarterly 1 (Dec. 1954):254-60.

Gilman, Charlotte Perkins. Concerning Children. London: Watts, 1907.

Guttman, David. "Women and the Conception of Ego Strength." Merrill-Palmer Quarterly 12 (1965):229-40.

Harrington, Charles. "Sexual Differentiation in Socialization and Some Male Genital Mutilations." American Anthropologist 70 (1968):951-56.

___, and Whiting, John W. M. "Socialization Process and Personality." In Psychological Anthropology. 2d ed. Cambridge, Mass.: Schenkman, 1972.

Hartley, Catherine G. "Sex-roles from a Child's Point of View." In Sourcebook on Marriage and the Family, ed. Marvin Sussman. Boston: Houghton Mifflin, 1968.

Hawes, Elizabeth. Fashion Is Spinach. New York: Random House, 1938.

___. It's Still Spinach. Boston: Little, Brown, 1954.

Heath, Dwight B. "Sexual Division of Labor and Cross-cultural Research." Social Forces 37 (1958):77-79.

Heiss, Jerold. "Degree of Intimacy and Male-Female Interaction." Sociometry 25 (June 1962):197-208.

Helfer, R. E., and Kemp, C. H. The Battered Child. Chicago: University of Chicago Press, 1969.

Hennessy, Caroline. The Strategy of Sexual Struggle. New York: Lancer Books, 1971.

Hilger, M. Inez. Field Guide to the Ethnological Study of Child Life. 2d rev. ed. New Haven: Human Relations Area Files Press, 1966.

Hoffman, Lois. "Effects of the Employment of Mothers on Parental Power Relations and the Division of Household Tasks." Marriage and Family Living 22 (Feb. 1960): 27-35.

Hollingworth, Leta S. "Social Devices for Compelling Women to Bear and Rear Children." American Journal of Sociology 22 (July 1916):28-29.

Jacobson, A. H. "Conflict of Attitudes toward the Roles of Husband and Wife in Marriage." American Sociological Review 17 (1952):146-50.

Jahoda, G., and Jahoda, Hovel. "Psychological Problems of Women in Different Social Roles." Educational Record 1 (Oct. 1955):36, 325-35.

Jarecki, Henry G. "Maternal Attitudes toward Child-rearing." Archives of General Psychiatry 4 (1961): 340-56.

Kagan, Jerome. "Acquisition and Significance of Sex Typing and Sex Role Identity." In Review of Child Development Research, vol. 1. New York: Russell Sage Foundation, 1964.

___. "The Emergence of Sex Differences." Women in Education. Special Issue. School Review 80 (1972): 217-28.

___, and Moss, Howard A. Birth to Maturity. New York: John Wiley, 1962.

Kargman, Marie W. "A Socio-legal Analysis of Family Role Conflict." Marriage and Family Living 21 (Aug. 1959): 275-78.

Kenkel, William F. "Husband-Wife Interaction in Decision-making and Decision Choices." Journal of Social Psychology 55 (1961):255-62.

Key, Ellen. The Morality of Woman and Other Essays. Chicago: Ralph Fletcher Seymour, 1911.

Kidd, Dudley. Savage Childhood. London: A. & C. Black, 1906.

Klein, Viola. The Feminine Character: History of an Ideology. First published, 1946. Urbana: University of Illinois Press, 1972.

Knight, Richard Payne, and Wright, Thomas. Sexual Symbolism: A History of Phallic Worship. First published, 1786. Reprint, New York: Julian Press, 1957.

Komarovsky, Mirra. "Cultural Contradictions and Sex Roles." American Journal of Sociology 20 (1946):42-47.

___. "Functional Analysis of Sex Roles." American Sociological Review 15 (Aug. 1960):508-16.

Kroeber, A. L. "On the Principle of Order in Civilization as Exemplified by Changes of Fashion." American Anthropologist 21 (1919):235-63.

___, and Richardson, R. J. "Three Centuries of Women's Dress Fashions: A Quantitative Analysis." University of California Anthropological Records 5 (1940):111-54.

Kurtz, Richard M. "Body Image--Male and Female." Transaction, Dec. 1968, pp. 25-27.

LaFontaine, J. S. "Ritualization of Women's Life Crises in Bugisu." In The Interpretation of Ritual, ed. J. S. LaFontaine, pp. 159-86. London: Tavistock, 1972.

Leslie, Gerald R., and Johnson, Kathryn P. "Changed Perceptions of the Maternal Role." American Sociological Review 28 (Dec. 1963):919-28.

Lessler, K. "The Anatomical and Cultural Dimensions of Sexual Symbols." Ph.D. dissertation, Michigan State University, 1963.
___. "Sexual Symbols, Structured and Unstructured." Journal of Consulting Psychology 26 (1962):44-49.
Lewis, Edwin C. "Emerging Social Patterns and the Potential of Women." Adult Leadership 18 (May 1969): 18-21.
Lewis, Michael. "Parents and Children: Sex Role Development." Women in Education. Special Issue. School Review 80 (1972):229-40.
Liby, Margaret. "The Biological Potential of Women." Adult Leadership 18 (May 1969):27-31.
Lopata, Helena Z. Occupation: Housewife. New York: Oxford University Press, 1971.
Lopate, Carol. "Sex Role Learning in Women's Liberation Child Care Centers." A paper presented at the 70th Annual Meeting of the American Anthropological Association, New York, 1971. Mimeo. Columbia University.
Low, Setha M. "Life Crises of Women." A paper presented at the 70th Annual Meeting of the American Anthropological Association, New York, 1971. Mimeo. University of California, Berkeley.
Ludovici, Laurence James. The Final Inequality: A Critical Assessment of Woman's Sexual Role in Society. New York: W. W. Norton, 1968.
Lynn, David B. "Determinants of Intellectual Growth in Women." Women in Education. Special Issue. School Review 80 (1972):241-60.
___. "A Note on Sex Differences in the Development of Masculine and Feminine Identification." Psychological Review 66 (1966):126-35.
___. "The Process of Learning Parental and Sex-role Identification." Journal of Marriage and the Family 28 (1966):466-70.
Maccoby, Eleanor. The Development of Sex Differences. Stanford: Stanford University Press, 1966.
___. "Role Taking in Childhood and Its Consequences for Social Learning." Child Development 30 (1959):239-52.
McKee, John P., and Sheriffs, Alex C. "Qualitative Aspects of Beliefs about Men and Women." Journal of Personality 25 (1957):451-54.
Michaelson, Evalyn Jacobson, and Goldschmidt, Walter. "Female Roles and Male Dominance among Peasants." Southwestern Journal of Anthropology 27 (1971):330-52.
Mill, John S., and Mill, Harriet T. Essays on Sex Equality, ed. Alice S. Rossi. Chicago: University of Chicago Press, 1970.
Minturn, Leigh. "A Cross-cultural Linguistic Analysis of Freudian Symbols." Ethnology 4 (1965):336-42.

Subject Topics

___; Grosse, Martin; and Haider, Santoah. "Cultural
Patterning of Sexual Beliefs and Behavior."
Ethnology 8 (1969):301-18.
Minturn, Leigh, and Lambert, William W. "Motherhood
and Child-rearing." In A Modern Introduction to the
Family, ed. Norman W. Bell and Ezra F. Vogel, pp.
551-57. New York: Free Press, 1968.
___. Mothers of Six Cultures: Antecedents of Child
Rearing. New York: John Wiley, 1964.
Moscovici, Marie. "Le changement social en milieu
rurale et le role des femmes." Revue Française de
Sociologie 1 (1960):314-22.
Moveh, James G. "Husband-Wife Interaction over Political
Issues." Public Opinion Quarterly 16 (Winter 1953-
54):461-70.
Nerlove, Sara, and Romney, A. Kimball. "Sibling Ter-
minology and Cross-sex Behavior." American
Anthropologist 69 (1967):179-87.
Norbeck, Edward. "The Interpretation of Data: Puberty
Rites." American Anthropologist 64 (1962):463-85.
Norton, Caroline. A Plain Letter to the Lord Chancellor
on the Infant Custody Bill. New York: Bruce Rogers,
1922.
Nye, F. I., and Berardo, F. M., eds. Emerging Conceptual
Frameworks in Family Analysis. New York: Macmillan,
1966.
Packard, Vance. The Sexual Wilderness: The Contem-
porary Upheaval in Male-Female Relationships. New
York: David McKay, 1968.
Park, George K. "Sons and Lovers: Characterological
Requisites of the Roles in Peasant Society." Ethnology
1 (1962):412-24.
Parsons, Talcott. "Family Structure and the Socialization
of the Child." In Family, Socialization and Interaction
Process, ed. T. Parsons and R. F. Bales. New York:
Free Press, 1955.
Patanjali, V. "Women's Role in Social Change." Social
Welfare, Apr. 1969, p. 30.
Plato. The Republic. Book 5: The Communal Rearing of
Children. New York: E. P. Dutton, 1950.
Prothro, E. Terry. "Patterns of Permissiveness among
Preliterate Peoples." Journal of Abnormal and Social
Psychology 61 (1960):151-54.
Raphael, Dana Louise. "Uncle Rhesus, Aunti Pachyderm,
and Mom: All Sorts and Kinds of Mothering." Per-
spectives in Biology and Medicine 13 (Winter 1969):
290-97.
Riegel, R. "Women's Clothes and Women's Rights."
American Quarterly 15 (Autumn 1963):390-401.
Roach, Mary Ellen, and Eicher, Joanne B., eds. Dress,
Adornment, and the Social Order. New York: John
Wiley, 1965.
Rocheblave-Spenle, Annemarie. Les rôles masculins et
féminins. Paris: Presses Universitaires de France,
1964.

Rose, Arnold. "The Adequacy of Women's Expectations for Adult Roles." Social Forces 30 (Oct. 1951):69-77.
Rosenblatt, Paul C. "A Cross-cultural Study of Child Rearing and Romantic Love." Journal of Personality and Social Psychology 41 (1966):336-38.
Rossi, Alice S. The Beginning of Ideology: Alternate Models of Sex Equality. Baltimore: Johns Hopkins University, Department of Social Relations, 1970.
___. "The Road to Sex Equality." A paper presented at the Social Inequality Seminar, Department of Sociology, University of Chicago, Feb. 1969.
___, ed. Essays on Sex Equality, by John Stuart Mill and Harriet Taylor Mill. Chicago: University of Chicago Press, 1970.
Rothschild, Nan. "Sex and Status: A Prehistoric Perspective." A paper presented at the 71st Annual Meeting of the American Anthropological Association, Toronto, 1972. Mimeo. New York University.
Ruderman, Florence. Child Care and Working Mothers: A Study of Arrangements Made for Daytime Care of Children. New York: Children's Welfare League of Americans, 1968.
Rudofsky, Bernard. Are Clothes Modern? An Essay on Contemporary Apparel. Chicago: Theobald, Paul, 1947.
Ryan, Mary S. Clothing: A Study in Human Behavior. New York: Holt, Rinehart & Winston, 1966.
Sacks, Karen. "Sexism: A Marxist View." A paper presented at the 70th Annual Meeting of the American Anthropological Association, New York, 1971. Mimeo. Oakland University.
Sanday, Peggy R. "A Cross-cultural Analysis of Sex Role Assignment: Sex, Religion and Politics." A paper presented at the 70th Annual Meeting of the American Anthropological Association, New York, 1971. Mimeo. Carnegie-Mellon University.
Sanger, Margaret. Motherhood in Bondage. New York: Brentano's, 1928.
Scheinfeld, Amram. Women and Men. New York: Harcourt, Brace, and World, 1944.
Schlegel, Alice. "The Socialization of the Hopi Girl." Ethnology 12 (1973):449-62.
Schoepf, Brooke Grundfest. "Cultural Implications of Biological Sex Differences: A Re-examination of the Evidence." A paper presented at the 70th Annual Meeting of the American Anthropological Association, New York, 1971. Mimeo. University of Connecticut.
Sears, P. "Doll Play Aggression in Normal Young Children: Influences of Sex, Age, Sibling Status, Father's Absence." Psychological Monographs 65, no. 6 (1951).
Sears, R. R.; Maccoby, E. E., and Levine, H. Patterns of Child Rearing. Evanston, Ill.: Row, Peterson, 1957.

Seligmann, Charles G. "Birth and Childhood Customs."
Reports of the Cambridge Anthropological Expedition
to the Torres Straits 5 (1904):194-200.
Silverman, Irwin. "Physical Attractiveness and Court-
ship." Sexual Behavior, Sept. 1971, pp. 22-25.
Skard, Aasa Gruda. "Maternal Deprivation: The Research
and Its Implications." Journal of Marriage and
the Family 27 (Aug. 1965):3.
Slater, Philip E. "Parental Role Differentiation."
American Sociological Review 67 (1961):296-311.
___, and Slater, Dori A. "Maternal Ambivalence and
Narcissism: A Cross-cultural Study." Merrill-Palmer
Quarterly of Behavior and Development 11 (1965):241-59.
Spindler, Louise, and Spindler, George. "Male and
Female Adaptations in Culture Change." American
Anthropologist 60 (1958):217-33. Reprinted in Man in
Adaptation: The Institutional Framework, ed. T. A.
Cohen, pp. 396-408. Chicago: Aldine, n.d.
Spock, Benjamin. Decent and Indecent. New York: McCall,
1970.
Stephens, William N. "A Cross-cultural Study of Modesty."
Behavioral Science Notes: Human Relations Area Files
Quarterly Bulletin 7 (1972):1-28.
Stoller, Robert J. Sex and Gender: On the Development
of Masculinity and Femininity. New York: Science
House, 1968.
Strodtbek, Fred, and Greelan, Paul. "The Interaction
Linkage between Family Size, Intelligence and Sex Role
Identity." Journal of Marriage and Family Living 30
(1968):301-7.
Stuart, Dorothy Margaret. The Girl through the Ages.
Philadelphia: J. B. Lippincott, 1933.
Swinehart, James S. "Socio-Economic Level, Status
Aspirations and Maternal Role." American Sociological
Review 28:391-99.
Symonds, P. M. "Changes in Sex Differences in Problems
and Interests of Adolescents with Increasing Age."
Journal of Genetic Psychology 50 (1937):83-89.
Talmon, Yonina. "Sex Role Differentiation in an
Egalitarian Society." In Life in Society, ed. T. E.
Lasswell, J. H. Bunne and S. H. Aronson. Chicago:
Scott, Foresman, 1965.
Terman, Lewis, and Miles, C. C. Sex and Personality:
Studies in Masculinity and Femininity. New York:
McGraw-Hill, 1936.
Terman, Lewis, and Tyler, L. E. "Psychological Sex
Differences." In Manual of Child Psychology, ed. L.
Carmichael. New York: John Wiley, 1954.
Thomas, Keith. "The Double Standard." In Ideas in
Cultural Perspectives, ed. Philip Wiener and Aaron
Nolan, pp. 446-67. New Brunswick, N.J.: Rutgers
University Press, 1962.

Thurber, Cheryl. "Sex Differentiation in Religious Movements." A paper presented at the 70th Annual Meeting of the American Anthropological Association, New York, 1971. Mimeo. University of British Columbia.

Thurber, James, and White, E. B. Is Sex Necessary? New York: Dell, 1964.

Trilling, Diana. "Female Biology in a Male Culture." Saturday Review 10 (Oct. 1970):16.

Turner, E. S. A History of Courting. New York: E. P. Dutton, 1955.

"UNICEF and the Changing Role of Women: A New Television Series." UNICEF News Issue 62 (Oct. 1969):15.

Van Gennep, A. The Rites of Passage. Ithaca: Cornell University Press, 1960.

Walkers, J. "Adolescent Attitudes towards the Role of Women." Journal of Social Psychology 35 (1952):101.

Wallin, P. "Cultural Contradictions and Sex Roles: A Repeat Study." American Sociological Review 40 (1950): 288-93.

Wax, Murray. "Themes in Cosmetics and Grooming." American Journal of Sociology 62 (1957):588-93.

Weitzman, Lenore J.; Eifler, Deborah; Hokada, Elizabeth; and Ross, Catherine. "Sex-Role Socialization in Picture Books for Preschool Children." American Journal of Sociology 7, 6 (May 1972). Reprint, Andover, Mass.: Warner Modular Publications #142, 1973.

Whiting, Beatrice B. "Folk Wisdom and Child Rearing." A paper presented at the meeting of the American Association for the Advancement of Science, December, 1971. Mimeo. Harvard University.

Whiting, John W., and Child, Irvin L. Child Training and Personality: A Cross-cultural Study. New Haven: Yale University Press, 1953.

Wiegand, Elisabeth. Use of Time by Full-time and Part-time Homemakers in Relation to Home Management. Ithaca: Cornell University Press, 1954.

Williams, F. E. "Sex Affiliation and Its Implications." Journal of the Royal Anthropological Institute of Great Britain and Ireland 62 (1932):51-82.

Winick, Charles. The New People. New York: Pegasus, 1968.

Women Studies Collective. "Power Strategies and Sex Roles." A paper presented at the 70th Annual Meeting of the American Anthropological Association, New York, 1971. Mimeo. Stanford University.

Young, Frank W. Initiation Ceremonies: A Cross-cultural Study of Status Dramatization. Indianapolis: Bobbs-Merrill, 1965.

FAMILY, MARRIAGE, KINSHIP, RESIDENCE, AND DIVORCE

Abbott, Lyman. The Home Builder. Boston: Houghton Mifflin, 1908.

Ackerman, Charles. "Affiliations: Structural Determinants of Differential Divorce Rates." American Journal of Sociology 69 (1963):13-20.

Aries, Philippe. Centuries of Childhood: A Social History of Family Life. New York: Alfred A. Knopf, 1962.

Astell, Mary. Some Reflections upon Marriage. New York: Collectors Editions, Source Books Press, 1970.

Babchuk, Nicholas, and Bates, Alan. "The Primary Relations of Middle-class Couples: A Study in Male Dominance." American Sociological Review 28 (June 1963):377-84.

Banks, J. A., and Banks, Olive. Feminism and Family Planning in Victorian England. New York: Schocken Books, 1964.

____. Prosperity and Parenthood: A Study of Family Planning among the Victorian Middle Classes. London: Routledge & Kegan Paul, 1954.

Bastock, Margaret. Courtship: An Ethological Study. Chicago: Aldine, 1967.

Bernard, Jessie. Marriage and Family among Negroes. Englewood Cliffs, N.J.: Prentice-Hall, 1966.

____. Remarriage: A Study of Marriage. New York: Dryden Press, 1956.

Blood, Robert O., Jr., and Wolfe, Donald M. Husbands and Wives: The Dynamics of Married Living. Glencoe, Ill.: Free Press, 1960.

Bohannan, Paul, ed. Divorce and After: An Analysis of the Emotional and Social Problems of Divorce. Garden City, N.Y.: Doubleday, 1970.

____, and Middleton, John, eds. Marriage, Family and Residence. New York: Natural History Press, 1968.

Bott, Elizabeth. Family and Social Network. 2d ed. London: Tavistock, 1971.

Briffault, R., and Malinowski, B. Marriage: Past and Present. Boston: Porter Sargent, Extending Horizons Books, 1956.

Caird, Mona. The Morality of Marriage and Other Essays on the Status and Destiny of Women. London: George Redway, 1897.

Cavan, Ruth Shonle. The American Family. New York: Thomas Y. Crowell, 1969.

"Changes in the Family." International Social Science Journal 14 (1962):411-549.

Collier, Jane F. "Women in Society: Kinship and Politics." A paper presented at the 71st Annual Meeting of the American Anthropological Association, Toronto, 1972. Mimeo. Stanford University.

Collins, Joseph. The Doctor Looks at Marriage and
   Medicine. Garden City, N.Y.: Doubleday, Doran, 1928.
Coser, Rose L., ed. The Family: Its Structure and
   Functions. New York: St. Martin's Press, 1964.
Crawley, A. E. "Man and Woman." In The Family, ed.
   E. B. Reuter and J. R. Runner. New York: McGraw-
   Hill, 1931.
____. The Mystic Rose: A Study of Primitive Marriage.
   London: Macmillan, 1902.
Dennis, Norman. "Modern Society and the Popularity of
   Marriage." In Comparative Perspectives on Marriage
   and the Family, ed. H. Kent Geiger. Boston: Little,
   Brown, 1968.
Ditzion, Sidney. Marriage, Morals, and Sex in America:
   A History of Ideas. New York: Bookman Associates,
   1953.
Ember, Melvin. "An Archeological Indicator of Matri-
   local vs. Patrilocal Residence." A paper presented
   at the 70th Annual Meeting of the American Anthro-
   pological Association, New York, 1971. Mimeo. Hunter
   College, CUNY.
____, and Ember, Carol R. "The Conditions Favoring
   Matrilocal versus Patrilocal Residence." American
   Anthropologist 73 (1971):571-93.
Engels, F. Origins of the Family, Private Property and
   the State. New York. International, 1942.
Farber, Anne. "Ego and Woman: A New Look at Kinship
   Theory." A paper presented at the 71st Annual Meeting
   of the American Anthropological Association, Toronto,
   1972. Mimeo. Columbia University.
Fishman, Nathaniel. Married Woman's Bill of Rights.
   New York: Liveright, 1943.
Folsom, Joseph Kirk. The Family and the Democratic
   Society. New York: John Wiley, 1943.
Fox, Robin. "Alliance and Constraint: Sexual Selection
   and the Evolution of Human Kinship Systems." In
   Sexual Selection and the Descent of Man, ed. Bernard
   Campbell, pp. 282-331. Chicago: Aldine, 1972.
____. Kinship and Marriage: An Anthropological Pers-
   pective. Baltimore: Penguin Books, 1967.
Funk, Nathalie O. "Social Mobility through Marriage."
   Ph.D. dissertation, University of Chicago, 1969.
Furstenberg, Frank. "Industrialization and the American
   Family: A Look Backward." American Sociological
   Review 31 (June 1966):326-37.
Goncalves, Maria Aparecida Ataliba de Lima. Mulher você.
   Petrópolis: Editôra Vozes, 1967.
Goode, William J. After Divorce. Glencoe, Ill.: Free
   Press, 1956.
____. The Family. Englewood Cliffs, N.J.: Prentice-Hall,
   1964.

___. "Marital Satisfaction and Instability: A Cross-cultural Class Analysis of Divorce Rates." International Social Science Journal 14 (1962):507-26.

___. Women in Divorce. First published, 1946. New York: Free Press, 1965.

___. World Revolution and Family Patterns. New York: Free Press, 1963.

Goody, Jack. "Inheritance, Property, and Marriage in Africa and Eurasia." Sociology 3 (1969):55-76.

___. "Sideways or Downwards? Lateral and Vertical Succession, Inheritance and Descent in Africa and Eurasia." Man, n.s. 5 (1970):627-38.

Gough, Kathleen. "The Nayars and the Definition of Marriage." Journal of the Royal Anthropological Institute 89 (1959):23-34.

___. "The Origin of the Family." Up from Under 1 (1971): 47-52.

Gould, Ethel P. "The Single-Parent Family Benefits in Parents without Partners." Journal of Marriage and the Family 30 (1968):666-70.

Hart, H., and Hart, E. Personality and the Family. Boston: D. C. Heath, 1941.

Hartland, S. "Matrilineal Kinship and the Question of Its Priority." American Anthropological Association Memoir 4, n.d.

Hartley, C. G. The Position of Women in Primitive Society: A Study of the Matriarchy. London: E. Nash, 1914.

Howard, George Elliot. A History of Matrimonial Institutions. 3 vols. New York: Humanities Press, 1964.

✗ Hsu, Francis L. K. "Kinship and Ways of Life: An Exploration." In Psychological Anthropology, pp. 509-72. Cambridge, Mass.: Schenkman, 1972.

James, Henry, and Greeley, Horace. Love, Marriage and Divorce, and the Sovereignty of the Individual: A Discussion between Henry James, Horace Greeley, and Stephen Pearl Andrews. First published, 1853. New York: Collectors Editions, Source Books Press, 1970.

___. Divorce: Being a Correspondence between Horace Greeley and Robert Dale Owen. First published, 1868. New York: Collectors Editions, Source Books Press, 1970.

Jorgensen, Joseph J. G. "Geographical Clusterings and Functional Explanations of In-law Avoidances: An Analysis of Comparative Method." Current Anthropology 7 (1966):161-69.

Keller, Suzanne. Does the Family Have a Future? Reprint 64. Andover, Mass.: Warner Modular Publications, 1973.

Kennedy, Robert Woods. The House and the Art of Its Design. New York: Reinhold, 1953.

Key, Ellen. Love and Marriage. First published, 1914. Reprint, New York: Collectors Editions, Source Books Press, 1970.

___. The Renaissance of Motherhood. First published,
1914. Reprint, New York: Collectors Editions,
Source Books Press, 1970.
Khare, R. S. "Hierarchy and Hypergamy: Some Interrelated
Aspects among the Kanya-Jubja Brahmans." American
Anthropologist 74 (1972):611-28.
Khuri, Foud I. "Parallel Cousin Marriage Reconsidered:
A Middle Eastern Practice That Nullifies the Effects
of Marriage on the Intensity of Family Relationships."
Man 5 (Dec. 1970):597-618.
Klein, Grace, and Cooper, Mae Klein [Farewell, Nina].
Every Girl Is Entitled to a Husband. New York:
McGraw-Hill, 1963.
Kluckhohn, Florence. "The American Family and the
Feminine Role." Human Relations, vol. 1, ed. Hugh
Cabot and Joseph A. Kahl. Cambridge: Harvard
University Press, n.d.
Komarovsky, Mirra. Blue-Collar Marriage. New York:
Random House, 1964.
___. "Blue-Collar Marriage: Barrier to Mental Com-
munication." In Structured Social Inequality: A
Reader in Comparative Social Stratification, ed.
Celia Heller, pp. 276-84. New York: Macmillan, 1967.
___. "Continuities in Family Research: A Case Study."
American Journal of Sociology 62 (July 1956):42-47.
___. Women in the Modern World. Boston: Little,
Brown, 1953.
Koos, Earl. Families in Trouble. New York: King's
Crown Press, 1946.
Kume, A. "Status of Women and the Family System."
United Asia 8 (1956):247-51.
Kunkel, Evalyn J., and Goldschmidt, Walter R. "Female
Roles and Male Dominance among Peasants." A paper
presented at the 69th Annual Meeting of the American
Anthropological Association, San Diego, 1970. Mimeo.
San Fernando Valley State College.
Landes, Ruth, and Zborowski, Mark. "The Context of
Marriage: Family Life as a Field of Emotions." In
Comparative Perspectives on Marriage and the Family,
ed. H. K. Geiger. Boston: Little, Brown, 1968.
Leacock, Eleanor Burke. "Women, Decision-making and the
Evolution of Social Structure." A paper presented at
the 71st Annual Meeting of the American Anthro-
pological Association, Toronto, 1972. Mimeo. City
College, CUNY.
Levi-Strauss, Claude. The Elementary Structures of
Kinship. Boston: Beacon Press, 1969.
Lipset, S. M., and Bendix, R. Social Mobility in
Industrial Society. Berkeley: University of
California Press, 1964.
Lynes, Russell. The Domesticated Americans. New York:
Harper & Row, 1963.

Maccoby, Eleanor E., and Gibbs, Patricia K. "Methods of
    Child-Rearing in Two Social Classes." In Readings in
    Child Development, ed. William E. Martin and Celia B.
    Stendler. New York, 1954.
McLenna, J. F. Primitive Marriage. Edinburgh: Adam &
    Charles Black, 1865.
Maine, H. S. Ancient Law. London: J. Murray, 1861.
Mair, Lucy. Marriage. Baltimore: Penguin Books, 1971.
Massari, C. "Nota sulla probabile età del matriarcato"
    [A note on the probable age of matriarchy]. Revista
    Etnologica 16 (1962):159-61.
Mehta, S. S. "A Consideration of the Position of Women
    in Primitive Society from the Standpoint of Marriage."
    Anthropological Society of Bombay Journal 10 (1917):
    377-99.
Murdock, George Peter. "Correlation of Matrilineal and
    Patrilineal Institutions." Studies in the Science of
    Society, ed. George Peter Murdock, pp. 445-70. New
    Haven: Yale University Press, 1937.
____. Social Structure. New York: Macmillan, 1949.
Myrdal, Gunnar. "A Parallel to the Negro Problem." In
    An American Dilemma: The Negro Problem and Social
    Structure, appendix 5. New York: McGraw-Hill, 1962.
Netting, Robert McC. "Marital Relations in the Jos
    Plateau of Nigeria: Women's Weapons: The Politics of
    Domesticity among the Kofyar." In You and Others:
    Readings in Introductory Anthropology, ed. A. Kimball
    Romney and Paul L. DeVore, pp. 203-11. Cambridge,
    Mass.: Winthrop, 1973.
Nye, F. I., and Berardo, F. M., eds. Emerging Conceptual
    Framework in Family Analysis. New York: Macmillan,
    1966.
O'Neill, William. Divorce in the Progressive Era. New
    Haven: Yale University Press, 1967.
Opler, M. K. "Woman's Social Status and the Forms of
    Marriage." American Journal of Sociology 49 (1943):
    144.
Osmond, Marie Withers. "Toward Monogamy: A Cross-
    cultural Study of Correlates of Types of Marriage."
    Social Forces 44 (1965):8-16.
Papashvily, Helen. All the Happy Endings. First pub-
    lished, 1956. Reprint, Port Washington, N.Y.:
    Kennikat Press, 1971.
* Parsons, Talcott, and Bales, Robert F. Family,
    Socialization and Interaction Process. Glencoe, Ill.:
    Free Press, 1955.
Peter, H. R. H., Prince of Greece and Denmark. Review of
    A Study of Polyandry. Current Anthropology 6 (1965):
    88-104.
____. "Polyandry and the Kinship Group." Man 55 (1955):
    179-81.
Pilpel, Harriet, and Zavin, Theodora. Your Marriage and
    the Law. New York: Macmillan, 1964.

Plautz, W. "Zur Frage des Mutterrechts im Alten Testament" [On the question of matriarchy in the Old Testament]. Zeitschrift für die alttestamentliche Wissenschaft 74 (1962):9-30.

Rainwater, Lee. Family Design: Marital Sexuality, Family Size, and Contraception. Chicago: Aldine, 1965.

Rao, G. R. S. "Emerging Role Pattern of Women in Family." Indian Journal of Social Work 26 (Oct. 1965):329-42.

Rappaport, Philip. Looking Forward: A Treatise on the Status of Woman and the Origin and Growth of the Family and the State. Chicago: C. H. Kerr, 1906.

Ronhaar, J. Woman in Primitive Motherright Societies. London: A. G. Berry, 1931.

Rosenblatt, Paul C. "Marital Residence and the Functions of Romantic Love." Ethnology 6 (1967):471-80.

Rubin, Zick. "Do American Women Marry Up?" American Sociological Review 33 (1968):750-59.

Russell, Bertrand. Marriage and Morals. New York: Liveright, 1929.

Schlegel, Alice. Male Dominance and Female Autonomy: Domestic Authority in Matrilineal Societies. New Haven: Human Relations Area Files Press, 1972.

Schneider, David H., and Gough, Kathleen. Matrilineal Kinship. Berkeley: University of California Press, 1961.

Schulz, David A. The Changing Family: Its Function and Future. Englewood Cliffs, N.J.: Prentice-Hall, 1972.

Schur, Edwin. The Family and the Sexual Revolution. Bloomington: Indiana University Press, 1964.

Scott, John Finley. "The Role of the College Sorority in Endogamy." American Sociological Review 30 (Aug. 1965):514-26.

Seidenberg, Robert. Marriage between Equals: Studies from Life and Literature. Garden City, N.Y.: Doubleday, 1973.
———. Marriage in Life and Literature. New York: Philosophical Library, 1970.

Skolnick, Arlene. "Families Can Be Unhealthy for Children and Other Living Things." Psychology Today, Aug. 1971, p. 18.

Stephens, William N. The Family in Cross-cultural Perspective. New York: Holt, Rinehart & Winston, 1963.

Wake, Charles. The Development of Marriage and Kinship, ed. Rodney Needham. First published, 1889. Chicago: University of Chicago Press, 1967.

Wallin, Paul. "Sex Differences in Attitudes to In-laws: A Test of a Theory." American Journal of Sociology 59 (Mar. 1954):466-69.

Westermarck, E. The History of Human Marriage. 3 vols. London: Macmillan, 1921.

Wolff, Peter H. "The Natural History of a Family." In
Tavistock Seminar on Mother-Infant Interaction:
Determinants of Infant Behavior; Proceedings, 2 vols.,
ed. Brian M. Foss. London: Tavistock Publications,
1961-63.
Young, Philip D. Ngawbe: Tradition and Change among the
Western Guaymí of Panama. Urbana: University of
Illinois Press, 1971.

HOMOSEXUALITY

Abbot, Sydney, and Love, Barbara. Sappho Was a Right-On
Woman. New York: Stein & Day, 1971.
Aldrich, Ann, ed. Carol in a Thousand Cities. New York:
Gold Medal, 1960.
____. We, Too, Must Love. New York: Fawcett World
Library, 1958.
____. We Walk Alone through Lesbos' Lonely Groves. New
York: Fawcett World Library, 1955.
Backett, E. Maurice. "Some Problems of Homosexuality."
In Penguin Science Survey 1965, ed. S. A. Barnett and
Ann McLaren, pp. 134-45. Baltimore: Penguin, 1965.
Beach, Frank A., ed. Sex and Behavior. New York: John
Wiley, 1965.
Benson, Patty. Lesbian Casebook: Women and Young Girls.
Hollywood, Calif.: Cameo Library, n.d.
Bergler, Edmund. "The Respective Importance of Reality
and Fantasy in the Genesis of Female Homosexuality."
Journal of Clinical Psychopathology 5 (1943):27.
Caprio, Frank S. Female Homosexuality. New York:
Citadel Press, 1954.
Cory, Donald Webster [pseud]. The Homosexual in America.
New York: Macfadden Bartell, 1951.
____. The Lesbian in America, intro. Albert Ellis. New
York: Citadel Press, 1964.
Ford, Laura M. Bittersweet: The Autobiography of a
Lesbian. Jericho, N.Y.: Exposition Press, 1969.
Gaultson, Helen. Casebook: Lesbianism and Sexual En-
vironments. Hollywood, Calif.: Cameo Library, n.d.
Humphreys, Laud. Tearoom Trade: Impersonal Sex in
Public Places. Chicago: Aldine, 1970.
Jacobs, Sue-Ellen. "Berdache: A Brief Review of the
Literature." Colorado Anthropologist 1 (1968):25-40.
Landes, Ruth. "A Cult Matriarchate and Male Homo-
sexuality." Journal of Abnormal and Social
Psychology 25 (1940):386-97.
Lepie, Lita. Lost in America: Odyssey of a Radical
Lesbian. Cambridge, Mass.: Bursk & Poor, 1971.
Magee, Bryan. One in Twenty: A Study of Homosexuality
in Men and Women. New York: Stein & Day, 1966.
Martin, Del, and Lyon, Phyllis. Lesbian Woman. New
York: Bantam Books, 1972.

___. "The Realities of Lesbianism." Motive, Mar.-Apr. 1969.

McCaghy, Charles A., and Skipper, James R., Jr. "Lesbian Behavior as an Adaptation to the Occupation of Stripping." Social Problems 17 (1969):262-70.

Pierce, Linda VanBroeke. "Ideologies of the Gay Liberation Movement." A paper presented at the 70th Annual Meeting of the American Anthropological Association, New York, 1971. Mimeo. University of Minnesota.

Querlin, Marise. Women without Men, trans. Malcolm McGraw. New York: Dell, 1965.

Ruitenbeek, Hendrik M., ed. The Problem of Homosexuality in Modern Society. New York: E. P. Dutton, 1963.

Simon, William, and Gagnon, John H. "The Lesbians: A Preliminary Overview." In Sexual Deviance, ed. John H. Gagnon and William Simon. New York: Harper & Row, 1967.

Sonenschein, David. "Homosexuality as a Subject of Anthropological Inquiry." Anthropological Quarterly 39 (1966):73-82.

Stearn, Jess. The Grapevine. Garden City, N.Y.: Doubleday, 1964.

Tanner, John. Sex and the Lesbian. New York: Macfadden-Bartell, 1971.

Ward, David Allen, and Kassebaum, Gene G. Women's Prison: Sex and Social Structure. Chicago: Aldine, 1965.

Wolff, Charlotte. Love between Women. New York: St. Martin's Press, 1971.

MENSTRUATION, PREGNANCY, ABORTION

Alk, Madelin, ed. Expectant Mother. Reprint, New York: Pocket Books, 1969.

Assali, N. S. Biology of Gestation. New York: Academic Press, 1968.

Association for the Study of Abortion. Bibliography Reprint List. Association for the Study of Abortion, 120 West 57 Street, New York, N.Y. 10019.

Auerbach, Aline B., and Arnstein, Helene S. Pregnancy and You. Rev. ed. New York: Department of Child Study Association, 1971.

Ayres, Barbara C. "Pregnancy Magic: A Study of Food Taboos and Sex Avoidances." Cross-cultural Approaches: Readings in Comparative Research, ed. Clellan S. Ford, pp. 111-25. New Haven: Human Relations Area Files Press, 1967.

Baker, Alex Anthony. Psychiatric Disorders in Obstetrics. Oxford: Blackwell Scientific Publications, 1967.

Subject Topics

Balint, Alice. "Psychology of Menstruation." Psycho-
analytic Quarterly 6 (May 1937):346-52.
Bannister, Constance. What to Expect When You're
Expecting. New York: Essandess Special Editions,
1969.
Bates, Jerome E., and Zawadzki, Edward S. Criminal
Abortion: A Study in Medical Sociology. Springfield,
Ill.: Charles C. Thomas, 1964.
Blake, Judith. "The Teenage Birth Control Dilemma and
Public Opinion." Science 180 (May 18, 1973):708-12.
Bleyer, Adrien. Childbearing before and after Thirty-
five: Biologic and Social Implications. A
Statistical Study of the Favored, and Less Favored
Years, for Human Procreation. New York: Vantage
Press, 1958.
Bock, Philip K. "Love Magic, Menstrual Taboos, and the
Facts of Geography." American Anthropologist 69
(1967):213-17.
Browne, Francis J., and Browne, John C. Advice to the
Expectant Mother. 13th ed. Baltimore: Williams &
Wilkins, 1967.
Calderone, Mary S., ed. Abortion in the United States.
Scranton: Harper & Row, Hoeber Medical Division, 1958.
Carrington, William John. Safe Convoy: The Expectant
Mother's Handbook. Philadelphia: J. B. Lippincott,
1944.
Carson, Ruth. Nine Months to Get Ready: The Importance
of Prenatal Care. New York: Public Affairs Committee,
1965.
Carter, Luther J. "New Feminism: Potent Force in Birth-
control Policy." Science 167 (1970):1234-36.
Castallo, Mario Alberto. Expectantly Yours: A Book for
Expectant Mothers and Expectant Fathers. New York:
Macmillan, 1943.
Chadwick, Mary. The Psychological Effects of Menstruation.
New York: Nervous & Mental Disease Publishing, 1932.
Ciba Foundation Study Group. Progesterone and the Defense
Mechanism of Pregnancy. Baltimore: Williams &
Wilkins, 1961.
Collver, Andrew. "Women's Work Participation and
Fertility in Metropolitan Areas." Demography 5 (1968):
55-60.
Colman, A. D. Pregnancy: Psychological Experience. New
York: Herder & Herder, n.d.
Davis, Morris Edward. Natural Child Spacing: The Body
Temperature Method of Child Planning. Garden City,
N.Y.: Hanover House, 1953.
Day, Beth, and Liley, H. I. Modern Motherhood: Preg-
nancy, Childbirth and the Newborn Baby. Rev. ed.
New York: Random House, 1969.
Devereux, George. A Study of Abortion in Primitive
Societies. New York: Julian Press, 1955.

Dick-Read, Grantly. Childbirth without Fear: The
    Principles and Practices of Natural Childbirth. First
    published, 1944. Reprint, New York: Dell, 1962.
Doctor X, The Abortionist. Garden City, N.Y.:
    Doubleday, 1962.
Eastman, Nicholson Joseph. Expectant Motherhood.
    Boston: Little, Brown, 1947.
Ehrman, Winston W. Premarital Dating Behavior. New
    York: Holt, Rinehart & Winston, 1959.
Eisner, Thomas. "Population Controls, Sterilization, and
    Ignorance." Science 167 (1970):1.
Ellis, Havelock. Erotic Symbolism, the Mechanism of
    Detumescence, the Psychic State in Pregnancy.
    Philadelphia: F. A. Davis, 1914.
Eloesser, Leo. Pregnancy, Childbirth, and the Newborn:
    A Manual for Rural Midwives. Mexico City: Instituto
    Indigenista Interamericana, 1959.
Evans, Lily. "What the Medical Profession Doesn't Tell
    Women's Lib." A paper presented at the 70th Annual
    Meeting of the American Anthropological Association,
    New York, 1971. Mimeo. New York University.
Featheringill, Eve S. Primer for Pregnancy: An In-
    formal and Practical Guide for the Expectant Mother.
    New York: Macmillan, 1962.
Fielding, Waldo L. Pregnancy and the Best State of the
    Union. Freeport, Me.: Bond Wheelwright, 1971.
Flanagan, Geraldine L. First Nine Months of Life. New
    York: Pocket Books, n.d.
Flugel, J. C. Men and Their Motives: Psycho-analytical
    Studies. First published, 1934. Reprint, New York:
    International Universities Press, 1947.
    . Population, Psychology, and Peace. London: C. A.
    Watts, 1947.
Food and Nutrition Board. Maternal Nutrition and Child
    Health. Washington, D.C.: National Academy of
    Sciences, 1951.
Ford, Clellan S. A Comparative Study of Human Repro-
    duction. First published, 1945. Reprint, New Haven:
    Yale University, Publications in Anthropology, 1964.
    . Field Guide to the Study of Human Reproduction.
    New Haven: Human Relations Area Files Press, 1964.
Frate, Dennis A. Geophasy: A Dietary Practice in
    Holmes County, Mississippi. Urbana: University of
    Illinois. Center for Advanced Computation, Document
    No. 85, 1973.
Freedman, Lawrence, and Ferguson, Vera M. "The
    Question of 'Painless' Childbirth in Primitive
    Cultures." American Journal of Orthopsychiatry 20
    (1950):363-72.
Fryer, Peter. The Birth Controllers. London: Secker
    & Warburg, 1965.
Fuchs, Fritz, and Klopper, Arnold. Endocrinology of
    Pregnancy. New York: Harper & Row, 1970.

Gallagher, Rory. Lady in Waiting: An Intimate Journal of a Labor of Love. New York: Frederick Ungar, n.d.

Gebhard, Paul H.; Pomeroy, Wardell B.; Martin, Clyde; and Christenson, Cornelia. Pregnancy, Birth, and Abortion. Scranton: Harper & Row, Hoeber Medical Division, 1958.

Goodrich, Frederick Warren. Natural Childbirth: A Manual for Expectant Mothers. New York: Prentice-Hall, 1950.

Grabin, William H., and Davidson, Maria. "Recent Trends in Child Spacing among American Women." Demography 5 (1968):212-25.

Graham, Harvey. Eternal Eve: The History of Gynecology and Obstetrics. Garden City, N.Y.: Doubleday, 1951.

Gray, Madeline. The Normal Woman. New York: Charles Scribner's, 1967.

Guttmacher, Alan F., ed. The Case for Legalized Abortion Now. Berkeley: Diablo Press, 1967.

Hall, Roberta L. "The Demographic Transition: Stage Four." Current Anthropology 13 (Apr. 1972):212-15.

Hamilton, Virginia C. "Medical Status and Psychologic Attitude of Patients following Abortion." American Journal of Obstetrics and Gynecology 41 (1941):285-88.

_____. "Some Observations on the Contraceptive Behavior of Abortion Patients." Human Fertility 5 (1941):37-41.

_____. "Some Sociologic and Psychologic Observations on Abortion." American Journal of Obstetrics and Gynecology 39 (1940):919-29.

Hardin, Garrett. "Abortion--or Compulsory Pregnancy?" Journal of Marriage and the Family 30 (May 1968):2. Reprint, Association for the Study of Abortion, 120 West 57 Street, New York, N.Y. 10019.

_____. "The History and Future of Birth Control." Perspectives in Biology and Medicine 10 (Autumn 1966):1. Reprint, Association for the Study of Abortion, 120 West 57 Street, New York, N.Y. 10019.

_____. "Semantic Aspects of Abortion." ETC 24 (Sept. 1967):3. Reprint, Association for the Study of Abortion, 120 West 57 Street, New York, N.Y. 10019.

Harrell, Ruth Flinn. The Effect of Mothers' Diets on the Intelligence of Offspring: A Study of the Influence of Vitamin Supplementation of the Diets of Pregnant and Lactative Women on the Intelligence of Their Children. New York: Columbia University, Teachers College, 1955.

Havemann, Ernest K. Birth Control. New York: Time-Life Books, 1967.

Heinz, Doris, and Bolt, Katherine Smith. Modeling for Motherhood: Heir Conditioning the Modern Mrs. New York: John Wiley, 1946.

Himes, Norman A. A Medical History of Contraception. First published, 1936. Rev. ed., New York: Gamut Press, 1963.

Hoeft, Douglas L. "A Study of the Unwed Mother in the Public Schools." Journal of Educational Research 61 (Jan. 1968):226-29.

Hudson, Jeffery. A Case of Need. Cleveland: World, 1968.

Hytten, Frank E., and Leitch, Isabella. The Physiology of Human Pregnancy. Oxford: Blackwell Scientific Publications, 1964.

Ibsen, Henrik. "Ghosts" and Two Other Plays. New York: E. P. Dutton, 1911.

Ingelman-Sundberg, Axel, and Wirsen, Claes. A Child Is Born: The Drama of Life before Birth. New York: Dell, Delacorte Press, 1966.

International Conference on Abortion. The Terrible Choice: The Abortion Dilemma. New York: Bantam Books, 1968.

Jayle, Max Fernand. Hormonology of Human Pregnancy. Elmsford, N.Y.: Pergamon Press, 1965.

Karmel, Marjorie. Thank You, Dr. Lamaze. Philadelphia: J. B. Lippincott, 1959.

Kennedy, David M. Birth Control in America: The Career of Margaret Sanger. New Haven: Yale University Press, 1970.

Kim, Taek II; Ross, John A.; and Worth, George C. The Korean National Family Planning Program: Population Control and Fertility Decline. Bridgeport, Conn.: Key Book Service, 1973.

Klein, Henriette R. Anxiety in Pregnancy and Childbirth. Scranton: Harper & Row, Hoeber Medical Division, 1950.

Lader, Lawrence. Abortion. Boston: Beacon Press, 1965. Reprint, Indianapolis: Bobbs-Merrill, 1966.

Lasagna, Louis. Life, Death, and the Doctor. New York: Alfred A. Knopf, 1968.

Lee, Nancy Howell. The Search for an Abortionist. Chicago: University of Chicago Press, 1969.

Lindburg, D. G., and Hazell, Lester Dessez. "Licking of the Neonate and Duration of Labor in Great Apes and Man." American Anthropologist 74 (1972):318-25.

Lipke, Jean. Pregnancy. Minneapolis: Lerner, 1971.

Lucas, Roy. "Federal Constitutional Limitations on the Enforcement and Administration of State Abortion Statutes." North Carolina Law Review 46 (June 1968): 4.

Marshall, John F.; Morris, Susan; and Polgar, Steven. "Culture and Natality: A Preliminary Classified Bibliography." Current Anthropology 13 (Apr. 1972): 268-77.

Marx, Jean L. "Drugs during Pregnancy: Do They Affect the Unborn Child?" Science 180 (1973):74-75.

Matthews, Washington. "Myths of Gestation and Parturition." American Anthropologist 4 (1902):737-42.

May, Edgar. The Wasted Americans. New York: Harper &
    Row, 1964.
Mead, Margaret. The Peaceful Revolution: Birth Control
    and the Changing Status of Women. New York: Planned
    Parenthood-- World Population, 1967.
Meeks, Dorothy K., and Kolafatich, Audrey. Maternal
    and Child Health. Totowa, N.J.: Littlefield, Adams,
    1960.
Mintz, Morton. The Pill: An Alarming Report. Boston:
    Beacon Press, 1970.
Moskin, J. Robert. "The New Contraceptive Society."
    Look, Feb. 4, 1969, pp. 50-53.
Murdock, George Peter. "Post-partum Sex Taboos."
    Paideuma 13 (1967):143-47.
Nag, Moni. Factors Affecting Human Fertility in Nonin-
    dustrial Societies: A Cross-cultural Study. First
    published, 1962. Reprint, New Haven: Human Relations
    Area Files Press, 1968.
Naroll, Frada; Naroll, Raoul; and Howard, Forrest.
    "Position of Women in Childbirth: A Study in Data
    Quality Control." American Journal of Obstetrics and
    Gynecology 82 (1961):943-54.
Neubardt, Selig. A Concept of Contraception. New York:
    Trident Press, 1967.
Newton, Niles. "Childbirth and Culture." Psychology
    Today, Nov. 1970, p. 75.
"The Number of Children Desired at the Time of Marriage."
    Milbank Memorial Fund Quarterly, 1956, pp. 287-312.
Osofsky, Howard J. The Pregnant Teen-ager: A Medical,
    Educational, and Social Analysis. Springfield, Ill.:
    Charles C. Thomas, 1968.
Parker, Elisabeth. Seven Ages of Woman, ed. Evelyn Broch.
    Baltimore: Johns Hopkins Press, 1960.
Petersen, William. The Politics of Population. Garden
    City, N.Y.: Doubleday, 1964.
Phelan, Lana Clarke, and Maginnis, Patricia. The
    Abortion Handbook for Responsible Women. North
    Hollywood, Calif.: Contact Books, 1969.
Pierce, Ruth I. Single and Pregnant. Boston: Beacon
    Press, 1970.
The Pill and Its Impact. Silver Springs, Md.: National
    Observer Newsbook, 1966.
Polgar, Steven. "Population History and Population
    Policies from an Anthropological Perspective." Current
    Anthropology 13 (Apr. 1972):203-11.
Rains, Prudence. Becoming an Unwed Mother: The
    Sociological Features of a Deviant Career. Chicago:
    Aldine, 1971.
Rainwater, Lee, and Weinstein, Karol. And the Poor Get
    Children. New York: Quadrangle Books, 1960.
Raphael, Dana. "The Lactation-suckling Process within a
    Matrix of Supportive Behavior." Ph.D. dissertation,
    Columbia University, 1966.

___. The Tender Gift: Breastfeeding. Englewood Cliffs, N.J.: Prentice-Hall, 1973.

Ratcliff, John Drury. Birth: New Medical Discoveries about Conception, Pregnancy and Childbirth. New York: Dodd, Mead, 1951.

Rodgers, David A., and Ziegler, Frederick J. "Social Role Theory: The Mental Relationship, and the Use of Ovulation Suppressers." Journal of Marriage and the Family 30 (Nov. 1968):584-91.

Roosevelt, Anna Eleanor, and Doyle, Leo. Your Pregnancy. New York: Holt, Rinehart & Winston, 1950.

Rosen, Harold, ed. Abortion in America. Boston: Beacon Press, 1970.

Rossi, Alice S. "Abortion and Social Change." Dissent, July-Aug. 1969.

___. "Abortion Laws and Their Victims." Transaction 3 (Sept.-Oct. 1966):7-12. Reprint, Association for the Study of Abortion, 120 West 57 Street, New York, N.Y. 10019.

Roth, Dennis M., and Urbanowitz, Charles F. "Scale Analysis of the Elaboration of Menstrual Taboos." A paper presented at the 67th Annual Meeting of the American Anthropological Association, 1968. Mimeo. University of Oregon, Portland.

Rugh, Roberts, and Shettles, Lardrum B. From Conception to Birth: The Drama of Life's Beginning. New York: Harper & Row, 1971.

Sadler, William Samuel. The Mother and Her Child. Chicago: A. C. McClurg, 1916.

Saucier, Jean-François. "Correlates of the Long Post-partum Taboo: A Cross-cultural Study." Current Anthropology 13 (Apr. 1972):238-48.

Schenk, Roy U. "Let's Think about Abortion." The Catholic World 207 (Apr. 1968):1237.

Schur, Edwin M. "Abortion." Annals of the American Academy of Political and Social Science 376 (Mar. 1968).

___. "Abortion and the Social System." Social Problems (Oct. 1955):94-99.

Scrimshaw, Susan. "The Demand for Female Sterilization in Spanish Harlem: Experiences of Puerto Ricans in New York City." A paper presented at the 69th Annual Meeting of the American Anthropological Association, San Diego, 1970. Mimeo. Columbia University.

Seligmann, Charles C. "Birth and Childhood Customs." Reports of the Cambridge Anthropological Expedition to the Torres Straits 5 (1904):194-200.

Seminar on Childbearing and Family Life: Prelude to Action. New York: Maternity Center, 1969.

Semmens, James P. Teen-age Pregnancy: Including Management of Emotional and Constitutional Problems. Springfield, Ill.: Charles C. Thomas, 1968.

Sherbon, Florence. The Child: His Origin, Development and Care. New York: McGraw-Hill, 1939.

Skultans, Vieda. "The Symbolic Significance of Menstruation and the Menopause." Man 5 (Dec. 1970): 639-51.

Smith, David L. Abortion and the Law. Cleveland: Press of Case Western Reserve University, 1967.

Stephens, William N. "A Cross-cultural Study of Menstrual Taboos." Genetic Psychological Monographs 64 (1961):385-416. Reprinted in Cross-cultural Approaches: Readings in Comparative Research, ed. Clellan S. Ford, pp. 67-94. New Haven: Human Relations Area Files Press, 1967.

Stevens, Barbara C. Marriage and Fertility of Women Suffering from Schizophrenia or Affective Disorders. New York: Oxford University Press, 1969.

Strean, Lyon P. Birth of Normal Babies. New York: Twayne, 1958.

Stycos, J. Mayonne, and Weller, Robert H. "Female Working Roles and Fertility." Demography 4 (1967): 210-17.

Tanzer, Deborah. "Natural Childbirth: Pain or Peak Experience?" Psychology Today 2 (Oct. 1968):2.

TenBerge, B. S., ed. Pregnancy. Springfield, Ill.: Charles C. Thomas, 1965.

Thompson, Richard W., and Robbins, Michael C. "Seasonal Variation in Conception in Rural Uganda and Mexico." American Anthropologist 75 (1973):676-86.

Tien, H. Yuan. "Mobility, Non-familial Activity and Fertility." Demography 4 (1967):218-27.

Wertenbaker, Lael Tucker. The Afternoon Women. New York: Bantam Books, 1970.

Westhoff, Charles. "The Structure of Attitudes toward Abortion." Milbank Memorial Fund Quarterly 47 (Jan. 1969):11-37.

White, Robert B. "Induced Abortions: A Survey of Their Psychiatric Implications, Complications, and Indications." Texas Reports of Biology and Medicine 24 (Winter 1966):531-58. Reprint, Association for the Study of Abortion, 120 West 57 Street, New York, N.Y. 10019.

Wilson, H. Clyde. "On the Origin of Menstrual Taboos." American Anthropologist 66 (1964):622-25.

Woodside, Moya. "Attitudes of Women Abortionists." Howard Journal 11 (1962):2.

Young, Frank W., and Bacdayan, Albert. "Menstrual Taboos and Social Rigidity." Ethnology 4 (1965): 225-40. Reprinted in Cross-cultural Approaches: Readings in Comparative Research, ed. Clellan S. Ford, pp. 95-110. New Haven: Human Relations Area Files Press, 1967.

PROSTITUTION

Abreu, Waldyr de. O submundo da prostitucão, vadiagem e jôgo do bicho aspectos socials, juridicos e psicológicos. Rio de Janeiro: Freitas Bastos, 1968.

Ackon, William. Prostitution. First published, 1857. Reprint, New York: Frederick A. Praeger, 1969.

Addams, Jane. A New Conscience and an Ancient Evil. New York: Macmillan, 1912.

Adler, Polly. A House Is Not a Home. New York: Rinehart, 1953.

Amelunxen, Clemen S. Der Zuhälter Wandlungen eines Tätertyps. Hamburg: Kriminalistek Verlag, 1967.

Avril de Sainte-Croix, Ghenia. League of Nations: Traffic in Women and Children. Report on the International Women's Associations. Geneva: Imprimerie Kundig, 1925.

Barday, Stephen. Bondage: The Slave Traffic in Women Today. New York: Funk & Wagnalls, 1968.

Bauer, Bernhard A. Women and Love. 2 vols. First published, 1949. Reprint, New York: Liveright, 1971.

Benjamin, Harry. Prostitution and Morality: A Definitive Report on the Prostitute in Contemporary Society and an Analysis of the Causes and Effects of the Suppression of Prostitution. New York: Julian Press, 1964.

Broughton, Philip Stephens. Prostitution and the War. New York: Public Affairs Committee, 1942.

Bullough, Vern L. The History of Prostitution. New Hyde Park, N.Y.: University Books, 1964.

Burgess, William. The World's Social Evil: A Historical Review and Study of the Problems Relating to the Subject. Chicago: Saul, 1914.

Chesser, Eustace. Live and Let Live: The Moral of the Wolfenden Report. London: Heinemann, 1958.

Chicago Vice Commission. The Social Evil in Chicago. First published, 1911. Reprint, New York: Arno Press, 1970.

Clark, William Lloyd. Hell at Midnight in Springfield: or, a Burning History of the Sin and Shame of the Capital City of Illinois. 4th ed. Milan, Ill:: Truth & Light, 1914.

Clouzet, Maryse. Psychoanalysis of the Prostitute. New York: Philosophical Library, 1961.

Cobden, John C. White Slaves of England. First published, 1860. Reprint, London: Mellicent Press, 1971.

Cousins, Sheila [pseud.]. To Beg I Am Ashamed. New York: Vanguard, 1938.

Cross, Harold H. U. The Lust Market. 3d ed. New York: Citadel Press, 1965.

Elliot, Albert Wells. The Cause of the Social Evil, and the Remedy. Atlanta: Webb & Vary, 1914.

161

Esselstyn, T. C. "Prostitution in the U.S." Annals of
the American Academy of Political and Social Science.
376 (Mar. 1968).
Feitz, Leland. A Quick History of Cripple Creek's Red
Light District. Denver: Golden Bell Press, 1968.
Fiaux, Louis. La police des moeurs devant la commission
extraparlementaire du régime des moeurs. Paris: F.
Alcan, 1907-10.
Fille de joie: The Book of Courtesans, Sporting Girls,
Ladies of the Evening, Madams, a Few Occasionals and
Some Royal Favorites. New York: Grove Press, 1967.
Flexner, Abraham. Prostitution in Europe. Montclair,
N.J.: Smith, Patterson, 1914.
Forjaz de Sampaio, Albino. O livro das courtesãs:
antologià de poetas portugueses e brasileiros.
Lisbon: Guimarães, 1920.
France. Ministere des Affaires Etrangères. Documents
diplomatiques. Conférence internationale pour la
répression de la traite des blanches. Paris:
Imprimerie Nationale, 1902.
Funk, John Clarence. Vice and Health: Problems,
Situations. Philadelphia: J. B. Lippincott, 1921.
Gauthier-Villars, Henry. Les bazars de la volupté.
Paris: Editions Montaigne, 1930.
Gentry, Curt. The Madams of San Francisco: An Ir-
reverent History of the City by the Golden Gate.
Garden City, N.Y.: Doubleday, 1969.
Glover, Edward. The Psycho-pathology of Prostitution.
London: Institute for the Study and Treatment of
Delinquency, 1945.
Gould, George, ed. Digest of State and Federal Laws
Dealing with Prostitution and Other Sex Offenses,
with Notes on the Control of the Sale of Alcoholic
Beverages as It Relates to Prostitution Activities.
New York: American Social Hygiene Association, 1942.
Great Britain. Committee on Homosexual Offences and
Prostitution. The Wolfenden Report. New York:
Stein & Day, 1962.
Greenwald, Harold. The Call Girl: A Social and
Psychoanalytic Study. First published, 1958. Re-
print, New York: Walker, 1970.
___. The Elegant Prostitute: A Social and Psycho-
analytic Study. New York: Ballantine, 1970.
Guyot, Yves. La prostitution. Paris: G. Charpentier,
1882.
Harland, Robert O. The Vice Bondage of a Great City:
or, the Wickedest City in the World. Chicago:
Young People's Civic League, 1912.
Harris, Sara. House of the Ten Thousand Pleasures: A
Modern Study of the Geisha and of the Streetwalker
of Japan. New York: E. P. Dutton, 1962.
Hay-Cooper, L. Josephine Butler and Her Work for Social
Purity. New York: Macmillan, 1922.

Hayward, C. The Courtesan: The Part She Has Played in Classic and Modern Literature and in Life. London: Casanova Society, 1926.

Henriques, Fernando. Prostitution and Society: A Survey. London: MacGibbon & Kee, 1962.

———. Stews and Strumpets: A Survey of Prostitution. London: MacGibbon & Kee, 1961.

International Agreement for the Suppression of the White Slave Traffic, Signed at Paris on 18 May 1904, Amended by the Protocol Signed at Lake Success, New York, 4 May 1949. Lake Success, N.Y.: United Nations Publications, 1950.

James, Jennifer. "Street Research: Prostitutes." A paper presented at the 70th Annual Meeting of the American Anthropological Association, New York, 1971. Mimeo. University of Washington.

Janney, Oliver Edward. The White Slave Traffic in America. New York: National Vigilance Committee, 1911.

Jeannel, Julien François. De la prostitution dans les grandes villes au deux-neuvième siècle et de l'extinction des maladies vénériennes, questions générales d'hygiène, de moralité publique. Paris: J. B. Baillière, 1868.

Kemp, Tage. Prostitution: An Investigation of Its Causes, Especially with Regard to Hereditary Factors. Copenhagen: Levin & Muhksgaard, 1936.

Kimball, Nell. Nell Kimball: Her Life as an American Madam, ed. Stephen Longstreet. New York: Macmillan, 1970.

Kneeland, George Jackson. Commercialized Prostitution in New York City. New York: Century, 1913.

Kumar, P. "Prostitution: A Socio-psychological Analysis." Indian Journal of Social Work 21 (Mar. 1961):425-30.

Lacroix, Paul. Geschichte der Prostitution. Berlin: J. Gnadenfeld, 1902.

———. History of Prostitution among All the Peoples of the World, from the Most Remote Antiquity to the Present Day, trans. Samuel Putnam. Chicago: P. Covici, 1926.

Lombroso, Cesare. Female Offender. New York: Philosophical Library, 1958.

Long, Mason. Save the Girls. Fort Wayne, Ind.: M. Long, 1888.

Longstreet, Stephen. Sportin' House: A History of the New Orleans Sinners and the Birth of Jazz. Los Angeles: Sherbourne Press, 1965.

McManus, Virginia. Not for Love. New York: G. P. Putnam, 1960.

Madeleine: An Autobiography. New York: Harper, 1919.

Marchant, James. The Master Problem. New York: Moffat, Yard, 1917.

Mayorca, Juan Manuel. Introducción al estudio de la prostitución. Caracas: Talleres de Gráfica Americana, 1967.

Murtagh, John M., and Harris, Sarah. Cast the First Stone. New York: McGraw-Hill, 1957.

Niemoeller, Adolph Fredrick. Sexual Slavery in America. New York: Panurge Press, 1935.

O'Callaghan, Sean. Damaged Baggage: The White Slave Trade and Narcotics Trafficking in the Americas. New York: Roy, 1970.

Pallavicino, Ferrante. Whore's Rhetorick. New York: Astor-Honor, 1961.

Passman, Hanns. Der Typus der Kurtisane im Elisabetha-nischen Drama. Borna-Leipzig: R. Noske, 1926.

Penzer, N. M. "Sacred Prostitution." In Poison-Damsels and Other Essays in Folklore and Anthropology, ed. N. M. Penzer, pp. 131-84. London: Charles J. Sawyer, 1952.

Powell, Hickmann. Ninety Times Guilty. New York: Harcourt, Brace, 1939.

Reckless, Walter Cade. Vice in Chicago. Chicago: University of Chicago Press, 1933.

Reitman, Ben Lewis. The Second Oldest Profession: A Study of the Prostitute's "Business Manager." New York: Vanguard Press, 1931.

Report of the Hartford Vice Commission. Hartford, Conn., 1913.

Robinson, William Josephus. The Oldest Profession in the World: Prostitution, Its Underlying Causes, Its Treatment and Its Future. New York: Eugenics, 1929.

Sanger, William W. The History of Prostitution: Its Extent, Causes and Effects throughout the World. New York: Medical Publishing, 1919.

Schreiber, Hermann. The Oldest Profession: A History of Prostitution, trans. James Cleugh. New York: Stein & Day, 1968.

Scott, George Dyley. A History of Prostitution from Antiquity to the Present Day. New York: Greenberg, 1936.

Seymour-Smith, Marhn. Fallen Women: A Skeptical En-quiry into the Treatment of Prostitutes, Their Clients, and Their Pimps, in Literature. New York: Inter-national Publications Service, 1970.

Spingarn, Arthur Barnett. Laws Relating to Sex Morality in New York City. New York: Century, 1926.

Stearn, Jess. Sisters of the Night: The Startling Story of Prostitution in New York Today. New York: Julian Messner, 1956.

Tappan, Paul Wilbur. Delinquent Girls in Court: A Study of the Wayward Minor Court of New York. New York: Columbia University Press, 1947.

U.N. Department of Economic and Social Affairs. Study of Traffic in Persons and Prostitution. Suppression of the Traffic in Persons and of the Exploitation of the Prostitution of Others. New York: United Nations Publication, 1959.

U.S. Public Health Service. What Representative Citizens Think about Prostitution. Washington, D.C.: U.S. Government Printing Office, 1927.

Warren, John H., Jr. Thirty Years' Battle with Crime; or, the Crying Shame of New York, as Seen under the Broad Glare of an Old Detective's Lantern. First published, 1875. Reprint, New York: Arno Press, 1970.

Waterman, Willoughby Cyrus. "Prostitution and Its Repression in New York City, 1900-1931." Master's thesis, Columbia University, 1932.

Willson, Robert Newton. The American Boy and the Social Evil, from a Physician's Standpoint. Philadelphia: J. C. Winston, 1905.

Wilson, Paul. Sexual Dilemma: Abortion, Homosexuality, Prostitution, and the Criminal Threshold. Portland, Ore.: International Scholarly Book Services, n.d.

Winick, Charles, and Kinsie, Paul M. The Lively Commerce: Prostitution in the United States. Chicago: Quadrangle Books, 1971.

Woolston, Howard B. Prostitution in the United States Prior to the Entrance of the United States into the World War. First published, 1921. Reprint, Montclair, N.J.: Patterson Smith, 1969.

Worthington, George E., and Topping, Ruth. Specialized Courts Dealing with Sex Delinquency: A Study of the Procedure in Chicago, Boston, Philadelphia and New York. New York: F. H. Hitchcock, 1925.

WOMEN AND RELIGION

Achtemeier, Elizabeth. Feminine Crisis in Christian Faith. Nashville: Abingdon Press, 1965.

Anderson, Evelyn M. It's a Woman's Privilege. Grand Rapids: Baker Book House, 1970.

Ardener, Edwin. "Belief and the Problem of Woman." In The Interpretation of Ritual, ed. J. S. LaFontaine, pp. 135-58. London: Tavistock, 1972.

Beaver, R. Pierce. All Loves Excelling. Grand Rapids: William B. Eerdmans, 1968.

Bocke, E. Wilbur. "The Female Clergy: A Case of Professional Marginality." American Journal of Sociology 72 (Mar. 1967):5.

Brunner, Peter. Ministry and the Ministry of Women. St. Louis: Concordia, 1971.

Chappell, Clovis G. Feminine Faces. Nashville: Abingdon Press, 1942.

Culver, Elsie Thomas. Women in the World of Religion. Garden City, N.Y.: Doubleday, 1967.

Cuneen, Sally S. Sex: Female, Religion: Catholic. New York: Holt, Rinehart & Winston, 1968.

Subject Topics

Daly, Mary. The Church and the Second Sex. New York:
Harper & Row, 1968.
Deen, Edith. All of the Women of the Bible. New York:
Harper & Row, 1955.
___. Bible's Legacy for Womanhood. New York:
Doubleday, 1970.
Deherme, Georges. Le pouvoir social des femmes. Paris:
Perrin, 1914.
De Lubac, Henry. Eternal Feminine. New York: Harper
& Row, 1971.
Douglas, Mary. Natural Symbols: Explorations in
Cosmology. London: Barrie and Rockliff, 1970.
___. Purity and Danger. London: Routledge and Kegan
Paul, 1966.
Drury, Clifford M. First White Women over the Rockies.
3 vols. Glendale, Calif.: Arthur H. Clark, 1956.
Faherty, William. The Destiny of Modern Woman in the
Light of Papal Teaching. Westminister, Md.: Newman
Press, 1952.
Farnell, L. R. "Sociological Hypotheses Concerning the
Position of Women in Ancient Religion." Archiv für
Religionswissenschaft 7 (1904):23-29.
Foster, Warren Dunham, ed. Heroines of Modern Religion.
Freeport, N.Y.: Books for Libraries Press, 1970.
Gage, Matilda Joslyn. Woman, Church, and State: A
Historical Account. New York: Truth Seeker, 1893.
Gibson, Elsie. When the Minister Is a Woman. New York:
Holt, Rinehart & Winston, 1970.
Harkness, Georgia. Women in Church and Society.
Nashville: Abingdon Press, 1971.
Hunt, Gladys. Does Anyone Here Know God? Grand Rapids:
Zondervan, 1968.
Kuyper, Abraham. Women of the New Testament. Grand
Rapids: Zondervan, 1968.
___. Women of the Old Testament. Grand Rapids:
Zondervan, 1968.
Leach, Edmund R. "Magical Hair." Journal of the Royal
Anthropological Institute (1958):147-64.
Lewis, I. M. Ecstatic Religion: An Anthropological
Study of Spirit Possession and Shamanism. Harmonds-
worth: Penguin Books, 1971.
Lindenbaum, Shirley. "Sorcerers, Ghosts, and Polluting
Women: An Analysis of Religious Belief and Population
Control." Ethnology 11 (1972):241-53.
Lockyer, Herbert. Women of the Bible. Grand Rapids:
Zondervan, 1967.
Lowie, Robert H. "Women and Religion." In The Making
of Men: An Outline of Anthropology, ed. F. V.
Calverton, pp. 744-57. New York: Modern Library,
1931.
Lundholm, Algot T. Women of the Bible. Philadelphia:
Fortress Press, 1948.

Marshall, Zona B. Certain Women. Jericho, N.Y.:
  Exposition Press, 1960.
Murrell, Gladys. Glimpses of Grace. Nashville:
  Abingdon Press, Apex Books, 1948.
Nelson, Martha. Christian Woman in the Working World.
  Nashville: Broadman Press, 1970.
Nelson, Ruth Y. Christian Women: Ten Programs for
  Women's Organization. Philadelphia: Fortress Press,
  1951.
Nyberg, Kathleen N. New Eve. Nashville: Abingdon
  Press, 1967.
Ockenga, Harold J. Women Who Made Bible History. Grand
  Rapids: Zondervan, 1971.
Patai, Raphael. "The Goddess Cult in Hebrew-Jewish
  Religion." Mimeo distributed at the 9th Inter-
  national Congress of Anthropological and Ethnological
  Sciences, Chicago, 1973.
Pinkham, Mildred Worth. Women in the Sacred Scriptures
  of Hinduism. New York: AMS Press, 1967.
Pitt-Rivers, Julian. "Women and Sanctuary in the
  Mediterranean." In Echanges et Communications, ed.
  Jean Pouillon and P. Maranda, II, 862-75. Paris:
  Mouton, 1970.
Rappaport, Roy. "Ritual, Sanctity, and Cybernetics."
  American Anthropologist 73 (1971):59-76.
Ryrie, Charles C. Role of Women in the Church. Chicago:
  Moody Press, 1968.
Sapir, J. David. "Kujaama: Symbolic Separation among
  the Diola-Fogny." American Anthropologist 72 (1970):
  1330-48.
Scudder, Vida D. The Church and the Hour: Reflections
  of a Socialist Churchwoman. New York: E. P. Dutton,
  1917.
Stendahl, Krister. Bible and the Role of Women.
  Philadelphia: Fortress Press, 1966.
Swantz, Marja-Liisa. Ritual and Symbol in Transitional
  Zaramo Society: With Special Reference to Women.
  Uppsala, Sweden: Studia Missionalia Upsalrensia XVI,
  1970.
Thrall, Margaret E. Ordination of Women to the Priest-
  hood. Naperville, Ill.: Alex R. Allenson, 1958.
Thurber, Cheryl. "Sex Differentiation in Religious
  Movements." A paper presented at the 70th Annual
  Meeting of the American Anthropological Association,
  New York, 1971. Mimeo. University of British
  Columbia.
Ulanov, Ann B. Feminine in Jungian Psychology and in
  Christian Theology. Evanston: Northwestern University
  Press, 1971.
van der Velde, Frances. She Shall Be Called Woman. First
  published, 1957. Reprint, Grand Rapids: Kregel, 1971.
Watts, Alan. Nature, Man, and Woman. New York:
  Pantheon, 1958.

WOMEN IN PRISON

Colebrook, Joan. The Cross of Lassitude. New York:
Alfred A. Knopf, 1967.

Deming, Barbara. Prison Notes. New York: Grossman,
1966.

DeRham, Edith. How Could She Do That? A Study of the
Female Criminal. New York: C. N. Potter, 1969.

Giallombardo, Rose. "Social Roles in a Prison for
Women." Social Problems 13 (Winter 1966):268-88.
___. Society of Women: A Study of a Women's Prison.
New York: John Wiley, 1966.

Lytton, Constance. Prisons and Prisoners: Some Personal Experience. London: Heinemann, 1914.

Pollak, Otto. The Criminality of Women. Philadelphia:
University of Pennsylvania Press, 1950.

Pringle, Patrick. Prisoner's Friend. New York: Roy,
n.d.

Sparrow, Gerald. Women Who Murder. New York: Abelard-
Schuman, 1970.

Ward, David, and Kassebaum, Gene G. Women's Prison: Sex
and Social Structure. Chicago: Aldine, 1971.

Wulffen, Erich. Woman as a Sexual Criminal. New York:
Falstaff Press, 1935.

POLITICAL ROLES, POWER, LEGAL STATUS
OF WOMEN(INCLUDES MATRIARCHY)

Acworth, Evelyn. New Matriarchy. Mystic, Conn.:
Lawrence Verry, 1965.

Alland, Alexander, Jr. Review of The Imperial Animal, by
Lionel Tiger and Robin Fox. American Anthropologist
75 (1973):1147-48.

Amundsen, Kirsten. The Silenced Majority: Women and
American Democracy. Englewood Cliffs, N.J.: Prentice-
Hall, 1971.

Anderson, Jack. "Washington Wives: How Much Should They
Talk?" Parade, Feb. 1970, p.1.

Aswad, Barbara C. "Key and Peripheral Roles of Nobel
Women in a Middle Eastern Plains Village." Anthropological Quarterly 40 (1967):139-52.

Bachofen, Johann J. Myth, Religion and Mother Right:
Selected Writings of Johann Jakob Bachofen. Princeton:
Princeton University Press, 1967.

Banks, Joseph A., and Banks, Olive. "Feminism and Social
Change." In Explorations in Social Change, ed. G. K.
Zollschan and W. Hirsch. Boston: Houghton Mifflin,
1964.

Bayles, George James, ed. Woman and New York Law. New
York: Law Press, 1911.

Beard, Mary Ritter. Woman as Force in History: A Study
in Traditions and Realities. New York: Macmillan,
1946.

Bebel, August. *Women under Socialism,* intro. Lewis A. Coser. Studies in the Life of Women Series. New York: Schocken Books, 1970.

Beckman, Gail. "Do Our Tax Laws Satisfy the Needs of the Working Woman?" *Women Lawyers Journal* 53 (Winter 1967):5-9.

Benedictis, Daniel J. de. *Legal Rights of Married Women.* New York: Cornerstone Library, 1969.

Bernard, Jessie. *Women and the Public Interest: An Essay on Policy and Protest.* Chicago: Aldine, 1971.

Boyd, Mary Brown Summer. *The Woman Citizen: A General Handbook of Civics with Special Consideration of Women's Citizenship.* New York: Frederick A. Stokes, 1918.

Briffault, Robert. *The Mothers: The Matriarchal Theory of Social Origins.* New York: Macmillan, 1931.

Bruce, H. Addington. *Woman in the Making of America.* Boston: Little, Brown, 1912.

Campbell, Angus. *The American Voter: An Abridgement.* New York: John Wiley, 1964.

Campbell, Enid. "Women and the Exercise of Public Functions." *Adelaide Law Review* 1 (1960-62):190-204.

Clignet, Remi. *Many Wives, Many Powers: Authority and Power in Polygynous Families.* Evanston: Northwestern University Press, 1970.

"La condition sociale et le statut juridique de la femme dans les pays de civilisations différentes [Social condition and legal status of women in countries with differing civilizations]." *Civilizations* 1 (1951): 9-68.

DuVerger, Maurice. *The Political Role of Women.* Paris: UNESCO Publications, 1955.

Evan, William M. "Dimensions of Participation in Voluntary Associations." *Social Forces* 36 (Dec. 1957):2.

Forman, Samuel Eagle. *The Woman Voter's Manual.* New York: Century, 1918.

Francis, Philip. *Legal Status of Women.* Dobbs Ferry, N.Y.: Oceana, 1963.

Fried, Morton H. *The Evolution of Political Society: An Essay in Political Anthropology.* New York: Random House, 1967.

Froman, Lewis. "Personality and Political Socialization." *Journal of Politics* 23 (1961):341-52.

Frumkin, Samuel. *A Women's Party.* London: E. Goldston, 1936.

Gehlen, Frieda L. "Women in Congress." *Transaction* 6 (Oct. 1969):36-40.

Greenstein, Fred I. "Sex-Related Political Differences in Childhood." *Journal of Politics* 25 (May 1961):353-71.

Gruberg, Martin. *Women in American Politics: An Assessment and Sourcebook.* Oshkosh: Academia Press, 1968.

Gusfield, Joseph R. Symbolic Crusade: Status Politics and the American Temperance Movement. Urbana: University of Illinois Press, 1963.

Haynes, M. "Fettered and Stunted by Patriarchy." Saturday Review 47 (Aug. 29, 1970):22-23, 28-29.

Hirvonen, Kaarle. Matriarchal Survivals and Certain Trends in Homer's Female Characters. Helsinki: Annales Academiae Secrentiarum Fennicae, 1968.

Hollister, Horace A. The Woman Citizen. New York: Appleton, 1918.

Hyman, Herbert. Political Socialization. Glencoe, Ill.: Free Press, 1959.

I.L.O. and Women. Geneva: International Labour Organization, 1953.

Inman, Mary. Woman Power. Los Angeles: Committee to Organize the Advancement of Women, 1942.

Jacobs, Sue-Ellen. "Women's Power: Real and Potential." A paper presented at the American Association of University Women, Fall Conference, 1972. Mimeo. University of Illinois.

Kagan, E. "Women." Adult Leadership 13 (Nov. 1964): 147-48.

Kanowitz, Leo. "Constitutional Aspects of Sex-based Discrimination in American Law." Nebraska Law Review 48 (Nov. 1968):131-82.

_____. "Legal Status of American Women." Family Law Quarterly 2 (1968):121-63.

_____. "Sex-based Discrimination in American Law: Law and the Single Girl." St. Louis University Law Journal 11 (Spring 1967):293-330; 12 (Fall 1967):3-73.

_____. "Sex-based Discrimination in American Law: Title VII 1964 of the Civil Rights Act and Equal Pay Act 1963." Hastings Law Journal 20 (Nov. 1968):305-60.

_____. Women and the Law: The Unfinished Revolution. Albuquerque: University of New Mexico Press, 1969.

Kelly, Amy. Eleanor of Aquitaine and the Four Kings. New York: Vintage Books, 1958.

Killham, John. Tennyson and the Princess: Reflections of an Age. London: Athlone, 1958.

Kulczycki, J. "Teoria matriarchatu w swietle prac radzieckich" [The theory of matriarchy in the work of Soviet ethnographers and archaeologists]. Lud 41 (1955):36-65.

Lamson, Peggy. Few Are Chosen. Boston: Houghton Mifflin, 1968.

Lipset, S. M. "The Psychology of Voting." In Handbook of Social Psychology, ed. G. Lindzey, pp. 1124-74. Reading, Mass.: Addison-Wesley, 1954.

Lucena, Luis de. Repetición de amores, ed. Jacob Ornstein. Chapel Hill: University of North Carolina Press, 1954.

Lutz, Alma. Crusade for Freedom: Women of the Antislavery Movement. Boston: Beacon Press, 1968.

McClees, Helen. A Study of Women in Attic Inscriptions. New York: Columbia University Press, 1920.

McVeety, Dean. "Law and the Single Woman." Woman Lawyers Journal 53 (Winter 1967):10-14.

Miller, Robert Stephans. "Sex Discrimination and Title VII of the Civil Rights Act of 1964." Minnesota Law Review 5 (Apr. 1967):877-97.

Morris, Richard B. Studies in the History of American Law. Philadelphia: J. M. Mitchell, 1959.

———. Studies in the History of American Law, with Special Reference to the Seventeenth and Eighteenth Centuries. New York: Columbia University Press, 1930.

Murray, Pauli, and Eastwood, Mary. "Jane Crow and the Law: Sex Discrimination and Title VII." George Washington Law Review 34 (Dec. 1965):232-56.

"My Lady Fair." Adult Leadership 18 (May 1969):32-36.

Newton, Esther; Webster, Paula; and Walton-Fischler, Shirley. "Matriarchy: Myth and Reality." A paper presented at the 71st Annual Meeting of the American Anthropological Association, Toronto, 1972. Mimeo. SUNY, Purchase.

Oldam, James C. "Sex Discrimination and State Protective Laws." Denver Law Review 44 (Summer 1967):344.

Philadelphia Women's Anthropology Collective. "Power and Participation in Feminist Organizations." A paper presented at the 71st Annual Meeting of the American Anthropological Association, Toronto, 1972. Mimeo. University of Pennsylvania.

Post, Alice. "The Role of Woman in the New Internationalism." National Educational Association of the U.S. Addresses and Proceedings, 1918, p. 74-77. Washington, D.C.: U.S. Government Printing Office, 1918.

Rachin, Helen. "Urban Institutions and Women's Leadership." Adult Leadership 18 (May 1969):22-26.

Rembaugh, Berta, ed. The Political Status of Women. New York: G. P. Putman, 1911.

Roosevelt, Anna Eleanor. It's up to the Women. New York: Frederick A. Stokes, 1933.

Root, Grace C. Women and Repeal: The Story of the Women's Organization for National Prohibition Reform. New York: Harper & Row, 1934.

Sampson, Ronald V. The Psychology of Power. New York: Pantheon Books, 1965.

Schlegel, Alice. Male Dominance and Female Autonomy: Domestic Authority in Matrilineal Societies. New Haven: Human Relations Area Files Press, 1972.

Schoepf, Brooke Grundfest, and Mariotti, Amelia M. "Personal and Political: Anthropology, Marxism and Women's Liberation." In Cross Cultural Perspectives on the Women's Movement, ed. Ruby Leavitt. The Hague: Mouton, in press.

Scott, Anne Firor, ed. The American Woman: Who Was She? Englewood Cliffs, N.J.: Prentice-Hall, 1971.

Slater, Carol. "Class Differences in Definition of Role and Membership in Voluntary Associations among Urban Women." American Journal of Sociology 65 (1961): 616-59.

Smith, Dorothy A. Justice Is a Woman. Philadelphia: Dorrance, 1966.

Tait, Marjorie. The Education of Women for Citizenship: Some Practical Suggestions. Paris: UNESCO Publications, 1954.

Taylor, Grace E. W. "Jury Service for Women." University of Florida Law Review 12 (1959):224-31.

Thayer, William M. Women Who Win; or, Making Things Happen. New York: Thomas Nelson, 1896.

Tiger, Lionel. Men in Groups. New York: Random House, Vintage Books, 1970.

____, and Fox, Robin. The Imperial Animal. New York: Holt, Rinehart & Winston, 1971.

Vaas, Francis J. "Title VII: Legislative History." Boston College Industrial and Commercial Law Review 7 (1966):431-72.

Vengris, Kandis. Legal Rights for Women. New York: Bantam Books, 1968.

Walden, May. Women and Socialism. Chicago: C. H. Kerr, n.d.

Wharton, Anne Hollingsworth. Colonial Days and Dames. Philadelphia: J. B. Lippincott, 1895.

White, E. M. Woman and Civilization. London: John Bale & Staples, 1940.

____. Woman in World History. London: H. Jenkins, 1924.

White, James J. "Women in the Law." Michigan Law Review 65 (Apr. 1967):1051.

"Women and the Law." Valparaiso University Law Review 5, no.2 (1971).

Women's Role in the Development of Tropical and Subtropical Countries. Brussels: Institut International des Civilisation Differentes, 1959.

Woodward, Helen. The Lady Persuaders. Stanford, Conn.: Astor-Honor, 1960.

ECONOMICS AND EMPLOYMENT

Abbott, Edith. Women in Industry: A Study in American Economic History. First published, 1910. Reprint, New York: Arno Press, 1969.

Access of Women to the Teaching Profession. Paris: UNESCO Publications, 1961.

Adams, Elizabeth Kemper. Women Professional Workers: A Study Made for the Women's Educational and Industrial Union. Chautauqua, N.Y.: Chautauqua Press, 1921.

Adams, Jean. Heroines of the Sky. Freeport, N.Y.:
   Books for Libraries, 1942.
Albrecht, Margaret. A Complete Guide for the Working
   Mother. Garden City, N.Y.: Doubleday, 1967.
Altman, Stuart H. "Factors Affecting the Unemployment
   of Married Women: A Study of the Dynamics of the
   Labor Force Behavior of Secondary Family Workers."
   Ph.D. dissertation, University of California, Los
   Angeles, 1969.
American Women: The Report of the U.S. President's
   Commission on the Status of Women and Other Publica-
   tions of the Commission. New York: Charles
   Scribner's, 1965.
American Working Women and the Class Struggle. New York:
   Workers Library, 1930.
Anderson, Frederic D. "Civil Rights and Fair Employ-
   ment." Business Lawyer 22 (1967):513-31.
Anderson, Mary. Woman at Work. Minneapolis: University
   of Minnesota Press, 1951.
Bailey, Beth. Young Woman in Business. Ames: Iowa
   State University Press, 1962.
Bailyn, Lotte. "Notes on the Role of Choice in Psychology
   of Professional Women." In The Women in America, ed.
   Robert J. Lifton, pp. 236-46. Boston: Houghton
   Mifflin, 1965.
Baker, Elizabeth. Protective Labor Legislation, with
   Special Reference to Women in the State of New York.
   New York: AMS Press, 1969.
   . Technology and Woman's Work. New York: Columbia
   University Press, 1964.
Baker, Melba. Women Who Work. S.R.W. (Seattle Radical
   Women), 3815 Fifth Ave. N.E., Seattle, Wash. 98103.
Balazs, G., and Poupard, A. "Girls in Training--What
   They Expect of the World of Work." CIRF Abstracts
   8 (section 13, B28098, 1969).
Bandler, Lucille, and Patterson, D. G. "Social Status
   of Women's Occupations." Occupations 26 (1947-48):
   421-24.
Basil, Douglas C. Women in Management: Performance,
   Prejudices, Promotion. New York: Dunellen, 1971.
Beauchamp, Joan. Women Who Work. New York: Inter-
   national, 1937.
Beecher, Catherine E. A Treatise on Domestic Economy.
   First published, 1841. Reprint, New York: Collectors
   Editions, Source Book Press, 1970.
Bellefords, Josette de. "Women and Engineering." Impact
   of Science on Society 9 (1964):249-67.
Belloc, Nedra R. "Labor Force Participation and Employ-
   ment Opportunities for Women." Journal of the
   American Statistical Association 9 (Sept. 1950):401-
   10.
Benigna, Rev. Sr. "Women Welfare Services, Ernokulam."
   Social Welfare 16 (Feb. 1970):8-22.

173

Berg, Richard K. "Equal Employment Opportunity under the Civil Rights Act of 1964." Brooklyn Law Review 31 (1964):62-97.

Berger, Bennett. Working-Class Suburb. Berkeley: University of California Press, 1960.

Bernard, Jessie. Academic Women. University Park: Pennsylvania State University Press, 1964.

_____. Women and the Public Interest: An Essay on Policy and Protest. Chicago: Aldine-Atherton, 1971.

Bernstein, Merton C. "Should Welfare Mothers Work?" America 21 (1969):704-6.

Berry, Jane. "Effects of Poverty on Culturally Disadvantaged Women." Adult Leadership 18 (May 1969): 9-13.

Beshiri, Patricia H. Woman Doctor: Her Career in Modern Medicine. Chicago: Cowles, 1969.

Bird, Caroline. Born Female: The High Cost of Keeping Women Down. New York: David McKay, 1968.

Blackwell, Elizabeth. Pioneer Work in Opening the Medical Profession to Women. First published, 1895. Reprint, New York: Collectors Editions, Source Books Press, 1970.

Blau, Peter, and Duncan, Otis. The American Occupational Structure. New York: John Wiley, 1967.

Bloch, Peter; Anderson, Deborah; and Gervais, Pamela. Policewomen on Patrol (Major Findings: First Report, Volume I). Washington, D.C.: Police Foundation, 1973.

Blood, Robert O., Jr. "Long-range Causes and Consequences of the Employment of Married Women." Journal of Marriage and the Family 27 (Feb. 1965): 43-47.

Boone, Gladys. The Women's Trade Union Leagues in Great Britain and the United States of America. New York: Columbia University Press, 1942.

Boserup, Ester. Women's Role in Economic Development. London: George Allen & Unwin, 1970.

Bosos, I. "Common Basic Training for Women's Clothing Manufacture." CIRF Abstracts 9 (section 4, 35348, 1970).

Branch, Mary Sydney. Women and Wealth. Chicago: University of Chicago Press, 1934.

Brandeis, Louis. Women in Industry. New York: Arno Press, 1969.

Breckinridge, Mary. Wide Neighborhoods: A Story of the Frontier Nursing Service. New York: Harper & Row, 1952.

Brown, David G. Mobile Professors. Washington, D.C.: American Council on Education, 1967.

Brown, Judith K. "Cross-cultural Ratings of Subsistence Activities and Sex Division of Labor: Retrospects and Prospects." Behavior Science Notes 4 (1969):281-90.

___. "A Note on the Division of Labor by Sex."
    American Anthropologist 72 (1970):1073-78.
Bureau of National Affairs. "Impact of the Equal Pay
    Act." Survey 75. Washington, D.C.: Bureau of
    National Affairs, 1964.
Business and Industry Discrimination Kit. N.O.W.
    (National Organization for Women), 5 S. Wabash, Suite
    1615, Chicago, Ill. 60603.
Butler, Elizabeth Beardsley. Women and the Trades. New
    York: Arno Press, 1969.
Byham, William C. Women in the Work Force: A Confron-
    tation with Change. New York: Behavioral
    Publications, 1972.
Cain, G. G. Married Women in the Labor Force. Chicago:
    University of Chicago Press, 1966.
Campbell, Helen. Prisoners of Poverty: Women Wage-
    workers, Their Trades and Their Lives. First pub-
    lished, 1887. Reprint, New York: Garrett Press, 1970.
Caplow, T., and McGee, Reece. The Academic Market Place.
    New York: Basic Books, 1958.
Carroll, Margaret S. "The Working Wife and Her Family's
    Economic Position." Monthly Labor Review 85 (1962):
    366-74.
Chase, Ilka. In Bed We Cry. New York: Doubleday, 1943.
Citizens' Advisory Council on the Status of Women.
    American Women 1968. Washington, D.C.: U.S. Depart-
    ment of Labor, 1968.
Clark, Alice. Working Life of Women in the Seventeenth
    Century. London: G. Routledge, 1919.
Clark, F. LeGros. Women, Work and Age: To Study the
    Employment of Working Women throughout Their Middle
    Lives. London: Nuffield Foundation, 1962.
Clymer, Eleanor, and Erich, Lillian. Modern American
    Career Women. New York: Dodd, Mead, 1959.
Cohen, Malcom S. "Married Women in the Labor Force: An
    Analysis of the Participation Rates." Monthly Labor
    Review 92 (1969):31-35.
College Placement Council. Women's Salary Survey.
    Bethlehem, Pa.: College Placement Council, 1970.
Cooksey, Frank C. "The Role of the Law in Equal Employ-
    ment Opportunity." Boston College Industrial and
    Commercial Law Review 7 (1968):778-98.
Cooper, Joseph D. A Woman's Guide to Part-time Jobs.
    Garden City, N.Y.: Doubleday, 1963.
Coppinger, Robert M., and Rosenblatt, Paul. "Romantic
    Love and Subsistence Dependence of Spouses." South-
    western Journal of Anthropology 24 (1968):310-19.
Cowan, John. Science of a New Life. First published,
    1874. Reprint, New York: Collectors Editions,
    Source Book Press, 1970.
Cowell, Margaret. Women and Equality. New York:
    Workers' Library, 1935.

Crowley, Joan. "Facts and Fictions about Working Women Explored; Several Stereotypes Prove False in National Study." University of Michigan Institute for Social Research Newsletter, Autumn 1972.

Dall, Caroline H. Women's Right to Labor; or, Low Wages and Hard Work; In Three Lectures, Delivered in Boston, November 1859. Boston: Walker, Wise, 1860.

Dalton, George. "'Bridewealth' vs. 'Brideprice.'" American Anthropologist 68 (1966):732-38. Reprinted in Economic Anthropology and Development: Essays on Tribal and Peasant Economics, ed. George Dalton, pp. 193-201. New York: Basic Books, 1971.

David, Deborah S. Career Patterns and Values: A Study of Men and Women in Scientific, Professional, and Technical Occupations. New York: Columbia University, Bureau of Applied Social Research, 1969.

Davis, H. "Economic, Legal, and Social Status of Teachers: Salaries of Women." Review of Educational Research 33 (Oct. 1963):399-400.

Davis, James. Great Aspirations: The Graduate School Plans of America's College Seniors. Chicago: Aldine, 1964.

Dexter, Elizabeth W. Career Women of America, 1776-1840. Francestown, N.H.: M. Jones, 1950.

___. Colonial Women of Affairs: Women in Business and the Professions in America before 1776. Reprint, Detroit: Gale Research, 1931.

Ditmore, Jack, and Prosser, W. R. A Study of Day Care's Effect on the Labor Force Participation of Low-Income Mothers. Washington, D.C.: Office of Economic Opportunity, 1973.

Dixon, Marlene. A Position Paper on Radical Women in the Professions; or, Up from Ridicule. 1968. V.W.L.M. (Voice of Women's Liberation Movement), 1940 Bissell, Chicago, Illinois 60614.

Dombusch, Sanford M., and Heer, David M. "The Evaluation of Work by Females, 1940-1950." American Journal of Sociology 63 (1957):27-29.

Dorsey, Susan Almira. "Position and Responsibility of Trained Women in Education." National Education Association of the U.S. Addresses and Proceedings (1921):413-16.

Durand, John D. "Married Women in the Labor Force." American Journal of Sociology 52 (1946):217-23.

Eisenberg, Leon. "Professional Performance of Women Physicians." Science 172 (1971):218-19.

Ellis, Evelyn. "Social Psychological Correlates of Upward Mobility among Unmarried Career Women." American Sociological Review 17 (1952):553-63.

"The Employment of Older Women." Geneva: International Labour Office, 1955. Reprint from International Labour Review 71 (July 1955).

Epstein, Cynthia Fuchs. Woman's Place; Options and
    Limits in Professional Careers. Berkeley: University
    of California Press, 1970.
____. "Women and Professional Careers: The Case of the
    Woman Lawyer." Ph.D. dissertation, Columbia
    University, 1968.
Etzioni, Amitai. Semi-professions and Their Organization.
    New York: Free Press, 1969.
Falk, Lawrence L. "Occupational Satisfaction of Female
    College Graduates." Journal of Marriage and the
    Family 28 (May 1966):177-85.
Fava, Sylvia F. "The Status of Women in Professional
    Sociology." American Sociological Review 25 (1960):
    271-76.
Fisch, Edith L., and Schwartz, Mortimer D. State Laws
    on the Employment of Women. Washington, D.C.:
    Scarecrow Press, 1953.
Fleischman, Doris E. An Outline of Careers for Women:
    A Practical Guide to Achievement. Garden City, N.Y.:
    Doubleday, 1929.
Fogarty, M. P.; Allen, A. J.; Allen, I.; and Walters, P.
    Women in Top Jobs. London: George Allen & Unwin,
    1971.
For Their Rights as Mothers, Workers, Citizens. Berlin:
    Women's International Democratic Federation, 1952.
Fuchs, Victor R. "Differences in Hourly Earnings between
    Men and Women." Monthly Labor Review 94 (May 1971):
    9-15.
Gereb, Sandor. "The ILO and Women Workers." Inter-
    national Labor Organization Panorama 37 (July-Aug.
    1969):80-83.
Gerin, Elizabeth. "Women and Television." Television
    and Adult Education 14 (July 1964):38-48.
Gildersleeve, Genieve N. Women in Banking. Washington,
    D.C.: Public Affairs Press, 1959.
Gilman, Charlotte Perkins. The Home: Its Work and
    Influence. First published, 1903. Reprint, intro.
    William L. O'Neill. Urbana: University of Illinois
    Press, 1972.
____. Women & Economics. First published, 1898. Reprint,
    New York: Collectors Editions, Source Book Press,
    1970.
Ginzberg, Eli. Life Styles of Educated Women. New York:
    Columbia University Press, 1966.
Giroud, Francoise. "The Awakening of Women." Way Forum
    59 (Apr. 1966):13-15.
Given, J. N. "Women in Executive Posts." Office
    Executive 35 (Dec. 1960):32-33.
Goldberg, Marylyn Power. The Economic Exploitation of
    Women. Reprint 53. Andover, Mass.: Warner Modular
    Publications. Reprinted from Review of Radical
    Political Economics 2, 1 (Spring 1970).

Gross, Edward. "Plus a Change? The Sexual Structure of
    Occupations Over Time." Social Problems 16 (1968):
    198.
Guilbert, Madeline. Les functions des femmes dans
    l'industrie. Paris: Mouton, 1966.
Haber, S. Female Labor Force Participation and Economic
    Development. Chicago: Rand McNally, 1958.
Hammond, Dorothy, and Jablow, Alta. Women: Their
    Economic Role in Traditional Societies. Addison-
    Wesley Module in Anthropology, no. 35. Reading,
    Mass.: Addison-Wesley, 1973.
Hapgood, Karen E. "Women in Planning: A Report on
    Their Status in Public Planning Agencies." American
    Society of Planning Officials (ASPO) Planning Advisory
    Service Report 273 (Oct. 1971).
Harbeson, Gladys. Choice and Challenge for the American
    Women. Cambridge, Mass.: Schenkman, 1967.
Harrison, Evelyn. "The Working Woman: Barriers to
    Employment." Public Administration Review 24 (1964):
    78-85.
Hedges, Janice N. "Women Workers and Manpower Demands
    in the 1970s." Women at Work. Monthly Labor Review
    93 (June 1970):19-29.
Henry, Alice. Women and the Labor Movement. New York:
    Dorna, 1923.
Hiestand, Dale L. Economic Growth and Employment Op-
    portunities for Minorities. New York: Columbia
    University Press, 1964.
Hill, Joseph A. Women in Gainful Occupations, 1870-
    1920. First published, 1929. Reprint, New York:
    Johnson Reprint, n.d.
Horner, M. S. "Sex Differences in Achievement Motiva-
    tion and Performance in Competitive and Non-
    competitive Situations." Ph.D. dissertation,
    University of Michigan, 1928.
Hunt, Harriett K. Glances and Glimpses; or, Fifty Years
    Social, Including Twenty Years Professional, Life.
    New York: Collectors Editions, Source Book Press,
    1970.
Hutchins, Grace. Women Who Work. International
    Pamphlets No. 27. New York: International Pamph-
    lets, 1932; London: Martin Lawrence, 1934.
___. What Every Working Woman Wants. New York: Workers
    Library, 1935.
Hutchinson, Emilie J. Women's Wages. New York: AMS
    Press, 1919.
International Labour Conference. 48th Session. Report
    6. Women Workers in a Changing World. Geneva:
    International Labour Office, 1963.
International Labour Office. The Apprenticeship of
    Women and Girls. Geneva: International Labour
    Office, 1956.

Jaffe, A. H. "Trends in the Participation of Women in the Working Force." Monthly Labor Review 79 (May 1965):559-65.

Jex-Blake, Sophia. Medical Women: A Thesis and a History. First published, 1886. Reprint, New York: Collectors Editions, Source Book Press, 1970.

Johnstone, Jenny Elizabeth. Women in Steel. New York: Workers' Library, 1937.

Khor, Thomas. "Women Teachers and Equal Pay." The Malayan Educator 8 (Apr. 1962):6.

Killian, R. A. The Working Woman: A Male Manager's Point of View. New York: American Management Association, 1971.

King, Alice G. Career Opportunities for Women in Business. New York: E. P. Dutton, 1963.

King, Karl. "Adolescents' Views of Maternal Employment as a Threat to the Marital Relationship." Journal of Marriage and the Family 30 (Nov. 1966):633-37.

Klein, Viola. Britain's Married Women Workers. New York: Humanities Press, 1965.

_____. Working Wives. London: Institute of Personnel Management, 1960.

_____, and Myrdal, Alva. Women's Two Roles: At Home and Work. Rev. ed. New York: Humanities Press, 1968.

Koontz, Elizabeth D. "The Women's Bureau Looks at the Future." Women at Work. Monthly Labor Review 93 (June 1970):3-9.

Kriesberg, Louis. Mothers in Poverty: A Study of Fatherless Families. Chicago: Aldine, 1971.

Laird, Donald A. The Psychology of Supervising the Working Woman. New York: McGraw-Hill, 1942.

Lajewsky, Henry C. "Working Mothers and Their Arrangements for Care of Their Children." Social Security Bulletin, Aug. 1959, pp. 8-13.

Lapin, Eva. Mothers in Overalls. New York: Workers Library, 1943.

Leslie, Gerald R., and Richardson, Arthur H. "Life-cycle, Career Pattern and Decision to Move." American Sociological Review 26 (1961):894-902.

Leuck, Miriam Simons. Fields of Work for Women. New York: Appleton-Century, 1938.

Lobsenz, Johanna. The Older Woman in Industry. New York: Charles Scribner's, 1929.

Lopate, Carol. Women in Medicine. Baltimore: Johns Hopkins Press, 1968.

Love, Barbara J., ed. Foremost Women in Communications. New York: R. R. Bowker, 1970.

Maccoby, Eleanor. "Feminine Intellect and the Demands of Science." Impact of Science on Society 1 (1970): 13-28.

McCune, Shirley D., and Schmidt, Ann D. Women, Management and Training. Houston: Gulf, 1971.

MacGibbon, Elizabeth G. Manners in Business. Rev. ed.
New York: Macmillan, 1954.

McLean, Beth B., and Paris, Jeanne. Young Woman in
Business. Ames: Iowa State University Press, 1962.

Mahoney, Thomas A. "Factors Determining the Labor Force
Participation of Married Women." Industrial and
Labor Relations Review 40 (July 1961):563-77.

Manning, Caroline. The Immigrant Woman and Her Job.
First published, 1930. Reprint, New York: Arno
Press, 1970.

Mattfeld, Jacquelyn A., and Van Aken, Carol, eds. Women
and the Scientific Professions. Cambridge, Mass.:
M.I.T. Press, 1967.

Maule, Frances. Executive Careers for Women. New York:
Harper, 1961.

Merriam, Eve. Mommies at Work. New York: Alfred A.
Knopf, 1961.

Merriam, Ida C. U.S. Social Security Administration.
Washington, D.C.: U.S. Government Printing Office,
1968.

Meyer, Annie Nathan. Woman's Work in America. New York:
Henry Holt, 1891.

Mezerick, A. G. "Getting Rid of the Women." Atlantic
Monthly 7 (June 1945):79-83.

Mincer, Jacob. "Labor Force Participation of Married
Women." In Aspects of Labor Economics: A Con-
ference of the Universities. Princeton: Princeton
University Press, 1962.

Montague, Richard. Oceans, Poles and Airmen. New York:
Random House, 1971.

Morau, Robert D. "Reducing Discrimination: Role of the
Equal Pay Act." Women at Work. Monthly Labor Review
93 (June 1970):30-34.

Murdock, George Peter. "Comparative Data on the Division
of Labor by Sex." Social Forces 15 (1937):551-53.
Reprinted in Culture and Society, ed. George Peter
Murdock, pp. 308-10. Pittsburgh: University of
Pittsburgh Press, 1937.

Myrdal, Alva, and Klein, Viola. Women's Two Roles: At
Home and Work. London: Routledge & Kegan Paul, 1956.

Narula, Uma. "Career Failure among Women." Social
Welfare 14 (May 1967):4-5.

Nash, Edmund. "The Status of Women in the U.S.S.R."
Women at Work. Monthly Labor Review 93 (June 1970):
39-44.

National Manpower Council. Womanpower. New York:
Columbia University Press, 1957.

National Science Foundation. Two Years after the College
Degree. Washington, D.C.: U.S. Government Printing
Office, 1963.

Neff, Wanda. Victorian Working Women. New York:
Columbia University Press, 1929.

Nestor, Agnes. Woman's Labor Leader. Rockford, Ill.:
    Bellevue Books, 1954.
New York State Department of Labor. Division of Women.
    Women Who Work in New York. Washington, D.C.: U.S.
    Government Printing Office, 1941.
Nurge, Ethel. "Birth Rate and Work Load." American
    Anthropologist 72 (1970):1434-39.
Nye, F. Ivan, and Hoffman, Lois W. The Employed Mother
    in America. New York: Rand McNally, 1963.
O'Laughlin, Bridget. "Women and the Economy." A paper
    presented at the 71st Annual Meeting of the American
    Anthropological Association, Toronto, 1972. Mimeo.
    Stanford University.
Olsen, Jack. The Girls in the Office. New York: Simon
    & Schuster, 1972.
O'Neill, William. Women at Work. New York: Quadrangle
    Books, 1972.
Oppenheimer, Valerie Kincade. "Demographic Influences
    on Female Employment and the Status of Women." A
    paper presented at the 137th Annual Meeting of the
    American Association for the Advancement of Science,
    Chicago, 1970. Mimeo. University of California,
    Los Angeles.
____. "The Interaction of Demand and Supply and·Its
    Effect on the Female Labor Force." U.S. Population
    Studies, Nov. 1967, p. 21.
Orden, Susan R., and Bradburn, Norman. "Working Wives
    and Marriage Happiness." American Journal of
    Sociology 74 (Jan. 1969):393-401.
Parrish, John B. "Professional Woman Power as a
    National Resource." Quarterly Review of Economics
    and Business 1 (1961):54-63.
Penny, Virginia. The Employments of Women. Boston:
    Walker & Wise, 1862.
____. How Women Can Make Money, Married or Single, in All
    Branches of the Arts and Sciences, Professions,
    Trades, Agricultural and Mechanical Pursuits. First
    published, 1870. Reprint, New York: Arno Press,
    1971.
____. Think and Act: A Series of Articles Pertaining to
    Men and Women, Work and Wages. First published, 1869.
    Reprint, New York: Arno Press, 1971.
Perella, Vera. "Women of the Labor Force." Monthly
    Labor Review 91 (1968):1-12.
Peterson, Ester. "Working Women." In The Woman in
    America, ed. Robert J. Lifton. Boston: Houghton
    Mifflin, 1965.
Phillips, Jean. "Women in Science." Science Journal,
    May 1966, pp. 77-81.
Pidgeon, Mary Elizabeth. Women in the Economy of the
    United States of America: A Summary Report. Washing-
    ton, D.C.: U.S. Government Printing Office, 1937.

Pinchbeck, Ivy. Women Workers in the Industrial Revolu-
tion. First published, 1930. Reprint, London:
Frank Cass, 1969.
Pogrebin, Letty C. How to Make It in a Man's World. New
York: Bantam Books, 1971.
Pollock, Nancy J. "Women and the Division of Labor: A
Jamaican Example." American Anthropologist 74 (1972):
689-92.
Rainwater, Lee; Coleman, Richard P.; and Handel, Gerald.
Workingman's Wife: Her Personality, World, and
Lifestyle. Dobbs Ferry, N.Y.: Oceana, 1959.
Ramsey, Glenn V. Women View Their Working World. Austin:
University of Texas Press, 1963.
Rand, Ayn. "Women and the Industrial Revolution." In
Capitalism: The Unknown Ideal. New York: New
American Library, 1967.
Rapoport, Rhona, and Rapoport, R. Dual-career Families.
Baltimore: Pelican, 1971.
"Reports on the Status of Women." United Nations
Monthly Chronicle 6 (Feb. 1969; Mar. 1969).
Robinson, Harriet H. Loom and Spindle; or Life among
the Early Mill Girls. New York: Crowell, 1898.
Roe, Marion. How Six Girls Made Money; and, Occupations
for Women. New York: Fowler & Wells, 1892.
Roethlisberger, Fritz. Management and the Worker.
Cambridge, Mass.: Harvard University Press, 1939.
Rolandis, Giuseppe Maria de. Le torinesi; saggio
statistico. Turin: Stamperia Alliana, 1829.
Rosenfeld, Carl, and Perella, Vera. "Why Women Start
and Stop Working: A Study in Mobility." Monthly
Labor Review 88 (Sept. 1965):1077-82.
Rossi, Alice. "Barriers to the Career Choice of
Engineering, Medicine, and Science among American
Women." In Women and the Scientific Professions, ed.
J. A. Mattfield and C. E. Van Aken, pp. 51-127.
Cambridge, Mass.: M.I.T. Press, 1965.
Russell, Thomas H. The Girl's Fight for a Living.
Chicago: Donohue, 1913.
Sartin, Pierrette. "Real and Pseudo Problems of the
Working Woman." UNESCO Courier 22 (1969):24-28.
Schmidt, W. "The Position of Women with Regard to
Property in Primitive Society." American Anthro-
pologist 37 (1935):244-56.
Schneider, Jane. "Of Vigilance and Virgins: Honor,
Shame and Access to Resources in Mediterranean
Societies." Ethnology 10 (1971):1-24.
Schreiner, Olive. Woman and Labor. New York:
Frederick A. Stokes, 1911.
Scofield, Nanette E., and Klarman, Betty. So You Want
to Go Back to Work. New York: Random House, 1968.
Scoresby, William. American Factories and Their Female
Operatives. First published, 1845. Reprint, New
York: Burt Franklin, 1967.

Sellin, T., ed. "Women's Opportunities and Responsibilities." Annals of the American Academy of Political and Social Science 651 (May 1947).

Severn, Jill. Women at Work. S.R.W. (Seattle Radical Women), 3815 Fifth Ave. N.E., Seattle, Wash. 98103.

Sison, Perfect S. "The Employment of Women Office Workers." Page Journal 2 (Jan.-June 1964):25-33.

Smith, Ellen. Wage Earning Women and Their Dependents. London: Fabian Society, 1915.

Smith, Georgina. Help Wanted: Female. New Brunswick, N.J.: Rutgers University Press, 1964.

Smuts, Robert W. Women and Work in America. First published, 1959. Reprint, New York: Schocken Books, 1971.

"Some Characteristics of the Achievement Motive in Women." Journal of Abnormal and Social Psychology 68 (Feb. 1964):119-28.

Soubiran, André. Open Letter to a Woman of Today, trans. E. Abbott. New York: James H. Heineman, 1968.

Spencer, Anna Garlin. Woman's Share in Social Culture. New York: Kennerley, 1913.

Standing Joint Committee of Industrial Woman's Organization. Labour Women's Report on Socialism and Our Standard of Living. London: Labour Publications Department, 1938.

Stant, Katherine. "Employment Problems of Women: Causes and Cures." Arizona Review 22 (May 1973):10-13.

Statistical Work: A Study of Opportunities for Women. New York: Bureau of Vocational Information, 1921.

Stimpson, Catherine R., ed. Discrimination against Women: Congressional Hearings on Equal Rights in Education and Employment. New York: Bowker, 1973.
_____. Women and the "Equal Rights" Amendment: Senate Subcommittee Hearings on the Constitutional Amendment, 91st Congress. New York: Bowker, 1972.

Swett, Maude. Summary of Labor Laws in Force 1909: Woman's Work. Madison: Parsons Printery, 1909.

Theodore, Athena, ed. Professional Woman. Cambridge, Mass.: Schenkman, 1971.

"Training for Girls and the Prospects Offered to the Belgian Working Class by This Training." CIRF Abstracts 9 (section 2, B34393, 1970).

Travell, Janet. Office Hours: Day and Night. New York: New American Library, 1971.

Udy, Stanley H., Jr. Organization of Work: A Comparative Analysis of Production among Nonindustrial Peoples. New Haven: Human Relations Area Files Press, 1967.

U.N. Department of Economic and Social Affairs. Civic and Political Education of Women. New York: United Nations Publications, 1964.
_____. Convention on the Nationality of Married Women, Historical Background and Commentary. New York: United Nations Publications, 1962.

_____. Nationality of Married Women: Report Submitted by the Secretary General. New York: United Nations Publications, 1963.
U.S. Citizens Advisory Council on the Status of Women. Task Force on Social Insurance and Taxes. Washington, D.C.: U.S. Government Printing Office, 1968.
_____. Women and Their Families in Our Rapidly Changing Society: Report. Washington, D.C.: U.S. Government Printing Office, 1968.
U.S. Department of Labor. Women's Bureau. Background Fact on Women Workers in the United States. Washington, D.C.: U.S. Government Printing Office, 1968.
_____. Background Facts on Women Workers in the United States. Washington, D.C.: U.S. Government Printing Office, 1970.
_____. The Fuller Utilization of the Woman Physician. Washington, D.C.: U.S. Government Printing Office, 1968.
_____. Handbook on Women Workers. Bulletin 285. Washington, D.C.: U.G. Government Printing Office, 1963.
_____. Handbook on Women Workers. Bulletin 290. Washington, D.C.: U.S. Government Printing Office, 1965.
_____. Handbook on Women Workers. Washington, D.C.: U.S. Government Printing Office, 1969.
_____. Handbook on Women Workers. Washington, D.C.: U.S. Government Printing Office, 1971.
_____. Job Horizons for College Women. Washington, D.C.: U.S. Government Printing Office, 1967.
_____. Job-Finding Techniques for Mature Women. Washington, D.C.: U.S. Government Printing Office, 1970.
_____. Negro Women in the Population and in the Labor Force. Washington, D.C.: U.S. Government Printing Office, 1967.
_____. Who Are the Working Mothers? Washington, D.C.: U.S. Government Printing Office, 1968.
_____. Women in Texas Industries. Bulletin 126. Washington, D.C.: U.S. Government Printing Office, 1936.
U.S. Interdepartmental Committee on the Status of Women. American Women 1963-1969. Washington, D.C.: U.S. Government Printing Office, 1968.
_____. Report on Progress on the Status of Women, 1963-1964. Washington, D.C.: U.S. Government Printing Office, 1964.
_____. Report on Progress in 1966. Washington, D.C.: U.S. Government Printing Office, 1967.
_____. 1968: Time for Action: Highlights. Washington, D.C.: U.S. Government Printing Office, 1969.
U.S. President's Commission on the Status of Women. American Woman: Report. Washington, D.C.: U.S. Government Printing Office, 1963.

____. Four Consultations. Washington, D.C.: U.S. Government Printing Office, 1963.

____. Report of the Committee on Civil and Political Rights. Washington, D.C.: U.S. Government Printing Office, 1964.

____. Report of the Committee on Education. Washington, D.C.: U.S. Government Printing Office, 1964.

____. Report of the Committee on Federal Employment. Washington, D.C.: U.S. Government Printing Office, 1963.

____. Report of the Committee on Home and Community. Washington, D.C.: U.S. Government Printing Office, 1963.

____. Report of the Committee on Private Employment. Washington, D.C.: U.S. Government Printing Office, 1964.

____. Report of the Committee on Protective Labor Legislation. Washington, D.C.: U.S. Government Printing Office, 1963.

U.S. President's Task Force on Women's Rights and Responsibilities. A Matter of Simple Justice: A Report. Washington, D.C.: U.S. Government Printing Office, 1970.

"Village Women Complete Training in Family and Child Welfare Project, Mehrauli." Social Welfare 16 (Dec. 1969):32.

Violette, Augusta. Economic Feminism in American Literature Prior to 1848. New York: Burt Franklin, 1925.

Vogel, Lise. Women Workers: Some Basic Statistics. Boston: New England Free Press, n.d.

Waldman, Elizabeth K. "Changes in the Labor Force Activity of Women." Women at Work. Monthly Labor Review 93 (June 1970):10-18.

____. "Marital and Family Characteristics of the U.S. Labor Force." Monthly Labor Review 93 (1970):18-25.

____, and Gover, K. R. "Children of Women in the Labor Force." Monthly Labor Review 94 (July 1971):19-25.

Walters, Patricia. Women in Top Jobs: Four Studies in Achievement. New York: Fernhill House, 1971.

Warrior, Betsy. Women and Welfare. Boston: New England Free Press, n.d.

Webb, Catherine. The Woman with the Basket: The History of the Women's Co-operative Guild 1883-1927. Manchester: Co-operative Wholesale Society's Printing Works, 1927.

Weil, Mildred W. "An Analysis of the Factors Influencing Married Women's Actual or Planned Work Participation." American Sociological Review 26 (Feb. 1961):91-96.

Weingarten, Violet. The Mother Who Works outside the Home. New York: Child Study Press, 1963.

White, James J. "Women in the Law." Michigan Law Review 65 (Apr. 1967):1051-1122.

Whiting, Beatrice B. "Work and the Family: Cross-
    cultural Perspectives." A paper prepared for "Women:
    Resource for a Changing World," International
    Conference, Radcliffe College, 1972.
Whittaker, Elvi, and Olesen, Virginia. "The Faces of
    Florence Nightingale." Human Organization 23 (1964):
    123-30.
Wiest, Raymond E. "Wage-Labor Migration and the Female-
    headed Household: Cases from Central Mexico." A
    paper presented at the 69th Annual Meeting of the
    American Anthropological Association, San Diego, 1970.
    Mimeo. University of Manitoba.
Wilensky, Harold L. "Women's Work: Economic Growth,
    Ideology, Structure." Institute of Industrial
    Relations Reprint 321. Berkeley: University of
    California, 1968.
Willacy, H. M., and Hilaski, H. J. "Working Women in
    Urban Poverty Neighborhoods." Monthly Labor Review
    93 (June 1970):35-38.
Willett, Jean Campbell. Women and Poverty. London:
    Social Credit Press, 1938.
Willett, Mabel H. Employment of Women in the Clothing
    Trade. First published, 1902. Reprint, New York:
    AMS Press, 1968.
Williams, Gertrude. Women and Work. New York: Essential
    Books, 1945.
Williams, Josephine Justice. The Professional Status of
    Women Physicians. Film. Chicago: University of
    Chicago Library, Department of Photographic Reproduc-
    tion, 1949.
Winkler, Ilene. Women Workers: The Forgotten Third of
    the Working Class. Boston: New England Free Press, n.d.
Winter, E. Women at Work. New York: Simon & Schuster,
    1967.
Wolff, Janet. What Makes Women Buy. New York: McGraw-
    Hill, 1958.
Wolfle, Dael, ed. "America's Resources of Specialized
    Talent." Commission on Human Resources and Advanced
    Training. New York: Harper & Row, 1954.
Wolfson, Theresa. The Woman Worker and the Trade Unions.
    New York: International Publishers, 1926.
"Women as a Source of Manpower." CIRF Abstracts 4
    (section 2, B3626, 1965).
"Women in the Age of Science and Technology." Impact of
    Science on Society 20 (Jan.-Mar. 1970):3-102.
"Women's Opportunities and Responsibilities." Annals of
    the American Academy of Political and Social Science
    251 (May 1947).
Women's Wages in England in the Nineteenth Century.
    London: Women's Industrial Council, 1906.
Wood, Myrna. We May Not Have Much, But There's a Lot of
    Us. Radical Education Project, Box 561-A, Detroit,
    Mich. 48232.

Wright, Carroll D. The Working Girls of Boston.
American Labor from Conspiracy to Collective Bar-
gaining Series. First published, 1889. Reprint,
New York: Arno Press, 1969.
Yenogoyan, Aram. "Sex Preferences, Fertility and
Economic Differentials." A paper presented at the
69th Annual Meeting of the American Anthropological
Association, San Diego, 1970. Mimeo. University of
Michigan.
Zetkin, Klara. Lenin on the Woman Question. New York:
International, 1934.
Znaniecki, Helena. Review of Women in Science and
Engineering, by Jacqueline Mattfield and Carold Van
Aken. Transaction 4 (1967):54.

EDUCATION

Abel, H., and Gingles, R. "Identifying Problems of
Adolescent Girls." Journal of Educational Research
58 (May 1965):389-92.
"Access of Women to Education: Steps Taken to Implement
Recommendation No. 34 to the Ministries of Education,
Adapted by the International Conference on Public
Education at Its 15th Session, 1952." International
Yearbook of Education 29 (1967):85-90.
Anderson, Kitty. "Women and the Universities: A
Changing Pattern." Fawcett Lecture. London: Bedford
College, 1963.
Astin, Helen S. The Woman Doctorate in America: Origins,
Careers and Family. New York: Russell Sage
Foundation, 1969.
____. Women: A Bibliography on Their Education and
Careers. Human Services, 4301 Connecticut Avenue,
N.W., Washington, D.C. 20521.
Babchuk, Nicholas, and Bates, Alan. "Professor or Pro-
ducer: The Two Faces of Academic Men." Social Forces
40 (1962):341-48.
Bailey, Larry Joe. "An Investigation of the Vocational
Behavior of Selected Women Vocational Education
Students." Master's thesis, University of Illinois,
1968.
Baker, Therese, and Fitzgerald, William. "Women and
Education." School Review 80 (1972):155-59.
Barton, A. Studying the Effects of College Education.
New Haven: Edward Hazer Foundation, 1959.
Batho, Edith C. A Lamp of Friendship: A Short History
of the I.F.U.W. London: International Federation of
University Women, 1968.
Baumrind, Diana. "From Each According to Her Ability."
Women in Education. Special Issue. School Review
80 (1972):161-97.

Subject Topics

Bennett, John. Strictures on Female Education, Chiefly as It Relates to the Culture of the Heart. First published, 1795. Reprint, New York: Collectors Editions, Source Book Press, 1970.

Bernard, Jessie. Academic Woman. First published, 1960. Reprint, New York: Meridian Books, 1964.

Boas, Louise S. Woman's Education Begins: The Rise of the Women's Colleges. First published, 1935. Reprint, New York: Arno Press, 1971.

Bolton, Sarah. Lives of Girls Who Became Famous. Rev. ed. New York: Crowell Collier & Macmillan, 1949.

Bondy, Stephen B., and Taylor, Romold G. "Validation of Factor Analytic Classification of the Women's Form of the SVIB: Implications for College Counseling." Journal of Educational Research 61 (Feb. 1968):273-74.

Borchers, G. "Some Investigations Concerning the Status of Faculty Women in America." In Women in College and University Teaching, ed. V. Totaro. Madison: University of Wisconsin, School of Education, 1963.

Borer, Mary. Women Who Made History. New York: Frederick Warne, 1963.

Brackett, Anna C. Woman and Higher Education. First published, 1893. Reprint, New York: Burt Franklin, n.d.

Calderone, Mary S. "New Roles for Women." Women in Education. Special Issue. School Review 80 (1972): 275-79.

Calixto, Julia. "Education of Women in Developing Countries." Science Review 10 (Feb. 1969):20-26.

Cathey-Calvert, Carolyn. "Sexism on Sesame Street." Reprint. Know, Inc., P.O. Box 10197, Pittsburgh, Pa. 15232.

Chaton, Jeanne. "Women in Pursuit of Their Rights." UNESCO Features 533-34 (Aug.-Sept. 1968):4-8.

Chattopadhyay, Kamaladevi. "Women's Rights and Controversy on Succession Act." Social Welfare 16 (Aug. 1969):8-24.

Chmaj, Betty E. American Women and American Studies. Pittsburgh: Know, Inc., 1972.

Crandall, J. J. "Parents' Attitudes and Behaviors on Grade School Children's Academic Achievement." Journal of Genetic Psychology 104 (1964):55-66.

Dale, R. R. "An Analysis of Research on Comparative Attainment in Mathematics in Single-sex and Co-educational Maintained Grammar Schools." Educational Research 5 (Nov. 1962):10-15.

_____. "A Critical Analysis of Research on the Effects of Co-education on Academic Attainment in Grammar Schools." Educational Research 4 (June 1962):207-17.

Davis, Anee. "Women as a Minority Group in Higher Academics." American Sociologist 5 (May 1969):95-99.

188

Davis, James. Undergraduate Career Decisions. Chicago: Aldine, 1965.

Dexter, Lewis A. The Tyranny of Schooling. New York: Basic Books, 1964.

Douvan, Elizabeth. Adolescent Girls. Ann Arbor: University of Michigan Survey Research Center, 1956.

_____. "Adolescent Girls: Their Attitude Toward Education." The Education of Women, ed. David D. Opal. Washington, D.C.: American Council on Education, 1959.

_____, and Raye, Carol. "Motivational Factors in College Entrance." In The American College, ed. N. Sanford, pp. 199-224. New York: John Wiley, 1962.

Edcentric. "Women in Education." December 1971. Center for Educational Reform, 2115 South Street, N.W., Washington, D.C. 20008.

"The Educated Woman." Student World 3 (1966).

"Education of Girls." Higher Education Journal 17 (Summer 1969):9-25.

The Education of Women and Girls: A List of Books and Articles in the Institute Library. Leeds: University cf Leeds, Institute of Education, 1966.

Feminists on Children's Media. "A Feminist Look at Children's Books." School Library Journal (1971): 19-24.

Fields, Rona M. "Public Education: Training for Sexism." Reprint. Know, Inc., P.O. Box 10197, Pittsburgh, Pa. 15232.

Fisher, Elizabeth. "The Second Sex, Junior Division." New York Times Book Review, May 24, 1970, p. 6.

Fleming, Alice. Doctors in Petticoats. Philadelphia: J. B. Lippincott, 1964.

_____. Great Women Teachers. Philadelphia: J. B. Lippincott, 1965.

Freedman, M. B. "The Passage through College." In The American College: A Psychological and Social Interpretation of Higher Learning, ed. N. Sanford. New York: John Wiley, 1962.

Frisof, Jamie Kelem. Textbooks and Channeling. Reprint. Know, Inc., P.O. Box 10197, Pittsburgh, Pa. 15232.

Gardner, Jo-Ann; Broverman, Inge; and Vogel, Susan. "Sesame Street and Sex-role Stereotypes." Reprint. Know, Inc., P.O. Box 10197, Pittsburgh, Pa. 15232.

Gersh, Harry. Women Who Made America Great. Philadelphia: J. B. Lippincott, 1962.

Gilford, Henry. Heroines of America. New York: Fleet Press, 1970.

Goldman, Freda H. A Turning to Take Next: Alternative Goals in the Education of Women. Boston: Center for the Study of Liberal Education for Adults, 1965.

Goldsen, Rose. What College Students Think. New York: Van Nostrand Reinhold, 1960.

Goodsell, Willystine, ed. Pioneers of Women's Education in the United States. New York: McGraw-Hill, 1931. Reprint. New York: AMS Press, 1970.

Gordon, C. W. The Social System of the High School: A Study in the Sociology of Adolescence. New York: Free Press, 1957.

Gupta, Venna Rani. "Ignorant Mothers: A Social Problem." Social Welfare 16 (Sept. 1969):32.

Havemann, E., and West, P. They Went to College. New York: Harcourt, Brace, 1952.

Hecker, Monique. "Access of Girls and Women to Technical and Vocational Education." UNESCO Chronicle 14 (July-Aug. 1968):279-84.

___. "Access of Girls to Higher Education." UNESCO Chronicle 8 (Apr. 1967):157-62.

Heilbrun, Carolyn G. "All Pregnant Girls Have Boy Babies." New York Times Book Review, Nov. 8, 1970, p. 8.

Himmelhock, Jerome. "Tolerance and Personality Needs: A Study of the Liberalization of Ethnic Attitudes among Minority Group College Students." American Sociological Review 15 (Feb. 1950):1.

Hopwood, Katherine. "Expectations of University College Women." Personnel and Guidance Journal 52 (1954): 464-69.

Hottel, Althea K. "Perspectives for the Education of Women." Educational Record 36 (1955):112-19.

Howe, Florence. "The Female Majority." In Conspiracy of the Young, ed. Paul Lauter and Florence Howe, pp. 288-319. New York: World, 1970.

___. "Sexual Stereotypes Start Early." Saturday Review, Oct. 16, 1971, p. 76.

Hunter, K. "Help Women Plan for Second Half." Adult Leadership 13 (Apr. 1965):311.

Husbands, Sandra Acker. "Women's Place in Higher Education." Women in Education. Special Issue. School Review 80 (1972):261-74.

International Conference on Public Education, Geneva, 1952. Access of Women Education. Paris: UNESCO Publications, 1952.

Isbister, C. "Education for Womanhood." Education News 11 (Feb. 1968):3-5.

Jacobs, Sue-Ellen. "Comments on the Position of Women in the State Colleges." In Alice in Academe, ed. Corinne Geeting. Sacramento: California Commission on the Status of Women in Higher Education, 1971.

Johnson, Dorothy. Some Went West. New York: Dodd, Mead, 1965.

Katz, J. Growth and Constraints on College Students. Stanford: Stanford Institute for the Study of Human Problems, 1967.

Kerr, W. D., and Johnston, R. L. "Self-Actualization for Women through Continuing Education." Adult Leadership 13 (Dec. 1964):174-78.

Key, Mary Ritchie. "The Role of Male and Female in Children's Books--Dispelling All Doubt." *Wilson Library Bulletin*, Oct. 1971, pp. 167-76.

Lander, Patricia. "AAA Membership Survey: Career Patterns of Anthropologists." A paper presented at the 70th Annual Meeting of the American Anthropological Association, New York, 1971. Mimeo. Columbia University.

———. "Report on the Activities of the AAA Committee on the Status of Women in Anthropology." A paper presented at the 69th Annual Meeting of the American Anthropological Association, San Diego, 1970. Mimeo. Columbia University.

LeFevre, Carol. "The Mature Woman as Graduate Student." Women in Education. Special Issue. *School Review* 80 (1972):281-97.

Lembo, John M. "Altruistic Attitudes among Catholic Lay and Religious Female College Students." *Journal of Educational Research* 61 (Oct. 1967):71-74.

Levitas, Gloria. "Case Material on Sexism in Anthropology." A paper presented at the 69th Annual Meeting of the American Anthropological Association, San Diego, 1970. Mimeo. Rutgers University.

Lewis, Edwin C. "Choice and Conflict for the College Woman." *Education Digest* 35 (Nov. 1969):52-54.

Lewis, Susan. "Exploding the Fairy Princess and Other Myths." Elementary Teacher's Edition, *Scholastic Teacher*, Nov. 1971, p. 11.

Lichtenstein, H., and Block, J. R. "Middle-aged Co-ed in Evening Colleges." *Adult Education* 13 (Summer 1963):234-39.

London, J. "Continuing Education of Women: A Challenge for Our Society." *Adult Leadership* 14 (Apr. 1966): 326-28.

Loring, Rosalind K. "Continuing Education for Women." *Adult Leadership* 18 (May 1969):5-8.

Lowie, Robert H., and Hollingworth, Leta Steller. "Science and Feminism." *Scientific Monthly* 3 (1916): 277-84.

Lutzker, Edythe. *Women Gain a Place in Medicine*, ed. Daniel Greenberg. New York: McGraw-Hill, 1969.

McFerran, Ann. *Elizabeth Blackwell, First Woman Doctor*. New York: Grossett & Dunlap, n.d.

Matthews, Ester. "Attitudes toward Career and Marriage and the Development of Life Styles in Young Women." *Journal of Counseling Psychology* 2 (Winter 1964): 375-84.

Meade, Marion. "A Mother Fights Back." *Woman's Day*, Mar. 1970, p. 64.

Mencher, Joan, and Hanchett, Suzanne. "Hidden Processes of Discrimination." A paper presented at the 69th Annual Meeting of the American Anthropological Association, San Diego, 1970. Mimeo. CUNY, Lehman.

Meyer, Carolyn. "Chiefly for Children." McCalls, Dec. 1970, pp. 8-11.

Miles, Betty. "Harmful Lessons Little Girls Learn in School." Redbook, Mar. 1971, p. 86.

———. "Women's Liberation Comes to Class." Elementary Teacher's Edition, Scholastic Teacher, Nov. 1971, pp. 9-10.

Minuchin, Patricia. "The Schooling of Tomorrow's Women." School Review 80 (1972):199-208.

Mitchell, B. "Oregon's Campus Day for Women Program." Adult Leadership 15 (Apr. 1967):359-60.

Mooney, J. D. "Attrition among Ph.D. Candidates: An Analysis of a Cohort of Recent Woodrow Wilson Fellows." Journal of Human Resources 3 (1968):47-62.

Nathan, Dorothy. Women of Courage. New York: Random House, 1964.

National Association of Women Deans and Counselors. Women's Roles, Labels, and Stereotypes. Washington, D.C.: National Education Association, 1971.

Neugarten, Bernice. "Education and the Life-cycle." Women in Education. Special Issue. School Review 80 (1972):209-16.

Newcomb, T. M. "Some Patterned Consequences of Membership in a College Community." In Public Opinion and Propaganda, ed. D. Katz, pp. 345-446. New York: Dryden Press, 1954.

Newcomber, Mabel. A Century of Higher Education for Women. New York: Harper & Row, 1959.

Nilsen, Aileen Pace. "Women in Children's Literature." College English (May 1971):918-26.

Palubinskas, Alice. "Personality Changes in College Women during Four Years." Proceedings of the Academy of Science 59 (1952):389-91.

Papashvily, Helen. Louisa May Alcott. Boston: Houghton Mifflin, 1965.

Perrault, Gerri. "Q: Do the Schools Need Women's Liberation? A: Yes, Yes, Yes, Yes, Yes..." Minnesota PTA News, Oct. 1971, pp. 14-17.

Pitcher, Evelyn Goodenough, and Prelinger, Ernst. Children Tell Stories: An Analysis of Fantasy. New York: International Universities Press, 1969.

Praderie, M. "Vocational Training for Girls and Women." CIRF Abstracts 9 (section 2, 17930, 1970).

President's Commission on the Status of Women. "Education of Women; Adaptation or Report." School Life 46 (Nov. 1963):17-19.

Rai, S. "Female Education in Villages." Social Welfare 16 (Sept. 1969):12.

"Rampant Sexism Found in Books for Children." St. Paul Dispatch, June 15, 1971, p. 20.

Rao, M. Subba. "Young Mothers' Training: Besides Syllabus." Social Welfare 16 (June 1969):30-31.

Reid, Marion. Woman, Her Education and Influence. New York, 1848.

Rice, Oliver. "Some Observations on the Women's Job Corps." Audio-Visual Instruction 13 (Feb. 1968): 131-37.

Riesman, D. "Some Dilemmas of Women's Education." Educational Record 46 (Fall 1965):424-34.

Rorke, M. W. Vocational Contributions of Women Graduates of the University of Queensland. Portland, Ore.: International Scholarly Book Services, n.d.

Rosenthal, Robert, and Jackson, Lenore. Pygmalion in the Classroom: Teacher Expectations and Pupil's Intellectual Development. New York: Holt, Rinehart & Winston, 1968.

Rossi, Alice. "The Utilization of Women Faculty in Colleges and Universities." A paper presented at the 37th Conference of Deans of Colleges and Universities of the Southern States, Dec. 3, 1968, Atlanta.

Russell, Dora. Hypatia; or, Woman and Knowledge. New York: E. P. Dutton, 1925.

Sanford, Nevitt, ed. The American College. New York: John Wiley, 1962.

———. Self and Society: Social Change and Individual Development. New York: Atherton Press, 1967.

"Schools' Sexual Stereotyping Angers Her." Minneapolis Tribune, Aug. 3, 1971, p. 8.

Seminar on the Role of Women's Non-Governmental Organizations in Literacy Teaching for Women and Girls in the Framework of Programme of Community Development, 18th Triennial Council Meeting, Teheran, 14-26 May 1966. Literacy: A Social Experience: Report on a Seminar. Paris: International Council of Women, 1966.

Severn, Bill. Free but Not Equal: How Women Won the Right to Vote. New York: Julian Messner, 1967.

Silverstein, Leni M., and Friedman, Elizabeth. "Graduate School Strategies." A paper presented at the 71st Annual Meeting of the American Anthropological Association, Toronto, 1972. Mimeo. New School for Social Research.

Simon, Rita J.; Clark, Shirley Merritt; and Galway, Kathleen. "The Woman Ph.D.: A Recent Profile." Social Problems 15 (Fall 1967):221-56.

Simon, Rita J.; Clark, Shirley Merritt; and Tifft, Larry L. "Of Nepotism, Marriage, and the Pursuit of an Academic Career." Sociology of Education 39 (Fall 1966):334-58.

Spinks, Sarah. "Sugar and Spice." This Magazine Is about Schools, Summer 1969, pp. 59-78. Reprint, Johnson Reprint, n.d.

Stavn, Diane Gersoni. "The Skirts in Fiction about Boys: A Maxi Mess." School Library Journal, Jan. 1971, pp. 66-70.

Stefflre, Buford. "Run, Mama, Run: Women Workers in Elementary Readers." Vocational Guidance Quarterly 18 (Dec. 1969):99-102.

Sternberg, C. "Personality Traits of College Students Majoring in Different Fields." Psychological Monographs 69 (1955).

Swarth, Lillian. "Profile of the Adult Females Student and Retraining." CIRF Abstracts 9 (section 2, B35777, 1970).

Tait, Marjorie. The Education of Women for Citizenship: Some Practical Suggestions. Problems in Education. Paris: UNESCO Publications, 1954.

Taylor, George. "Universal Co-education?" Times Educational Supplement 2651 (Mar. 11, 1966):743.

Tegner, Bruce, and McGrath, Alice. Self-Defense for Girls: A Secondary School and College Manual. Rev. ed. Ventura, Calif.: Thor, 1961.

Thibert, Margherite. "The Vocational Training of Women and Its Problems." CIRF Abstracts 8 (section 2, B25471, 1968).

Tinker, A. H. "Programs for Mature Co-eds." Adult Leadership, Mar. 1965, pp. 283-84.

Trecker, Janice Law. "Woman's Place Is in the Curriculum." Saturday Review, Oct. 16, 1971, p. 83.

___. "Women in U.S. History High School Textbooks." Social Education, Mar. 1971, p. 249.

Tripathi, Kalawati. Access of Girls to Primary, Secondary and Higher Education. Mimeo. Sacramento: California State University Library, 1967.

Tucker, Alan; Gottlieb, David; and Prease, J. Attrition of Graduate Students. Publication 8. East Lansing: Office of Research Development and Graduate Schools, Michigan State University, 1964.

UNESCO. Access of Girls and Women to Education in Rural Areas: A Comparative Study. Educational Studies and Documents. Paris: UNESCO Publications, 1964.

___. Access of Girls and Women to Higher Education. Paris: UNESCO Publications, 1966.

___. Access of Girls and Women to Technical and Vocational Education: Questionnaire. Paris: UNESCO Publications, 1967.

___. Access of Women to Out-of-School Education: Report Prepared for the United Nations Commission on the Status of Women. Paris: UNESCO Publications, 1961.

___. Comparative Study on Access of Girls and Women to Higher Education. Paris: UNESCO Publications, 1967.

___. Comparative Study on Access of Girls and Women to Technical and Vocational Education. Paris: UNESCO Publications, 1968.

___. Comparative Study on Access of Girls to Elementary Education. Paris: UNESCO Publications, 1962.

_____. Equality of Access to Education of Girls and
Women: Resolutions and Work Plans Adopted by the
General Conference of UNESCO and Its Fourteenth
Session (1966). Paris: UNESCO Publications, 1967.
_____. Reports of Member States on the Implementation of
the Convention and Recommendation against Discrimina-
tion in Education: Report of the Special Committee
of the Executive Board of Discrimination in Education.
Paris: UNESCO Publications, 1968.
_____. Study Grants and Courses for Women. Paris:
UNESCO Publications, 1969.
_____. Study of Co-education. Paris: UNESCO Publications,
1969.
_____. Study on Equal Access of Girls and Women to
Literacy. Paris: UNESCO Publications, 1970.
_____. Women and Education. Paris: UNESCO Publications,
1963.
_____. Regional Office for Education in Asia. Documents
on Women's Education and Women in Public Life.
Bangkok: UNESCO Publications, 1970.
_____. Secretariat. Access of Women to Education,
UNESCO Activities in 1965-1966 of Special Interest to
Women and Main Activities Proposed for 1967-1968.
Paris: UNESCO Publications, 1967.
_____. Secretariat. Women and Education in the World
Today. Paris: UNESCO Publications, 1968.
U.N. Department of Economic and Social Affairs. "Women
and Technical Assistance: First-person stories."
United Nations Review 4, nos. 11, 12; 5, nos. 1, 2
(1958).
UNICEF. Assessment of Projects for the Education and
Training of Women and Girls for Family and Community
Life. New York: UNESCO Publications, 1970.
U.S. Department of Health, Education and Welfare.
Special Report on Women and Graduate Study. Report
13 (June 1968).
U.S. Department of Labor, Women's Bureau. Continuing
Education Programs and Services for Women. Washington,
D.C.: U.S. Government Printing Office, n.d.
Vance, Carole. "Sexual Stratification in Academic
Anthropology." A paper presented at the 69th Annual
Meeting of the American Anthropological Association,
San Diego, 1970. Mimeo. Columbia University.
Walawender, Marge Lisowski. The Behavior and Role Ex-
pectations of Foreign and American Graduate Women.
Ann Arbor: University Microfilms, 1964.
Weitzman, Lenore J.; Eifler, Deborah; Hokada, Elizabeth;
and Ross, Catherine. "Sex Role Socialization in
Picture Books for Pre-school Children." A paper pre-
sented at the American Sociological Association
Meeting, Denver, 1971. Mimeo. University of
California, Davis.

195

West, Anne Grant. Report on Sex Bias in the Public
Schools. New York City Chapter of the National Or-
ganization for Women (N.O.W.), A. West, 453 Seventh
Street, New York 11215.

White, Lynn. Educating Our Daughters. New York:
Harper & Row, 1950.

White, William F. "Personality Correlates of Cheating
among College Women under Stress of Independent,
Opportunistic Behavior." Journal of Educational
Research 61 (Oct. 1967):68-70.

Wilson, Pauline. College Women Who Express Futility: A
Study Based on Fifty Selected Life Histories of Women
College Graduates. New York: Columbia University,
Teachers College, Bureau of Publications, 1950.

"Women in Training." CIRF Abstracts 8 (section 8,
B29605, 1969).

Women on Words and Images. Task Force of Central New
Jersey Chapter of N.O.W. Dick and Jane as Victims:
Sex Stereotyping in Children's Readers. Women on
Words and Images, 25 Cleveland Lane, RD 4, Princeton,
N.J. 08540.

Woody, Thomas H. A History of Women's Education in the
United States. 2 vols. New York: Octagon Books,
1929.

Yost, Edna. American Women of Nursing. 2d ed. Philadelphia: J. B. Lippincott, 1965.

____. American Women of Science. Rev. ed. Philadelphia:
J. B. Lippincott, 1955.

____. Women of Modern Science. New York: Dodd, Mead,
1959.

Young, Michael. The Rise of the Meritocracy, 1870-2033:
An Essay on Education and Equality. Baltimore:
Penguin Books, 1959.

Zahm, John Augustine. Women in Science. New York:
Appleton-Century-Crofts, 1913.

WOMEN AND WAR

Alsop, Gulielma Fell, and McBride, Mary F. Arms and the
Girl: A Guide to Personal Adjustment in War Work and
War Marriage. New York: Vanguard Press, 1943.

Anthony, Susan B. Out of the Kitchen into the War. New
York: Stephen Daye, 1943.

Baer, Clara Gregory. "Women and the War." National
Education Association of the U.S. Journal of Addresses
and Proceedings, 1918, pp. 355-57.

Degen, Marie L. History of the Women's Peace Party.
First published, 1939. Reprint, New York: Burt
Franklin, n.d.

Elmendorf, Mary L. "The Role of Women as Agents for
Peaceful Social Change." A paper presented at the 12th
World Conference of the Society for International
Development, Ottawa, 1971.

Flynn, Elizabeth Gurley. Women in the War. New York:
    Workers Library, 1942.
Grant, Zalin. "Mobilization of Women in Vietnam." New
    Republic 158 (June 1, 1968):11-13.
Heiman, Leo. "Warriors in Skirts." Military Review 42
    (Mar. 1962):13-22.
Ibarruri, Dolores. They Will Not Pass: The Autobiography
    of La Pasionaria. New York: International Publishers,
    1966.
_____. The Women Want a People's Peace. New York:
    Workers Library, 1941.
International Conference on the Role of Women in the
    Struggle for Peace and Development, Nov. 29-Dec. 6,
    1964. Report. Jerusalem: Department of Public Infor-
    mation, 1964.
International Seminar in Norway on UNESCO's East-West
    Major Project. East-West Cultural Existence. Mimeo.
    Oslo: Women's International League for Peace and
    Freedom, 1961.
Key, Ellen. War and Peace and the Future. New York: G.
    P. Putnam, 1916.
Laffin, John. Women in Battle. New York: Abelard
    Schuman, 1968.
McConnell, Dorothy. Women, War and Fascism. New York:
    American League against War and Fascism, 1935.
McLaren, Barbara. Women of the War. London: Hodder &
    Stoughton, 1917.
"Military Service: An Open Door to Learning for America's
    Young Women." Adult Leadership 14 (Jan. 1966):229.
Polster, Elizabeth. "Conscription: The War on Women and
    Children." March 1967 Speech. Women's International
    League for Peace and Freedom, 2006 Walnut St.,
    Philadelphia, Pa. 19103.
Schaffter, Dorothy. What Comes of Training Women for War.
    Washington, D.C.: American Council on Education, 1948.
Severn, Jill. Women and Draft Resistance: Revolution in
    the Revolution. S.R.W. (Seattle Radical Women), 3815
    Fifth Ave. N.E., Seattle, Wash. 98103.
Snowden, Ethel Annakin. "Woman and War." National
    Education Association of the U.S. Journal of Addresses
    and Proceedings, 1915, pp. 54-56.
Treadwell, Mattie. The Women's Army Corps. Washington,
    D.C.: Office of the Chief of Military History,
    Department of the Army, 1954.
Wakefield, Dan. Supernation at Peace and War. Boston:
    Little, Brown, Atlantic Monthly Press, 1968.
Young, Agatha. The Women and the Crisis. New York:
    McDowell, Oblensky, 1959.

MISOGYNY

Belfort-Bax, E. The Fraud of Feminism. London: Grant
    Richards, 1913.

Bennett, Dan. "Who Says It's a Man's World?" Family
    Weekly, Mar. 15, 1970, p. 4.
Centers, Richard. "Authoritarianism and Misogyny."
    Journal of Social Psychology 61 (1963):81-85.
Deutsch, Helene. The Psychology of Women. New York:
    Grune & Stratton, 1944.
Dingwall, E. J. The American Woman: A Historical Study.
    London: Duckworth, 1956.
Fast, Julius. Incompatibility of Men and Women and How
    to Overcome It. New York: M. Evans, 1971.
Goldberg, P. "Are Women Prejudiced against Women?"
    Transaction, Apr. 1, 1968.
Hays, H. R. The Dangerous Sex: The Myth of Feminine
    Evil. New York: Simon & Schuster, 1965.
    . From Ape to Angel: An Informal History of Social
    Anthropology. New York: G. P. Putnam, Capricorn
    Books, 1962.
Hernton, Calvin. Sex and Racism in America. New York:
    Grove Press, 1966.
Hinckle, Warren, and Hinckle, Marianne. "A History of the
    Rise of the Unusual Movement for Women Power in the
    United States, 1961-1968." Ramparts, Feb. 1968, pp.
    22-31.
Kamiat, Arnold H. Feminine Superiority and Other Myths.
    New York: Twayne, 1907.
Kaplan, Justin, ed. With Malice toward Women: A Handbook
    for Women-haters Drawn from the Best Minds of All
    Times. London: W. H. Allen, 1953.
Ludovici, Anthony M. Enemies of Women. London: Carroll
    & Nicholson, 1948.
Lundberg, Ferdinand, and Farnham, Marynia F. Modern
    Woman: The Lost Sex. New York: Harper & Row, 1947.
Mailer, Norman. "The Time of Her Time." In Advertisements
    for Myself. New York: G. P. Putnam, 1959.
Moore, Josslyn. "Hetaerism among American Anthropologists:
    A Study of the 1970 AAA Meeting." A paper presented at
    the 70th Annual Meeting of the American Anthropological
    Association, New York, 1971. Mimeo. Hunter College,
    CUNY.
Reeve, Tapping. The Law of Baron and Femme. 3d ed. First
    published, 1862. Reprint, New York: Collectors
    Editions, Source Book Press, 1970.
Sacks, Karen. "Sexism: A Marxist View." A paper pre-
    sented at the 70th Annual Meeting of the American
    Anthropological Association, New York, 1971. Mimeo.
    University of Oakland.
Seltman, Chris. Women in Antiquity. London: Thames &
    Hudson, 1956.
Strecker, Edward. Their Mother's Sons. Philadelphia:
    J. B. Lippincott, 1946.
Wylie, Philip. Generation of Vipers. Rev. ed. New York:
    Simon & Schuster, 1968.

WOMEN IN HISTORY

Abbot, Willis J. Notable Women in History. Philadelphia:
    John C. Winston, 1913.
Adams, Henry. Historical Essays. 2 vols. New York:
    Adler, 1891.
Agrippa, Cornelius. Ancient and Modern Ladies Oracle.
    Los Angeles: Price, Stern, Sloan, 1967.
Annals of the American Academy of Political and Social
    Science, May 1947.
Aries, Philippe. Centuries of Childhood. New York:
    Alfred A. Knopf, 1962.
Baer, Thelma. "Women in the History of Anthropology." A
    paper presented at the 71st Annual Meeting of the
    American Anthropological Association, Toronto, 1972.
    Mimeo. New School for Social Research.
Barney, Laura. Women in a Changing World: The Story of
    the International Council of Women since 1888. New
    York: Fernhill House, 1966.
Beard, Mary Ritter. Woman as Force in History: A Study
    in Traditions and Realities. New York: Macmillan,
    1946.
Benson, Mary S. Women in Eighteenth-Century America.
    Port Washington, N.Y.: Kennikat Press, 1935.
Bland, James. An Essay in Praise of Women: Marks Upon
    Music and Dancing and Other Recreations Fit for
    Ladies, Exhortations to the Knowledge of One's Self.
    Also, Observations and Reflections in Defense of the
    Fair Sex, against Base and Satyrical Authors: The
    Whole Being a Composition of Wit and Humor, Morality
    and Divinity, Fit to Be Perused by All the Curious and
    Ingenious, Especially the Ladies. London: Jane
    Bland, 1733.
Borgese, Elisabeth Mann. The Ascent of Woman. New
    York: George Braziller, 1963.
Bradford, Gamaliel. Elizabethan Women. Freeport, N.Y.:
    Books for Libraries, 1936.
Brittain, Vera. Lady into Woman: A History of Women
    from Victoria to Elizabeth II. New York: Macmillan,
    1953.
Brown, Dee. Gentle Tamers: Women in the Old Wild West.
    Lincoln: University of Nebraska Press, 1968.
Bugan, Kenneth Gregory. "Women in the Public Affairs of
    Illinois, 1916-1920." Master's thesis, University of
    Illinois, 1959.
Bullough, Vern L., and Bullough, Bonnie. The Subordinate
    Sex: A History of Attitudes toward Women. Urbana:
    University of Illinois Press, 1973.
Chamberlin, Hope. Women in Congress, 1917-71. New York:
    Praeger, 1972.
Clark, Alice. Working Life of Women in the Seventeenth
    Century. Clifton, N.J.: Augustus M. Kelley, 1919.

Commetti, Elizabeth. "Women in the American Revolution." New England Quarterly 20 (Sept. 1947):329-46.

Cuddeford, Gladys. Women and Society from Victorian Times to the Present Day. New York: Fernhill House, 1967.

Cunnington, C. Willett. Feminine Attitudes in the Nineteenth Century. New York: Macmillan, 1936.

Daniels, Jonathan. Washington Quadrille: The Dance beside the Documents. Garden City, N.Y.: Doubleday, 1968.

Davis, Elizabeth Gould. The First Sex. New York: G. P. Putnam, 1972.

Degler, Carl N. Out of Our Past. New York: Harper & Row, 1959.

Diner, Helen. Mothers and Amazons: The First Feminine History of Culture. First published, 1938. Garden City, N.Y.: Doubleday, 1973.

Douthit, Mary Osborn, ed. The Souvenir of Western Women. Portland, Ore.: Anderson & Duriway, 1905.

Drury, Clifford Merrill. First White Women over the Rockies: Diaries, Letters, and Biographical Sketches of the Six Women of the Oregon Mission Who Made the Overland Journey in 1836 and 1838. Glendale, Calif.: A. H. Clark, 1963-66.

Earle, Alice M. Colonial Dames and Goodwives. Frederick Ungar, 1962.

Ellet, Elizabeth. Women of the American Revolution. 3 vols. New York: Haskell House, 1969.

Fuller, Margaret. Woman in the Nineteenth Century, and Kindred Papers Relating to the Sphere, Condition and Duties of Women. First published, 1855. Reprint, New York: Collectors Editions, Source Book Press, 1970.

Gleason, Caroline Joanna. Legislation for Women in Oregon. Washington, D.C.: Catholic University of America, 1924.

Greenville Ladies' Association in Aid of the Volunteers of the Confederate Army. Minutes of the Proceedings. Durham, N.C.: Duke University Press, 1937.

Hagood, Margaret Jarman. Mothers of the South: Portraiture of the White Tenant Farm Woman. Chapel Hill: University of North Carolina Press, 1939.

Hale, Sarah Josepha. Women's Record; or, Sketches of All Distinguished Women, from the Creation to A.D. 1854. Arranged in Four Eras with Selections from Female Writers of Every Age. First published, 1855. 2 vols. Reprint, New York: Collectors Editions, Source Book Press, 1970.

Hankins, Marie Louise. Women of New York. New York: M. L. Hankins, 1861.

Harkness, David James. Southern Heroines of Colonial Days. Knoxville: University of Tennessee, Extension Series, 1963.

Hecker, Eugene Arthur. A Short History of Woman's Rights from the Days of Augustus to the Present Time. New York: G. P. Putnam, 1910.

Henry, Alice. Women and the Labor Movement. First published, 1923. Reprint, New York: Arno Press, 1971.

Hill, Kate A. Home Builders of West Texas. San Antonio: Naylor, 1970.

Himmelfarb, Gertrude. Victorian Minds. New York: Alfred A. Knopf, 1968.

Hirsch, A. H. The Love Elite: The Story of Woman's Emancipation and Her Drive for Sexual Fulfillment. New York: Julian Press, 1963.

Holliday, Carl. Woman's Life in Colonial Days. First published, 1922. Reprint, Detroit: Gale Research, 1970.

Humphrey, Grace. Women in American History. Freeport, N.Y.: Books for Libraries, 1919.

Illinois Commission on the Status of Women. Report on the Status of Women. Springfield: Governor's Office, 1965.

Irwin, Inez Hayes. Angels and Amazons: One Hundred Years of American Women. Garden City, N.Y.: Doubleday, Doran, 1934.

Johnson, G. W. Evolution of Woman from Subjection to Comradeship. London: Holden, 1926.

Jones, Katharine M. Heroines of Dixie: Confederate Women Tell Their Story of the War. Indianapolis: Bobbs-Merrill, 1955.

____. When Sherman Comes: Southern Women and the "Great March." Indianapolis: Bobbs-Merrill, 1969.

Josephson, Hannah. Golden Threads: New England's Mill Girls and Mandates. First published, 1949. Reprint, New York: Russell & Russell, 1967.

Judek, Stanislaw. Women in the Public Service: Their Utilization and Employment. Ottawa: Canada Department of Labour, Economics and Research Branch, 1968.

Juliet, Mitchell. Women: The Longest Revolution. R.E.P. (Radical Education Project), Box 561-A, Detroit, Mich., 48232.

Kemp-Welch, Alice. Of Six Medieval Women. First published, 1903. Reprint, London: Corner House, 1972.

Kraditor, Aileen S., ed. Up from the Pedestal: Selected Documents from the History of American Feminism. New York: Quadrangle Books, 1968.

Langdon-Davies, John. A Short History of Women. New York: Viking, 1927.

Leonard, Eugenie A. American Woman in Colonial and Revolutionary Times, 1565-1800. Philadelphia: University of Pennsylvania Press, 1961.

Lerner, Gerda. The Woman in American History. Reading, Mass.: Addison-Wesley, 1971.

Subject Topics

Letourneau, Ch. "La femme à travers les ages." Revue
 de l'Ecole d'Anthropologie 11 (1901):273-90.
Longwell, Marjorie R. America and Women. Philadelphia:
 Dorrance, 1962.
Lutz, Alma. Crusade for Freedom: Women of the Anti-
 Slavery Movement. Boston: Beacon Press, 1968.
McHer, Keith. "The Beginnings of Women's Movements,
 1800-1840." Ph.D. dissertation, Yale University, 1963.
Marble, Annie Russell. The Women Who Came in the
 Mayflower. Boston: Pilgrim Press, 1920.
Martines, Julia, and Martines, Lauro. Women in History.
 New York: Harper & Row, 1972.
Massey, Mary Elizabeth. Bonnet Brigades. New York:
 Alfred A. Knopf, 1966.
Meakin, Annette M. B. Women in Transition. London:
 Methuen, 1907.
Morgan, David. Suffragists and Democrats: The Politics
 of Woman Suffrage in America. East Lansing: Michigan
 State University Press, 1971.
Morgan, Elaine. The Descent of Women. New York: Stein
 & Day, 1972.
Nichols, Thomas Low. Woman: In All Ages and Nations.
 New York: Fowlers & Wells, 1849.
North Carolina Historical Commission. Addresses to the
 Unveiling of the Memorial to the North Carolina Women
 of the Confederacy, Presented to the State by the Late
 Ashley Horne. Raleigh: Edwards & Broughton Printing
 Co., 1914.
Noyes, Ethel J. R. C. The Women of the Mayflower and the
 Women of Plymouth Colony. Plymouth, Mass.: Memorial
 Press, 1921.
O'Connor, Lillian. Pioneer Women Orators. New York:
 Columbia University Press, 1954.
O'Neill, William L. Everyone Was Brave: The Rise and
 Fall of Feminism in America. New York: Quadrangle
 Books, 1969.
___. The Woman Movement: Feminism in the United States
 and England. London: Allen & Unwin, 1969.
Ossoli, Sarah M. Woman in the Nineteenth Century and
 Kindred Papers Relating to the Sphere, Condition, and
 Duties of a Woman. First published, 1874. Reprint,
 Westport, Conn.: Greenwood Press, 1968.
Power, Eileen. "The Position of Women." In The Legacy
 of the Middle Ages. London: Oxford University Press,
 1962.
Putnam, Emily James. The Lady: Studies of Certain
 Significant Phases of Her History. First published,
 1910. Reprint, Chicago: University of Chicago Press,
 1970.
Rappaport, Philip. Looking Forward: A Treatise on the
 Status of Woman and the Origin and Growth of the
 Family and the State. Chicago: C. H. Kerr, 1913.

Reeve, Tapping. The Law of Baron and Femme. 3d ed.
First published, 1862. New York: Collectors Editions,
Source Book Press, 1970.
Riegel, Robert E. American Feminists. Lawrence:
University of Kansas Press, 1968.
    . American Women: A Story of Social Change.
Rutherford, N.J.: Fairleigh Dickinson University
Press, 1970.
Ross, Isabel. Sons of Adam, Daughters of Eve: The Role
of Women in American History. New York: Harper &
Row, 1969.
Ross, Nancy. Westward the Women. Freeport, N.Y.: Books
for Libraries, n.d.
    . Heroines of the Early West. New York: Random
House, 1960.
Rossi, Alice S. The Feminist Papers: From Adams to de
Beauvoir. Irvington, N.Y.: Columbia University
Press, 1973.
Sargent, Shirley. Pioneers in Petticoats: Yosemite's
First Women, 1856-1900. Costa Mesa, Calif.:
Trans-Anglo Books, n.d.
Scott, Anne Firor. "After Suffrage: Southern Women in
the '20s." Journal of Southern History 30 (Aug.
1964):298-318.
    . The Southern Lady: From Pedestal to Politics,
1830-1930. Chicago: University of Chicago Press,
1970.
    , ed. The American Woman: Who Was She? Englewood
Cliffs, N.J.: Prentice-Hall, 1971.
Seltman, Chris. Women in Antiquity. New York:
Macmillan, Collier Books, 1957.
Seton, Cynthia. Special and Curious Blessing. New
York: W. W. Norton, 1968.
Sillen, Samuel. Women against Slavery. New York:
Masses & Mainstream, 1955.
Simkins, Francis Butler. The Women of the Confederacy.
First published, 1936. Reprint, St. Clair Shores,
Mich.: Scholarly Press, 1971.
Sinclair, Andrew. The Better Half: The Emancipation
of the American Woman. New York: Harper & Row, 1965.
Smith, Page. Daughters of the Promised Land: Women in
American History. Boston: Little, Brown, 1970.
Sprague, William. Women and the West. North Quincy,
Mass.: Christopher, 1940.
Spruill, Julia Cherry. Women's Life and Work in the
Southern Colonies. First published, 1938. Reprint,
New York: Russell & Russell, 1969.
Stern, Madeleine. We the Women: Career Firsts of
Nineteenth-century America. New York: Schulte, 1963.
Taylor, Gordon Rattray. Sex in History. New York:
Vanguard Press, 1954.
Texas Governor's Commission on the Status of Women.
Report. Austin: Governor's Office, 1967.

203

Trahey, Jane, ed. Harper's Bazaar: 100 Years of the
   American Female. New York: Random House, 1967.
Trecker, Janice Law. "Women in U.S. History in High
   School Textbooks." Social Education 35 (1971):249-
   61, 338.
U.S. Civil Service Commission. Bureau of Management
   Services. Study of Employment of Women in the
   Federal Government. Washington, D.C.: Manpower
   Statistics Division, U.S. Civil Service Commission,
   n.d.

SUFFRAGE, HISTORICAL FEMINISM

Adams, Mildred. The Right to Be People. Philadelphia:
   J. B. Lippincott, 1967.
Anthony, Susan B.; Stanton, Elizabeth Cady; and Harper,
   I. H., eds. History of Women's Suffrage. 6 vols.
   First published, 1881. Reprint, New York: Arno
   Press, 1972.
Association for the Advancement of Women. Historical
   Account of the Association for the Advancement of
   Women, 1873-1893. Dedham, Mass.: Transcript, 1893.
Astell, Mary. A Serious Proposal to the Ladies for the
   Advancement of Their True and Greatest Interest.
   First published, 1694. Reprint, New York: Collectors
   Editions, Source Book Press, 1970.
Barton, Ann. Mother Bloor. New York: Workers Library,
   1935.
_____. Mother Bloor: The Spirit of 76. New York:
   Workers Library, 1937.
Bell, Ralcy Husted. Woman from Bondage to Freedom. New
   York: Critic Guide, 1921.
Bennett, Arnold. Our Women: Chapters on the Sex-Discord.
   London: Cassell, 1920.
Blackburn, Helen. Women's Suffrage: A Record of the
   Women's Suffrage Movement in the British Isles. First
   published, 1902. Reprint, Millwood, N.Y.: Kraus
   Reprint, 1970.
Blackwell, Alice Stone. Lucy Stone: Pioneer of Women's
   Rights. Boston: Little, Brown, 1930.
Brockett, L. P. Woman: Her Rights, Wrongs, Privileges
   and Responsibilities; Her Present Legal Status in
   England, France and the United States, and Woman Suf-
   frage and Its Folly. First published, 1869. Reprint,
   Freeport, N.Y.: Books for Libraries, 1970.
Bushnell, Horace. Women's Suffrage: The Reform against
   Nature. New York: Charles Scribner's, 1869.
Catt, Carrie Chapman. Woman Suffrage and Politics: The
   Inner Story of the Suffrage Movement. First published,
   1923. Reprint, Seattle: University of Washington
   Press, 1969.

Clark, David L. _Brockden Brown and the Rights of Women_.
Folcroft, Pa.: Folcroft Press, 1912.

Convention on Women's Rights, Akron, Ohio, 1851.
Proceedings. First published, 1851. Reprint, New
York: Burt Franklin, 1969.

Coolidge, Olivia. _Women's Rights: The Suffrage Movement in America, 1848-1920_. New York: E. P. Dutton,
n.d.

Courtney, Janet. _Adventurous Thirties: A Chapter in
the Women's Movement_. Freeport, N.Y.: Books for
Libraries, 1933.

Davis, Paulina Wright. _A History of the National
Women's Rights Movement_. First published, 1871.
Reprint, New York: Collectors Editions, Source Book
Press, 1970.

Duniway, Abigail Scott. _Path Breaking: An Autobio-
graphical History of the Equal Suffrage Movement in
Pacific Coast States_. First published, 1915.
Reprint, New York: Collectors Editions, Source Book
Press, 1970.

Eastman, Max. _Is Woman Suffrage Important?_ New York:
Men's League for Woman Suffrage, 1911.

_Equal Rights for All: George William Curtis in the New
York State Constitutional Convention_. Rochester,
N.Y.: New York State Constitutional Campaign
Committee, 1867.

Faber, Doris. _Petticoat Politics: How Women Won the
Right to Vote_. New York: Lothrop, Lee & Shepard,
1967.

Farrar, Rowena. _A Wondrous Moment Then_. New York:
Holt, Rinehart & Winston, 1968.

Fawcett, Millicent G. _Women's Suffrage_. First published, 1912. Reprint, New York: Collectors Editions,
Source Book Press, 1970.

Flexner, Eleanor. _A Century of Struggle: The Woman's
Rights Movement in the U.S.A._ New York: Atheneum,
1968.

Foster, G. Allen. _Votes for Women_. New York:
Criterion, 1966.

Fulford, Roger. _Votes for Women: The Story of Struggle_.
London: Faber & Faber, 1958.

Goodwin, Grace Duffield. _Anti-Suffrage: Ten Good
Reasons_. New York: Duffield, 1913.

Grimes, Alan. _The Puritan Ethic and Women Suffrage_.
New York: Oxford University Press, 1967.

Grimké, Sarah N. _Letters on the Equality of the Sexes,
and the Condition of Woman_. First published, 1838.
Reprint, New York: Collectors Editions, Source Book
Press, 1970.

Hale, Beatrice Forbes-Robertson. _What Women Want_. New
York: Frederick A. Stokes, 1914.

Haskell, Oreola Williams. _Banner Bearers_. New York:
W. F. Humphrey, 1920.

Howe, Julia Ward. _Julia Ward Howe and the Woman Suf-
frage Movement_. Boston: D. Estes, 1913.
Ireland, William. "The Rise and Fall of the Suffrage
Movement." _Leviathan_, May 1970.
Jacobi, Mary Putnam. _Common Sense Applied to Woman
Suffrage_. New York: G. P. Putnam, 1915.
Keniston, Ellen, and Keniston, Kenneth. "An American
Anachronism: The Image of Women and Work."
American Scholar 33 (Summer 1965):355-78.
Kraditor, Aileen S. _Ideas of the Woman Suffrage Move-
ment, 1890-1920_. New York: Columbia University
Press, 1965.
Lemons, J. Stanley. _The Woman Citizen: Social Feminism
in the 1920s_. Urbana: University of Illinois Press,
1972.
Leonard, Clara T. _Woman Suffrage: Letter from Mrs.
Clara T. Leonard_. 1884.
Martin, Edward Sanford. _The Unrest of Women_. New York:
Appleton, 1913.
Maude la Claviere, Marie. _The Women of the Renaissance:
A Study of Feminism_. New York: G. P. Putnam, 1901.
Maule, Frances. _Woman Suffrage History: Arguments and
Results_. New York: National Woman Suffrage Pub-
lishing, 1911.
Mencken, H. L. _In Defense of Women_. New York: Alfred
A. Knopf, 1922.
National American Woman Suffrage Association. _Report of
the International Council of Women_. Washington,
D.C.: National American Woman Suffrage Association,
1888.
_____. _Victory: How Women Won It: A Centennial
Symposium, 1840-1940_. New York: H. W. Wilson, 1940.
_____. _Woman Suffrage, Arguments and Results_. 2 vols.
First published, 1911. Reprint, Milwood, N.Y.: Kraus
Reprint, 1970.
Nevinson, Mary. _Ancient Suffragettes_. London, 1911.
Noun, Louise R. _Strong-Minded Women: The Emergence of
the Women Suffrage Movement in Iowa_. Ames: Iowa
State University Press, 1970.
Owen, Harold. _Woman Adrift: A Statement of the Case
against Suffragism_. New York: E. P. Dutton, 1912.
Ozer, Jerome, ed. _Woman Suffrage in America_. 13 vols.
New York: Arno Press, 1969.
Pankhurst, Christabel. _Plain Facts about a Great Evil_.
London: Nutt, 1913.
Pankhurst, Estelle Sylvia. _The Life of Emmeline
Pankhurst: The Suffragette Struggle for Women's
Citizenship_. New York: Kraus Reprint, 1969.
_____. _Save the Mothers_. London: Alfred A. Knopf, 1930.
_____. _The Suffrage Movement: An Intimate Account of
Persons and Ideals_. New York: Longmans Green, 1931.
_____. _The Suffragette: The History of the Women's
Militant Suffrage Movement 1905-1910_. First pub-
lished, 1911. Reprint, New York: Collectors Editions,
Source Book Press, 1968.

Park, Maud Wood. "The Woman of America and the Demo-
cratic Awakening." In National Education Association
of the U.S., Addresses and Proceedings, 1922, pp.
216-17. Washington, D.C.: U.S. Government Printing
Office, 1922.
Parker, Gail, ed. The Oven Birds: American Women on
Womanhood, 1820-1920. Garden City, N.Y.: Doubleday,
1972.
Parsons, Alice Beal. Woman's Dilemma. New York:
Crowell, 1926.
Paul, Nanette B. The Great Woman Statesman. New York:
Hogan-Paulus, 1925.
Porter, Kirk H. History of Suffrage in the United
States. New York: AMS Press, 1918.
Rivington, Ann. Women Vote for Life! New York: Workers
Library, 1940.
Rover, Constance. Women's Suffrage and Party Politics
in Britain, 1866-1914. Toronto: University of
Toronto Press, 1967.
Schirmacher, Kaethe. Modern Woman's Rights Movement.
New York: Macmillan, 1912.
Shaw, Frederick John, ed. The Case for Women's Suffrage.
London: T. Fisher Unwin, 1907.
Simons, May Wood. Woman and the Social Problem. Chicago:
C. H. Kerr, 1890.
Smith, Thomas Robert. Woman Question. New York: Boni
& Liveright, 1919.
Sophocles. "Elektra." In Chief Patterns of World Drama,
ed. W. S. Clark, pp. 29-58. Boston: Houghton
Mifflin, 1946.
Spencer, Sara Jane. Problems on the Woman Question.
Washington, D.C.: Langran, Ogilvie, 1871.
Squire, Belle. The Woman Movement in America: A Short
Account of the Struggle for Equal Rights. Chicago:
A. C. McClurg, 1911.
Stanton, Elizabeth Cady. Eighty Years and More (1815-
1897). First published, 1898. Reprint, New York:
Collectors Editions, Source Book Press, 1970.
_____. History of Woman Suffrage (1881-1922). Reprint,
New York: Collectors Editions, Source Book Press,
1970.
_____. The Revolution, 1868-1872. Reprint, New York: Collectors
Editions, Source Book Press, 1971.
Stanton, Theodore, ed. The Woman Question in Europe.
First published, 1884. Reprint, New York: Collectors
Editions, Source Book Press, 1970.
Strachey, Rachel Conn Costelloe. Our Freedom and Its
Results, by Five Women. London: Hogarth Press, 1936.
Strutt, Elizabeth. The Feminine Soul. Boston: Henry
H. & T. W. Carter, 1870.
Swisshelm, Jane Grey. Half a Century. First published,
1880. Reprint, New York: Collectors Editions,
Source Book Press, 1970.

Tarbell, Ida. The Business of Being a Woman. New York: Macmillan, 1912.

___. The Ways of Women. New York: Macmillan, 1915.

Taylor, A. Elizabeth. The Woman Suffrage Movement in Tennessee. New York: Bookman Associates, 1957.

Thompson, William. Appeal of One Half the Human Race, Women, against the Pretensions of the Other Half, Men, to Retain Them in Political, and Thence in Civil and Domestic Slavery, in Reply to a Paragraph of Mr. (James) Mill's Celebrated "Article on Government." First published, 1825. Reprint, New York: Collectors Editions, Source Book Press, 1970.

Tuttle, Florence Guertin. The Awakening of Woman: Suggestions from the Psychic Side of Feminism. New York: Abingdon Press, 1915.

___. Women and World Federation. New York: R. M. McBride, 1919.

U.S. Senate Committee on the District of Columbia. Women's Suffrage and the Police: Three Senate Documents. First published, 1913. Reprint, New York: Arno Press, 1971.

Wadia, A. R. The Ethics of Feminism: A Study of the Revolt of Woman. London: Allen & Unwin, 1923.

Wallas, Ada. Before the Bluestockings. New York: Macmillan, 1930.

Wieth-Knudsen, K. A. Feminism, A Sociological Study of the Woman Question from Ancient Times to the Present Day. London: Constable, 1928.

Wollstonecraft, Mary. A Vindication of the Rights of Women. First published, 1792. Reprint, New York: Collectors Editions, Source Book Press, 1970.

Woman's Rights Convention, Seneca Falls, New York, 1848. Woman's Rights Convention. New York: Arno Press, 1970.

Woodbury, Helen Laura Summer. Equal Suffrage: The Results of an Investigation in Colorado Made for the Collegiate Equal Suffrage League of New York State. New York: Harper Press, 1909.

Woodward, Helen Beal. The Bold Women. New York: Farrar, Straus & Young, 1953.

MODERN FEMINISM

Abbott, Sydney, and Love, Barbara. Sappho Was a Right-on Woman. New York: Stein & Day, 1971.

Adams, Elsie, and Briscoe, Mary L. Up against the Wall, Mother: A Women's Liberation Reader. New York: Free Press, 1971.

Adams, Mildred. The Right to Be People. Philadelphia: J. B. Lippincott, 1967.

Adelstein, Michael, and Pival, Jean C. Women's Liberation. New York: St. Martin's Press, 1972.

Allen, Pamela. Free Space: A Perspective on the Small
  Group in Women's Liberation. New York: Times Change
  Press, 1971.
Altbach, Edith H., ed. From Feminism to Liberation.
  Cambridge, Mass.: Schenkman, 1971.
"The American Woman." Transaction, Nov.-Dec., 1970.
Andreas, Carol. Sex and Caste in America. Englewood
  Cliffs, N.J.: Prentice-Hall, 1971.
"Are We a Nation of Breast Worshippers?" Sexual Behavior,
  Apr. 1971, pp. 50-53.
Babcox, Deborah, and Belkin, Madeline. Liberation Now.
  New York: Dell, 1971.
Becker, Beril. Fiery Feminists. New York: Pyramid,
  1971.
Bem, Sandra L., and Bem, Daryl J. "Training the Woman to
  Know Her Place: The Power of a Nonconscious Ideology."
  In Beliefs, Attitudes, and Human Affairs, ed. Daryl J.
  Bem. Belmont, Calif.: Wadsworth, Brooks-Cole Division,
  1970.
____. "We're All Nonconscious Sexists." Psychology Today,
  Nov. 1970.
Berscheid, Ellen, and Walster, Elaine. "Beauty and the
  Best." Psychology Today, Mar. 1972, p. 42.
Black Panther Sisters Talk about Women's Liberation.
  Boston: New England Free Press, n.d.
Bragdon, Elizabeth, ed. Women Today. Indianapolis:
  Bobbs-Merrill, 1953.
Brown, Judith, and Jones, Beverley. Toward a Female
  Liberation Movement. First published, 1940. V.W.L.M.
  Reprint. Voice of the Women's Liberation Movement,
  1940 Bissell, Chicago, Ill. 60614.
Browning, Harley L. "Timing of Our Lives." Transaction,
  Oct. 1969, pp. 22-27.
Brown-Miller, Susan. "Sisterhood Is Powerful." New York
  Times Magazine, Mar. 15, 1970, pp. 27, 128-40.
____. "Where American Women Are Now." Vogue 153 (1969):
  176-85.
Chesler, Phyllis. "Men Drive Women Crazy." In The
  Female Experience, ed. Carol Tavris, pp. 79-83. Del
  Mar, Calif.: CRM Publishers, 1973.
Colon, Clara. Enter Fighting: Today's Woman. New York:
  New Outlook, 1970.
Conway, Bill. From Joan to Angela: A Bitter Ballad of
  Oppression and Martyrs. Los Angeles: F.A.D., 1970.
Cooke, Joanne, ed. The New Women: A Native Anthology of
  Women's Liberation. New York: Fawcett World Library,
  1971.
Crathern, Alice T. In Detroit, Courage Was the Fashion.
  Detroit: Wayne State University Press, 1954.
Cudlipp, Edythe. Understanding Women's Liberation. New
  York: Paperback Library, 1971.
DeCrow, Karen. The Young Woman's Guide to Liberation.
  New York: Pegasus, 1971.

Dixon, Marlene. "Why Women's Liberation?" Ramparts 8
    (1969):58-63.
Dunbar, Roxanne. Poor White Women. Boston: New
    England Free Press, n.d.
Dunn, Nell. Talking to Women. New York: International,
    1965.
Ehrenfels, U. R. von. "Feminism and Traditional
    Matriliny." Mimeo distributed at the 9th Inter-
    national Congress of Anthropological and Ethnological
    Sciences, Chicago, 1973.
Ellis, Julie. Revolt of the Second Sex. New York:
    Lancer Books, 1970.
Ellmann, Mary. Thinking about Women. New York:
    Harcourt, Brace & World, 1968.
Epstein, Cynthia, and Goode, William J., eds. The Other
    Half: Roads to Women's Equality. Englewood Cliffs,
    N.J.: Prentice-Hall, 1971.
Epstein, Cynthia, and Tiger, Lionel. "Debate: Will
    Women's Lib Really Help Women?" Sexual Behavior,
    Sept. 1971, pp. 56-57.
Equal Opportunity Employment Commission. Guidelines on
    Discrimination because of Sex. Federal Register 5999,
    1967.
Ermarth, Margaret. Adam's Fractured Rib. Philadelphia:
    Fortress Press, 1970.
Farber, Seymour M., and Wilson, Roger H. L., eds. The
    Potential of Women. New York: McGraw-Hill, 1963.
Farrell, Barry. "You've Come a Long Way, Buddy." Life
    71 (Aug. 27, 1971):52-59.
Farrell, Warren. "Debate: How Men Really Feel about
    Women's Lib." Sexual Behavior, Feb. 1972, pp. 26-32.
"The Feminist Movement." Gallup Opinion Index, Report
    63, Sept. 1970.
Figes, Eva. Patriarchal Attitudes: The Case for Women
    in Revolt. Greenwich, Conn.: Fawcett, 1970.
Firestone, Shulamith. The Dialectic of Sex: The Case
    for Feminist Revolution. New York: William Morrow,
    1970.
_____, ed. "Notes from the Second Year." Women's
    Liberation. 1970. Old Chelsea Station, P.O. Box AA,
    New York, N.Y. 10011.
Fraser, Clara. The Emancipation of Women. S.R.W.
    (Seattle Radical Women), 3815 Fifth Ave. N.E.,
    Seattle, Wash. 98103.
_____. Which Road toward Women's Liberation? The Move-
    ment as a Single Issue Coalition or a Radical
    Vanguard. S.R.W. (Seattle Radical Women), 3815 Fifth
    Ave. N.E., Seattle, Wash. 98103.
Freeman, Jo. Building the Gilded Cage. Pittsburgh:
    Know, Inc., n.d.
_____. "The New Feminists." Nation 208 (Feb. 24, 1969):
    241-44.

Freud, Sigmund. "Femininity." In New Introductory
   Lectures on Psychoanalysis. New York: W. W. Norton,
   1965.
Friedan, Betty. The Feminine Mystique. New York: Dell,
   1963.
Garskof, Michele Hoffnung. Roles Women Play: Readings
   toward Women's Liberation. Belmont, Calif.: Brooks-
   Cole, 1971.
Gershenfeld, Matti. Achieve Your Full Potential as a
   Woman. New York: Cornerstone Library, 1971.
Gilman, Richard. "Where Did It All Go Wrong?" Life 71
   (Aug. 13, 1971):40-55.
Goldman, Emma. "On Love." In Anarchism and Other Essays.
   1917. Reprint. New York: Dover, 1971.
   . Traffic in Women and Other Essays on Feminism.
   Reprint. New York: Times Change Press, 1971.
Goncharov, Ivan. Oblomov. Baltimore: Penguin, 1954.
Gornick, Vivian, and Moran, Barbara K. Woman in Sexist
   Society: Studies in Power and Powerlessness. New
   York: Basic Books, 1971.
Graham, Abbie. Ladies in Revolt. New York: Woman's
   Press, 1934.
Green, Arnold W., and Melnick, Eleanor. "What Has Hap-
   pened to the Feminist Movement." In Studies in
   Leadership: Leadership and Democratic Action, ed.
   Alvin W. Gouldner. New York: Russell & Russell, 1965.
Greer, Germaine. The Female Eunuch. New York: McGraw-
   Hill, 1971.
Grimes, Alan P. The Puritan Ethic and Woman Suffrage.
   New York: Oxford University Press, 1967.
Gross, Louise, and MacEwan, Phyllis. On Day Care.
   Boston: New England Free Press, n.d.
Halonen, Kae. Man's World and Welcome to It! R.E.P.
   (Radical Education Project), Box 561-A, Detroit, Mich.
   48232.
Harris, Janet. Single Standard. New York: McGraw-Hill,
   1971.
Hart, Marie. "Women Sit in the Back of the Bus."
   Psychology Today, Oct. 1971, pp. 64-66.
Helman, Patricia K. Complete Woman: A Christian View of
   Women's Lib. Garden City, N.Y.: Doubleday, 1971.
Hennesey, Caroline. I, B.I.T.C.H. New York: Lancer,
   1970.
Hobbs, Lisa. Love and Liberation: Up Front with the
   Feminists. New York: McGraw-Hill, 1971.
Hole, Judith, and Levine, Ellen. Rebirth of Feminism.
   New York: Quadrangle Books, 1971.
Hopper, Peggy, and Foldz, Steve. I Don't Want to Change
   My Lifestyle. I Want to Change My Life. Boston: New
   England Free Press, n.d.
Howard, Jane. "Is Women's Lib a Dirty Word in Milwaukee?"
   Life 71 (Aug. 27, 1971):46-51.

Hudson, Kenneth. Men and Women: Feminism and Anti-Feminism Today. New York: Transatlantic Arts, 1969.

Janeway, Elizabeth. Man's World, Woman's Place: A Study in Social Mythology. New York: William Morrow, 1970.

Kamm, Josephine. Rapiers and Battleaxes: The Women's Movement and Its Aftermath. New York: Humanities Press, 1966.

Kenealy, Arabella. Feminism and Sex-Extinction. New York: E. P. Dutton, 1920.

Kern, Edward. "An Outrageous Demand Touched Off a Crusade." Life 71 (Aug. 20, 1971):40-49.

Key, Ellen. The Woman Movement. New York: G. P. Putnam, 1912.

Kirkpatrick, Clifford. "A Comparison of Generations in Regard to Attitudes toward Feminism." Journal of Genetic Psychology 49 (Dec. 1936):343-61.

Komisar, Lucy. "The New Feminism." Saturday Review, Feb. 21, 1970, pp. 27-30.

La Follette, Suzanne. Concerning Women. New York: Boni, 1926.

Lamb, Myrna. "The Mod Donna" and "Scyklon Z": Plays of Women's Liberation. New York: Pathfinder Press, n.d.

Larger, Ellie. Women of the Telephone Company. Boston: New England Free Press, n.d.

Lasch, Christopher. The New Radicalism in America, 1889-1963. New York: Alfred A. Knopf, 1965.

Leavitt, Ruby, ed. Cross-cultural Perspectives on the Women's Movement. The Hague: Mouton, in press.

The Lib Game. Gini Scott, Creative Communications and Research, Del Mar, Calif.

The Liberated Woman's Appointment Calendar and Field Manual. New York: Universe Books, 1971, 1972, 1973.

Liberation Now! Writings on the Women's Liberation Movement. New York: Dell, 1971.

Ludovici, Anthony M. Woman: A Vindication. New York: Alfred A. Knopf, 1923.

Mainardi, Pat. The Politics of Housework. Boston: New England Free Press, n.d.

Marhn, Gloria. Women in the Revolutionary Struggle. S.R.W. (Seattle Radical Women), 3815 Fifth Ave. N.E., Seattle, Wash. 98103.

Mathis, James L. "Distorted Views of Women." Sexual Behavior, July 1971, pp. 75-80.

McAfee, Kathy, and Ward, Myrna. What Is the Revolutionary Potential of Women's Liberation? Boston: New England Free Press, n.d.

McClesky, Donna. "The New Woman." Newsletter of the Ecumenical Institute, Jan. 1967. Ecumenical Institute, 3444 Congress Parkway, Chicago, Ill. 60624.

McCrimmon, A. L. The Woman Movement. Philadelphia: Griffith & Rowland, 1915.

Merriam, Eve. After Nora Slammed the Door: American Women in the 1960's: The Unfinished Revolution. Cleveland: World, 1964.

Miller, Ruth Ann. <u>In Defense of the Women's Movement</u>.
New York: Pathfinder Press, 1971.
Millett, Kate. <u>Sexual Politics</u>. Garden City, N.Y.:
Doubleday, 1970.
___, director. <u>Three Lives</u>. Impact Films. Women's
Liberation Cinema Co., n.d.
Mitchell, Juliet. <u>Women's Estate</u>. New York: Pantheon
Books, 1972.
<u>Modern Woman: The Uneasy Life</u>. Film. Minneapolis:
University of Minnesota, Audio-Visual Department, n.d.
Morgan, Robin. <u>The Hand That Cradles the Rock</u>. New
York: Random House, 1970.
___. <u>New Sisterhood</u>. New York: Random House, 1970.
___, ed. <u>Sisterhood Is Powerful</u>. New York: Random
House, Vintage Books, 1970.
___. <u>Women in Revolt</u>. New York: Random House, 1969.
Morrison, Denton E., and Holden, Carlin Paige. "The
Burning Bra: The American Breast Fetish and Women's
Liberation." In <u>Deviance and Change</u>, ed. Peter K.
Manning. Englewood Cliffs, N.J.: Prentice-Hall, 1971.
___. "Why Are Women Burning Their Bras?" <u>Sexual Be-
havior</u>, Feb. 1972, pp. 18-25.
Muir, Willa. <u>Women: An Inquiry</u>. London: L. & V.
Woolf, 1925.
Mull, Brenda. <u>Our Struggle against Levi-Strauss</u>. Boston:
New England Free Press, n.d.
Negrin, Su. <u>Graphic Notebook on Feminism</u>. New York:
Times Change Press, 1971.
Newton, Esther, and Walton, Shirley. "The Person Is
Political: Consciousness Raising and Personal Change
in the Women's Liberation Movement." A Paper Pre-
sented at the 70th Annual Meeting of the American
Anthropological Association, New York, 1971. Mimeo.
SUNY, Purchase.
North, Sandie. "Women's Liberation Hits the Suburbs."
<u>Family Circle</u>, Nov. 1970, p. 18.
Noun, Louise R. <u>Strong-Minded Women</u>. Ames: Iowa State
University Press, 1969.
Novac, George. <u>Revolutionary Dynamics of Women's
Liberation</u>. New York: Pathfinder Press, n.d.
O'Neill, William L. "Feminism as a Radical Ideology."
In <u>Dissent: Explorations in the History of American
Radicalism</u>, ed. Alfred E. Young, pp. 273-300. DeKalb:
Northern Illinois University Press, 1968.
___. <u>Woman Movement: Feminism in the United States and
England</u>. New York: Barnes & Noble, 1969.
Parturier, Francoise. <u>An Open Letter to Men</u>, trans. J.
Bernstein. New York: James Heineman, 1968.
Paterson, Dorothy. <u>Family Woman and the Feminist: A
Challenge</u>. London: Heinemann Medical Books, 1945.
Petrova, Lidia. <u>Together with Women Everywhere</u>. Moscow:
Novosti Press, n.d.

Piercy, Marge. Grand Coulee Damn: Women's Oppression in the Movement. Boston: New England Free Press, n.d.

Radical Women: Program and Structure. S.R.W. (Seattle Radical Women), 3815 Fifth Ave. N.E., Seattle, Wash. 98103.

Ramey, Estelle. "Well, Fellows, What Did Happen at the Bay of Pigs? And Who Was in Control?" McCall's, Jan. 1971, p. 28.

Reed, Evelyn. The Myth of Women's Inferiority: Women's Role in Prehistoric Societal Development. Boston: New England Free Press, n.d.

_____. Problems of Women's Liberation: A Marxist Approach. New York: Pathfinder Press, 1970.

Riegel, Robert E. American Feminists. First published, 1963. Reprint, Lawrence: University Press of Kansas, 1968.

Rollin, Betty. "Motherhood, Who Needs It?" Look, Sept. 22, 1970, pp. 15-17.

Rosen, Ruth. "What Women Want to Be Liberated From." Sacramento Bee 15 (Nov. 1970):67.

Rover, Constance. The Punch Book of Women's Rights. Cranbury, N.J.: A. S. Barnes, 1970.

Schneir, Miriam, ed. Feminism: The Essential Historical Writings. New York: Random House, Vintage Press, 1972.

Sexton, Anne. To Bedlam and Part Way Back. Boston: Houghton Mifflin, 1960.

Shell, Louise. The Lonely Girl in the Big City. Boston: New England Free Press, n.d.

Showalter, Elaine. Women's Liberation and Literature. New York: Harcourt, Brace Jovanovich, 1971.

Snowden, Ethel. The Feminist Movement. London: Collins' Clear Type Press, n.d.

Solanas, Valerie. SCUM Manifesto. New York: Olympia Press, 1968.

Sontag, Susan. Styles of Radical Will. New York: Farrar, Straus & Giroux, 1969.

Stambler, Sookie, ed. Women's Liberation: Blueprint for the Future. New York: Ace Books, 1970.

Steinem, Gloria. "After Black Power, Women's Liberation." New York, Apr. 7, 1969, pp. 8-10.

Stevenson, Janet. Women's Rights. New York: Franklin Watts, 1972.

Sunegrin. A Graphic Notebook on Feminism. New York: Times Change Press, n.d.

Tanner, Leslie, ed. Voices from Women's Liberation. New York: New American Library, 1970.

Tavris, Carol. "Woman and Man." Psychology Today, Mar. 1972, p. 57.

Tax, Meredith. Woman and Her Mind: The Assaults of Daily Life: Female Schizophrenia, Consumerism: A Marxist Analysis. Boston: New England Free Press, n.d.

The Teen-Age Boy. Film. Bloomington: Indiana University Audio-Visual Center, n.d.

The Teen-Age Girl. Film. Bloomington: Indiana University Audio-Visual Center, n.d.
Teitz, Joyce. What's a Nice Girl Like You Doing in a Place Like This? New York: Crowell, 1971.
Thompson, Mary Lou, ed. Voices of the New Feminism. Boston: Beacon Press, 1970.
Uesugi, Thomas C., and Vinacke, W. Edgar. "Strategy in a Feminine Game." Sociometry 26 (Mar. 1963):75-88.
Ware, Cellestine. Woman Power: The Movement for Women's Liberation. New York: Tower, 1970.
Waters, Mary A. Politics of the Women's Liberation Movement Today. New York: Pathfinder Press, n.d.
Wells, Lyn. American Women: Their Use and Abuse. Boston: New England Free Press, n.d.
West, Anthony. "Who Takes Advantage of American Women? Men." Vogue, May 1968, p. 198.
Woman and Man. Game. Psychology Today Games, Del Mar, Calif. 92014.
"The Woman Problem: A Historical Pictorial Essay." Life, Aug. 1971, pp. 40-47.
"Women and Socialism"; "Women in the Liberation Struggle: An Overview"; "Ma Bell Has Fleas," and "A Lot of Angry Workers." Boston: New England Free Press, n.d.
Woolf, Virginia. A Room of One's Own. New York: Harcourt, Brace & World, 1929.
Worell, Judith, and Worell, Leonard. "Supporters and Opposers of Women's Liberation: Some Personality Correlates." A paper presented at the Annual Convention of the American Psychological Association, Washington, D.C., 1971. Mimeo. University of Kentucky.

WOMEN IN LITERATURE, MYTHOLOGY, AND FOLK TRADITION

Aldridge, John W. In Search of Heresy: American Literature in an Age of Conformity. Port Washington, N.Y.: Kennikat Press, 1956.
Asimov, Isaac. Uncertain, Gay, and Hard to Please: The Myth of Femininity. Boston: New England Free Press, n.d.
Auchincloss, Louis. Pioneers and Caretakers: A Study of Nine American Women Novelists. New York: Dell, 1966.
Ayres, Barbara. "Pregnancy Magic: A Study of Food Taboos and Sex Avoidances." In Cross-cultural Approaches: Readings in Comparative Research, ed. Clellan S. Ford, pp. 111-25. New Haven: Human Relations Area Files Press, 1967.
Bald, Marjory. Women Writers of the Nineteenth Century. First published, 1923. Reprint, Russell & Russell, 1963.

Barnard, Mary, trans. Sappho: A New Translation.
    Berkeley: University of California Press, 1958.
Beauvoir, Simone de. The Woman Destroyed. New York:
    G. P. Putnam, 1969.
Benson, Ruth Crego. Women in Tolstoy: The Ideal and the
    Erotic. Urbana: University of Illinois Press, 1973.
Bettelheim, Bruno. Symbolic Wounds: Puberty Rites and
    the Envious Male. Rev. ed. New York: Macmillan,
    1962.
Brophy, Brigid. Don't Never Forget: Collected Views
    and Reviews. New York: Holt, Rinehart & Winston, 1966.
Chabrol, Claude. Le récit féminin: contribution à
    l'analyse sémiologique du courrier du coeur et des
    entrevues ou 'enquêtes' sur la femme dans la presse
    féminine actuelle. The Hague: Mouton, 1971.
Chamberlain, A. F. "Primitive Woman as Poet." Journal
    of American Folklore 16 (1903):205-21.
Champerlain, I. C. "Contributions toward a Bibliography
    of Folklore Relating to Women." Journal of American
    Folklore 12 (1899):32-37.
Chopin, Kate. The Awakening. First published, 1899.
    Reprint, New York: Garrett Press, 1971.
Colby, Vineta. Singular Anomaly: Women Novelists of the
    Nineteenth Century. New York: New York University
    Press, 1970.
Crandall, Coryl, ed. Swetnam, The Woman-Hater: The
    Controversy and the Play. Lafayette, Ind.: Purdue
    University Studies, 1967.
Deegan, Dorothy. Stereotype of the Single Woman in
    American Novels. New York: Octagon Books, 1968.
DePrima, Diane. Dinners and Nightmares. New York:
    Corinth Books, 1961.
Dickinson, Emily. Complete Poems. Boston: Little,
    Brown, 1960.
Drinker, Sophie. Music and Women. New York: Coward-
    McCann, 1948.
Fiedler, Leslie. Love and Death in the American Novel.
    New York: Criterion Books, 1960.
Fletcher, Jefferson Butler. The Religion of Beauty in
    Women and Other Essays on Platonic Love in Poetry.
    New York: Haskell House, 1966.
Forrest, Mary, ed. Women of the South Distinguished in
    Literature. First published, 1861. Reprint, New
    York: Garrett Press, 1969.
Freud, Phil. Myths of Creation. London: W. H. Allen,
    1964.
Gagen, Jean E. New Woman. New York: Twayne, 1969.
Gloag, Julian. Our Mother's House. New York: Simon &
    Schuster, 1963.
Gough, Kathleen. "The Origin of the Family." Up from
    Under 1 (1971):47-52.
Gressain, Robert. Le motif vagina dentata. Copenhagen:
    32nd International Congress of Americanists, 1958.

Grisay, Auguste; Lavis, G.; and Dubois-Stasse, M. Les
dénominations de la femme dans les anciens textes
littéraires français. Gembloux: J. Duculot, 1969.
Griswold, R. W., ed. Female Poets of America. First
published, 1873. Reprint, New York: Garrett Press,
1969.
Harding, Esther. Woman's Mysteries. New York: Pantheon,
1955.
Hart, John. Female Prose Writers of America. Detroit:
Gale Research, 1852.
Hawkes, Jacquetta. "A Woman as Great as the World." In
The Subversive Science: Essays toward an Ecology of
Man, ed. Paul Shepard and Daniel McKinley, pp. 437-39.
Boston: Houghton Mifflin, 1970.
. A Woman as Great as the World and Other Fables.
New York: Random House, 1953.
Hays, H. R. The Dangerous Sex: The Myth of Feminine
Evil. New York: Pocket Books, 1965.
Heilbrun, Carolyn. "The Masculine Wilderness of the
American Novel." Saturday Review, Jan. 29, 1972,
pp. 41-44.
Hentsch, Alice. De la littérature didactique du moyen
âge s'adressant spécialement aux femmes. Cahors:
A. Coueslant, 1903.
Hinkley, Laura L. Ladies of Literature. Freeport, N.Y.:
Books for Libraries, n.d.
Howard, Sidney. The Silver Cord. New York: Samuel
French, 1928.
Ibsen, Henrik. A Doll's House. New York: E. P. Dutton,
1958.
Jayal, S. Status of Women in Epics. Mystic, Conn.:
Lawrence Verry, 1966.
Jessup, Josephine. Faith of Our Feminists. First pub-
lished, 1950. Reprint, New York: Biblo & Tannen, 1965.
Johnson, Reginald B. Some Contemporary Novelists: Women.
Freeport, N.Y.: Books for Libraries, 1920.
. Women Novelists. First published, 1919. Reprint,
Freeport, N.Y.: Books for Libraries, 1967.
Kaufmann, Sue. Diary of a Mad Housewife. First published,
1967. Reprint, New York: Bantam Books, 1970.
Kelly, George. Craig's Wife. Boston: Little, Brown, 1926.
Kennard, Joseph S. "Friar in Fiction," "Sincerity in Art,"
and Other Essays. Freeport, N.Y.: Books for Libraries,
1923.
Lawrence, Margaret. School of Femininity. Port
Washington, N.Y.: Kennikat Press, 1936.
Lederer, Wolfgang. Fear of Women. First published, 1968.
Reprint, New York: Harcourt, Brace Jovanovich, 1970.
Lee, Anna. Memoirs of Eminent Female Writers, of All Ages
and Countries. Ann Arbor: Midway Press, 1927.
Legman, Gershon. The Rationale of the Dirty Joke: An
Analysis of Sexual Humor. New York: Grove Press, 1968.
Lessing, Doris. Five. Toronto: William Collins Sons &
Co., 1953.

____. The Four-Gated City. Children of Violence Series. New York: Alfred A. Knopf, 1969.
____. The Habit of Loving. New York: Thomas Y. Crowell, 1957.
____. Landlocked. Children of Violence Series. London: MacGibbon & Kee, 1964.
____. Martha Quest. Children of Violence Series. London: MacGibbon & Kee, 1952.
____. A Proper Marriage. Children of Violence Series. London: MacGibbon & Kee, 1954.
____. Retreat to Innocence. First published, 1956. Reprint, London: M. Joseph, 1959.
____. A Ripple from the Storm. Children of Violence Series. London: MacGibbon & Kee, 1958.
Lewis, Sinclair. Main Street. First published, 1920. Reprint, New York: Harcourt, Brace & World, 1920.
MacCarthy, B. G. Women Writers. 2 vols. Mystic, Conn.: Lawrence Verry, 1946-47.
Masefield, Muriel A. Women Novelists from Fanny Burney to George Eliot. Freeport, N.Y.: Books for Libraries, 1934.
May, Caroline, ed. American Female Poets. First published, 1869. Reprint, New York: Garrett Press, 1969.
Merriam, Eve. The Double Bed from the Feminine Side. New York: Marzani & Munsell, 1958.
____. "The Matriarchal Myth." The Nation, Nov. 1958.
Mews, Hazel. Frail Vessels: Woman's Role in Women's Novels from Fanny Burney to George Eliot. New York: Oxford University Press, 1969.
Millay, Edna St. Vincent. Collected Sonnets of Edna St. Vincent Millay. New York: Harper & Row, 1941.
Murasaki, Lady. The Tale of Genji. Garden City, N.Y.: Doubleday, n.d.
Nabokov, Vladimir. Lolita. New York: G. P. Putnam, 1958.
Olsen, Tillie. Tell Me a Riddle. London: Faber & Faber, 1961.
O'Neill, Eugene. "Abortion: A Play in One Act." In Lost Plays of Eugene O'Neill, pp. 11-34. New York: New Fathoms Press, 1950.
Overton, Grant. Women Who Make Our Novels. Freeport, N.Y.: Books for Libraries, 1928.
Papashvily, Helen. All the Happy Endings. First published, 1956. Reprint, Port Washington, N.Y.: Kennikat Press, 1971.
Parker, Dorothy. The Collected Poetry of Dorothy Parker. New York: Modern Library, 1936.
Passeron, René. Io lourde (notes pour une légende). Paris: R. Julliard, 1952.
Pattee, Fred L. Feminine Fifties. Port Washington, N.Y.: Kennikat Press, 1940.
Pendry, E. D. The New Feminism of English Fiction: A Study in Contemporary Women-Novelists. Tokyo: Kenkyusha, 1956.

Plath, Sylvia. _Ariel._ London: Faber & Faber, 1965.
Read, Thomas B., ed. _Female Poets of America._ New York: Garrett Press, 1969.
Riley, Madeleine. _Brought to Bed._ Cranbury, N.J.: A. S. Barnes, 1968.
Rogers, Katharine M. _The Troublesome Helpmate: A History of Misogyny in Literature._ Seattle: University of Washington Press, 1966.
Rosaldo, Michelle. "Women in Belief, Symbol and Ideology." A paper presented at the 71st Annual Meeting of the American Anthropological Association, Toronto, 1972. Mimeo. Stanford University.
Sarashina, Lady. _As I Crossed a Bridge of Dreams: The Recollections of a Woman in Eleventh-century Japan,_ trans. Ivan Morris. New York: Dial, 1971.
Sartre, Jean-Paul. _Saint Genet: Actor and Martyr,_ trans. B. Frechtman. New York: George Braziller, 1963.
Schinnerer, Otto P. _Woman in the Life and Works of Gutzkow._ New York: AMS Press, 1924.
Seidenberg, Robert. _Marriage in Life and Literature._ New York: Philosophical Library, 1970.
Siclier, Jacques. _Le mythe de la femme dans le cinema Americain; de "La Divine" à Blanche Dubois._ Paris: Editions Ducerf, 1956.
Smith, Lillian. _Killers of the Dream._ New York: W. W. Norton, 1949.
Sonstroem, David. _Rossetti and the Fair Lady._ Middletown, Conn.: Wesleyan University Press, 1970.
Stead, Christina, and Blake, William. _Modern Women in Love._ New York: Dryden, 1955.
Stebbins, Lucy P. _Victorian Album._ New York: AMS Press, 1946.
Strainchamps, Ethel. _Women's Guide to the Man's World of Media._ New York: Quadrangle Books, 1972.
Thomson, P. _The Victorian Heroine: A Changing Ideal, 1837-1873._ New York: Oxford University Press, 1956.
Van Middendorp, Gerarda. _Hero in the Feminine Novel._ New York: Haskell House, 1931.
Walsh, William S. _Heroes and Heroines of Fiction._ First published, 1915. Reprint, Detroit: Gale Research, 1966.
Wasserstrom, William. _Heiress of All the Ages: Sex and Sentiment in the Genteel Tradition._ Minneapolis: University of Minnesota Press, 1959.
Williams, M. A. _Our Early Female Novelists._ Folcroft, Pa.: Folcroft Press, 1904.
Woolf, Virginia. _Three Guineas._ First published, 1938. Reprint, New York: Harcourt, Brace & World, 1963.
Wright, Frederick. _Feminism in Greek Literature._ Port Washington, N.Y.: Kennikat Press, 1969.
Young, Sherman Plato. _The Women of Greek Drama._ New York: Exposition Press, 1953.

MISCELLANEOUS CLASSICS

Ackermann, Jessie. The World through a Woman's Eyes.
    Chicago: William E. Curtis, 1896.
All Colors: A Study Outline on Woman's Part in Race Re-
    lations. New York: Woman's Press & Association Press,
    1926.
Anderson, Sherwood. Perhaps Women. Mamaroneck, N.Y.:
    Paul P. Appel, 1970.
Aristophanes. Lysistrata, trans. Dudley Fitts. New York:
    Harcourt, Brace & World, 1954.
Asbury, Herbert. Carry Nation. New York: Alfred A.
    Knopf, 1929.
Bachofen, J. J. Das Mutterrecht. Stuttgart: Krais &
    Hoffman, 1861.
Barnes, Earl. Woman in Modern Society. New York: B. W.
    Huebsch, 1912.
Barton, Clara. A Story of the Red Cross. New York:
    Airmont, 1868.
Beard, Mary Ritter. On Understanding Women. First pub-
    lished, 1931. New York: Greenwood Press, 1968.
Bebel, August. Women and Socialism. First published,
    1879. New York: Collectors Editions, Source Book
    Press, 1970.
_____. Woman in the Past, Present, and Future. London:
    Modern Press, 1885.
Brantôme, Pierre de Bourdeille. Les dames galantes:
    nouvelle édition publiée d'après les manuscrits de la
    Bibliothèque Nationale. First published, 1901. Re-
    print, Paris: Garnier, 1955.
Breckinridge, Sophonisba P. Women in the Twentieth
    Century: A Study of Their Political, Social and
    Economic Activities. New York: McGraw-Hill, 1933.
Briffault, Robert. The Mothers. New York: Humanities
    Press, 1959.
Bristol, Augusta Cooper. The Present Phase of Woman's
    Advancement and Other Addresses. Boston: Christopher,
    1916.
Burton, John. Lectures on Female Education and Manners.
    First published, 1794. Reprint, New York: Collectors
    Editions, Source Book Press, 1970.
Buytendijk, Frederik Jacobus Johannes. Woman: A Con-
    temporary View. Glen Rock, N.J.: Newman Press, 1968.
Carpenter, Edward. The Intermediate Sex: A Study of
    Some Transitional Types of Men and Women. London:
    George Allen & Unwin, 1908.
Cooper, J. M. "The Position of Woman in Primitive
    Culture." Primitive Man 5 (1932):32-47.
Daudet, Léon. La femme et l'amour, aspects et visages.
    Paris: E. Flammarion, 1930.

De Kay, John Wesley. Women and the New Social State.
    Basel: C. A. Junger, 1918.
De Koven, Anna. Women in Cycles of Culture. New York:
    G. P. Putnam, 1941.
De Leon, Daniel. The Ballot and the Class Struggle. New
    York: New York Labor News, 1933.
Densmore, Emmet. Sex Equality: A Solution of the Woman
    Problem. New York: Funk & Wagnalls, 1907.
Farmer, Lydia Hoyt. The National Exposition Souvenir:
    What America Owes to Women. Buffalo: C. W. Moulton,
    1893.
Fawcett, Millicent Garrett. What I Remember. London:
    T. F. Unwin, 1924.
Gamble, Eliza Burt. Evolution of Woman. New York: G. P.
    Putnam, 1894.
Gilman, Charlotte Perkins. The Living of Charlotte
    Perkins Gilman. New York: Appleton-Century, 1935.
    . The Man-made World; or Our Androcentric Culture.
    First published, 1911. Reprint, New York: Collectors
    Editions, Source Book Press, 1970.
    . The Home: Its Work and Influence. First published,
    1903. Reprint, Urbana: University of Illinois Press,
    1972.
Glasgow, Maude. Subjection of Woman and Traditions of
    Men. New York: M. I. Glasgow, 1940.
Gordon, Elizabeth Putnam. Women Torchbearers. Evanston,
    Ill.: National Woman's Christian Temperance Union
    Publishing House, 1924.
Haldane, Charlotte. Truth Will Out. New York: Vanguard,
    1950.
Hartley, Catherine Gasquorine. The Truth about Women.
    New York: Dodd, Mead, 1913.
Holtby, Winifred. Women and a Changing Civilization.
    New York: Longmans, Green, 1936.
International Congress of Charities. The Organization of
    Charities. Baltimore: Johns Hopkins Press, 1894.
International Congress of Women. Report: Our Common
    Cause, Civilization. Chicago: National Council of
    Women, 1933.
International Council of Women. Report 1888. Washington,
    D.C.: R. H. Darby, 1888.
International Council of Women. Report of Transactions
    during the Third Quinquennial Term. Boston: Inter-
    national Council of Women, 1909.
The Lady's Preceptor; or, a Letter to a Young Lady of
    Distinction upon Politeness. Taken from the French
    of the Abbe d'Ancourt, and Adapted to the Religion,
    Customs, and Manners of the English Nation. 3d ed.
    London: J. Watts, 1745.
Letourneau, Charles. La condition de la femme dans les
    diverses races et civilizations. Paris: V. Giard
    and E. Brière, 1903.

Lombroso-Ferrero, Gina. La femme aux prises avec la vie, trans. Le Hénaff. Paris: Payot, 1924.
___. The Soul of Woman: Reflections on Life. New York: E. P. Dutton, 1923.
Lowie, Robert Henry. Primitive Society. First published, 1920. Reprint, New York: Liveright, 1947.
Menon, Lakshmi N. The Position of Women. New York: Oxford University Press, 1944.
Mill, John Stuart. On the Subjection of Women. First published, 1869. Reprint, New York: Collectors Editions, Source Book Press, 1970.
Ploss, Hermann; Bartels, M. C. A.; and Bartels, P. R. A. Woman: An Historical, Gynaecological and Anthropological Compendium. 3 vols. London, 1935.
Schmidt, Wilhelm. Das Mutterrecht. Studia Instituti Anthropos 10. Vienna-Midlingen: Missionsdruckerei St. Gabriel, 1955.
World Congress of Women. Copenhagen, 1953. Reports, Speeches (extracts), Documents. Berlin: Women's International Democratic Federation, 1953.

BIOGRAPHIES AND AUTOBIOGRAPHIES

Adams, Henry Gardner. Cyclopaedia of Female Biography: Consisting of Sketches of All Women Who Have Been Distinguished by Great Talents, Strength of Character, Piety, Benevolence, or Moral Virtues of Any Kind. London: G. Routledge, 1869.
Adams, Jean. Heroines of the Sky. Garden City, N.Y.: Doubleday, Doran, 1942.
Adams, William Henry Davenport. Celebrated Women Travellers of the Nineteenth Century. London: W. S. Sonnenschein, 1883.
Adelman, Joseph Ferdinand Gottlieb. Famous Women: An Outline of Feminine Achievement through the Ages with Life Stories of Five Hundred Noted Women. New York: Ellis N. Lonow, 1926.
Adler, Polly. A House Is Not a Home. New York: Popular Library, 1955.
Aikman, Duncan. Calamity Jane and the Lady Wildcats. New York: Henry Holt, 1927.
America's Twelve Great Women Leaders during the Past Hundred Years as Chosen by the Women of America: A Compilation from the Ladies' Home Journal and the Christian Science Monitor. Chicago: Associated Authors Service, 1933.
Anderson, Margaret. The Fiery Fountains: Continuation and Crisis to 1950. New York: Horizon Press, 1970.
___. My Thirty Years' War. New York: Horizon Press, 1970.

___. The Strange Necessity. New York: Horizon Press,
  1970.
Anderson, Mary. Woman at Work: The Autobiography of
  Mary Anderson as Told to Mary Winstow. Minneapolis:
  University of Minnesota Press, 1951.
Balabanoff, Angelica. My Life as a Rebel. First pub-
  lished, 1938. Reprint, Westport, Conn.: Greenwood
  Press, 1968.
Balfour, Frances. Dr. Elsie Englis. London: Hodder &
  Stoughton, 1918.
Bäumer, Gertrud. Bildnis der Liebenden: Gestalt und
  Wandel der Frau. Tübingen: Rainer Winderlich Verlag,
  1958.
Beach, Seth C. Daughters of the Puritans: A Group of
  Brief Biographies. First published, 1905. Reprint,
  Freeport, N.Y.: Books for Libraries, 1970.
Beaunier, André. Visages des femmes. 5th ed. Paris:
  Plon-Nowrit, 1913.
Beauvoir, Simone de. Memoirs of a Dutiful Daughter.
  Cleveland: World, 1959.
___. A Very Easy Death. New York: G. P. Putnam, 1966.
Besant, Annie. An Autobiography. London: Fisher Unwin,
  1893.
Biddle, Gertrude, ed. Notable Women of Pennsylvania.
  Philadelphia: University of Pennsylvania Press, 1942.
Biographical Cyclopaedia of American Women. New York:
  Halvord, 1924-25.
Birney, Catherine. The Grimké Sisters. First published,
  1885. Reprint, New York: Haskell, 1969.
Blackwell, Elizabeth. "A Military Genius." In
  Cyclopedia of American Biography, 5. New York: Press
  Association Compilers, 1918-31.
Blake, Katherine Devereux. Champion of Women. New York:
  Revell, 1943.
Blashfield, Evangeline. Portraits and Backgrounds. New
  York: Charles Scribner's, 1917.
Bleakley, Horace William. Ladies Fair and Frail:
  Sketches of the Demi-monde during the Eighteenth
  Century. New York: J. Lane, 1909.
Bloomer, Dexter C. Life and Writings of Amelia Bloomer.
  Boston: Arena, 1895.
Bloor, Ella Reeve. We Are Many: An Autobiography. New
  York: International, 1940.
Bloss, Celestia Angenette. Heroines of the Crusades.
  Peoria, Ill.: S. H. & G. Burnett, 1853.
Blunt, Hugh Francis. The Great Magdalens. New York:
  Macmillan, 1928.
Boccaccio, Giovanni. Concerning Famous Women. New
  Brunswick, N.J.: Rutgers University Press, 1963.
Bracken, Peg. I Try to Behave Myself: Peg Bracken's
  Etiquette Book. First published, 1964. Reprint,
  Greenwich, Conn.: Fawcett, 1966.

Bradford, Gamaliel. Daughters of Eve. First published,
    1930. Reprint, Port Washington, N.Y.: Kennikat Press,
    1969.
    ___. Portraits of American Women. First published, 1919.
    Reprint, Freeport, N.Y.: Books for Libraries, n.d.
Brown, Alice. Mercy Warren. Women of Colonial and
    Revolutionary Times Series. Reprint, Spartanburg,
    S.C.: Reprint, 1968.
Brown, Mary Milbank. The Secret Life of Jeanne d'Arc.
    New York: Vantage Press, 1962.
Browne, William Hardcaste. Famous Women of History:
    Containing Nearly Three Thousand Brief Biographies and
    Over One Thousand Female Pseudonyms. Philadelphia:
    Arnold, 1895.
Buckmaster, Henrietta. Women Who Shaped History. New
    York: Macmillan, 1966.
Bullard, Laura C. Our Famous Women: An Authorized Record
    of the Lives and Deeds of Distinguished Women of Our
    Times, by Twenty Eminent Authors. New York: Garrett
    Press, 1883.
Burnett, Constance. Five for Freedom. Westport, Conn.:
    Greenwood Press, 1953.
Castelar y Ripoll, Emilio. Galería histórica de mujeres
    célebres. Madrid: Alvarez Hermanos, 1886-89.
Chace, Elizabeth Buffum, and Lovell, Lucy Buffum. Two
    Quaker Sisters. New York, 1937.
Child, Lydia María. Biographies of Good Wives. Boston:
    J. H. Francis, 1850.
Clarke, Mary Cowden. World-Noted Women; or, Types of
    Womanly Attributes of All Lands and Ages. New York:
    D. Appleton & Co., 1867.
Clough, Emma. Study of Mary Wollstonecraft and the
    Rights of Woman. First published, 1846. Reprint,
    Detroit: Gale Research Co., n.d.
Code, Joseph Bernaid. Great American Foundresses.
    Freeport, N.Y.: Books for Libraries, 1929.
Comte, Auguste. The Positive Philosophy of Auguste Comte,
    trans. and ed. Harriet Martineau. New York: Calvin
    Blanchard, 1858.
Costello, Louisa Stuart. Memoirs of Eminent Englishwomen.
    London: R. Bentley, 1849.
Courtney, Janet Elizabeth. The Women of My Time. London:
    L. Dickinson, 1934.
Cowley, Joyce. Pioneers of Women's Liberation. New York:
    Pathfinder Press, n.d.
Crouch, Nathaniel. Female Excellency; or, the Ladies
    Glory. Illustrated in the Worthy Lives and Memorable
    Actions of Nine Famous Women Who Have Been Renowned
    either for Virtue or Valour, in Several Ages of the
    World. London: A. Bettesworth, 1728.
Custer, Elizabeth. Boots and Saddles. Norman: Uni-
    versity of Oklahoma Press, 1961.

Daniel, Sadie Iola. Women Builders. Washington, D.C.: Associated Publishers, 1931.

Dantas, Julio. Revoada de musas; as mulheres na vida dos homen's célebres. Lisbon: Portugália Editora, 1905.

Dark, Sidney. Twelve More Ladies: Good, Bad and Indifferent. Freeport, N.Y.: Books for Libraries, 1969.

D'Auvergne, Edmund Basil Francis. Adventuresses and Adventurous Ladies. London: Hutchinson & Co., 1927.

Day, Dorothy. The Long Loneliness: The Autobiography of Dorothy Day. New York: Harper & Row, 1952.

Decaux, Alain. Les grandes favorites de toutes les époques et dans tous les pays. Paris: Grasset, 1960.

Dell, Floyd. Women as World Builders: Studies in Modern Feminism. Chicago, 1913.

Demeuse, Pierre. Les amoureses de l'amour; ou les immoralités légendaires. Paris: P. de Meyere, 1963.

Domenuchi, Lodovico. La nobiltà delle donne. Venice: Appresso G. Giolito di Ferrarii e Fratelli, 1552.

Dorr, Rheta Childe. Susan B. Anthony: The Woman Who Changed the Mind of a Nation. New York: AMS Press, 1970.

Douglas, Emily Taft. Margaret Sanger: Pioneer of the Future. New York: Holt, Rinehart & Winston, 1970.

_____. Remember the Ladies: The Story of Great Women Who Helped Shape America. New York: G. P. Putnam, 1966.

Drago, Harry S. Notorious Ladies of the Frontier. New York: Dodd, Mead, 1969.

Dreier, Mary. Margaret Dreier Robins: Her Life, Letters, and Work. New York: Island Press Cooperative, 1950.

Drinnon, Richard. Rebel in Paradise. Chicago: University of Chicago Press, 1961.

Du Bois, Ellen. Struggling into Existence: The Feminism of Sarah and Angelina Grimké. Boston: New England Free Press, n.d.

Duncan, Isadora. My Life. New York: Boni & Liveright, 1927.

Duniway, Abigail Scott. Path Breaking: An Autobiographical History of the Equal Suffrage Movement in Pacific Coast States. Studies in the Life of Women Series. New York: Schocken, 1970.

Dunnahoo, Terry. Emily Dunning: A Portrait. Chicago: Reilly & Lee, 1970.

Duster, Alfreda. Crusade for Justice: A Biography of Ida B. Wells. Chicago: University of Chicago Press, 1970.

Eliot, George [Mary Ann Evans]. The Mill on the Floss. First published, 1867. Boston: Houghton Mifflin, Riverside Editions, 1961.

Ellet, Elizabeth Fries. Pioneer Women of the West. New York: Charles Scribner's, 1852.

____. The Queens of American Society. New York: Charles
Scribner & Co., 1867.
____. The Women of the American Revolution. First pub-
lished, 1849. Reprint, New York: Haskell House, 1969.
Ets, Marie Hall. Rosa. Minneapolis: University of
Minnesota Press, 1970.
Flynn, Elizabeth Gurley. The Anderson Story: My Life as
a Political Prisoner. New York: Northwest Inter-
national Press, 1963.
____. Daughters of America: Ella Reeve Bloor and Anita
Whitney. New York: Workers Library, 1942.
____. I Speak My Own Piece. New York: Masses & Main
Stream, 1955.
Foster, Warren Dunham. Heroines of Modern Religion.
Freeport, N.Y.: Books for Libraries, 1970.
Fowler, William Worthington. Woman on the American
Frontier: A Valuable and Authentic History of the
Heroism, Adventures, Privations, Captivities, Trials,
and Noble Lives and Deaths of the "Pioneer Mothers of
the Republic." Hartford: S. S. Scranton, 1879.
Fox, Richard Michael. Rebel Irishwomen. Dublin: The
Talbot Press, 1935.
Frank, Anne. The Diary of a Young Girl, trans. B. M.
Mooyaart. Garden City, N.Y.: Doubleday, 1952.
Frederick, Pauline. Ten First Ladies of the World. New
York: Hawthorn Books, 1967.
Frost, John. Heroic Women of the West: Comprising
Thrilling Examples of Courage, Fortitude, Devotedness,
and Self-Sacrifice among the Pioneer Mothers of the
Western Country. Philadelphia: A. Hart, 1854.
George, Margaret. One Woman's "Situation": A Study of
Mary Wollstonecraft. Urbana: University of Illinois
Press, 1970.
Gérard, Jo. Belles gisantes. Avelgem, Belgium: J.
Delrue, 1965.
Giglio, Vittorio. Donne celebri. Milan: Societa
Editrice Libraria, 1950.
Gilder, Rosamond. Enter the Actress: The First Women in
the Theatre. Boston: Houghton Mifflin, 1931.
Gilman, Agness Geneva. Who's Who in Illinois: Women—
Makers of History. Chicago: Eclectic, 1927.
Ginzberg, Eli, and Yohalem, Alice M. Educated American
Women: Self-Portraits. New York: Columbia Uni-
versity Press, 1966.
Glendinning, Victoria. A Suppressed Cry: Life and Death
of a Quaker Daughter. London: Routledge & Kegan Paul,
1969.
Goldman, Emma. Living My Life. First published, 1930.
Reprint, New York: AMS Press, 1970.
Goldmark, Josephine. Impatient Crusader: Florence
Kelley's Life Story. University of Illinois Press, 1953.

Goodrich, Samuel Griswold. <u>Lives of Celebrated Women.</u>
  Philadelphia: Brodbury, Soden, 1844.
Gorsse, Pierre de. <u>Aimables inconstantes.</u> Paris: Plon,
  1961.
Gracey, Annie Ryder. <u>Eminent Missionary Women.</u> New York:
  Eaton & Mains, 1898.
Gribble, Francis Henry. <u>Women in War.</u> London: S. Low,
  Marston, 1916.
Guedalla, Philip. <u>Bonnet and Shawl: An Album.</u> New York:
  G. P. Putnam, 1928.
Guimarães, Ruth. <u>Mulheres célebres.</u> São Paulo: Editora
  Cultrix, 1960.
Harper, Ida Husted. <u>The Life and Work of Susan B. Anthony.</u>
  3 vols. New York: Arno Press, 1969.
Hasted, Jane-Eliza. <u>Unsuccessful Ladies.</u> Freeport, N.Y.:
  Books for Libraries, 1950.
Hays, Elinor R. <u>Lucy Stone: One of America's First and</u>
  <u>Greatest Feminists.</u> New York: Tower, 1971.
  ───. <u>Morning Star: A Biography of Lucy Stone, 1818-1893.</u>
  New York: Harcourt, Brace & World, 1961.
Heyn, Leah. <u>Challenge to Become a Doctor.</u> Columbia, Mo.:
  Feminist Press, n.d.
Holmes, Marjorie. <u>Love and Laughter.</u> Garden City, N.Y.:
  Doubleday, 1970.
  ───. <u>To Treasure Our Days.</u> Kansas City: Hallmark Cards,
  1971.
Hoyt, Mary. <u>American Women of the Space Age.</u> New York:
  Atheneum, 1966.
Hug-Hellmuth, H. <u>A Young Girl's Diary,</u> preface by Sigmund
  Freud. Seltzer, 1921.
Hull, Florence. <u>Julia Ward Howe and the Woman Suffrage</u>
  <u>Movement.</u> Woman Suffrage in America Series. First
  published, 1913. Reprint, New York: Arno Press, 1969.
Hume, Ruth. <u>Great Women of Medicine.</u> New York: Random
  House, 1964.
Hunt, Harriett K. <u>Glances and Glimpses; or, Fifty Years</u>
  <u>Social, Including Twenty Years Professional Life.</u> First
  published, 1856. Reprint, New York: Collectors
  Editions, Source Book Press, 1970.
Ireland, Norma O. <u>Index to Women.</u> Westwood, Mass.: F.
  W. Faxon, 1970.
Jacobs, Helen. <u>Famous American Women Athletes.</u> New York:
  Dodd, Mead, 1964.
James, Edward, and James, Janet Wilson. <u>Notable American</u>
  <u>Women, 1607-1950: A Biographical Dictionary.</u>
  Cambridge, Mass.: Harvard University Press, 1971.
Kent, John. <u>Elizabeth Fry.</u> London: B. T. Batsford,
  1962.
Kooiman, Helen. <u>Cameos.</u> Wheaton, Ill.: Tyndale House,
  n.d.

Koren, Elizabeth. The Diary of Elizabeth Koren: 1853-1855. Northfield, Minn.: Norwegian-American Historical Association, 1955.

Lader, Lawrence. The Margaret Sanger Story, and the Fight for Birth Control. New York: Doubleday, 1955.

Ladies' Home Journal and Christian Science Monitor. America's Twelve Great Women Leaders during the Past Hundred Years as Chosen by the Women of America. Freeport, N.Y.: Books for Libraries, 1933.

Lash, Joseph P. Eleanor and Franklin. New York: W. W. Norton, 1971.

Lawrence, Catherine S. Autobiography. Albany: Amasa J. Parker, 1893.

Lerner, Gerda. The Grimké Sisters from South Carolina: Pioneers for Woman's Rights and Abolition. Studies in the Life of Women Series. New York: Schocken Books, 1971.

Levinger, Elma E. Great Jewish Women. New York: Behrman House, 1940.

Lidderdale, Jane, and Nicholson, Mary. Dear Miss Weaver. New York: Viking, 1971.

Livermore, Mary A. The Story of My Life. Hartford: A. D. Worthington & Co., 1897.

Love, Cornelia Spencer. Famous Women of Yesterday and Today. Chapel Hill: University of North Carolina Press, 1936.

Lutz, Alma. Created Equal. New York: John Day, 1940.
_____. Emma Willard: Daughter of Democracy. Boston: Houghton Mifflin, 1929.
_____. Emma Willard: Pioneer Educator of American Women. Boston: Beacon Press, 1964.
_____. Susan B. Anthony. Boston: Beacon Press, 1959.

Luxemburg, Rosa. Rosa Luxemburg Speaks, intro. Mary Alice Waters. Lakeside, Calif.: Pathfinder Press, n.d.

McCarthy, Mary. Memories of a Catholic Girlhood. New York: Harcourt, Brace & World, 1957.

Marberry, M. M. Vicky: A Biography. New York: Funk & Wagnalls, 1967.

Marder, Herbert. Feminism and Art: A Study of Virginia Woolf. Chicago: University of Chicago Press, 1968.

Marshall, Helen. Dorothea Dix: Forgotten Samaritan. First published, 1937. Reprint, New York: Russell & Russell, 1967.

Mead, Margaret. Blackberry Winter: My Earlier Years. New York: William Morrow, 1972.

Menzies, Sutherland. Political Women. 2 vols. Port Washington, N.Y.: Kennikat Press, 1970.

Merriam, Eve, ed. Growing Up Female in America: Ten Lives. New York: Doubleday, 1971.

Milner, Esther. Dialogue of Women. Indianapolis: Bobbs-
Merrill, 1967.
Minnigerode, Meade. Some American Ladies. Freeport,
N.Y.: Books for Libraries, 1926.
Mitchell, Geoffrey, ed. Hard Way Up: The Autobiography
of Hannah Mitchell, Suffragette and Rebel. New York:
Fernhill House, 1969.
Mitchell, Hannah. The Hard Way Up. New York: Fernhill
House, 1968.
Mitford, Nancy. Zelda. New York: Harper & Row, 1970.
Moore, Virginia. Distinguished Women Writers. First
published, 1934. Reprint, Port Washington, N.Y.:
Kennikat Press, 1968.
Mora, Constancia de la. In Place of Splendor: The
Autobiography of a Spanish Woman. New York: Harcourt,
Brace, 1939.
Musil, Robert. Five Women. New York: Delacorte Press,
1966.
Nathan, Dorothy. Women of Courage. New York: Random
House, 1964.
Nettl, J. P. Rosa Luxemburg. 2 vols. New York: Oxford
University Press, 1966.
Nin, Anaïs. The Diary of Anaïs Nin. 2 vols. New York:
Harcourt, Brace & World, 1966.
Noble, Iris. First Woman Ambulance Surgeon: Emily
Barringer. New York: Julian Messner, 1962.
Nystrom-Hamilton, Louise. Ellen Key: Her Life and Her
Work. New York: G. P. Putnam, 1913.
Oakley, Mary Ann B. Elizabeth Cady Stanton. New York:
Feminist Press, 1972.
Orpen, Adella Elizabeth. Memories of the Old Emigrant
Days in Kansas, 1862-1865. Edinburgh: William
Blakewood & Sons, 1926.
Pankhurst, Emmeline. My Own Story. First published,
1914. Reprint, New York: Collectors Editions, Source
Book Press, 1970.
Parkman, Mary K. Heroines of Service. First published,
1917. Reprint, Freeport, N.Y.: Books for Libraries,
1968.
Parton, James. Eminent Women of the Age: Being Nar-
ratives of the Lives and Deeds of the Most Prominent
Women of the Present Generation. Hartford: S. M.
Betts, 1869.
Phillips, Emma M. Dedicated to Serve. Independence, Mo.:
Herald House, 1970.
Randall, Mercedes M. Improper Bostonian: Emily Green
Balch. New York: Twayne, 1964.
Richardson, Dorothy. Pilgrimage. 4 vols. London:
Dent, 1967.
Richmond, Alexander. Native Daughter: The Story of
Anita Whitney. San Francisco: A. Whitney 75th Annual
Committee, 1942.

Roosevelt, Eleanor. On My Own: The Years since the White House. New York: Curtis Books, 1958.

Ross, Isabel. Angel of the Battlefield. New York: Harper & Row, 1956.

Ross, Nancy. Heroines of the Early West. New York: Random House, 1960.

St. John, Christopher Marie. Christine Murrell. London: Williams & Norgate, 1935.

Sanger, Margaret. Margaret Sanger: Autobiography. New York: W. W. Norton, 1938.

_____. My Fight for Birth Control. Elmsford, N.Y.: Pergamon Press, n.d.

_____. Woman and the New Race. Elmsford, N.Y.: Pergamon Press, n.d.

Seaver, James E. A Narrative of the Life of Mrs. Mary Jemison. 1823. Reprint, New York: Corinth Books, 1961.

Sergeant, Philip W. Dominant Women. Freeport, N.Y.: Books for Libraries, 1929.

Shaw, Anna Howard. The Story of a Pioneer. First published, 1915. Reprint, Millwood, N.Y.: Kraus Reprint, n.d.

Sickels, Eleanor M. Twelve Daughters of Democracy. Freeport, N.Y.: Books for Libraries, 1941.

Simmons, Dawn Langley. A Rose for Mrs. Lincoln. Boston: Beacon Press, 1970.

Sokolnikova, Galina O. Nine Women, trans. H. C. Stevens. Freeport, N.Y.: Books for Libraries, 1932.

Stanton, Elizabeth Cady. Eighty Years and More: Reminiscences 1815-1897, intro. Gail Parker. Studies in the Life of Women Series. New York: Schocken, 1970.

Stanton, Theodore. Elizabeth Cady Stanton as Revealed in Her Letters, Diary, and Reminiscences. New York: Harper & Row, 1922.

Sterling, Philip. Sea and Earth: The Life of Rachel Carson. New York: Crowell, 1970.

Stevens, William. Famous Women of America. New York: Dodd, Mead, 1950.

Stocks, Mary D. Eleanor Rathbone: A Biography. London: Gollancz, 1949.

Suhl, Yuri. Ernestine L. Rose and the Battle for Human Rights. Clifton, N.J.: Reynal, 1959.

Thane, Elswyth. Dolley Madison: Her Life and Times. New York: Crowell-Collier Press, 1970.

Thomas, Henry, and Lee, Dana. Living Biographies of Famous Women. New York: Doubleday, 1959.

Thorp, Margaret. Female Persuasion: Six Strong-minded Women. First published, 1949. Reprint, Hamden, Conn.: Shoe String Press, 1971.

_____. Sarah Orne Jewett. First published, 1949. Reprint, Minneapolis: University of Minnesota Press, 1971.

Two Thousand Women of Achievement. 2 vols. New York:
    Rowman & Littlefield, 1969.
Vorse, Mary Heaton. A Footnote to Folly: Reminiscences
    of Mary Heaton Vorse. New York: Farrar & Rinehart,
    1935.
Vorst, Mrs. John Van. The Woman Who Toils: Being the
    Experiences of Two Gentlewomen as Factory Girls. New
    York: Doubleday & Page, 1903.
Wade, Mason. Margaret Fuller: Whetstone of Genius.
    First published, 1940. Reprint, New York: Augustus
    M. Kelly, 1970.
Wald, Lillian. The House on Henry Street. First pub-
    lished, 1915. Reprint, New York: Dover, 1969.
Walsh, James, ed. These Splendid Sisters. Essay Index
    Report Series. Freeport, N.Y.: Books for Libraries,
    n.d.
Wardle, Ralph. Mary Wollstonecraft: A Critical Bio-
    graphy. Lawrence: University of Kansas Press, 1951.
Webb, Beatrice. Diaries, 1912-1932, ed. Margaret I.
    Cole. New York: Longmans Green, 1952.
____. My Apprenticeship. New York: Longmans Green, 1926.
____. Our Partnership. New York: Longmans Green, 1948.
Willard, Frances E. Glimpses of Fifty Years: The Auto-
    biography of an American Woman. First published, 1889.
    Reprint, New York: Collectors Editions, Source Book
    Press, 1970.
____, and Livermore, Mary A., eds. American Women: A
    Comprehensive Encyclopedia of the Lives and Achieve-
    ment of American Women during the Nineteenth Century.
    2 vols. Women of the Century Series. Reprint,
    Detroit: Gale Research, 1967.
Wise, Winifred. Fanny Kemble. New York: G. P. Putnam,
    1966.
____. Harriet Beecher Stowe. New York: G. P. Putnam,
    1965.
____. Jane Addams of Hull House. New York: Harcourt,
    Brace, 1935.
Wyse, Lois. Mrs. Success. New York: World, 1970.

FUTURISM, UTOPIANISM

Baker, T., and Bird, M. "Urbanization and the Position
    of Women." Sociological Review 1 (July 1959):99-122.
Bell, Daniel, ed. Toward the Year 2000: Work in
    Progress. Boston: Houghton Mifflin, Daedalus
    Library, 1968.
Bellamy, Edward. Looking Backward: 2000-1887.
    Cambridge, Mass.: Harvard University Press, Belknap
    Press, 1967.
Day, Lincoln H., and Day, Alice Taylor. Too Many
    Americans: Tomorrow's Issue. Boston: Houghton
    Mifflin, 1964.

Etzioni, Amitai. "Sex Control, Science, and Society."
  Science 13 (Sept. 1968):1107-12.
Flynn, Elizabeth Gurley. Women Have a Date with Destiny.
  New York: Workers Library, 1944.
  ___. Women's Place in the Fight for a Better World. New
  York: New Century, 1947.
Goodman, Percival, and Goodman, Paul. Communitas: Means
  of Livelihood and Ways of Life. Chicago: University
  of Chicago Press, 1947.
Hinds, William Alfred. American Communities. First
  published, 1878. Reprint, New York: Corinth Books,
  1961.
Jacobs, Sue-Ellen. "Toward Polyocular Anthropology." In
  Human Futuristics, ed. Magorah Maruyama and James
  Dator, pp. 151-70. Honolulu: University of Hawaii
  Social Science Research Institute, 1971.
Keller, Suzanne. "The Future Role of Women." Annals of
  the American Academy of Political and Social Science
  408 (1973):1-12.
Ludovici, Anthony M. Lysistrata; or, Woman's Future and
  Future Woman. London: Kegan Paul, Trench, Trubner,
  1924.
Otto, Herbert A., ed. The Family in Search of a Future.
  New York: Appleton-Century-Crofts, 1970.
Skinner, B. F. Walden Two. New York: Macmillan, 1949.
Toffler, Alvin. Future Shock. New York: Random House,
  1970.

BIBLIOGRAPHIES

Aldous, Joan, and Hill, Reuben. International Biblio-
  graphy of Research in Marriage and the Family.
  Minneapolis: University of Minnesota Press, 1967.
Bibliography on Abortion. A.S.A. (Association for the
  Study of Abortion), 120 West 57 St., New York, N.Y.
  10019.
Bibliography on Twentieth-century Women Writers Who Write
  about Women. Bread and Roses, 1151 Massachusetts
  Ave., Cambridge, Mass.
Books for Women's Liberation. Lenora Lloyd, London
  Socialist Woman Group, 40 Inverness Road, Southall,
  Middlesex, London, England.
Boston Public Library. Galatea Collection. Catalogue
  of the Galatea Collection of Books Redatry to the
  History of Woman. 1898. Boston Trustees.
Chiñas, Beverly. "Bibliography: Anthropology of Women."
  Mimeo. Chico, California: Chico State College,
  Department of Anthropology, 1971.
Fifty Years After the 1912 Amendment: A Bibliography on
  the Elusive Struggle for Women's Liberation. Rohnert
  Park, Calif.: Sonoma State College, 1970.

Freeman, Leah, ed. The Changing Role of Women: A
    Selected Bibliography. Bibliographic Series No. 9.
    Sacramento: Sacramento State College Library, 1971.
Gay, Jules. Bibliographie des ouvrages relatifs à
    l'amour, aux femmes, au mariage, et des livres
    facétieux, pantagruéliques, scatologiques, saty-
    riques, etc., contenant les titres détaillés de ces
    ouvrages, les noms des auteurs, un aperçu de leur
    sujet, leur valeur et leur prix dans les ventes, etc.
    Turin: J. Gay, 1871-73.
Gerritsen, Alelta Henriette. La femme et le féminisme.
    Collection des livres, périodiques etc. sur la
    condition sociale de la femme et le mouvement
    féministe. Paris: V. Giard et Brière, 1900.
Hughes, Marija, ed. Bibliography on Women's Rights in
    Employment. Sacramento: California State Library,
    Law Library, 1969.
International Bibliography of Women's Writers. Center
    for Women's Studies, San Diego State College, San
    Diego, Calif.
Jacobs, Sue-Ellen. Women in Cross-cultural Perspective:
    A Preliminary Sourcebook. Urbana: University of
    Illinois, Department of Urban and Regional Planning,
    1971.
Kirkpatrick, Joanna. "Tutorial on Woman: Selected
    Bibliography." Mimeo. Bennington College, Depart-
    ments of Psychology and Anthropology, 1970.
Leonard, E. A. The American Woman in Colonial and
    Revolutionary Times, 1565-1800: A Syllabus with
    Bibliography. Philadelphia: University of Pennsylvania
    Press, 1962.
Moore, Louise. Occupations for Girls and Women: Selected
    References, July 1943-June 1948. Bulletin 229. U.S.
    Department of Labor, Women's Bureau. Washington, D.C.:
    U.S. Government Printing Office, 1942.
Morgan, Robin. "Bibliography." In Sisterhood Is
    Powerful, pp. 567-83. New York: Random House, 1970.
Oetzel, Roberta M. "Annotated Bibliography." In The
    Development of Sex Differences, ed. Eleanor Maccoby,
    pp. 223-321. Stanford: Stanford University Press,
    1966.
O'Leary, Timothy J. "Bibliography of Cross-Cultural
    Studies: Supplement II." Behavior Science Notes 8
    (1973):123-34.
Publications of the Women's Bureau. U.S. Department of
    Labor, 1371 Peachtree St., N.E., Atlanta, Ga. 30309.
Sex Role Concepts: Selected Annotated Bibliography.
    Business and Professional Women, 2012 Massachusetts
    Ave., N.W., Washington, D.C. 20036.
Tabaku, Faire. Bibliografia e letërsisë për fëmijë dhe
    të rinj (1945-1964). Tiranë: Instituti Studimeve
    dhe Botimeve Shkollore, 1965.

The Women's Collection: A Bibliography of Material in
    All Matters Pertaining to Women's Interests Added to
    the Woman's College Library of the University of N.C.
    Greensboro: University of North Carolina, Women's
    College Library, n.d.
Women's Rights in Employment: A Bibliography. California
    State Library, Law Library, Sacramento, Calif. 95814.
Women's Studies Program. Carol Rowell, Coordinator,
    College of Arts & Letters, San Diego State College,
    San Diego, Calif. 92115.

PUBLICATIONS OF WOMEN'S STUDIES
COLLECTIVES AND CENTERS

"Ain't I a Woman?" Women's Collective of Iowa, Box 1169,
    Iowa City, Iowa 52240.
APHRA: A Literary Journal. Amazon Bookstore, 3240 Cedar
    Ave. South, Minneapolis, Minn.
Archives. Women's History Research Center, 2325 Oak St.,
    Berkeley, Calif. 94708.
Association for the Study of Abortion Newsletter, 120
    West 57th St., New York, N.Y. 10019.
Battle Acts. YAWF Women, 58 West 25th St., New York,
    N.Y. 10010.
C.W.L.U. News. Chicago Women's Liberation Union, 2875
    West Cermak, Room 9, Chicago, Ill. 60623.
Canadian Women's Educational Press, 280 Bloor Street West,
    Suite 305, Toronto, Ontario, Canada.
Citizen's Advisory Council on Status of Women Newsletter.
    U.S. Department of Labor, Washington, D.C. 20210.
Clearinghouse on Women's Studies. Feminist Press. Box
    334, Old Westbury, N.Y. 11568.
Every Woman. 1043B W. Washington Blvd., Venice, Calif.
    90291.
F.E.W.: News and Views. Federally Employed Women, Suite
    487, National Park Station, Washington, D.C.
Feminist Publications: The Archetypal Woman. Class
    Structure in the Women's Movement. Dangers of the Pro-
    Woman Line and Consciousness Raising. History of the
    Equality Issue in the Contemporary Women's Movement.
    The Institution of Sexual Intercourse. Man-Hating.
    Marriage. Notes from the Lower Classes. Notes from
    the Lower Classes, II. Power as a Function of the
    Group. Radical Feminism. Radical Feminism and Love.
    The Rise of Man. Rules and Responsibilities in a
    Leaderless Revolutionary Group. The Twig-Benders.
    Vaginal Orgasm as a Mass Hysterical Survival Response.
    The Feminist History. The Feminist Organization
    Principles and Structure. The Feminist, 120 Liberty
    St., New York, N.Y. 10006.

Feminist Studies. Ann Calderwood, 294 Riverside Dr., New
York, N.Y. 10025.
Know, Inc., Publications: Female Studies I. Female
Studies II. New Guide to Female Studies. Know, Inc.,
Box 10197, Pittsburgh, Pa. 15232.
The Ladder. Box 5025, Washington Station, Reno, Nevada
89503.
Ms. 370 Lexington Ave., New York, N.Y. 10017.
No More Fun and Games. 371 Somerville Ave., Somerville,
Mass. 02143.
Off Our Backs. P.O. Box 4859, Cleveland Park Station,
Washington, D.C. 20008.
Pandora: The Seattle Women's Newspaper. P.O. Box 94,
Seattle, Wash., 98105.
Second Wave. Female Liberation, Box 303, Kenmore Square
Station, Boston, Mass. 02215.
Sex Role Materials. Shari Etzkowitz, A.W.S. National
Coordinator of Sex Role Curricula, Box 1113,
Department of Sociology, Washington University, St.
Louis, Mo. 63130.
Society for Humane Abortion: Newsletter, P.O. Box 1862,
San Francisco, Calif., 94101.
Sophie Smith Collection: A Printed Book Catalog. West-
port, Conn.: Greenwood Press, Resource Library, n.d.
Source Library of the Women's Movement. New York: Source
Book Press, 1970.
The Spokeswoman. Urban Research Corporation, 5464 South
Shore Drive, Chicago, Ill. 60615.
Up from Under. 339 Lafayette St., New York, N.Y. 10012.
Velvet Glove Magazine. P.O. Box 188, Livermore, Calif.
94550.
Voice of the Women's Liberation Movement Newsletter.
1940 Bissell, Chicago, Ill. 60614.
Women Lawyers Journal 1-54. 1911-68. Reprint,
Hackensack, N.J.: Fred B. Rothman, 1971.
Women's Rights Law Reporter. Vol. 1, July-Aug. 1971.
Bimonthly.
Women's Studies Abstracts. P.O. Box 1, Rush, N.Y.
Women's Studies Newsletter. Clearinghouse on Women's
Studies. Feminist Press, Box 334, Old Westbury, N.Y.
11568.

PUBLICATIONS USEFUL FOR DEALING
WITH SEX DISCRIMINATION

Fraser, Leila. Guidelines on Filing Complaints of Sex
Discrimination in Educational Employment. 2d ed.
Women's Caucus for Political Science, 1972. Mimeo.
Hughes, Marija Matich. The Sexual Barrier: Legal and
Economic Aspects of Employment. Supplement 1. San
Francisco: Hastings College of Law, 1971.

Jiagge, Annie R. "An Introduction to the Declaration on
  Elimination of Discrimination against Women." U.N.
  Monthly Chronicle 7 (Mar. 1968):55-61.
Miller, Robert S. "Sex Discrimination and Title VII of
  the Civil Rights Act of 1964." Minnesota Law Review
  51 (1967):877-97.
Murray, Pauli, and Eastwood, Mary O. "Jane Crow and the
  Law: Sex Discrimination and Title VII." George
  Washington Law Review 34 (1965):232-56.
National Organization for Women. Campus Coordinating
  Committee. Academic Discrimination Kit. Chicago:
  National Organization for Women, 1971.
Nevada Commission on the Status of Women. Interim
  Report, Sept. 1967-Dec. 1968.
Oldam, James C. "Sex Discrimination and State Protective
  Laws." Denver Law Journal 44 (1967):344-76.
Pressman, Sonia. "Sex Discrimination in Employment and
  What You Can Do about It." Women Lawyers Journal 54
  (Fall 1968):6-10.
Sigworth, Heather. The Legal Aspects of Sex Discrimina-
  tion against Female Faculty. University of Indiana
  Law School.
Stimpson, Catherine R., ed. Discrimination against Women:
  Congressional Hearings on Equal Rights in Education and
  Employment. New York: Bowker, 1973.
  ___. Women and the "Equal Rights" Amendment: Senate Sub-
  committee Hearings on the Constitutional Amendment,
  91st Congress. New York: Bowker, 1972.
Taylor, Grace. "Equal Rights for Women." University of
  Florida Review 15 (Summer 1962):134.
U.N. Department of Economic and Social Affairs. Declaration
  on the Elimination of Discrimination against Women. New
  York: Office of Public Information, 1968.
U.S. Department of Labor. Women's Bureau. Laws on Sex
  Discrimination in Employment. Washington, D.C.: U.S.
  Government Printing Office, 1970.
  ___. Bulletin 10. Washington, D.C.: U.S. Government
  Printing Office, n.d.
  ___. Know Your Rights. Washington, D.C.: U.S. Government
  Printing Office, n.d.
U.S. Equal Employment Opportunity Commission Hearings.
  Washington, D.C.: U.S. Government Printing Office, 1969.
Who Will Listen If You Have a Civil Rights Complaint?
  Washington, D.C.: U.S. Government Printing Office, 1969.
"Women and the Law." Valparaiso University Law Review 5
  (1971).
Women's Equity Action League. Summary of Executive Order
  11246 as Amended by Executive Order 11375: How These
  Orders Relate to Sex Discrimination in Universities and
  Colleges That Have Federal Contracts. 1504 44th St.,
  N.W., Washington, D.C. 20007.

Anthony, Katharine Susan, 60,73
Anthony, Susan B., 196,204
Anthony, Sylvia, 49
Antin, Mary, 64
Antoun, Richard T., 21
Anzoategui, Yderla G., 84
Apysheva, Apal, 64
Apuleius, Madaurensis, 126
Ardener, Edwin, 165
Arduini, Alberto, 34
Arens, Hanns, 60
Arensberg, C. M., 56
Aries, Philippe, 146,199
Ariga, A. Kizaeman, 29
Aristophanes, 220
Ariwoola, O., 10
Armstrong, Ruth Gallup, 40
Arnaiz Amigo, Aurora, 98
Arnstein, Helene S., 153
Aron, Albert William, 60
Arregger, Constance, 49
Arroyo, Cesar Emilio, 88
Asbury, Herbert, 220
Asimov, Isaac, 215
Assa, Janine, 62
Assali, N. S., 153
Astell, Mary, 146,204
Astin, Helen S., 108,187
Aswad, Barbara C., 94,168
Athavale, Parvatibai, 41
Atienza, Maria Fe G., 77
Auber, J., 19
Auchincloss, Louis, 215
Auclert, Habertine, 56
Auerbach, Aline B., 153
Auerbach, H. A., 22
Aufenanger, H., 81
Austregesilo, Antonio, 84
Avril de Sainte-Croix, Ghenia, 161
Avsarova, M. P., 64
Awad, B. A., 7
Ayling, Keith, 108
Ayres, Barbara, 153,215
Ayscough, Florence, 34
Aziz, Wahida, 40
Azizbekova, P. O., 64
Azman, Y., 25
Azume, T., 29

Baba of Karo, 10
Babb, Lawrence A., 40
Babchuk, Nicholas, 146,187
Babcox, Deborah, 209

Bacdayan, Albert, 160
Bachofen, Johann J., 168,220
Backett, E. Maurice, 152
Bacon, Alice M., 29
Bacon, Margaret K., 137
Bader, Clarisse, 41
Baer, Clara Gregory, 196
Baer, Thelma, 199
Bahr, Howard M., 109
Bailey, Beth, 173
Bailey, Garrick, 94
Bailey, Larry Joe, 187
Bailyn, Lotte, 173
Bainton, Roland H., 60
Baker, Alex Anthony, 153
Baker, Elizabeth, 173
Baker, Luther G., 137
Baker, Melba, 173
Baker, Roger G., 124
Baker, T., 231
Baker, Therese, 187
Balabanoff, Angelica, 64,223
Balandier, Georges, 14
Balazs, G., 173
Bald, Marjory, 215
Baldensperger, Philip J., 22
Bales, Robert F., 150
Balfour, Frances, 223
Balint, Alice, 154
Balsan, F., 14
Balsdon, J. P., 62
Bandler, Lucille, 173
Bandura, Albert, 126
Banks, Joseph A., 49,146,168
Banks, Olive, 49,146,168
Banning, Margaret, 108
Bannister, Constance, 154
Banton, M., 10
Barad, Mirriam, 23
Bar Joseph, Rikvah, 23
Barbey d'Aurevilly, Jules Amedee, 56
Barday, Stephen, 161
Bardwick, Judith M., 126
Barnard, Mary, 216
Barnes, Earl, 220
Barney, Laura, 199
Barnouw, Victor, 93
Baroni, Albert, 106
Barrow, Tui Terence, 83
Barry, Herbert, III., 137
Bartels, Lambert, 16
Bartels, M. C. A., 222
Bartels, P. R. A., 222

240

Barton, A., 187,204
Barton, Clara, 220
Barton, Margaret Ruby, 60
Basden, G. T., 10
Basil, Douglas C., 173
Baskakov, N. A., 64
Bastock, Margaret, 146
Bates, Alan, 146,87
Bates, Jerome E., 154
Bateson, Gregory, 78,81
Batho, Edith C., 187
Bauer, Bernhard A., 161
Bauer, Max, 60
Baumann, Hermann, 10
Baumer, Gertrud, 60,223
Baumrind, Diana, 187
Bax, Ernest Belfort, 49
Baxter, Richard, 60
Bayles, George James, 168
Beach, Frank A., 134,152
Beach, Seth C., 223
Beall, Elizabeth, 125
Beals, Ralph L., 98
Beard, Mary Ritter, 29,108,168,199,220
Beardsley, Richard, 29,33
Bearne, Catherine Mary, 56
Beatty, Jerome, Jr., 108
Beauchamp, Joan, 173
Beaunier, Andre, 223
Beauvoir, Simone de, 23,119,216,223
Beavan, Keith, 49
Beaver, R. Pierce, 165
Bebel, August, 60,169,220
Becker, Beril, 209
Beckman, Gail, 169
Bednarik, Karl, 126
Beecher, Catherine Esther, 108,173
Beidelman, T. O., 16
Beier, H. U., 10
Belden, Jack, 34
Belfort-Bax, E., 197
Belfrage, Sally, 64
Belkin, Madeline, 209
Bell, Clair Hayden, 60
Bell, Daniel, 231
Bell, F. L. S., 16
Bell, Ralcy Husted, 204
Bell, Willis H., 94
Bellah, R., 29
Bellamy, Edward, 231
Bellefonds, Linant de, 20
Bellefords, Josette de, 173
Belloc, Nedra R., 173

Belo, Jane, 77
Bem, Daryl J., 209
Bem, Sandra L., 209
Bender, Marylin, 137
Bendix, R., 149
Benedek, Therese, 132
Benedict, Burton, 19
Benedict, Ruth, 29,91,126
Benedictis, Daniel J. de, 169
Benfer, Robert A., 123
Ben-Gurion, David, 23
Benigna, Rev. Sr., 173
Benitez, Helena Z., 37
Benjamin, Harry, 161
Benn, Rachel R., 34
Bennett, Arnold, 204
Bennett, Dan, 198
Bennett, Kay, 94
Bennett, John, 188
Bennigsen, A., 64
Benson, Mary Sumner, 108,199
Benson, Patty, 152
Benson, Ruth Crego, 216
Bentwich, Norman, 23
Ben-Yosef, A. C., 23
Beokovic, Mila, 74
Beran, Janice Ann, 77
Berardo, F. M., 142,150
Berg, Richard K., 174
Berger, Bennett, 174
Bergler, Edmund, 126,132,152
Berman, Joan, 89
Bernard, Jessie, 132,146,169,174,188
Berndt, Catherine H., 76
Berndt, Ronald Murray, 81
Bernstein, Lionel Mardel, 125
Bernstein, Merton C., 174
Berry, Jane, 174
Berreman, Gerald D., 41
Berscheid, Ellen, 209
Besant, Annie, 223
Beshiri, Patricia H., 174
Best, Elsdon, 83
Bettelheim, Bruno, 108,137,216
Bhattacharyya, Panchanan, 41
Bianquis, G., 60
Bick, Mario, 132
Biddle, Gertrude, 223
Bier, William C., 108,126
Bil'shai-Pilipenko, Vera L'vovna, 65
Binet, J., 14
Binyon, Michael, 49
Biocca, Ettore, 84
Bird, Caroline, 174

Bird, M., 231
Birdwell, Russell, 49
Birmingham, W., 10
Birney, Catherine, 223
Bista, Khem Bahadur, 41
Bittencourt, Adalzira, 84
Black, C. E., 65
Black, Lydia T., 30
Blackburn, Helen, 49,204
Blacking, John, 18
Blackman, Winifred, 7
Blackwell, Alice Stone, 204
Blackwell, Elizabeth, 174,223
Blake, Judith, 89,154
Blake, Katherine Devereux, 223
Blake, William, 219
Blanc, Marie Therese, 108
Blanchard, Kendall, 94
Bland, James, 199
Blashfield, Evangeline, 223
Blau, Peter, 174
Bleakley, Horace William, 223
Blease, W. Lyon, 49
Bleumen, Jean, 137
Bleyer, Adrien, 154
Bloch, Iwan, 132
Bloch, Peter, 174
Block, J. R., 191
Blomberg, Hector Pedro, 86
Blood, Robert O., Jr., 108,146,174
Bloomer, Dexter C., 223
Bloor, Ella Reeve, 65,223
Bloss, Celestia Angenette, 223
Blum, Eva, 71
Blum, Richard, 71
Blumenthal, Walter Hart, 108
Blunt, Hugh Francis, 223
Boas, Louise S., 188
Bobr'onok, Serhii Tykhonovych, 65
Boccaccio, Giovanni, 223
Bochkareva, Ekaterina Ivanovna, 65
Bock, E. Wilbur, 165
Bock, Philip K., 154
Boggs, Lucinda Pearl, 34
Bohannan, Laura, 10
Bohannan, Paul, 3,146
Bolton, Sarah, 188
Bomli, P. W., 72
Bonaparte, Marie, 132
Bondy, Stephen B., 188
Boone, Gladys, 174
Borchers, G., 188
Bordeaux, Henry, 56

Borer, Mary, 188
Borgese, Elisabeth Mann, 199
Borton, Hugh, 30
Boserup, Ester, 174
Bosos, I., 174
Bott, Alan John, 49
Bott, Elizabeth, 146
Bochereau, M. G., 89
Boulting, William, 62
Bourgignon, Erika, 93
Bouvat, L., 20
Bowen, Eleanor Smith, 10
Bowerman, Charles, 138
Bowman, Mary Jean, 87
Boyd, Mary Brown, 169
Brace, C. Loring, 123
Bracken, Peg, 223
Brackett, Arna C., 188
Bradburn, Norman, 181
Bradford, Gamaliel, 199,224
Bradinska, Radka N., 74
Bragdon, Elizabeth, 209
Bramblett, Claud A., 123
Branch, Mary Sydney, 174
Brandeis, Louis, 174
Brandel, M., 14,18
Branscomb, Susan, 123
Brant, Charles S., 37
Brantome, Pierre de Bourdeille, 57,220
Braunstein, Otto, 71
Brayne, Frank Lugard, 41
Brecher, Edward, 132
Brecher, Rugh, 132
Breckinridge, Mary, 174
Breckinridge, Sophonisba P., 108,220
Breer, Paul E., 126
Breitenbach, Josef, 28
Bremme, Gabriele, 60
Brenton, Myron, 132
Briceno Vasquez, Ramon Maria, 89
Briffault, R., 146,169,220
Briggs, Jean L., 92
Brim, Orville G., 126,137
Briscoe, Mary L., 208
Bristol, Augusta, 220
Brittain, Vera, 199
Brochett, L. P., 204
Bronfenbrenner, Urie, 65,126
Brooks, Geraldine, 57
Brophy, Brigid, 119,216
Brose, Alberta J., 137
Broughton, Philip Stephens, 161
Broverman, Inge, 189

Brown, Alice, 224
Brown, Daniel, 126,137
Brown, David G., 174
Brown, Dee, 199
Brown, Demetra Vaka, 25,26
Brown, Donald R., 65
Brown, Grant R., 37
Brown, Helen Gurley, 132,133
Brown, J. S., 133
Brown, Judith K., 98,119,133,137,138,174,175,209
Brown, Mary Milbank, 224
Brown, Nona B., 127
Brown, P. E., 53
Browne, Francis J., 154
Browne, John C., 154
Browne, William Hardcaste, 224
Browning, Harley L., 209
Brown-Miller, Susan, 209
Bruce, Henry Addington Bayley, 108,169
Bruere, Martha S., 119
Bruning, Elfriede, 60
Brunner, Peter, 165
Bruno, Emilio, 62
Bruns, Ivo, 71
Buchbinder, Georgeda, 81
Buck, H. H., 77
Buckmaster, Henrietta, 224
Bugan, Kenneth Gregory, 199
Buhrig, Marga, 60
Bullard, Laura C., 224
Bullough, Bonnie, 199
Bullough, Vern L., 133,161,199
Buniatov, Grigorii, 65
Burch, Thomas, 30
Buresch-Riebe, Ilse, 60
Burgess, William, 161
Burke, P. E., 73
Burness, H. M., 10
Burnett, Constance, 224
Burniaux, Jeanne, 57
Burton, Frances, 123
Burton, John, 220
Burton, Margaret Ernestine, 28,30,34
Burton, Roger V., 127
Bushnell, Horace, 204
Busia, K. H., 10
Bussman, Hanna, 60
Butler, Elizabeth Beardsley, 175
Buxton, J., 10
Buytendijk, Frederik Jacobus Johannes, 127,220
Byham, William C., 175

Caar, L., 93
Cain, Glen G., 175

Caird, Mona, 146
Calame-Griaule, G., 8
Calderone, Mary S., 154,188
Caldwell, John Charles, 10
Calera, Ana Maria, 72
Calhoun, Arthur, 108
Calixto, Julia, 188
Callahan, Sidney Cornelius, 109,119
Camarano, Chris, 89
Cambert, William W., 129
Camden, Charles Carroll, 50
Campbell, Angus, 169
Campbell, Bernard, 133
Campbell, Enid, 169
Campbell, Helen, 175
Campbell, Henry D., 14
Campo de Alange, Maria, 72
Cannon, Mary Minerva, 85,87
Caplow, Theodore, 109,175
Caprio, Frank S., 152
Carlebach, J., 16
Carley, Verna A., 3
Carluci, M. A., 84
Carpenter, Edward, 133,220
Carpi, Leone, 62
Carrasco Puente, Rafael, 98
Carreira, A., 9,11
Carrington, William John, 154
Carroll, Margaret S., 175
Carson, Josephine, 103
Carson, Ruth, 154
Carstairs, G. M., 133
Carter, Luther J., 154
Carter, M., 11
Cary, Alice, 57
Casagrande di Villaviera, Rita, 62
Cash, W. J., 109
Cassara, Beverly Benner, 109
Castallo, Mario Alberto, 154
Castelar y Ripoll, Emilio, 224
Castellani, Maria, 62
Castetter, Edward F., 94
Castro, Fidel, 89
Catalino del Amo, Severo, 72
Cathey-Calvert, Carolyn, 188
Catling, Patrick Skene, 133
Catt, Carrie Chapman, 204
Caudill, William, 30,109
Cavan, Ruth Shonle, 146
Celarie, Henriette, 5
Centers, Richard, 198
Cerati, Marie, 57
Chabrol, Claude, 138,216

Chace, Elizabeth Buffum, 224
Chadwick, Mary, 154
Chagnon, Napoleon, 85
Chakraborty, Usha, 41
Chakravarty, Syam Sunder, 41
Chaltopadhyaya, Kamaladevi, 41
Chamberlain, A. F., 216
Chamberlin, Hope, 199
Champerlain, I. C., 216
Chance, Norman A., 92
Chao, Pu-Wei Youg, 34
Chapman, Joseph Dudley, 127
Chappell, Clovis G., 165
Chartham, Robert, 135
Chase, Ilka, 175
Chassequet-Smirgel, J., 133
Chaton, Jeanne, 188
Chattopadhyaya, Kamaladevi, 188
Chaudhary, Roop Lal, 41
Chavarriaga Meyer, Jose Luis, 88
Chayes, A. H., 50
Chazaro, Gabriel, 98
Chelhod, J., 21
Chepurkovskii, E. M., 65
Chesler, Phyllis, 209
Chesnut, Mary Boykin, 109
Chesser, Eustace, 50,161
Child, H. F., 16
Child, Irvin L., 137,145
Child, Lydia Maria, 224
Chimnabai II, Maharani of Baroda, 41
Chiñas, Beverly Litzler, 98,232
Chisolm, Shirley, 103
Chmaj, Betty E., 188
Chodorow, Nancy, 138
Chombart de Lauwe, Marie-Jose, 57,119
Chombart de Lauwe, Paul, 57,119
Chopin, Kate, 216
Chopra, Sharda, 42
Chowning, Ann, 76
Christensen, Jean, 109
Christenson, Cornelia, 156
Christenson, Harold T., 73,109
Christian, A., 11
Christy, Howard Chander, 109
Chudinov, Aleksandr Nikolaevich, 65
Chughtie, Ghayas-u-din, 39
Chumacero, Rosalia de, 98
Chun Koh, Hesung, 34
Chung, Shou-Ching, 34
Chung-Cheng, Chow, 34
Ciccacci, I., 8
Clancey, Richard W., 50

Clancy, Elizabeth Durack, 81
Clark, Alice, 50,175,199
Clark, David L., 205
Clark, F. LeGros, 175
Clark, Frances Ida, 57
Clark, Margaret, 109
Clark, Shirley Merritt, 193
Clark, William Lloyd, 161
Clarke, A., 138
Clarke, Edith, 89,119
Clarke, Ida Gallagher, 109,224
Clarke, Mary Gowden, 224
Clarkson, Frank E., 138
Claus, Claire, 65
Clauson, John A., 127
Cleaver, Eldridge, 103
Clemente Travieso, Carmen, 89
Cleverdon, Catherine L., 97
Clignet, Remi, 3,11,169
Clough, Emma, 224
Clouzet, Maryse, 161
Clymer, Eleanor, 175
Cobden, John C., 161
Cochrane, D. G., 80
Cocteau, Jean, 57
Code, Joseph Bernaid, 224
Codere, Helen, 14
Cohen, Lucy M., 88
Cohen, Mabel Blake, 133
Cohen, Malcom S., 175
Cohen, Ronald, 11
Cohen, Yehudi A., 89,133,138
Cohn, B. S., 47
Cohn, David L., 109
Colby, Kenneth M., 127
Colby, Vineta, 216
Cole, Johnetta B., 103
Cole, Margaret Postgate, 50
Cole, William, 119
Colebrook, Joan, 168
Coleman, James, 127
Coleman, Richard P., 182
Colguhoun, A. R., 34
Collard, J., 14
Collier, Jane F., 146
Collins, Joseph, 146
Collins, S., 50
Collver, Andrew, 154
Colman, A. D., 154
Colon, Clara, 209
Colon Ramirez, Consuleo, 98
Colson, Elizabeth, 94
Comhaire-Sylvain, Suzanne, 14

Crowley, Joan, 176
Crozier, Michel, 57
Cuddeford, Gladys M., 50,200
Cudlipp, Edythe, 209
Culhs, Winifred Clare, 50
Culver, Elsie Thomas, 165
Cummings, Gwenna, 103
Cuneen, Sally S., 165
Cunnington, Cecil Willett, 50,200
Curson, Peter, 83
Cusack, Dymphna, 35
Custer, Elizabeth, 224
Cutler, John H., 119

Dahlstrom, Edmund, 73,138
Dale, R. R., 188
Dall, Caroline H., 176
Dalton, G., 176
Daly, Mary, 166
D'Andrade, Roy G., 103,138
Dandridge, Dorothy, 103
Dangerfield, George, 50
Daniel, Sadie Iola, 225
Daniels, Jonathon, 200
Danilina, K., 65
Danilova, Ekatenina Zakharovna, 65
Dannett, Sylvia G. L., 103
Dantas, Julio, 225
Dark, Sidney, 225
Darwin, Charles, 138
Das, M. N., 42
Das, Parimal, 42
Das, Sonya Sklar, 110
Daudet, Leon, 220
Daumas, General Eugene, 5
D'Auvergne, Edmund Basil Francis, 225
David, Deborah S., 103,176
David, Jay, 106
David, Nicholas, 14
Davidson, Maria, 156
Davis, Allison W., 110
Davis, Anee, 188
Davis, Elizabeth Gould, 119,200
Davis, H., 176
Davis, James, 176,189
Davis, Katherine B., 133
Davis, Morris Edward, 154
Davis, Paulina Wright, 205
Dawson, M., 76
Day, Alice Taylor, 231
Day, Beth, 154
Day, Dorothy, 225
Day, Lincoln H., 231

Dick-Read, Grantly, 155
Diebold, A. R., Jr., 98
Dieks, Henry, 65
Diner, Helen, 200
Dingwall, Eric John, 110,198
Dinitz, S., 138
Dipoko, Mbella, 3
Ditmore, Jack, 176
Ditzion, Sidney, 147
Dixon, Marlene, 176,210
Dju, D. C., 39
Dobert, Margarita, 11
Dobkin, Marlene, 26
Dodge, Norton T., 65
Dollard, John, 110
Dolz y Arango, Maria Luisa, 89
Dombusch, Sanford M., 176
Domenuchi, Lodovico, 225
Dore, R. P., 30
Dorjahn, Vernon R., 11
Dornstreich, Mark D., 81
Dorr, Rheta Childe, 110,225
Dorsey, Susan Almira, 176
Dorsingfang-Smets, A., 15
Douglas, Emily Taft, 225
Douglas, James, 97
Douglas, Mary, 3,15,166
Douglass, Joseph H., 7,103
Douglass, Katherine W., 7
Douthit, Mary Osborn, 200
Douvan, Elizabeth, 127,189
Dowty, Nancy, 23
Doyle, Leo, 159
Drabkin, Haim, 23
Drachmann, Emmy, 73
Drago, Harry S., 225
Draper, Patricia, 18
Dreier, Mary, 225
Dreiser, Theodore, 110
Driberg, J. H., 8
Drinker, Sophie, 216
Drinnon, Richard, 225
Driver, Harold E., 91,94,98
Driver, Wilhelmine, 98
Drower, E. S., 22
Drury, Clifford Merrill, 166,200
Dube, S. C., 42
Dubisch, Jill, 71
DuBois, Cora, 78,127
DuBois, Ellen, 225
Dubois-Stasse, M., 217
DuBroca, Louis, 57
Duche, Natacha, 57

Dunbar, Janet, 50
Dunbar, Roxanne, 210
Duncan, Isadora, 225
Duncan, Otis, 174
Duniway, Abigail Scott, 205,225
Dunn, Nell, 50,210
Dunnahoo, Terry, 225
Dupire, Marguerite, 9
Durand, E. M., 176
Durand, John D., 42
Durham, M. Edith, 66
Durkheim, Emile, 119
Duster, Alfreda, 225
Dutt, Beulah, 42
Duval, Paul Alexandre Martin, 57
DuVerger, Maurice, 48, 169
Dvorsky, Frantisek, 75
Dynes, R., 138

Earengey, Florence, 50
Earle, Alice M., 200
Earthy, Emily Dora, 16
Eastman, Nicholson Joseph, 155
Eastman, Max, 205
Eastwood, Mary, 171,236
Eaton, Clement, 110
Eaton, Joseph W., 23,110
d'Eaubonne, Francoise, 133
Eby, O., 15
Edgerton, Robert E., 17
Edif, Halide, 26
Edwardes, Stephen Meredyth, 42
Efimenko, P. P., 119
Ehrenfels, U. R. von, 3,42,210
Ehrman, Winston W., 155
Eicher, Joanne B., 142
Eichinger, F., 35
Eifler, Deborah, 145,195
Eiselen, Werner M., 18
Eisenberg, Leon, 176
Eisner, Thomas, 155
Elder, Joseph, 42
Eliot, George [Mary Ann Evans], 225
Eliot, Thomas, 73
Ellet, Elizabeth Fries, 110,200,225
Elliot, Albert Wells, 161
Ellis, Albert, 138
Ellis, Evelyn, 176
Ellis, Havelock, 133,138,155
Ellis, Julie, 210
Ellis, Sarah Stickney, 51
Ellison, Grace Mary, 26
Ellmann, Mary, 210

Elmendorf, Mary Lindsay, 98,196
Elnett, Elaine, 66
Eloesser, Leo, 155
Elston, D. R., 23
Ember, Carol, 17,147
Ember, Melvin, 147
Engels, F., 147
Engle, Bernice Attis, 133
Epstein, Cynthia Fuchs, 103,177,210
Epstein, Israel, 35
Epstein, T. S., 42
Erdland, August, 80
Erdmann, Walter, 71
Erikson, Erik H., 125,127,138
Ermarth, Margaret, 210
Escobedo, Raquel, 99
Esenkova, P., 26
Espinosa, Juan de, 63
Essai, Brian, 81
Esselstyn, T. C., 162
Ets, Marie Hall, 226
Etzioni, Amitai, 23,177,232
Evan, William M., 169
Evans, Lily, 155
Evans, Maurice S., 17
Evans-Pritchard, E. E., 15,119
Expilly, Charles, 85
Eyman, Francis, 94

Faber, Doris, 205
Faguet, Emile, 57
Faherty, William, 166
Fairbank, John K., 28
Fairchild, Johnson E., 134
Falade, Solange, 9
Falk, Lawrence L., 177
Fand, Alexandra Botwinik, 139
Fanon, Frantz, 119
Farber, Anne, 147
Farber, Seymour M., 139,210
Farmer, Lydia Hoyt, 110,221
Farnell, L. R., 166
Farnham, Marynia F., 198
Farnsworth, William Oliver, 57
Faron, Louis C., 84
Farrar, Rowena, 205
Farrell, Barry, 210
Farrell, Warren, 210
Fast, Julius, 198
Fauset, Arthur, 103
Faust, Allen Klein, 30
Fava, Sylvia F., 134,177

Fawcett, Millicent Garrett, 205,221
Featheringill, Eve S., 155
Feitz, Leland, 162
Feldman, Harold, 127
Felkin, R. W., 17
Ferguson, Charles W., 127
Ferguson, Vera M., 155
Fernando, Sylvia, 46
Fernea, Elizabeth Warnock, 22
Feroze, M. R., 20
Ferrero, Guglielmo, 63
Feshback, M., 70
Fetz, Jennifer, 110
Fiaux, Louis, 162
Fichter, Joseph Henry, 103
Fiedler, Leslie, 216
Field, Alice, 66
Field, Harry Hubert, 42
Fielding, Waldo L., 155
Fields, Rona M., 189
Figes, Eva, 127,210
Finlayson, Angela, 54
Firestone, Shulamith, 210
Firth, Raymond, 51
Firth, Rosemary, 78
Fisch, Edith L., 177
Fischer, Ann, 80,120
Fischer, John L., 80
Fisher, Elizabeth, 189
Fisher, Marguerite J., 28
Fisher, Welthy Honsinger, 35
Fishman, Nathaniel, 147
Fitch, Charles Luther, 57
Fitch, Florena Mary, 23
Fitzgerald, William, 187
Fitzpatrick, William, 26
Fitzsimons, John, 120
Fjeld, Harriet, 127
Flanagan, Geraldine L., 155
Flannery, Regina, 94
Fleischman, Doris E., 177
Fleisher, Frederic, 73
Fleming, Alice, 189
Fletcher, Jefferson Butler, 216
Flexner, Eleanor, 162,205
Flory, Vera E., 20
Flugel, J. C., 139,155
Flynn, Elizabeth Gurley, 197,226,232
Fock, Niels, 84
Fogarty, M. P., 139,177
Foldz, Steve, 211
Folsom, Joseph Kirk, 147
Fongeyrallas, Pierre, 9

Foote, Nelson, 139
Forget, Nelly, 6
Ford, Clellan S., 125,134,155
Ford, Edward, 81
Ford, Laura M., 152
Forde, Daryll, 4,11
Foreman, Carolyn Thomas, 91
Forjaz de Sampaio, Albino, 162
Forman, Samuel Eagle, 169
Forrest, Mary, 216
Fortes, Meyer, 11
Fortsch, Barbara, 63
Foster, Anna, 93
Foster, G. Allen, 205
Foster, Warren Dunham, 166,226
Fowler, William Worthington, 111,226
Fox, David, 131
Fox, L. K., 17
Fox, Richard Michael, 56,226
Fox, Robin, 134,147
Francis, Philip, 169
Francos Rodriguez, Jose, 72
Frank, Anne, 226
Frank, Avis Rae, 125
Fraser, Clara, 210
Fraser, Leila, 235
Frate, Dennis A., 155
Frazier, E. Franklin, 103
Frederick, Pauline, 226
Freed, Ruth S., 94
Freed, Stanley A., 94
Freedman, Lawrence, 155
Freedman, M. B., 189
Freeman, J. D., 78
Freeman, Jo, 210
Freeman, Julia Deane, 111
Freeman, Leah, 233
Freeman, T. W., 56
Freud, Phil, 216
Freud, Sigmund, 127,134,211
Frick, J., 35
Fried, Morton H., 169
Friedan, Betty, 211
Friedl, Ernestine, 71,120
Friedman, Alfred S., 136
Friedman, Elizabeth, 193
Frisof, Jamie Kelem, 189
Froman, Lewis, 169
Fromm, Erich, 127
Frost, David, 51
Frost, John, 226
Frost, Lois, 30,109
Frumkin, Samuel, 169

Fryer, Peter, 3,51,155
Fuchs, Fritz, 155
Fuchs, K. L., 6
Fuchs, Victor R., 177
Fueto, Toshi, 30
Fugita, Stephen S., 136
Fujita, Taki, 30
Fulford, Roger, 205
Fuller, Margaret, 200
Funk, John Clarence, 162
Funk, Nathalie O., 147
Furlong Cardiff, Guillermo, 86
Furman, Lucile N., 111
Furstenberg, Frank, 147
Fussell, George, 51

Gab, 57
Gadgil, D. R., 42
Gafarova, M. K., 66
Gage, J., 63
Gage, Matilda Joslyn, 166
Gagen, Jean E., 216
Gagnon, John H., 134,152
Gale, Fay, 76
Gallagher, Rory, 159
Galway, Kathleen, 193
Gamarekian, E., 35
Gamble, D. P., 9
Gamble, David, 11
Gamble, Eliza Burt, 221
Gamio de Alba, Ana Margarita, 99
Gancourt, Edmond Louis Antoine Huot de, 58
Gandhi, Mohandas Karamchand, 42,43
Gans, Herbert, 111
Garandy, Roger, 120
Garcia y Garcia, Elvira, 87
Gardner, Jo-Ann, 189
Garnett, Lucy M., 26
Garofalo, Anna, 63
Garskof, Michele Hoffnung, 211
Gasiorowska, Zenia, 66
Gaudefroy-Demombynes, Jean, 111
Gaudio, A., 20
Gaudry, Mathea, 6
Gaultson, Helen, 152
Gauthier-Villars, Henry, 162
Gavron, Hannah, 127
Gay, Jules, 233
Gebhard, Paul H., 134,155
Gedge, Evelyn C., 43
Geertz, Clifford, 78
Geertz, Hildred, 78
Gehlen, Frieda L., 169

Gehman, Richard, 111
Geiger, H. Kent, 66
Geiss, Anne, 111
Geldens, Maria, 43
Gemini, P., 43
Gendall, Murray, 73
Gentry, Curt, 162
George, Margaret, 226
George, W. L., 127
Gerard, Jo, 226
Gereb, Sandor, 177
Gerin, Elizabeth, 177
Gerritsen, Alelta Henriette, 233
Gersdorff, Ursula von, 61
Gersh, Harry, 189
Gershenfeld, Matti, 211
Gervais, Pamela, 174
Gervasi, Frank, 23
Gessain, Monique, 9
Gheusi, Pierre Barthelemy, 57
Giallombardo, Rose, 168
Gibbs, James L., 3
Gibbs, Patricia K., 150
Gibson, Elsie, 166
Gideon, Helen, 43
Giese, Hans, 134
Giglio, Vittorio, 226
Gilder, Rosamond, 226
Gildersleeve, Genieve N., 177
Gilevskaya, S., 68
Gilford, Henry, 189
Gillin, J. P., 111
Gilman, Agness Geneva, 226
Gilman, Charlotte Perkins, 139,177,221
Gilman, Richard, 211
Gilmore, M. R., 94
Gingles, R., 187
Gini, Corrado, 63
Ginzburg, Eli, 177,226
Gipson, Theodore H., 103
Giroud, Francoise, 177
Given, J. N., 177
Gladwin, Thomas, 76,80
Glasgow, Maude, 221
Glasse, Robert, 81
Glazier, Jack, 17
Gleason, Caroline Joanna, 200
Gleason, Judith, 85
Glendinning, Victoria, 226
Gloag, Julian, 216
Glover, Edward, 162
Gluckman, Max, 3,15
Goggin, John M., 93

Goichon, Amelia-Marie, 6
Gokulanathan, K. S., 43
Goldberg, Marylyn Power, 177
Goldberg, Philip, 128,198
Goldberg, Steven, 120
Golde, Peggy, 120
Goldenweiser, A. A., 93
Goldman, Emma, 211,226
Goldman, Freda H., 189
Goldman, George D., 134
Goldmark, Josephine, 226
Goldschmidt, Walter,141,149
Goldsen, Rose, 189
Gollock, Georgina A., 103
Goncalves, Maria Aparecida Ataliba de Lima, 147
Goncharov, Ivan, 217
Gonzalez, Nancie L., 103
Goodale, Jane C., 76
Goodall, Jane van Lawick, 124
Goodman, Mary Ellen, 30
Goodman, Paul, 232
Goodman, Percival, 232
Goode, William J., 128,147,148,210
Goodenough, Ward, 81
Goodrich, Frederick Warren, 156
Goodrich, Samuel Griswold, 227
Goodsell, Willystine, 190
Goodwin, Grace Duffield, 205
Goody, Esther N., 11
Goody, Jack, 134,148
Gordon, C. W., 190
Gordon, David C., 6
Gordon, Elizabeth Putnam, 221
Gordon, Eugene, 104
Gordon, Linda, 89
Gorman, Mary Rosaria, 71
Gornick, Vivian, 211
Gorsse, Pierre de, 227
Goshen-Gottstein, Esther R., 23
Gottlieb, David, 194
Gough, Kathleen, 43,148,151,216
Gould, Ethel P., 148
Gould, Flo, 104
Gould, George, 162
Grabin, William H., 156
Gracey, Annie Ryder, 227
Graham, Abbie, 211
Graham, Harvey, 156
Graham, Maxtome, 51
Grandmaison, Colette LeCour, 9
Granquist, Hilma Natalia, 23
Grant, Zalin, 38,197
Graves, A. J., 111

Gray, Madeline, 156
Gray, R. F., 17
Grebler, Leo, 106
Greco, Oscar, 63
Greelan, Paul, 144
Greeley, Horace, 148
Green, Arnold W., 211
Green, J., 51
Green, M. M., 11
Greenburg, Dan, 111
Greene, Felix, 35
Greene, Gael, 134
Greenfield, Richard, 16
Greenstein, Fred I., 169
Greenwald, Harold, 162
Greer, Germaine, 211
Greg, William Rathbone, 51
Gregor, Thomas, 85
Grenett, Lucy M. J., 63
Gressain, Robert, 216
Grez, Vicente, 87
Gribble, Francis Henry, 227
Griffin, Naomi Musmaker, 92
Grimes, Alan, 205,211
Grimké, Sarah, 205
Grisay, Auguste, 217
Griswold, R. W., 217
Groenman, S., 61
Gromova, Galina Mikhailovna, 66
Grosbois, 35
Gross, Edward, 178
Gross, Louise, 211
Grosse, Martin, 141
Grossman, Edward, 111
Groves, Ernest Rutherford, 111
Gruberg, Martin, 111,169
Gruening, Ernest, 99
Gubser, Nicholas J., 92
Guedalla, Philip, 227
Gueland-Leridon, Francoise, 58
Guemple, D. L., 92
Guilbert, Madeline, 178
Guimaraes, Ruth, 227
Guiteras-Holmes, Colexe, 99
Gulick, John, 27
Gulick, Sidney Lewis, 30
Gunson, N., 83
Guntekin, Resat Nuri, 26
Gupta, Verna Rani, 190
Gusfield, Joseph R., 170
Guttmacher, Alan F., 156
Guttman, David, 139
Guyot, Yves, 162

Haar, B., 78
Haas, Mary, 93
Haavio-Mannila, Elina, 73
Haber, S., 178
Haberland, Helga, 61
Habicht, Jean-Pierre, 99
Habliekuk, J., 51
Hacker, Helen, 120
Hagood, Margaret Jarman, 111,200
Haider, Santoah, 142
Haldane, Charlotte, 221
Haldeman, C., 31
Hale, Beatrice Forbes-Robertson, 205
Hale, Sarah Josepha, 200
Hall, Evelyn Beatrice, 58
Hall, Geoffrey F., 58
Hall, Oswald, 97
Hall, Roberta L., 156
Halle, Fannina W., 66
Hallowell, A. Irving, 91,93,128
Halonen, Kae, 211
Hamburg, David A., 125
Hamilton, Cicely Mary, 51
Hamilton, Virginia C., 156
Hammel, Eugene A., 75
Hammond, Dorothy, 178
Hammsy, Laila Shukry, 95
Hanaford, Phebe A., 111
Hanchett, Suzanne, 191
Handel, Gerald, 182
Hankins, Marie Louise, 200
Hannerz, Ulf, 104
Hanry, P., 9
Hansen, Edward, 99
Hansen, Henry Harold, 21,22
Hanson, F. Allan, 83
Hansson, Laura, 128
Hapgood, Karen E., 178
Harbeson, Gladys, 178
Harby, Mohammed Khayri, 7
Hardin, Garrett, 156
Harding, Mary Esther, 128,217
Harding, Nina, 104
Hare, Julia, 104
Hare, Nathan, 104
Harkness, David James, 200
Harkness, Georgia, 166
Harland, Robert O., 162
Harper, Edward B., 43
Harper, Ida Husted, 204,227
Harrell, Ruth Flinn, 156
Harrington, Charles, 139
Harris, Adelaide E., 51

Harris, Grace, 15
Harris, Janet, 51,211
Harris, Sarah, 162,164
Harrison, Evelyn, 178
Hart, Charles W., 76
Hart, Donn V., 38
Hart, E., 148
Hart, H., 148
Hart, John, 217
Hart, Marie, 211
Hartland, S., 148
Hartley, Catherine G., 128,139,148,221
Hasegawa, Nyozekan, 31
Haskell, Oreola Williams, 205
Hassum, H. C., 20
Hasted, Jane-Eliza, 227
Hatcher, Orie Latham, 111
Hate, Chandrakala Anandrao, 43
Hatsumi, Reiko, 31
Hausnecht, E. G. Murray, 112
Havemann, Ernest K., 156,190
Haviland, Laura S., 104
Hawes, Bess Lomax, 104
Hawes, Elizabeth, 112,120,139
Hawkes, Jacquetta, 217
Hay-Cooper, L., 162
Hayden, Casey, 134
Hayner, Norman S., 99
Haynes, M., 170
Hays, Elinor Rice, 227
Hays, H. R., 198,217
Hayward, C., 163
Hazell, Lester Dessez, 157
Headland, Isaac Taylor, 35
Healy, William J., 97
Hearn, Lafcadio, 31
Heath, Dwight B., 139
Hebard, Grace Raymond, 95
Hecker, Eugene Arthur, 201
Hecker, Monique, 190
Hedges, Janice N., 178
Heer, David M., 176
Hegeler, Inge, 73
Hegeler, Sten, 73
Heidensohn, Frances, 51
Heilbrun, Carolyn G., 190,217
Heiman, Leo, 197
Heinrich, Joachim, 51
Heinz, Doris, 156
Heiss, Jerold, 139
Held, J. L., 82
Helfer, R. E., 139
Hellbon, Anna-Britta, 99

Heller, Otto, 61
Hellerman, Marcia, 89
Hellman, Florence S., 112
Helman, Patricia K., 211
Henderson, Helen, 11
Henkle, Henrietta, 112
Hennessy, Caroline, 139,211
Hennig, Hilke, 14
Henriques, F. Figueira, 17
Henriques, Fernando, 163
Henry, Alice, 178,201
Henry, Jules, 86
Hentsch, Alice, 217
Hernandez, Isabel, 107
Hernton, Calvin, 198
Heron, A., 112
Herredsvela, K., 73
Herreshoff, David, 112
Herschberger, Ruth, 120
Herschfeld, Magnus, 134
Herskovits, Melville, 11
Heuer, Berys N., 83
Hewitt, J. N. B., 93
Hewitt, Margaret, 51
Heymans, Gerardus, 128
Heyn, Leah, 227
Hibbert, Eloise Talcott, 35
Hicks, Judy, 120
Hiestand, Dale L., 178
Higgins, Chester, 104
Highbaugh, Irma, 35
Hilaski, H. J., 186
Hilger, M. Inez, 87,93,95,139
Hill, Joseph, 178
Hill, Kate A., 201
Hill, Reuben, 232
Hilliard, Marion, 125
Himmelfarb, Gertrude, 201
Himmelhock, Jerome, 134,190
Himes, Joseph S., 104
Himes, Norman, A., 156
Hinckle, Marianne, 198
Hinckle, Warren, 198
Hinds, William Alfred, 232
Hingston, A., 80,81,83
Hinkle, Beatrice, 128
Hinkley, Laura L., 217
Hinshaw, Robert, 99,102
Hinton, William, 35
Hippler, Arthur E., 92
Hirsch, A. H., 201
Hirvonen, Kaarle, 170
Hobbs, Lisa, 211

Hobson, Elizabeth Kimball, 112
Hodzaeva, R. D., 66
Hoeft, Douglas L., 157
Hoffer, Carol P., 12
Hoffman, Lois, 139,181
Hoffman, Susannah, 71
Hoffsten, Ruth Bertha, 63
Hogbin, Ian H., 82
Hohenwart-Gerlachstein, A., 7
Hokada, Elizabeth, 145,195
Holden, Carlin Page, 213
Holden, Dronie, 120
Hole, Christina, 52
Hole, Judith, 211
Holland, Beverley, 83
Holland, Clive, 6,31,58,61
Holliday, Carl, 201
Hollingsworth, Leta Steller, 139,191
Hollister, Horace A., 112,170
Holmes, Marjorie, 227
Holtby, Winifred, 221
Honigmann, Irma, 92
Honigmann, John J., 40,90,92
Hooper, Peggy, 211
Hope, Marjorie, 3
Hoppe, E., 31
Hopwood, Katherine, 190
Horner, Isaline Blew, 35
Horner, M. S., 178
Horney, Karen, 128
Horton, Patricia Marttila, 112
Hosie, Dorothea Soothill, 35
Hosteler, John A., 122
Hotchkiss, John C., 99
Hottel, Althea K., 90
Hough, Walter, 114
Houghton, Ross C., 28
Howard, Forrest, 158
Howard, Jane, 211
Howard, George Eliot, 52,148
Howard, Sidney, 217
Howe, Florence, 190
Howe, Julia Ward, 206
Howe, S. E., 6
Howell, Norma A., 93
Hoyt, Mary, 227
Hsu, Francis L. K., 148
Huang, Jen Lucy, 35
Hubbell, Linda J., 99
Huber, H., 12
Huber, Joan, 120
Hudson, Jeffrey, 157
Hudson, Kenneth, 52

Jacobi, Mary Putnam, 206
Jacobs, Helen, 227
Jacobs, Jane, 112
Jacobs, Milton, 6
Jacobs, Sue-Ellen, 91,121,152,170,190,232,233
Jacobson, A. H., 140
Jacoby, Susan, 66
Jaffe, A. H., 179
Jahoda, Gustav, 12,128,140
Jahoda, Hovel, 140
Jakande, L. K., 12
Jambagi, Sadanand, 44
Jambagi, Sulochana, 44
James, Edward T., 227
James, Henry, 148
James, Janet W., 227
James, Jennifer, 134,163
James, Thomas Egbert, 52
Janney, Oliver Edward, 163
Jarecki, Henry G., 140
Jarnow, Jeannette A., 121
Jaschke, G., 26
Jay, Anthony, 51
Jayal, S., 217
Jayle, Max Fernand, 157
Jean, C. F., 22,26
Jeannel, Julien Francois, 163
Jeanniere, Abel, 134
Jenkins, David, 73
Jenkins, Hester Donaldson, 26
Jenness, Linda, 89
Jennings, Jesse, 91
Jensen, Oliver Ormerod, 112
Jenzer, Annemarie, 71
Jephcott, Pearl, 52
Jessup, Josephine, 217
Jex-Blake, Sophia, 17
Jiagge, Annie R., 236
Johnson, Clarence R., 26
Johnson, Dallas, 112
Johnson, Dorothy, 190
Johnson, G. W., 201
Johnson, Kathryn P., 140
Johnson, Reginald B., 217
Johnson, Virginia, 135
Johnston, R. L., 190
Johnstone, Jenny Elizabeth
Joly, Gertrude, 27
Jones, Bessie, 104
Jones, Beverly, 209
Jones, Emrys, 56
Jones, Ernest, 134
Jones, Katharine M., 201

Jones, Robert C., 107
Jones, Violet, 44
Joran, Theodore, 58
Jorgensen, Joseph J. G., 148
Joseph, Alice, 95
Joseph, Ceston, 12
Joseph, Joyce, 52
Josephson, Hannah, 201
Josephy, Alvin M. Jr., 91
Joyce, Thomas, 83,121
Judek, Stanislaw, 201
Judells, Beatrice, 121
Juliet, Mitchell, 201
Jumunabai, J., 44

Kaberry, Phyllis M., 15,76
Kadono, Chakuro, 31
Kagan, E., 170
Kagan, Jerome, 140
Kahle, P., 7
Kahn, Franz, 63
Kaibara, Ekken, 31
Kalchycka, Lydia, 70
Kalvesten, Ana-Lisa, 73
Kamiat, Arnold H., 198
Kamii, Constance K., 105
Kamm, Josephine, 52,212
Kammeyer, Kenneth, 128
Kannangara, Inrogen, 44
Kanowitz, Leo, 170
Kaplan, Bert, 113
Kaplan, Frances B., 114
Kaplan, Justin, 198
Kaplan, M. R., 90
Kaps, Johannes, 61
Kardiner, Abram, 128
Kargman, Marie W., 140
Karlsson, Georg, 73
Karmel, Marjorie, 157
Karovsky, Eliyahu, 24
Kartini, Raden Adjeng, 78
Karush, Aaron, 128
Kashif, H., 8
Kass, Babette, 113
Kassebaum, Gene G., 136,153,168
Katasheva, L., 66
Katz, J., 190
Kaufman, Sue, 217
Kaur, M., 44
Kawai, Michi, 31
Kaye, Barrington, 12
Kazantzis, Judith, 52
Kazem, Mohamed I., 8

Kearney, Belle, 104
Kehoe, Alice B., 113
Keiiser, J. L. M. de, 121
Keller, Suzanne, 148,232
Kellogg, Charlotte Hoffman, 61
Kelly, Amy, 170
Kelly, George, 217
Kelly, Isabel, 95,99
Kelly, John V., 12
Kemp, Tage, 163
Kemp-Welch, Alice, 201
Kenealy, Arabella, 212
Keniston, Ellen, 206
Keniston, Kenneth, 206
Kenkel, William F., 140
Kennard, Joseph S., 217
Kennedy, David M., 128,157
Kennedy, John G., 8
Kennedy, Raymond, 78,89
Kennedy, Robert Woods, 148
Kent, John, 227
Kerekhoff, Richard, 104
Kern, Edward, 212
Kerr, W. D., 190
Key, Ellen, 140,148,149,197,212
Key, Mary Ritchie, 191
Khairullah, Ibrahim A., 27
Khalaf, Samir, 27
Khare, R. S., 149
Khor, Thomas, 179
Khoreva, G., 66
Khuri, Faud I., 20,149
Khwaja, B. A., 44
Kidd, Dudley, 140
Kilibanov, L. A., 20
Killham, John, 170
Killian, R. A., 179
Kim, Taek Il, 157
Kimball, Nell, 163
Kimpins Ka-Tat' siun, Oleksandra, 66
King, Alice G., 179
King, Karl, 179
Kingsbury, Susan Myra, 66
Kinsey, Alfred C., 134
Kinsie, Paul M., 164
Kirkpatrick, Clifford, 61,128,212
Kirkpatrick, Joanna, 36,44,233
Kisosonkole, P., 17
Klarman, Betty, 182
Klein, Grace, 120,149
Klein, Henriette R., 157
Klein, N. H., 12
Klein, Viola, 52,121,140,179,180

Klemensiewiczowa, Jadwiga Sikorska, 75
Klima, G., 17
Klima, J., 27
Klimpel Alvarado, Felicitas, 87
Kloos, Peter, 85
Kloos, Werner, 61
Klopper, Arnold, 155
Kloskowska, Antonina, 75
Kluckhohn, Clyde, 95
Kluckhohn, Florence, 113,149
Klunzinger, C. B., 8
Knebel, Fletcher, 104
Kneeland, George Jackson, 163
Knight, Richard Payne, 140
Knowlson, H., 52
Knudsen, Mary, 113
Knysh, Irena, 67
Koch-Grunberg, Theodor, 84,85
Koedt, Anne, 134
Kohlberg, Lawrence, 128
Kolafatich, Audrey, 158
Kollontai, Alexandra Mikhailovna, 67
Komarovsky, Mirra, 140,149
Komisar, Lucy, 212
Kong, Y. S., 78
Konopczynski, Wladyslaw, 75
Konopka, G., 129
Kooiman, Helen W., 227
Koontz, Elizabeth D., 179
Koos, Earl, 149
Koren, Elizabeth, 228
Korevanova, Agrippina Garilovna, 67
Korshunora, Ekaterina Nikolaevna, 67
Kortlandt, Adriann, 124
Koya, 31
Koyama, Takashi, 31
Kraditor, Aileen S., 201,206
Krause, Wolfgang, 73
Krauss, F. S., 61,75
Kreps, Juanita, 134
Krieg, Eileen Jensen, 18
Kriege, J. D., 18
Kriesberg, Louis, 179
Kroeber, A. L., 140
Krog, Gina, 73
Kroger, William S., 132
Kronhausen, Eberhard, 134
Kronhausen, Phyllis, 134
Kuchler, L. W., 31
Kulczycki, J., 170
Kumar, P., 163
Kume, A., 149
Kummer, Hans, 124

Kunkel, Evalyn J., 149
Kunstadter, Peter, 104
Kuper, Hilda, 17
Kuper, Leo, 4
Kurganov, Ivan Alekseevich, 67
Kurtz, Richard M., 140
Kuyper, Abraham, 166
Kuznets, Simon, 31,44,85

Labarca Hubertson, Amanda, 113
Labram, G. W., 52
Lacroix, Paul, 163
Lader, Lawrence, 157,229
Ladner, Joyce A., 104
Laffin, John, 197
LaFollette, Cecile Tipton, 113
LaFollette, Suzanne, 212
La Fontaine, J. S., 140
LaHire, Marie Weyrich de, 58
Laing, R. D., 129
Laird, Donald A., 179
Lajewsky, Henry, 179
Lajpat Rai, Lala, 44
Lallier, Roger, 71
Lamb, Felicia, 52
Lamb, Myrna, 212
Lambert, William W., 142
Lambin, Jane, 71
Lambiri, Ioanna, 71
Lampman, E. S., 95
Lamson, Peggy, 113,170
Lancaster, Alice Cunningham, 106
Lancaster, Jane B., 124
Landberg, Pamela, 17
Lander, Patricia, 191
Landes, Ruth, 85,93,104,149,152
Landres, Albert, 86
Landy, Avrom, 121
Lane, E. W., 8
Lang, Elsie M., 52
Langdon-Davies, John, 201
Langner, T. S., 99
Langness, Lewis L., 76,82
Lanham, Betty B., 31
Lanoux, Armand, 58
Lantis, Margaret, 92
LaPiere, Richard, 129
Lapin, Eva, 179
Lardizabal, A. S., 78
Larger, Ellie, 212
Larson, Barbara, 6
Larteguy, Jean, 24
LaRue, Linda J. M., 104

Lasagna, Louis, 157
Lasch, Christopher, 212
Lash, Joseph P., 228
Laufer, P. C., 80
Laurentin, Anne, 15
Lausky, Leonard, 129
Lavis, G., 217
Lawman, T., 15
Lawrence, Catherine S., 228
Lawrence, Margaret, 217
Lazarte, J., 121
Leach, Edmund R., 44,166
Leacock, Eleanor, 91,93,149
Leavitt, Ruby, 121,212
LeBar, Frank M., 38
Lebeson, Anita Libman, 113
Lebeuf, Annie M. D., 4
Leblanc, Maria, 38
Lechner, 61
Lederer, Wolfgang, 217
Lee, Anna, 217
Lee, Dana, 230
Lee, Nancy Howell, 157
LeFebvre, G., 6,191
Legman, Gershon, 217
Legouve, Joseph Wilfred Ernest Gabriel, 58
LeGros, Clark F., 52
Lehner, Stephan, 82
Leighton, Dorothea, 95
Leijon, Anna-Greta, 73
Leis, Nancy B., 6,12
Leitch, Isabella, 157
Leith-Ross, Sylvia, 4,12
Lelong, M., 6
Lembo, John M., 191
Lemons, James Stanley, 113,206
Lenin, Vladimir Ilich, 67
Lenski, Gerhard, 121
Leon, D., 24
Leonard, Clara T., 206
Leonard, Eugenie A., 113,201,233
Leong, Stephen Mun-Yoon, 67
Leonov, N., 67
Lepie, Lita, 152
Lerner, Gerde, 228,201
Lescure, Marthurin Francois Adolphe de, 58
Leser, C. E. V., 48
Leslie, C. M., 100
Leslie, Gerald R., 140,179
Lessing, Doris, 17,52,217,218
Lessler, K., 141
Letourneau, Charles, 4,202,221
Leuck, Miriam Simons, 179

LeVine, Barbara B., 17
Levine, Donald N., 16
Levine, Ellen, 211
Levine, H., 143
Levine, Irving R., 67
LeVine, Robert A., 4,12,17
Levinger, Elma E., 228
Levi-Strauss, Claude, 129,149
Levitas, Gloria, 191
Levy, Howard Seymour, 36
Levy, L. H., 129
Lewin, J., 19
Lewis, Claudia, 92
Lewis, Edwin C., 129,141,191
Lewis, Helen Matthews, 113
Lewis, Hylan, 104
Lewis, Ida Belle, 36
Lewis, I. M., 166
Lewis, Jose Guillermo, 100
Lewis, Michael, 141
Lewis, Oscar, 90,95,100
Lewis, Sinclair, 218
Lewis, Susan, 191
Liby, Margaret, 140
Lichtenstadter, Ilse, 20,21
Lichtenstein, H., 8,191
Lidderdale, Jane, 228
Liebow, Elliot, 104
Liebowitz, Lila, 124
Lifton, R. J., 31,113
Liley, H. I., 154
Lilienthal, Meta, 113
Lin, W. T., 131
Lindberg, D. G., 157
Lindenbaum, Shirley, 166
Linner, Birgitta, 74
Linton, Sally, 121
Lipke, Jean, 157
Lipset, S. M., 149,170
Lison Tolosana, C., 12
Lissak, M., 25
Little, Kenneth L., 12
Litzler, Beverly N., 100
Liubimova, Serafima Timofeevna, 67
Livermore, Mary A., 228,231
Li, Yu, 36
Llewellyn-Jones, Derek, 125
Lobsenz, Johanna, 179
Locke, Amy, 61,75
Locke, Edwin, 126
Lockwood, Douglas, 77
Lockyer, Herbert, 166
Logan, William, 52

Lombardo Otero de Soto, Rosa Maria, 100
Lombroso, Cesare, 163
Lombroso-Ferrero, Gina, 222
London, J., 191
Long, Mason, 163
Longbell, Marjorie R., 113
Longford, Joseph H., 32
Longmore, Laura, 19
Longstreet, Ethel, 163
Longstreet, Stephen, 32
Longwell, Marjorie R., 202
Loomis, Charles P., 114
Lopata, Helena Znaniechi, 114,141
Lopate, Carol, 141,179
Loring, Rosalind K., 191
Lougee, Dora Aileen, 63
Love, Barbara, 152,179,208
Lovell, Lucy Buffum, 224
Low, Seth, 114, 41
Lowie, Robert H., 95,166,191,222
Lucas, Roy, 157
Lucena, Luis de, 170
Luckey, Eleanor B., 48
Ludovici, Anthony M., 198,212,232
Ludovici, Laurence James, 141
Lugrin, N. de Bertrand, 97
Lundberg, Ferdinand, 198
Lunde, Donald T., 125
Lundholm, Algot T., 166
Lungo, Isidoro del, 63
Lurie, Nancy O., 91,93,121
Lurin, G., 9
Luschinsky, Mildred Stroop, 44
Lutz, Alma, 114,170,202,228
Luxemburg, Rosa, 228
Luzbetak, Louis, 67
Lynes, Russell, 149
Lynn, David B., 74,141
Lyon, Phyllis, 152,153
Lytton, Constance, 168

Mabille, Paul, 71
Macabee, June Marilyn, 125
MacCarthy, B. G., 52,218
MacEwan, Phyllis, 211
MacGibbon, Elizabeth G., 180
MacKenzie, Norman, 77
MacLean, Una, 12
McBride, Mary F., 196
McCaghy, Charles A., 153
McCall, Daniel F., 12
McCarthy, Mary, 228
McClees, Helen, 171
McClelland, David, 114
McClesky, Donna, 212

McClung, Jean, 87
McConnell, Dorothy, 197
McCord, William, 104
McCracken, Elizabeth, 114
McCrimmon, A. L., 212
Maccoby, Eleanor E., 129,141,143,150,179
McCune, Shirley D., 179
McDonald, James G., 24
McDougall, Harold, 104
McDowell, Kenneth V., 136
McElroy, Ann, 92
McElroy, W. W., 129
McFerran, Ann, 191
McGee, Reece, 175
McGrath, Alice, 194
McGregor, O. R., 53
McHer, Keith, 202
Mack, Dolores, 104
McKee, John P., 129,141
McLaren, Barbara, 197
McLean, Beth B., 180
McLenna, J. F., 150
McManus, Virginia, 163
McPartland, John, 134
Macphail, Andrew, 114
McVeety, Jean, 171
McVicar, Thomas, 17
McWilliams, Carey, 107
Madison, Bernice G., 67
Madsen, William, 100,107
Mafud, Julio, 87
Magee, Bryan, 152
Maginnis, Patricia, 158
Magner, James A., 100
Mahludji, M., 22
Mahoney, Thomas A., 180
Mailer, Norman, 198
Maillart, Ella K., 67
Mainardi, Pat, 212
Maine, H. S., 150
Mair, Lucy, 150
Maistriaux, Robert, 4
Majors, Monroe A., 104
Majumder, D. N., 44
Malcolm X, 105
Malik, Fida Hussain, 20
Malinowski, Bronislaw, 77,135,146
Mandach, Laure de, 58
Mandel, William, 67
Mandelbaum, David G., 44
Mann, R. S., 44

Maurer, Rose, 67
Maurois, Andre, 58
May, Caroline, 218
May, Edgar, 158
Mayer, Iona, 4
Mayer, Philip, 4
Mayhew, Henry, 53
Mayorca, Juan Manuel, 163
Meachem, A. B., 91
Mead, Kate Campbell, 114
Mead, Margaret, 32,26,76,78,82,83,95,114,129,135,158,228
Meade, Marion, 191
Meakin, Annette, 26,67,202
Meeks, Dorothy K., 158
Meggitt, J. J., 77
Meggitt, M. J., 81,82
Mehta, S. S., 150
Mehta, S. V., 45
Mehta, Sushila, 45
Meikle, Wilma, 53
Melek-Hanum, 20
Melnick, Eleanor, 211
Melo Lancheros, Livia Stella, 88
Mencher, Joan, 191
Mencken, H. L., 206
Menken, Alice Davis, 129
Menon, Lakshmi N., 222
Menzies, Sutherland, 228
Merriam, Eve, 114,180,212,218,228
Merriam, Ida C., 180
Messenger, John C., 56
Messing, Simon D., 16
Metraux, Alfred, 86
Metraux, Rhoda, 32
Mews, Hazel, 218
Meyer, Annie Nathan, 114,180
Meyer, Carolyn, 192
Meyer, Johann Jakob, 45
Meyers, Thomas, 129
Mez'er, Augusta Vladimirovna, 67
Mezerick, A. G., 180
Michaelson, Evalyn Jacobson, 141
Michelson, Truman, 95,97
Middleton, John, 146
Middleton, Russell, 105
Miles, Betty, 192
Miles, C. C., 144
Mill, Harriet T., 141
Mill, John Stuart, 141,222
Millan, Verna Carleton, 100
Millay, Edna St. Vincent, 218
Miller, Benjamin F., 129

Miller, Irving, 24
Miller, Robert Stephans, 171,236
Miller, Ruth Ann, 213
Millett, Kate, 213
Milner, Esther, 114,229
Mi Mi Khaing, Daw, 38
Mincer, Jacob, 180
Minnigerode, Meade, 229
Minturn, Leigh, 129,141,142
Mintz, Morton, 158
Mintz, Sidney, 90
Minuchin, Patricia, 192
Mirza, Sarfaraz Hussain, 40
Mischel, Walter, 130
Mishima, Sumie Seo, 32
Misra, Rekha, 45
Mitchell, B., 192
Mitchell, Geoffrey, 229
Mitchell, Hannah, 229
Mitchell, J. C., 15
Mitchell, Juliet, 213
Mitford, Nancy, 229
Mitter, Dwarka Nath, 45
Modiano, Nancy, 100
Mohsen, Safia, 6
Moller, H., 130
Molnos, A., 18
Money, John, 135
Monsalve, Jose Delores, 88
Montagu, Ashley, 125,135
Montague, Richard, 180
Montalban, L., 100
Montely, Henri De, 6
Monti, Antonio, 63
Moody, Anne, 105
Mooney, J. D., 192
Moore, Josslyn, 198
Moore, Lillian Mary, 125
Moore, Louise, 233
Moore, Virginia, 229
Moore, Wilbert, 31,85
Morais, Vamberto, 85
Mora, Constancia de la, 229
Moran, Barbara K., 211
Morau, Robert D., 180
Morgan, David, 202
Morgan, Edmund, 114
Morgan, Elaine, 202
Morgan, Robin, 213,233
Morgan, W. P., 36
Morris, Homer L., 53
Morris, Ivan, 32
Morris, Richard B., 171

Morris, Susan, 157
Morrison, A., 53
Morrison, Denton E., 213
Morrison, M., 53
Morton, Ward M., 100
Morvay, J., 75
Moscovici, Marie, 142
Moskin, J. Robert, 158
Moss, Howard A., 140
Moss, Leonard W., 63
Mountfard, Charles P., 77
Moustakas, Clark E., 135
Moveh, James G., 142
Moynihan, Daniel Patrick, 105
Muhyi, Ibrahim Abdulla, 21
Muir, Willa, 213
Mukherjee, P., 45
Mukhopadhyay, A., 45
Mull, Brenda, 213
Muller, Jean-Claude, 13
Mulligan, D. G., 83
Munroe, Robert L., 4,135
Munroe, Ruth H., 4,135
Muraro, Rose Marie, 85
Murasaki, Lady, 32,218
Murdock, George Peter, 3,91,135,150,158,180
Murphy, Robert F., 85,130
Murray, Pauli, 171,236
Murrell, Gladys, 167
Murtagh, John M., 164
Musil, Robert, 229
Myrdal, Alva, 74,180
Myrdal, Gunnar, 114,150

Nabokov, Vladimir, 218
Nadel, S. F., 4,8
Nader, Laura, 100
Nag, Moni, 45,114,158
Nakane, Chie, 32
Nakayama, Eiji, 92
Nanda, Savitri Devi, 45
Naroll, Frada, 158
Naroll, Raoul, 158
Narula, Uma, 180
Nash, E., 68,180
Nath, Kamla, 45
Nathan, Dorothy, 192,229
Naumann, Ida Blum, 61
Navarre, Octave Lucien Louis, 48
Nearing, Scott, 114
Nefertiti, 79
Neff, Wanda, 180
Negrin, Su, 213

Nehru, Shyam Kumari, 45
Nelson, Cynthia, 8
Nelson, E., 130
Nelson, Martha, 167
Nelson, Ruth Y., 167
Nemecek, Ottokar, 135
Nerlove, Sara, 142
Nervall, Gerard de, 8
Nestor, Agnes, 181
Netting, Robert McC., 13,150
Nettl, J. P., 229
Neubardt, Selig, 158
Neubauer, Peter B., 24
Neugarten, Bernice, 192
Neumann, Erich, 130
Neustadt, I., 10
Nevinson, Mary, 206
Newcomb, T. M., 192
Newcomer, Mabel, 192
Newman, Philip L., 82
Newton, Esther, 115,130,135,171,213
Newton, Niles, 130,158
Nichols, Thomas Low, 202
Nicholas, Maria, 85
Nielsen, Dorise Winnifred Webber, 97
Niemoeller, Adolph Fredrick, 164
Nilsen, Aileen Pace, 192
Nil'skii, Ivan Fedorovich, 68
Nimbkar, Krishna Bai, 45
Nimmo, H. Arlo, 79
Nin, Anaïs, 229
Noble, Iris, 229
Noble, Jeanne L., 105
Noble, Margaret, 45
Nock, A. J., 115
Norbeck, Edward, 142
Noronha, George, 45
North, Sandie, 213
Norton, Caroline Sheridan, 53,142
Nortor, G., 71
Noualer, K., 6
Noun, Louise R., 206,213
Novac, George, 213
Novak, Emil, 125
Noyes, Ethel J. R. C., 202
Nuita, Yoko, 32
Nurge, Ethel, 79,181
Nurina, F., 68
Nussbaum, Elizabeth, 24
Nyberg, Kathleen N., 167
Nye, F. I., 142,150,181
Nystrom-Hamilton, Louise, 229

279

Oakley, Ann, 121,229
Obeyesekere, G., 46
O'Brien, Denise, 68
O'Callaghan, Sean, 164
O-Chev, 68
Ockenga, Harold J., 167
O'Connor, Lillian, 202
Oetzel, Roberta M., 233
Ogot, Grace, 4
Ogunsheye, F. A., 13
O'Hara, Albert Richard, 36
Ohnuki-Tierney, Emiko, 32
Okamura, Kimi, 32
Okediji, F. O., 13
Okpewho, Isidore, 13
O'Laughlin, Bridget, 181
Oldam, James C., 171,236
O'Leary, Timothy J., 84,233
Olesen, Virginia, 186
Oliphant, Alexander (Mrs.), 53
Olmsted, D. L., 100
Oloo, Celina Nyai, 18
Olsen, Jack, 181
Olsen, Tillie, 218
Omaboe, E. N., 10
Omari, Peter, 13
O'Meara, Walter, 96
O'Neill, William L., 150,181,202,213
O'Nell, Carl, 100,101
Opler, Marvin K., 105,150
Opler, Morris E., 96
Oppenheimer, Valerie Kincade, 181
Orden, Susan R., 181
Orenstein, Henry, 46
Orga, Irfan, 27
Orpen, Adella E., 229
Orshansky, Mollie, 105
Ortner, Sherry B., 122
Osmond, Marie Withers, 150
Osnos, R., 116
Osofsky, Howard J., 158
Ossoli, Sarah M., 202
O'Sullivan-Beare, Nancy, 101
Ottenberg, Phoebe, 3
Ottenberg, Simon, 3,13
Otterbein, Keith F., 90
Otto, Herbert A., 232
Overton, Grant, 218
Ovesey, Lionel, 128
Ovsiannikova, Mariĭa Dmitrievna, 68
Owen, Harold, 206
Owusu, Maxwell, 13

Ozer, Jerome, 206

Pachmuss, Temira, 68
Pachucka, Romana, 75
Packard, Vance, 142
Page, John W., 123
Pak, Hwa-song, 34
Pallavicino, Ferrante, 164
Palson, Charles, 135
Palson, Rebecca, 135
Palubinskas, Alice, 192
Palvanova, Bibi, 68
Panbanyong, S., 38
Pankhurst, Christabel, 206
Pankhurst, Emmeline, 229
Pankhurst, Estelle Sylvia, 206
Paoli, U. E., 72
Papanek, Hannah, 40
Papanek, Mariam L., 130
Papashvily, Helen, 150,192,218
Paranavitana, S., 46
Parca, Gabriella, 63
Paredes de Salazar, Elssa, 86
Paris, Pierre, 27
Park, George K., 142
Park, Maud Wood, 207
Parker, Dorothy, 218
Parker, Elisabeth, 158
Parker, Gail, 207
Parkman, Mary K., 229
Parrish, John B., 181
Parsons, Alice Beal, 207
Parsons, Elsie Clews, 96,135
Parsons, Talcott, 115,142,150
Parton, James, 229
Partorino, Carlos Juliano Torres, 122
Parturier, Francoise, 213
Paskaleva, Virzhiniia, 75
Passeron, Rene, 218
Passman, Hanns, 164
Patai, Raphael, 24,122,167
Patanjali, V., 142
Paterson, Dorothy, 213
Patrick, G. T. W., 130
Patrick, Mary Mills, 8,20
Pattee, Fred L., 218
Patterson, D. G., 173
Paul, Nanette B., 207
Paul, Radha, 28
Paulme, Denise, 4,13
Paz, Octavio, 101
Peacock, N., 62
Pecchiai, Pio, 63

Pecson, Geronima T., 79
Peerbhoy, Homai, 28
Peiris, W., 46
Pelzer, Karl J., 38
Pendry, E. D., 218
Penny, F., 46
Penny, Virginia, 181
Penzer, Norman Mosley, 27,164
Pereira, Armando, 85
Perella, Vera, 181,182
Perlman, Melvin L., 18
Pernell, Ruby B., 28
Perrault, Gerri, 192
Pestalozza, U., 59
Peter, Prince of Greece and Denmark, 46,150
Petersen, William, 158
Peterson, Ester, 181
Petrova, Lidia, 68,213
Petrullo, Vincenzo M., 63
Phansi Wichakorakun, 38
Phelan, Lana Clarke, 158
Phillips, Arthur, 4
Phillips, Derek L., 130
Phillips, Emma M., 229
Phillips, Jean, 181
Picard, Roger, 59
Pichel, Vera, 87
Pickthorn, Helen, 52
Pidgeon, Mary Elizabeth, 181
Pierce, Linda Van Broeke, 153
Pierce, Ruth I., 158
Piercy, Marge, 214
Pieroni Bortolotti, Franca, 63
Pierre, Andre, 68
Pilling, Arnold A., 77
Pilling, Richard A., 77
Pilpel, Harriet, 150
Pinch, Trevor, 46
Pinchbeck, Ivy, 182
Pinckney, Eliza, 115
Pinkham, Mildreth Worth, 46,167
Pitcher, Evelyn Goodenough, 192
Pitkin, Donald S., 64
Pitt-Rivers, Julian, 167
Pival, Jean C., 208
Plant, Thomas A., 113
Plath, Sylvia, 219
Plato, 142
Plattner, Stuart, 101
Plautz, W., 151
Plisnier-Ladame, F., 4
Ploss, Herman Heinrich, 136,222
Poehlmann, Christof Ludwig, 62

Pogrebin, Letty C., 182
Polgar, Steven, 157,158
Pollak, Otto, 136,168
Pollock, Nancy J., 90,182
Polonska-Vasylenko, Nataliia Dmytrivna, 68
Polster, Elizabeth, 197
Pomelova, Anotonina Nikolaevna, 68
Pomeroy, Wardell B., 134,156
Poole, Ernest, 68
Popova, Nina Vasilevna, 68
Poppleton, P. K., 53
Portal, Magda, 87
Porter, Kirk H., 207
Possenti, Eligio, 65
Post, Alice, 171
Potter, David, 115
Powdermaker, Hortense, 15
Powell, Hickmann, 164
Power, Eileen, 202
Pownall, Evelyn, 79
Pozas, Ricardo Arciniega, 101
Praderie, M., 192
Prakash, P., 46
Prakash, Ram, 46
Prasad, T., 46
Pratt, Edwin A., 53
Prawirodihardjo, Tartib, 79
Prease, J., 194
Prelinger, Ernst, 192
Pressel, Esther J., 130
Pressman, Sonia, 236
Prevost, Marcel, 59
Price, Richard, 87
Pringle, Patrick, 168
Pritchina, Efrosiniîa Akimovna, 68
Prittle, Terence, 24
Proft, Gabriele, 75
Prohaska, Dragutin, 75
Prosser, W. R., 176
Prothro, E. T., 27,142
Pruitt, Ida, 36
Puckett, Hugh Wiley, 62
Punekar, S. D., 46
Putnam, Emily James, 202
Pyeatt, Patrick, 99

Qoyawagma, Polingaysi (Elizabeth White), 96
Querlin, Marise, 153

Rabin, A. I., 24
Rabkin, L. Y., 24
Rachin, Helen, 171
Radcliffe-Brown, A. R., 4

Raden, Norma, 105
Radhakrishnan, Sarvepalli, 46
Rai, S., 192
Rains, Prudence Mors, 158
Rainwater, Lee, 105,115,151,182
Rama Devi, B., 46
Ramabai, Sarasvati, 46
Remey, Estelle, 214
Ramos, Maria, 97
Ramsey, Glenn V., 182
Ramsey, Lady, 27
Ranade, R., 46
Rand, Ayn, 182
Randall, Mercedes M., 229
Rao, G. R. S., 151
Rao, M. Subba, 192
Raper, Arthur, 32
Raphael, Dana Louise, 122,142,158,159
Rapoport, R., 182
Rapoport, Rhonda, 182
Rappaport, Philip, 151,202
Rappaport, Roy, 167
Rat, Maurice, 59
Ratcliff, John Drury, 159
Ravenel, Florence Leftwich, 59
Ravenel, Harriott Horry, 115
Raya, Gino, 122
Razafyadriamihaingo, S., 19
Read, Kenneth E., 82
Read, Thomas B., 219
Reay, Marie, 82
Reca, Telma, 115
Reckless, Walter Cade, 164
Reed, Evelyn, 214
Reeve, Tapping, 198,203
Reeves, Nancy, 130
Reich, Wilhelm, 125
Reichard, G., 96
Reid, Marion, 193
Reina, Ruben, 101
Reischauer, Edwin, 28
Reiss, I. L., 136
Reitman, Ben Lewis, 164
Rembaugh, Berta, 171
Reminick, Ronald A., 16
Rendel, Margherita N., 53
Retif, A., 15
Revesz, Andres, 122
Reyes, Antonio, 90
Reyes, Felina, 79
Reyher, Rebecca Houruich, 19
Reyna, Stephen, 8
Reynolds, Myra, 53

Reynolds, Vernon, 124
Rham, Edith de, 110,130,168
Rheingold, Joseph C., 130
Rice, Charles S., 115
Rice, Clara Colliver Hammond, 22
Rice, Margery Spring, 53
Rice, Oliver, 193
Richards, Audrey I., 15
Richards, Cara E., 94,122
Richardson, Arthur H., 179
Richardson, Dorothy, 229
Richardson, Joanna, 59
Richardson, Lula McDowell, 59
Richardson, R. J., 140
Richmond, Alexander, 229
Richter, Lina Spiess, 62
Rico, Heidi K. de, 86
Riegel, R., 142
Riegel, Robert E., 115,203,214
Riegelhaupt, Joyce F., 72
Riesman, D., 193
Riley, Madeleine, 219
Rischbieth, Bessie Mabel, 77
Ritchie, Jane, 83
Rivington, Ann, 207
Rizal y Alonso, Jose, 79
Roach, Mary Ellen, 142
Roark, Sue, 91
Robbins, Michael C., 160
Robertson, Ruth, 80
Robinson, Harriet H., 182
Robinson, Marie N., 136
Robinson, William Josephus, 164
Roche, Charles E., 115
Rocheblave-Spenle, Annmarie, 142
Rocher, Guy, 97
Rodgers, David A., 159
Rodriguez, Joao Batista Cascudo, 85
Roe, Dorothy, 115
Roe, Marion, 182
Roethlisberger, Fritz, 182
Rogers, Agnes, 115
Rogers, Katharine M., 219
Roheim, Geza, 77,131
Rolandis, Giuseppe Maria de, 182
Rollin, Betty, 214
Romero de Terreos y Vinent, Manuel, 101
Romero de Valle, Emilia, 101
Romney, A. Kimball, 131,142
Romney, Romaine, 101
Ronhaar, J., 151
Root, Grace C., 171
Rorabacher, Louis Elizabeth, 53

Rorke, M. W., 193
Roosevelt, Anna Eleanor, 159,171
Roosevelt, Eleanor, 115,230
Rosaldo, Michelle, 219
Rose, Arnold, 143
Rosen, Daniel, 122
Rosen, Harold, 159
Rosen, Lawrence, 105
Rosen, Ruth, 214
Rosenblatt, Paul C., 136,143,151
Rosenfeld, Carl, 182
Rosenfeld, E., 24
Rosenfeld, Henry, 20,24
Rosenfels, Paul, 131
Rosenthal, Robert, 193
Rosenzweig, J., 95
Rosner, M., 24
Ross, Catherine, 145,195
Ross, Isabel, 115,203,230
Ross, J. A., 82,157
Ross, Mary Steele, 115
Ross, Nancy, 115,203,230
Ross, S. V. B., 13
Rossel, Agda, 74
Rossel, James, 74
Rossi, Alice S., 143,159,182,193,203
Roth, Dannis M., 159
Rothfield, Otto, 46
Rothschild, Nan, 143
Rougemont, Denis de, 131
Roussier, J., 20
Rover, Constance, 207,214
Rubel, Arthur J., 107
Rubenius, Anna, 53
Rubenstein, Dale Ross, 68
Rubin, Zick, 151
Ruderman, Florence, 143
Rudofsky, Bernard, 143
Rugh, Robert, 159
Ruitenbeek, Hendrick M., 136,153
Rumianseva, Mariia Stepanorna, 68
Rusova, Sofiia Fedorivna, 69
Russell, Bertrand, 151
Russell, Dora, 193
Russell, Maude, 36
Russell, Thomas H., 182
Rustow, D. A., 33
Ryan, Bryce, 46
Ryan, Mary S., 143
Ryder, Alice Elizabeth, 125
Ryrie, Charles C., 167

St. John, Christopher Marie, 230
Sabino, Ignez, 85
Sacks, Karen, 143,198
Sadler, William Samuel, 159
Saffiot, Heleieth'lara Bongiovani, 85
Safilios-Rothschild, Constantina, 122
Sagarin, Edward, 136
Salas, Irma, 40
Salman, A., 20
Salomon, Louis, 54
Saloutos, Theodore, 115
Salovesh, Michael, 101
Sampson, Ronald V., 171
Samuel, Edwin, 24
Sand, Chiye, 32
Sanday, Peggy R., 91,122,143
Sanderson, Lillian, 9
Sandoz, Mari, 96
Sanford, Nevitt, 193
Sanger, Margaret, 143,230
Sanger, William W., 164
Sangree, Walter H., 14
Sapir, J. David, 167
Saran, Raksha, 46
Sarashina, Lady, 32,219
Sargent, Shirley, 203
Sartin, Pierrette, 182
Sartre, Jean-Paul, 219
Sato, Toshihiko, 33
Saucier, Jean-Francois, 159
Saunders, Louise, 115
Sawrey, W. I., 74
Sayers, P., 56
Scarbrough, E. M., 14
Schaffter, Dorothy, 197
Schapera, I., 4,19
Schein, Muriel, 72
Scheinfeld, Amram, 143
Schenk, Roy U., 159
Scherer, Alice, 122
Schinnerer, Otto P., 219
Schirmacher, Kaethe, 207
Schlegel, Alice, 143,151,171
Schlesinger, Rudolf, 69
Schmidt, Wilhelm S. V. D., 182,222
Schneider, David H., 151
Schneider, Jane, 182
Schneir, Miriam, 214
Schoepf, Brooke Grundfest, 125,143,171
Schreiber, Hermann, 164
Schreiber, William, 116
Schreiner, George Abel, 27
Schreiner, Olive, 182

Singer, M., 47
Singh, Amrit Kaur, 47
Singleton, John, 33
Siraj, M., 79
Sison, Perfect S., 79,183
Sivachandra, Vasu, 47
Skard, Aasa Gruda, 144
Skeat, Walter W., 38,79
Skerlj, Bozo, 62
Skinner, B. F., 232
Skipper, James R., 153
Skolnick, Arlene, 151
Skultans, Vieda, 160
Slater, Carol, 172
Slater, Dori A., 143
Slater, Eliot, 54
Slater, Philip Elliot, 72,144
Slaughter, Diana T., 105
Smelser, Neil, 54
Smirnova, Raisa Mikhailovna, 5
Smith, Annie S., 116
Smith, David L., 160
Smith, Dorothy A., 172
Smith, Ellen, 183
Smith, Georgina, 183
Smith, Jessica, 69
Smith, Lillian, 219
Smith, Mary, 14
Smith, Page, 203
Smith, R. F., 33
Smith, Raymond T., 86,90
Smith, Thomas Robert, 207
Smulevich, Boleslav Iakovlevich, 69
Smuts, Robert W., 182
Snow, Edgar, 36
Snow, Helen, 36
Snow, L. W., 36
Snowden, Ethel, 197,214
Sofue, Takao, 33
Sokolnikova, Galina O., 230
Solanas, Valerie, 214
Sonenschein, David, 153
Sonmez, Emel, 27
Sonstroem, David, 219
Sontag, Susan, 214
Sophocles, 207
Sorabji, Cornelia, 47
Sorokin, Pitrim, 136
Sosa de Newton, Lily, 87
Soubiran, Andre, 183
Sourgen, H., 59
Soustelle, Jacques, 102
Southall, Aiden, 5

Stevens, Barbara C., 131,160
Stevens, William, 230
Stevenson, Janet, 214
Steward, Julian H., 84
Stewart, C. M., 54
Stewart, Marjorie, 80,82
Stimpson, Catherine R., 183,236
Stirling, A. Paul, 27
Stocks, Mary D., 230
Stoddard, Hope, 116
Stoetzel, Jean, 33
Stoller, Robert J., 144
Stone, Calvin P., 124
Stoodley, Bartlett H., 79
Stopes, Charlotte, 54
Storey, Robert G., 69
Strachey, Rachel, 54,207
Straelen, Henricus van, 33
Strainchamps, Ethel, 219
Strange, Helene, 74
Strangway, A. K., 15
Strasser, Nadja, 69
Strathern, Andrew, 82
Strathern, Marilyn, 82
Stratton, F., 14
Strean, Lyon P., 160
Strecker, Edward, 198
Strodtbeck, Fred L., 106,144
Strong, Anna Louise, 36
Strutt, Elizabeth, 207
Stuart, Dorothy Margaret, 144
Stuart, M., 131
Sturtevant, William C., 93
Stycos, J. Mayonne, 160
Sufa, Icken, 116
Suggs, Robert C., 83,135
Sugimoto, Etsu Inagaki, 33
Suhl, Yuri, 230
Sullerno, Evelyne, 122
Sunegrin, 214
Sunons, Harold, 5
Susman, Margarete, 62
Sussman, Robert W., 124
Suter, K., 7
Sutherland, Elizabeth, 90
Suyin, Han, 36,79
Svalastoga, Kaare, 74
Sverdlov, G. M., 70
Swantz, Maria-Liisa, 167
Swarth, Lillian, 194
Swartz, Marc J., 81
Sweet, Louise E., 21
Swett, Maude, 27,183

Swinehart, James S., 144
Swisshelm, Jane Grey, 207
Sykes, Barbara, 121
Sykes, Ella C., 22
Sykes, John, 33
Symonds, P. M., 144
Syrkin, Marie, 25
Sysiharja, Anna-Liisa, 74

Tabaku, Faire, 233
Tait, Marjorie, 172,194
T'ai T'ai, Ning L., 36
Takei, Yoko, 32
Talbot, D. Amaury, 14
Talmon, Yonina, 144
Talmon-Garber, Yonina, 25
Tampoe, R., 47
Tanner, John, 153
Tanner, Leslie, 214
Tanner, Nancy, 79,106
Tanzer, Deborah, 16
Tappan, Paul Wilbur, 164
Tarbell, Ida, 208
Tatarinova, Nadazhda, 70
Tatybekora, Zhanetta Saimasaevna, 70
Tavris, Carol, 131,214
Tax, Meredith, 214
Tax, Sol, 102
Taylor, A. Elizabeth, 208
Taylor, George, 194
Taylor, Gordon Rattray, 203
Taylor, Grace, 172,236
Taylor, Romold G., 188
Taylor, Sidney, 5
Taylor, Susan D., 116
Tchernavin, Tatiana, 70
Tcholakian, Arthur, 106
Teer, Barbar Ann, 106
Tegner, Bruce, 194
Teitz, Joyce, 215
TenBerge, B. S., 160
Terman, Lewis, 144
Terra, Stuart, 84
Thane, Elswyth, 230
Thayer, William M., 172
Theal, George McCall, 19
Theobald, Robert, 122
Theodore, Athena, 183
Thibert, Margherite, 194
Thomas, Edith, 59
Thomas, Henry, 230
Thomas, Keith, 144
Thomas, Northcote Whitridge, 14,79

Thomas, Paul, 47
Thomas, William Isaac, 122,136
Thome, Yolanda Bettencourt, 122
Thompson, Barbara, 54
Thompson, Clara, 131
Thompson, Helen Bradford, 131
Thompson, Margaret Patricia N., 54
Thompson, Mary Lou, 215
Thompson, Richard, 160
Thompson, William, 208
Thomson, Patricia, 54,219
Thomson, Walker H., 63
Thorp, Margaret, 230
Thrall, Margaret E., 167
Thurber, Cheryl, 145,167
Thurber, James, 145
Thurnwald, H., 18,80
Tickner, Frederick Windham, 55
Tien, H. Yuan, 160
Tiffany, Warren I., 91
Tifft, Larry L., 193
Tiger, Lionel, 172,210
Tingston, Herbert, 49
Tinker, A. H., 194
Tirabutana, P., 39
Titmyss, Richard, 55
Tkadleckova-Vantuchova, Jarmila, 75
Tobias, R. B., 136
Toffler, Alvin, 232
Tomich, Nada, 8
Topley, Marjorie, 36
Topping, Ruth, 165
Torday, Emil, 15
Toro¡Godoy, Julia, 87
Torres de Ianello, Reina, 102
Toshchakova, E. M., 70
Tovar, Beatriz, 86
Trahey, Jane, 204
Tralins, Robert, 8
Travell, Janet, 183
Treadwell, Mattie, 197
Trecker, Janice Law, 194,204
Trilling, Diana, 145
Trimmer, Eric, 125
Tripathi, Kalawati, 194
Trouillot, H., 90
Truefitt, Alison, 55
Tucker, Alan, 194
Tuden, A., 5
Turgeon, Charles Marie Joseph, 59
Turnbull, Colin M., 15
Turner, E. S., 145
Turner, Victor, 16

Tuttle, Florence Guertin, 208
Tuxen, Paul, 47
Tweker, Sylvia, 131
Tyler, L. E., 144
Tymchenko, Zhanaa Pavlivna, 70

Uberoi, N., 55
Udy, Stanley H. Jr., 183
Uesugi, Thomas C., 215
Ulanov, Ann B., 167
Underhill, Ruth M., 96
Underwood, John Levi, 116
Urbanowitz, Charles F., 159
Urbieta Rojas, Pastor, 86
Uribe de Acosta, Ofelia, 88
Urquhart, Margaret M., 47
Urquida, Jose Macedonio, 86
Usoro, E. J., 14
Uzanne, Louis Octave, 59

Vaas, Fransis J., 172
Vaca, Victor Hugo, 88
Vagabov, Mustafa Vagabovich, 70
Van Aken, Carol G., 180
Vance, Carole, 195
Van Den Berg, J. H., 131
Van Den Berghe, Pierre, 19,122,124
van der Velde, Frances, 167
Van Gennep, Arnold, 19,145
Van Middendorp, Gerarda, 219
Van Waters, Miriam, 132
Varigry, Charles Victor Grosnier de, 117
Vasilgevna, G. P., 70
Vasquez, Enriqueta, 107
Vatuk, Sylvia J., 47
Vatuk, Ved Prakash, 27
Vayda, A. P., 83
Vengris, Kandis, 172
Vernier, Pierre, 21
Viirsalu, Erika, 70
Villard, Leonie, 55
Villa Rojas, Alfonso, 102
Vinacke, W. Edgar, 215
Vincent, Clark, 106,136
Vinelas, Estrella, 90
Violette, Augusta, 86,185
Vladimorov, Leonid, 70
Voegelin, C. F., 97
Vogel, Ezra, 33
Vogel, Lise, 185
Vogel, Susan, 33,189
Voipio-Juvas, Anni, 74
Vorcarattorta, Elisabeth, 86

Webb, Beatrice, 231
Webb, Catherine, 185
Webster, Paula, 171
Wedgwood, Camilla H., 82
Weil, Mildred W., 185
Weiler, Ludwig, 84
Weingarten, Murray, 25
Weingarten, Violet, 185
Weinhold, Karl, 62
Weininger, Otto, 136
Weinstein, Karol, 158
Weintraub, D., 25
Weiss, Kenneth M., 124
Weisstein, Naomi, 132
Weitzman, Lenore J., 195
Weitzman, S., 70,145
Welch, Galbraith, 5
Weller, Robert H., 160
Wenig, Steffen, 8
Werner, Alice, 19
Werner, E., 123
Wertenbaker, Lael Tucker, 160
West, Anne Grant, 196
West, Anthony, 215
West, P., 190
Westermarck, Edvard Alexander, 7,151
Westhoff, Charles, 160
Whale, Winifred Stephens, 59
Wharton, Anne Hollingsworth, 172
Wheeler, Susan Anna Brookings, 70
White, E. B., 145
White, E. M., 172
White, James J., 172,185
White, Lynn, 196
White, Robert B., 160
White, William F., 196
Whiteman, J., 82
Whiting, Beatrice B., 18,132,145,186
Whiting, Gerald, 55
Whiting, John W. M., 18,127,132,139,145
Whittaker, Elvi, 186
Whitten, Norman E., 88
Whittington, James, 89
Wiegand, Elisabeth, 145
Wiest, Raymond E., 186
Wieth-Knudsen, K. A., 208
Wilde, Frank (Mrs.), 48
Wilensky, Harold L., 186
Wilionson, T. O., 33
Willacy, H. M., 186
Willard, Frances E., 231
Willett, Jean Campbell, 186

Willett, Mabel H., 186
Williams, Barbara Ruth, 55
Williams, F. E., 145
Williams, Gertrude, 48,186
Williams, Herbert H., 27
Williams, Josephine Justice, 186
Williams, Maxine, 106
Williams, M. A., 219
Williams, Sharlotte Neely, 124
Willmott, Peter, 55
Willner, Dorothy, 25
Willson, Robert Newton, 165
Wilson, Jeannie Lansley, 117
Wilson, H. Clyde, 160
Wilson, Mona, 55
Wilson, Paul, 165
Wilson, Pauline, 196
Wilson, R. McNair, 60
Wilson, Roger H. L., 139,210
Wilton, M., 116
Win, Kyi Kyi, 39
Winick, Charles, 136,145,165
Winkler, Ilene, 186
Winter, E., 186
Wirsen, Claes, 157
Wise, Winifred, 231
Wiser, Charlotte, 48
Wiser, William, 48
Wit, G. A. de, 132
Wolf, Arthur P., 37
Wolf, Deborah, 136
Wolf, Margery, 37
Wolfe, Donald M., 108,146
Wolff, Charlotte, 153
Wolff, Janet L., 117,186
Wolff, Peter H., 151
Wolfle, Dael, 186
Wolfson, Theresa, 186
Wollstonecraft, Mary, 208
Wong, Su-ling, 37
Wood, Myrna, 186
Woodbury, Helen Laura Sumner, 208
Woodham-Smith, Cecil, 55
Woods, Frances Jerome, 106
Woodside, Moya, 160
Woodsmall, Ruth Frances, 21
Woodsworth, Sheila, 97
Woodward, Helen, 117,172,208
Woodwide, Moya, 54
Woody, Thomas H., 196
Woolf, Virginia, 215,219
Woolson, Abba Louisa, 117
Woolston, Howard B., 165

Worell, Judith, 215
Worell, Leonard, 215
Worth, George C., 157
Worthington, George E., 165
Wright, Carroll D., 187
Wright, Frederick, 219
Wright, Harold Bell, 97
Wright, Norman Pelham, 102
Wright, Thomas, 140
Wrochno, Krystyna, 76
Wulffen, Erich, 168
Wylie, Philip, 198
Wynne, Mervyn L., 80
Wyse, Lois, 231

Yalman, Nur O., 48
Yanagida, Kunio, 33
Yang, Chiing-K'un, 37
Yengoyan, Aram, 187
Yieni Tsao Li, 37
Yohalem, Alice M., 226
Yohannan, Jacob Baba, 22
Yoors, Jan, 117
Yost, Edna, 196
Young, Agatha, 197
Young, Frank W., 145,160
Young, Louise M., 107
Young, Michael, 55,196
Young, Miriam, 48
Young, Philip D., 151
Young, Sherman Plato, 219
Young, Virginia H., 106,107
Young, Wayland, 136

Zabelin, Ivan Egorovich, 71
Zahm, John Augustine, 196
Zapp, Eduard, 62
Zavalloni, M., 90
Zavin, Theodora, 150
Zawadzki, Edward S., 154
Zborowski, Mark, 149
Zeinab, Mahmoud Mehrez, 7
Zendejas, Adelina, 102
Zetkin, Klara, 187
Zevi, Elena, 72
Zeyneb, Lanum, 27
Ziegler, Frederick J., 159
Zinkin, Taya, 28
Znaniecki, Helena, 187
Zucconi, Angela, 55
Zweig, Ferdynand, 25

5236

LEWIS AND CLARK COLLEGE LIBRARY
PORTLAND, OREGON 97219

DATE DUE

APR 28 2009	

BRODART   Cat. No. 23-221

Lewis and Clark College - Watzek Library   wmain
HQ1180 .J33 1974
Jacobs, Sue-Ellen/Women in perspective :

3 5209 00369 2643